D1066092

botha

BIG BOWL
FOOTBALL

The Great Postseason
Classics

FRED RUSSELL

and

GEORGE LEONARD
Both of the *Nashville Banner*

THE RONALD PRESS COMPANY • NEW YORK

Southern Baptist College
BRUST
LIBRARY
Walnut Ridge, Ark.

Copyright © 1963 by
THE RONALD PRESS COMPANY

———

All Rights Reserved

No part of this book may be reproduced
in any form without permission in writing
from the publisher.

Library of Congress Catalog Card Number: 63–22417

PRINTED IN THE UNITED STATES OF AMERICA

Preface

Of course, the very fact we have written a book of this size about the bowl games is evidence we approve of them.

In truth, we shudder to think of a New Year's Day without football (the pomp and circumstance suit us fine, too).

After a few trips to Pasadena to cover the Rose Bowl game, the late Franklin Lewis of the *Cleveland Press* wrote: "I love all this stuff. I think it's terrific."

So do we.

An exciting, often criticized, but overwhelmingly popular encore to each season—that's the bowls. They're entertaining, enthralling, enriching.

The big bowl games, attracting nearly 500,000 fans, mean extra jobs, life-prolonging vacations, a thrill and an honor for most players, pleasure for millions, and profits in the millions also.

Certainly bowl games are big business. But rigid regulations discourage get-rich-quick schemers.

The major bowls gross more than $3,000,000 annually from ticket, television-radio, and concession rights. Most of these revenues go to the colleges. Competing schools are handsomely rewarded but many others benefit. Schools belonging to conferences must apportion shares among all members.

If evils exist, they seem to have been magnified by those who profess to see them.

Quite a long time ago Graham McNamee, the first great sports announcer, rhapsodized about the entrancing scenery surrounding the Rose Bowl. Sometimes the game description suffered as McNamee's gaze strayed to the lofty, white-browed San Gabriel mountains overlooking the bowl. He also frequently referred to the mild climate of the charming California city of Pasadena.

Still, nobody listening in parts of the United States where the countryside was bleak and the air intensely cold minded. We were vicariously warmed.

Nowadays most of us take delight in all of the bowl games, including their fanfare, floats, and turf-tearing combat.

We find the bowls a proper, sensible way of celebrating New Year's Day.

FRED RUSSELL
GEORGE LEONARD

Nashville, Tennessee
October, 1963

iii

Southern Baptist College
BRUSH
LIBRARY
Walnut Ridge, Ark.

Acknowledgments

The authors express their thanks to the following for permission to reprint the pictures appearing on the pages shown.

ASUCLA Photography Department. Page 177.
Atlanta Journal-Constitution, photo by Marion Johnson. Page 318.
Columbus (Ohio) *Dispatch,* photo by Bill Foley. Page 308.
Daily Oklahoman. Page 321. Photo by Al McLaughlin. Page 306.
Florida Times-Union. Pages 191, 296.
Dick Whittington, Los Angeles. Page 108.
Fort Worth Star-Telegram. Pages 263, 264. Photos by Al Panzera. Pages 206, 210, 223, 238, 379.
Gator Bowl Association. Page 376.
Harper Leiper Studios, Houston. Page 347.
Hearst Metrotone News, Inc. Page 54.
Laughead Photographers, Dallas. Page 299.
Liberty Bowl Charities, photo by the City of Philadelphia. Page 350.
Los Angeles Herald-Examiner. Pages 26, 44. Photo by Samuel Sansone. Page 53.
Los Angeles Times. Page 324.
Lou Witt Photography, Houston. Page 388.
Miami Herald. Page 171.
Miami News. Page 139.
Nashville Banner. Page 279.
New Orleans Mid-Winter Sports Association, photos by Leon Trice. Pages 77, 112, 115, 126, 335.
New Orleans States-Item. Page 382.
New Orleans Times-Picayune. Page 226.
Squire Haskins, Dallas. Page 207.
Syracuse University. Page 330.
Tournament of Roses Association. Pages 5, 7.
United Press International. Pages 70, 283.
University of Colorado. Page 99.
University of Michigan. Page 10.
University of Southern California. Page 120.
University of Tennessee, photo by Thompson's Studios, Knoxville. Page 121.
Wide World Photos, Inc. Pages 86, 187, 201, 258, 269, 286, 315, 331, 337, 341, 345, 351, 362, 385.

Contents

BIG BOWL FOOTBALL

How It All Started

On January 1, 1902, the University of Michigan met Leland Stanford University in a football contest played at Tournament Park in Pasadena. There, on a dusty field at California Street and Wilson Avenue in that charming, beautiful city of sunshine and flowers, they pioneered the Rose Bowl game—and all bowl games.

However, it wasn't the first postseason intersectional game held on the Pacific coast.

Coach Amos Alonzo Stagg of the University of Chicago brought his team west in an obsolete, condemned Pullman in 1894. That was the year, incidentally, Stagg originated the tackles back formation that put six men in the backfield and threw heavy mass interference ahead of the ball carrier.

Stagg's 1894 team defeated Stanford 24 to 4 on Christmas Day in San Francisco. Three days later Stanford beat Chicago 12 to 0 at Los Angeles. Then Stagg took his men to San Francisco again where they lost to the Reliance Athletic Club of Oakland 6 to 0. That was on January 1, 1895—the first intersectional game on New Year's Day.

Mr. and Mrs. Stagg spent their honeymoon, surrounded by football players, on that creaky, ancient Pullman. One night Stagg grabbed his wife's head rather roughly. He had dreamed he was falling on a fumbled ball.

Gay tourists joining with Pasadena folks swarmed in the streets for the festivities planned that first day of 1902. Only 8,000 turned out for the football game. Most of them came to see the flower-bedecked carriages, tallyhos, buggies, and (that year) automobiles in the already traditional morning parade known as the Tournament of Roses.

An Easterner, Dr. Charles Frederick Holder, proposed the idea of the parade many years before football was also featured each New Year's Day. Dr. Holder, a Massachusetts-born naturalist, moved to Pasadena in 1885 to accept a position as professor of zoology at Throop College of Technology, now California Institute of Technology.

If Dr. Holder was the originator of the parade, the exclusive Valley

3

Hunt Club, which he joined, was the first sponsor. To members of the club, Dr. Holder broached a project that found instant favor. To celebrate the ripening of California fruit, to herald the new year, and to tell the world that, far from having snow and ice or freezing weather, in Pasadena it was balmy and verdant, the citizens would bring roses and other flowers to Sportsmen's Park at the corner of Walnut Street and Los Robles Avenue for a display. Three thousand came. Enthusiasm was high. The idea caught on. The name "Tournament of Roses" was consequently adopted.

Tournament of Roses people date the floral pageantry from January 1, 1890. Actually, the first parade was held in 1891. In the nineties Valley Hunt Club members and other Pasadenans adorned carts, saddle horses, and bicycles with blooms and garlands from their own gardens. Families vied to design the most interestingly decorated vehicles. The Tournament of Roses was a community celebration in the beginning.

The popularity and scope of the Tournament increased swiftly. The thought of a rose parade in midwinter proved an irresistible lure to many in the East and Midwest, warming themselves by a fireside and contemplating the latest plunge of the thermometer. As a tourist attraction it may never have been equaled.

By 1895 fresh problems were popping up. The show had become so famous that during the next year the Valley Hunt Club, feeling the event had outgrown the club, handed over sponsorship to an organization representing the entire citizenry. On September 7, 1896, the Tournament of Roses Association was formed. It ran things henceforth.

This nonprofit association, numbering several hundred public-spirited members, is devoted to the perpetuation of a civic promotion enjoyed by untold millions. Citizens from many walks of life pay modest dues to work for nothing. They get their satisfaction in trying to make each parade as good or better than the one of the year before, an almost impossible task. Approximately 50,000 hours of service are contributed yearly.

Sweet-smelling floral floats now form an almost indescribably beautiful two-hour parade extending five miles. Exquisite floats, sixty of them in each spectacle, are covered by millions of blossoms. Some may require as many as 350,000 flowers. There are really more chrysanthemums than roses. But many other kinds of fresh flowers are used to fashion the mosaics.

These ingenious and expensive creations of the float builders represent organizations, business and industry, communities, even nations. Spectacular masterpieces compete for awards in several classi-

The spectacularly beautiful Tournament of Roses parade, Pasadena's way of beginning the New Year.

fications, each float harmonizing with the theme of the parade, which is selected far in advance.

Interspersed among the mechanized chassis with their frameworks of flowers are twenty-one bands and handsomely accoutered equestrians astride scores of fine horses with silver trappings worth a fortune.

More than a thousand persons ride or march in the parade, usually held in soft, sunny weather. Between one and two million spectators throng the sides of Colorado Street. Perhaps seventy-five million view the pageant as relayed by two national television networks.

Seldom does rain dampen the Tournament of Roses. It has happened less than a dozen times since the floral fete began.

In 1934, when Columbia sprang the biggest upset in bowl history by surprising Stanford 7 to 0, torrential downpours fell in Pasadena for two days before the game. The theme of the parade was "Tales of the Seven Seas." Water has not been mentioned in subsequent titles.

Dr. Holder had suggested that the parade be followed in the afternoon by a sports program. Townsfolk participated in races on foot and bicycles. Races for burros, ponies, and horses were also carried on. A somewhat strange Spanish game called "Tourney at the Rings" was another important event. Pasadena "knights," riding spirited horses at full speed, tried to thrust a wooden lance through wreaths of roses hung from posts.

Another early day Pasadena citizen, also from the East, found the athletic entertainment too tame. In 1901 dynamic James H. Wagner was elected president of the Tournament of Roses Association. This is considered a greater honor than becoming mayor. President Wagner gets the credit for founding the East-West football game in his city. This was the forerunner of the Rose Bowl game.

Despite criticism, skepticism, and obstacles he brought together two prominent football teams, one representing the Far West and the other from a state east of the Mississippi River, in a then unique sort of postparade diversion.

The game between Michigan and Stanford netted the Tournament Association nearly $4,000, which was even more than President Wagner's guarantee to the schools.

Although football then was a young game with no steady grip on American sports fans and there were doubts about that first Pasadena affair, his foresight and business judgment were proved keen. But the gross receipts were a far cry from today's figure, exceeding $1,-000,000, of which about half comes from television income.

By the time Coach Fielding H. Yost's Wolverines from Ann Arbor, Mich., crushed the Indians from Palo Alto, Calif., in a game cut short at the entreaty of Stanford, Pacific Coast football had touched a sad nadir.

The Tournament of Roses parades continued, more and more breathtaking in variegated floral beauty, but the game was forgotten. In place of football, chariot races became the rage in the early 1900's. Pasadenans attempted to introduce a twentieth-century version of the Roman chariot races with all their excitement. Again, the idea was Dr. Holder's. Starting in 1904, they drew large crowds for several years. But interest gradually waned.

About that time, football was finding increasing favor. The game was more absorbing and thrilling now that the forward pass, legalized in 1906, and other reforms opened up the offense. West Coast football was perking up and in 1915 it was time again to challenge the East. The game has gone on each year since the renewal on New Year's Day, 1916.

Early games were played at Tournament Park, seating only 1,000 when first used in 1900. By 1922, when the last East-West contest was held there, capacity of the bleachers was 40,000. The Tournament of Roses Association purchased this property in 1901. The land was donated to the City of Pasadena, then leased from the city, with privilege of renewal, at a nominal rental. Thus, the pattern for friendly city-Tournament cooperation was set. The city later sold the 14-acre grounds to California Tech as an addition to the campus.

When it became evident the event had outgrown Tournament Park, the Association decided in early 1922 to build a concrete stadium on city land in a great natural gorge known as the Arroyo Seco. This was the Rose Bowl. It was built to seat 52,000 at the original cost of $272,198.26.

The Rose Bowl with seating capacity of 100,631.

The stadium, designed as an oval by Pasadena architect Myron Hunt, was first horseshoe-shaped with the south end open. It was officially and happily named "The Rose Bowl" following the suggestion of Harlan W. Hall, Tournament publicist.

After raising the money to build the stadium, the Tournament deeded it to the city, which leases it back for the football game. The Rose Bowl was financed through the sale of ticket privileges over ten- and five-year periods. Tournament funds also paid for a series of enlargements.

The Tournament receives fifteen per cent of the take from ticket sales, television rights, and concessions of the Rose Bowl game. This pays for parade expenses, the salary of the Tournament Association's only full-time employee, manager and executive director Max Colwell, and secretarial help. Excess money is turned over to the city for upkeep of the bowl and public improvements.

The Rose Bowl has its own Hall of Fame located in the southeast corner of the stadium between tunnels 1 and 28. Exhibits were assembled by the Helms Athletic Foundation under the supervision of managing director Bill Schroeder.

Here, in a grand setting in a stadium seating 100,631 and built—counting additions—at a total cost of approximately $1,000,000, the Rose Bowl football game has been played with only one interruption since January 1, 1923. In 1942, shortly after the United States entered World War II, the government would not permit large assemblies of people on the Pacific Coast. So the game was held in faraway Durham, N. C.

The Tournament of Roses parade is an American tradition. The Rose Bowl game has become a renowned sports classic. And thus we were shown a much more zestful, admirable, wonderful way of observing the first day of the year than ever before.

– 1902 –

The First Game at Pasadena

ROSE BOWL

At Michigan shortly after the turn of the century, Willie Heston played left halfback on some of the most astonishingly successful football teams in history.

He made 93 touchdowns in his fabulously successful career. He scored in all of the Wolverines' 44 games in that 1901–4 period (they won 43, tied one) except the first Tournament of Roses classic in 1902 in which Stanford was manhandled 49 to 0.

And in that game Heston set a Rose Bowl game record for most individual yardage gained that stood for 57 years—170 yards in 18 tries, an average of 9.4 yards per carry.

Michigan challenged California (undefeated and conqueror of Stanford) in 1901, Coach Fielding H. (Hurry Up) Yost's first year at Ann Arbor, and was refused. When James H. Wagner, president of the Tournament of Roses, conceived the idea of a football game to entertain Pasadena visitors and parade viewers on New Year's Day, the Wolverines eagerly accepted an invitation to meet Stanford.

"It took us 23 minutes to score," recalled Heston, "but after that there was no holding us. We led at halftime, 17–0. There were several Stanford casualties. We didn't use a single substitute. Stanford weakened rapidly in the second half. Finally, Ralph Fisher, Stanford's captain, came across the field and informed Yost, 'We can't continue. We haven't enough able-bodied men.' Yost let us play three or four more minutes. Then, as I remember, the game was called with several minutes still left."

Michigan rushed the ball for the staggering total of 503 yards. The Wolverines got off 111 plays, including 21 punts by Everett Sweeley, right end, for a 38.9 average. Fullback Neil Snow scored five touchdowns.

"The night of the game we had our dinner at the Raymond House

9

Willie Heston, Michigan's immortal halfback who gained 170 yards in the first Tournament of Roses game.

in Pasadena and were sitting in the lobby enjoying ourselves," Heston said. "Yost suddenly became aware that our three substitutes were missing. He asked Dan McGugin, our left guard, and me to look them up. We found them in back of the hotel turning a garden hose on each other and rolling in the dirt—in full uniform. They told us they were ashamed to go back to Michigan and have the folks think they hadn't played."

This was the first of Yost's famed "point-a-minute" teams. In 1901 the Wolverines scored 501 points to 0 in ten regular season games. In 1902 they made 644 against 12 in eleven games. In 1903 it was 565 to 6 in twelve games and in 1904, 567 to 22 in ten games.

Yost coached twenty-five football teams at Michigan. They won 165 games, lost 29, and tied 10.

"We had every play used today except the pass," Heston said. "We ran from the T. We shifted. We used balanced and unbalanced lines. We learned assignments for 52 plays.

"Yost instructed our quarterback, Boss Weeks, to call signals for the next play as we were getting up from the last one. He emphasized speed and more speed. They didn't call him 'Hurry Up' for nothing. There was one series of four or five plays we ran without signal. Everyone knew what to do and what play was next. Our opponents didn't have much chance to get set."

Sweeley, later judge of the Twin Falls, Idaho, Probate Court (Heston also became a judge), remembers one embarrassing occurrence.

"I was coming up the sidelines returning a punt and going all-out when Big Bill Traeger, Stanford's fine tackle, dove from the side and hit me so hard he couldn't hold me," the superlative punter said. "He sent me flying over the rail of a box for a perfect three-point

Michigan vs. Stanford, January 1, 1902, in the forerunner of the Rose Bowl classics and postseason football games everywhere.

landing in the laps of four people sitting peacefully there. One of the occupants was a very pretty young lady. I left them all a souvenir of field dust, apologized and withdrew. I met the young lady at the country club ball that evening, but she wouldn't give me a dance until I promised to stay out of her lap."

Stanford was in a bad way in the second half. Traeger, a convalescent from a long illness, emerged with a shattered collar bone. End Joe Sefton played with a broken collar bone supported by a harness. Alan McGilvray, the fullback who performed phenomenally on defense, had to leave because of sheer exhaustion.

Guard William K. Roosevelt, second cousin of President Theodore

Roosevelt, felt something snap in his leg and so informed halfback Frank Slaker, who with Fisher had the task of preparing Stanford when Coach Charlie Fickert was unable to finish the assignment.

"I sure was hoping we could hold them here," said Slaker.

"I'll stay," Roosevelt answered. He stood his ground despite a broken leg and two fractured left ribs. Three times Stanford held Michigan with less than a foot to go for a touchdown. This was in the first half before the Wolverines scored.

"It was one of the most heroic stands I ever saw in football," Slaker said. "When Roosevelt was taken out and Michigan hit the guard I had to put in, he popped out of the line like a melon seed squeezed between your fingers."

When Yost came to Michigan in 1901, after one-year stops at Ohio Wesleyan, Nebraska, Kansas, and Stanford, Director of Athletics Charles Baird met him at the station. "Young man," he asked, "why are you so sure you can produce winning teams in this conference?"

"Mr. Baird," Yost replied, "there are three things that make a winning football team—spirit, manpower and coaching. If your boys love Michigan, they've got the spirit. If they'll turn out, that takes care of the manpower. I'll take care of the coaching."

WEDNESDAY, JANUARY 1, 1902
(Game not divided into quarters until 1910)

Michigan	17	32	49
Stanford	0	0	0

Michigan—Touchdowns: Snow 5 (5, 2, 6, 15, 3, center rushes), Redden 2 (25, punt return; 25, run with recovered fumble), Herrnstein (22, right tackle). Field goal: Sweeley (20, placekick). Points after touchdown: Shorts 4.

STATISTICS

Michigan		Stanford	Michigan		Stanford
Redden	LE	Clark	27	First downs	5
White (c)	LT	Traeger	503	Net yards rushing	67
McGugin	LG	Roosevelt	21	Number of punts	16
Gregory	C	Lee	38.9	Punting average	31
Wilson	RG	Thompson	1	Fumbles lost	8
Shorts	RT	McFadden	10	Yards penalized	15
Sweeley	RE	Cooper			
Weeks	QB	Tarpay			
Heston	LH	Slaker			
Herrnstein	RH	Fisher (c)			
Snow	FB	McGilvray			

Substitutions—Michigan: none. Stanford: Preston, Sefton, ends; Hauverman, tackle; Van Sickle, guard; Allen, halfback.

– 1916 –

ROSE

Rising fervor for football and sentiment for the Allies were sweeping the country in the ebbing months of 1915.

It was, if ever, the time for the Tournament of Roses Association to stage another gridiron festival to round off its gala New Year's Day show.

Strength on the Pacific slope was centered in the Northwest. Washington and Washington State were both undefeated and untied. The Tournament people felt that Washington State was stronger.

Washington State was coached by a man both extremely able and colorful, William H. (Lone Star) Dietz. In his first year as coach he elevated Washington State football to its highest stature. He wrought a minor miracle with virtually the same players who won only two games the year before.

Dietz's mother was a Sioux Indian. His father was a Union Pacific railroad surveyor. The young coach was a highly intelligent, many-sided, debonair dandy with a flair for the stage, movies, art, fancy clothes, thoroughbred dogs, Indian lore, music, and writing, as well as football.

Lone Star was a teammate of Jim Thorpe's at Carlisle. When he was graduated, he remained at the Indian school three years as assistant to Glenn S. (Pop) Warner, soaking up everything he could learn from the master of the single and double wingback formations.

It was said of Dietz, after he arrived in Pullman, Wash., that he often appeared on the practice field wearing a silk hat, Prince Albert cutaway, yellow gloves, and spats and jauntily swinging a Malacca cane. Long afterward, Dietz debunked the story, saying "My so-called sartorial splendor was greatly overplayed."

He added, "Those boys learned football because I taught them. I got in and scrimmaged with them. I was in good condition then and could outcharge and outrun any man on my squad and they were tough pioneer boys from Washington's ranches and lumber woods.

All they needed to know was how to play the game and I had the answers."

Brown, picked as the Eastern representative, lost three games and tied one. But when Dietz arrived in Pasadena on Christmas morning, he told the press, "Brown will simply wipe the dirt with us." He always regarded optimism as the arch enemy of good football.

The only reporter he couldn't throw off was Damon Runyon who wrote: "I don't agree that Brown will win. Washington State is faster and acts like it wants to play football and is not here just for the trip. I think they mean business and are going to win."

Runyon was right, 14 to 0.

It was an overconfident Brown team. Eastern football was rated far superior to the Western game.

It was an unexciting contest in the mud. Firm footing might have produced a real tingler because Brown's finest runner, Fritz Pollard, one of the shiftiest, fastest backs in the country, would have had a chance to display his shiftiness. In the mire Pollard was held to 46 yards in 15 carries.

Ken Sprague, Brown center, always maintained, "With Pollard's running and Buzz Andrews' passing, we would have been three or four touchdowns ahead on a dry field. The sea of mud which we hardly expected of California changed everything. They even had snow two days before the game."

Most of the game was played on the Brown-defended side of the field. However, the Cougars, who outweighed their Eastern foes approximately 13 pounds per man, didn't score until the second half, when Brown was able to operate from scrimmage only fourteen times.

Sticking mostly to straight football inside the tackles, Washington State backs Ralph Boone, Carl Dietz (no relation to the coach), and Benton Bangs put pulverizing pressure on the whipped-down Brown linemen in the last two quarters.

Boone scored on a three-yard penetration in the third period. Dietz got the second touchdown late in the struggle on a four-yard plunge. Washington State amassed 301 yards rushing.

A crowd of 20,000 had been forecast. But it turned up rain and only 7,000 dampened spectators appeared. The Tournament's net loss came to $11,000.

The next time Brown's right guard returned, ten years later, it was a much happier occasion. He was the head coach of a victorious Alabama team. His name was Wallace Wade.

The train taking Brown players back to Providence stopped at a water tank in the desert.

"Wally got out to chase a jackrabbit which he saw in the sage brush," Sprague remembered. "The train started as he jumped the rabbit. He just had time to catch our coach where I was holding the vestibule door open. He lost his gold watch in the sprint. Some Indians sitting in the shade of the tank must have picked it up because he got the watch in the mail a few days after we reached Providence."

SATURDAY, JANUARY 1, 1916

Washington State	0	0	7	7	14
Brown	0	0	0	0	0

Washington State—Touchdowns: Boone (3, left tackle), Dietz (4, right tackle). Points after touchdown: Durham 2.

STATISTICS

Washington State		Brown	Washington State		Brown
Loomis	LE	Butner	19	First downs	7
Clark (c)	LT	R. Ward	301	Net yards rushing	79
Applequist	LG	Staff	2	Passes attempted	3
Langdon	C	Sprague	0	Passes completed	2
Fishback	RG	Wade	2	Passes had intercepted	0
Brooks	RT	Farnum	0	Net yards passing	19
Zimmerman	RE	Weeks	301	Total net yards	98
Durham	QB	Purdy	5	Number of punts	8
Bangs	LH	Pollard	37	Punting average	29.3
Hanley	RH	Andrews (c)	2	Fumbles lost	1
Dietz	FB	Saxton	55	Yards penalized	10

Substitutions—Washington State: Stites, Finney, guards; Boone, halfback; Doane, fullback. Brown: Ormsby, end; Maxwell, guard; Murphy, quarterback; Hillhouse, S. Ward, halfbacks; Fraser, Jemail, fullbacks.

– 1917 –

ROSE

Undismayed by the abominable weather, poor attendance, and deficit of the 1916 East versus West renewal, the Tournament of Roses Association plunged ahead with plans for the next year.

To guarantee the appearance of an outstanding team from a well-respected eastern university, the Association got an early fall commitment from Pennsylvania. The Quakers finished with a creditable 7–2–1 record. But they were not rated one of their section's strongest teams.

In the Pacific Northwest, Washington and Oregon were unbeaten. They fought to a scoreless tie. Which was stronger? A majority of experts voted for the Webfoots.

Hugo Bezdek, the Oregon coach, was a stocky, brawny, Bohemian-born product of the University of Chicago where he played halfback and fullback under Amos Alonzo Stagg.

Hollis Huntington, Oregon fullback in 1916 who participated in every minute of three Tournament of Roses (Rose Bowl) games, called Bezdek "a fanatical slave driver who demanded perfection.

"He actually tried to pick fights before the games with opposing coaches, such as Gil Dobie and Andy Smith. He criticized so much at Pasadena they said they would never have one of his teams again. He always complained about meals when on the road with his boys. A cook in a Portland hotel chased him out of the kitchen with a knife.

"He didn't believe in injuries. Only broken bones would get a man relieved. One thing about him—I never heard him swear."

Bezdek's near fight with Coach Elmer Henderson of Southern California in the center of the field before the 1923 Rose Bowl game is famous. His brawl with Burleigh Grimes in the washroom of a Pullman going from Pittsburgh to Cincinnati during the 1917 baseball season was one of baseball's most celebrated. At that time Bezdek was manager of the Pirates.

Pennsylvania's 1916 coach, Robert C. Folwell, had just returned to his alma mater after four excellent seasons at Washington and Jefferson. Some, including Stagg, credited him with originating the screen pass while at W&J.

"We didn't look on the game with Oregon as important as some of those we had played during the season," said J. Howard Berry, Pennsylvania's great punting fullback. "Our spirit was what I'd call holiday spirit."

In contrast, "We regarded it as the most important game of our lives," said Huntington. "Remember, the West Coast was not recognized in football at that time. Bezdek kept reminding us of that all the time as we worked every day from Thanksgiving to New Year's Day. Before the game he had practically every man crying."

Old Tournament Park was jammed with 26,000 spectators on a gorgeous New Year's Day afternoon, 1917. Financially, the game was a striking success.

The game followed the pattern of the one before. The eastern team threatened but didn't score in the first half. Oregon punched over touchdowns in the third and fourth quarters and won by the same score as Washington State had, 14 to 0.

The Ducks stepped off 70 yards to break the tie. They got the march under way when Charles (Shy) Huntington, Hollis' quarterback brother in Bezdek's single wingback offense, intercepted a pass. Huntington picked off three Penn aerials in the second half.

A carefully rehearsed, trickily executed pass off a reverse brought the touchdown from the 19. Shy Huntington, after taking the ball from right halfback Johnny Parsons, passed in the end zone to right end Lloyd Tegert, who had no one to contend with for the ball.

"They used our own play to beat us," moaned Quaker quarterback Bert Bell, who piloted professional football to its peak years later as commissioner of the National Football League. The reverse-pass maneuver was a carbon copy of one of Folwell's favorites.

Another interception by Shy Huntington in the fourth quarter settled the issue. Parsons sped 42 yards to the 1 on the first play. Shy headed for the right corner and made it for the second touchdown.

"The Penn team was wonderful," said Bezdek a few years before his death in 1952. "But Stagg personally scouted the Philadelphians and we worked up a defense to stop them. We had only 13 players. But oh, my, those 13 were men."

MONDAY, JANUARY 1, 1917

Oregon	0	0	7	7	14
Pennsylvania	0	0	0	0	0

Oregon—Touchdowns: Tegert (19, pass from C. Huntington), C. Huntington (1, right tackle). Points after touchdown: C. Huntington 2.

STATISTICS

Oregon		*Pennsylvania*	*Oregon*		*Pennsylvania*
Mitchell	LE	Crane	10	First downs	13
Beckett (c)	LT	Mathews (c)	209	Net yards rushing	109
Snyder	LG	Henning	10	Passes attempted	27
Risley	C	Wray	3	Passes completed	13
Spellman	RG	Ertresvaag	2	Passes had intercepted	5
Bartlett	RT	Little	38	Net yards passing	130
Tegert	RE	Miller	247	Total net yards	239
C. Huntington	QB	Bell	16	Number of punts	10
Monteith	LH	Light	37.2	Punting average	39.1
Parsons	RH	Derr	1	Fumbles lost	1
H. Huntington	FB	Berry	45	Yards penalized	75

Substitutes—Oregon: Cook, end; Williams, tackle. Pennsylvania: Young, end; Titzel, tackle; Bryant, quarterback; Williams, halfback; Quigley, fullback.

– 1918 and 1919 –

ROSE

With the United States at war, football teams representing the armed forces provided the entertainment at Tournament Park on January 1, 1918.

The marines from Mare Island met the soldiers from Camp Lewis and defeated them 19 to 7 before a crowd of 25,000 on a sunny, hot afternoon.

Superb generalship by Walter (Jap) Brown, the hard, inside running of Hollis Huntington, and the field-goal kicking of Keith Ambrose overcame the battling doughboys who were pushed around by a huge line (for the times) averaging 207 pounds per man.

Ambrose had never before attempted to placekick a field goal. But he booted 31- and 33-yard kicks in a game in which he ordinarily wouldn't have played. He started at left end.

Ambrose was a substitute. Brick Mitchell would have started except for a badly injured knee. C. F. Hobson, the right end, was crippled on the first play and carried off with a broken leg. Ambrose shifted to right end and Mitchell hobbled onto the gridiron. He played the remainder of the game, practically on one leg.

Late in the first half the marines' goal line, never crossed during the season, was reached and passed on a six-yard sprint around left end by Dick Romney. Now the Army boys were on top, 7 to 3.

Hugo Bezdek had agreed to serve as coach for this game and had given his team a spread formation for use in an emergency.

This was it.

In one of the variations left tackle John Beckett was an eligible pass receiver because he lined up on one flank as the end dropped into the backfield and a halfback moved into the line. Beckett as player-coach had organized the team and handled it all season.

The flip to Beckett succeeded for 14 yards on a touchdown drive that began on the marines' 43. Then, from the same formation, Brown threw the ball to Lawson Sanderson, the left halfback, for 32 yards. Brown turned right end from the 5 for the touchdown.

The Brown to Sanderson pass was regarded as the key play of the game.

Huntington advanced 111 yards in twenty bruising smashes and scored the last touchdown on a one-yard jab. Ambrose frosted the victory cake with another field goal in the fourth quarter.

Each marine player was kissed by his commanding officer's wife as he entered the crowded Maryland Hotel lobby after the game. Liberty, three days of it in the Los Angeles area, was another sweet reward.

The Tournament of Roses Association contributed part of the net receipts to the Red Cross.

With World War I over and travel restrictions relaxed, the Tournament selection committee invited the unbeaten Great Lakes Naval Training Station team from near Chicago to oppose Mare Island in the 1919 game.

The sailor squad included George Halas, Jimmy Conzelman, Paddy Driscoll, and Charley Bachman, famous names in football for many years. Both Halas and Conzelman coached world professional championship teams.

Conzelman rivaled Lone Star Dietz, the Mare Island coach, in his many sided gifts. He was a football player, owner of a professional team, amateur boxer, song writer, sculptor, vaudeville performer, opera singer, actor, pianist, artist's agent, band leader, owner of a country weekly newspaper, magazine contributor, radio announcer, minor league baseball manager, executive of a trucking line, assistant to the president of a major league baseball club (the old St. Louis Browns), popular after-dinner speaker, and a winning pro and college coach.

On New Year's Day the field was in perfect condition and there were 27,000 fans present. Most of them were shivering. The temperature was a brisk 25 degrees.

The 158-pound Driscoll drew blood early with a 25-yard field goal, neatly drop kicked.

Pass interceptions, five of them, ruined several marine scoring threats. On one of them, in the second quarter, 220-pound left tackle Lawrence Eklund thundered 65 yards to the Mare Island 15. Halas called that run the turning point. Two swift strikes produced the touchdown.

Halas himself scored the second touchdown when he seized a 22-yard pass from Driscoll. Halas, from right end, charged across the line a few steps, then headed diagonally left and took the toss in the clear at the 10. Late in the game Halas galloped 77 yards with an interception.

The plucky marines outgained the sailors on the ground but suffered tragically in the air. Great Lakes amassed 192 yards by pass interceptions. The final score was 17 to 0.

"Little Paddy Driscoll turned in one of the outstanding individual performances in Rose Bowl history," said Halas.

On the last play of the first half, Hugh Blacklock, the sailors' 222-pound right tackle and extra point artist, was knocked cold. He remained senseless throughout the intermission but regained consciousness a moment before the kickoff and rushed onto the field to play the full 60 minutes.

Driscoll remembers the big crowd the talented Conzelman drew one night about 11 P.M. high in the Rocky Mountains when the train stalled in a snow storm.

"And what did Jimmy do but give an impromptu concert on his ukelele," said Paddy.

TUESDAY, JANUARY 1, 1918

Mare Island	0	9	0	10	19
Camp Lewis	0	7	0	0	7

Mare Island—Touchdowns: Brown (5, right end), Huntington (1, center plunge). Field goals: Ambrose 2 (31, 33, placekicks). Point after touchdown: Ambrose.

Camp Lewis—Touchdown: Romney (6, left end). Point after touchdown: McKay.

STATISTICS

Mare Island Marines		Camp Lewis Army		Mare Island	Camp Lewis
Ambrose	LE	Turner	12	First downs	9
Beckett (c)	LT	Cook	224	Net yards rushing	115
Ridderhof	LG	Snyder	6	Passes attempted	6
Teberg	C	Russell (c)	3	Passes completed	1
Hall	RG	Christensen	0	Passes had intercepted	0
Bailey	RT	Bartlett	49	Net yards passing	6
Hobson	RE	McRae	273	Total net yards	121
Brown	QB	Sharpe	6	Number of punts	8
Sanderson	LH	McKay	36	Punting average	34.6
Gardner	RH	Romney	1	Fumbles lost	1
Huntington	FB	Craig	30	Yards penalized	5

Substitutes—Mare Island: Mitchell, end. Camp Lewis: Dee, Gard, McKinney, ends; Lynch, Hunt, tackles; Green, Lane, guards; Kapple, halfback; Monteith, fullback.

WEDNESDAY, JANUARY 1, 1919

Great Lakes	3	7	7	0	17
Mare Island	0	0	0	0	0

Great Lakes—Touchdowns: Reeves (3, center), Halas (32, pass from Driscoll of 22, run of 10). Field goal: Driscoll (25, drop kick). Points after touchdown: Blacklock 2.

STATISTICS

Great Lakes Navy		Mare Island Marines	Great Lakes		Mare Island
Reichle	LE	Zimmerman	8	First downs	9
Eklund	LT	Budd	71	Net yards rushing	119
Keefe (c)	LG	Lodell	13	Passes attempted	21
Bachman	C	Risley (c)	6	Passes completed	4
Jones	RG	Moran	1	Passes had intercepted	5
Blacklock	RT	Pike	120	Net yards passing	66
Halas	RE	Hanley	191	Total net yards	185
Driscoll	QB	Steers	12	Number of punts	13
Ericksen	LH	Adams	34	Punting average	33.5
Eielson	RH	Glover	1	Fumbles lost	1
Reeves	FB	Gillis	55	Yards penalized	0

Substitutes—Great Lakes: C. Barnard, L. Barnard, ends; Knight, center; Abrahamson, Conzelman, halfbacks; Willaman, fullback. Mare Island: Mohr, end; Cozetto, guard; Galloway, quarterback; Blewett, Bangs, Calhoun, halfbacks.

– 1920 –

ROSE

When World War I ended and demobilization orders were issued, the caliber of college football improved immeasurably. Teams across the land were stocked with matured service veterans. Many had played outstandingly before the United States went to war. Developed beyond the usual degree and eager for a rugged outlet for their energies, they returned to play with extreme distinction.

Football in the twenties reached a high level of player skill and player enthusiasm. More schools turned out their greatest teams in history than ever before.

The golden era of sport, with Grange, Jones, Ruth, Dempsey, Tilden, Wills, and Rockne, was appropriately ushered in by the Tournament of Roses game.

Harvard, then a power in the East, won, 7 to 6, and the Oregon players have never got over it.

"It was my most frustrating experience," said Oregon fullback Hollis Huntington forty years later. "I still lay awake nights thinking of how easily this game might have been won."

Bill Steers, Oregon's flashy quarterback, was savagely tackled after a 28-yard gain in the second quarter. The crowd booed.

"For a moment it seemed as if the people in the stands were starting on the field," Huntington said. "No foul was called although Steers was hit hard after the whistle. He was carried from the game and our bread and butter player was gone."

All the scoring was compressed into the second quarter. Steers and Clifford (Skeet) Manerud, who replaced him, dropkicked field goals. But between these three-point efforts Harvard inserted a touchdown and the decisive extra point.

The Crimson worked the ball down the field after Steers' 58-yard punt to the 15. It was returned 25 yards by Captain Billy Murray. From the 40 the Ivy Leaguers moved forward for the game's only touchdown.

Quarterback Murray attempted only six passes. He completed two of them, for 20 and 10 yards, to All-America halfback Eddie Casey to put the ball on Oregon's 20. Soon it rested on the 13 after an offside penalty and rushes by Casey and Arnold Horween.

Delicate skill characterized the 13-yard touchdown run by Freddie Church, 180-pound substitute fullback for Ralph Horween, who suffered a shoulder injury.

Church received the snap while moving to his left. He fled into the secondary, dodged two Oregonians, and crossed the goal line in the corner. Then he darted back sharply and placed the ball between the goal posts. Under the rules the conversion try had to be attempted from a spot passing through the point where the touchdown was declared and parallel to the sideline. Thus, from directly in front, Arnold Horween was able to bisect the posts for the vital point after touchdown.

Steers, knocked cold earlier, returned in the final quarter to try another dropkick. It was blocked.

Moments later Oregon had its last chance. The Lemon and Yellow recovered a Harvard fumble on the 18. Stalled on the ground, the Webfoots called on Manerud's toe. Dropping back to the 24, the lightest player ever to perform in the Rose Bowl game—at 128 pounds —thumped the ball with good height toward the bar.

The crowd of 30,000 cheered loudly. It looked true. The scoreboard operator prematurely hung up the figure nine.

"Harvard players threw their head gears to the ground," Manerud recalled. "I thought it was good, too. But referee George Varnell ruled no. He said it was wide. We've argued about it through the years but have remained friends."

Manerud mentioned another turning point.

"As the first quarter ended we completed a forward pass for what we thought was a first down on the Harvard four," he said. "But the timekeeper came on the field and told the referee time was out before the play started. His gun would not go off."

Approximately five hundred adherents of the Crimson, including former athletes and prominent alumni, gathered at the Harvard Club in New York City late on a cold afternoon. Lawrence Perry reported in the *New York Evening Post* the next day:

"When Oregon failed of success in all but two of her many attempts (six) at field goals, the cheers which greeted the failure were the full-lunged sounds of strong men knowing vast relief. And when Harvard made her advance that resulted in a touchdown—well, this was no longer a club room; it was a segment of the Stadium at Cambridge at the supreme moment."

At the end of the game, Langdon P. Marvin, class of '98, led cheers.

Tom Woods, Harvard's 222-pound All-America left guard, returned with a cherished souvenir, the game ball. At 2:15 P.M., half an hour before the kickoff, an airplane piloted by Al St. Johns, a movie comedian, buzzed the gridiron. St. Johns dropped a football decorated with the colors of both teams. Woods caught it and kept it.

Another treasured souvenir was the red jersey with white numbers worn by Casey. A happy bellboy at the Raymond Hotel in Pasadena sported it after the game.

THURSDAY, JANUARY 1, 1920

Harvard	0	7	0	0	7
Oregon	0	6	0	0	6

Harvard—Touchdown: Church (13, left end). Point after touchdown: A. Horween.

Oregon—Field goals: Steers (25, drop kick), Manerud (30, drop kick).

STATISTICS

Harvard		Oregon	Harvard		Oregon
Desmond	LE	Howard	9	First downs	13
Sedgwick	LT	E. Leslie	146	Net yards rushing	285
Woods	LG	Williams	7	Passes attempted	2
Havemeyer	C	K. Leslie	5	Passes completed	0
Faxon	RG	Mautz	0	Passes had intercepted	0
Brown	RT	Bartlett	68	Net yards passing	0
Phinney	RE	Anderson	214	Total net yards	285
Murray (c)	QB	Steers	10	Number of punts	9
A. Horween	LH	Brandenburg	36.9	Punting average	36.3
Casey	RH	V. Jacobberger	3	Fumbles lost	1
R. Horween	FB	Huntington	37	Yards penalized	40

Substitutes—Harvard: Steele, Ryan, ends; Kane, tackle; Hubbard, guard; Felton, quarterback; Church, fullback. Oregon: Manerud, quarterback; Chapman, halfback.

– 1921 –

ROSE

The first and probably greatest of Coach Andy Smith's "wonder teams" at California startled the transcontinental sphere of American football by flattening favored Ohio State 28 to 0 in the East-West attraction on January 1, 1921.

Because of certain significant aspects, the game clearly ranks with the most memorable of all time.

After taking note of the superlative all-around showing of Harold (Brick) Muller, California's right end, Walter Camp was pleased the following season to put him on his first All-America eleven. It was the first time Camp looked west of Minnesota for an All-American.

In the light of California's overwhelming victory over the Big Ten champions, national rankings were hastily revised. Most authorities agreed that the Golden Bears, who scored 510 points to 14, deserved the No. 1 spot.

The East was now convinced, if never before, a rugged brand of football was played on the western shores. It apparently took a man of Andy Smith's caliber to develop the wonderful material in California, ready for the molding. In a few years, Howard Jones at California and Glenn Warner at Stanford would solidify further the Golden State's stature as a producer of some of the most formidable teams in the land.

Smith's four qualifications for success were aggressiveness, obedience, concentration, and determination. He considered spirit and fight worth sixty per cent of a team's effectiveness.

Between 1920 and 1924, Smith's succession of "wonder teams" never lost. They won four straight Pacific Coast Conference championships. They won 44 games and were tied four times. Two seasons, 1920 and 1922, were perfect.

In 1920, Ohio State, coached by Dr. John W. Wilce, stirred a football-crazy nation by the way it achieved a spotless record. The Buckeyes gained the consent of the Big Ten to appear in Pasadena.

Three seeming frustrations were plucked from the coals in the last minute or two. In fact, the pass that beat Illinois, from quarterback Harry (Hoge) Workman to left end Cyril Myers, was in the air when the final whistle blew.

Camp himself saw Ohio State trail Wisconsin, 7 to 0, with four minutes to play, score on a Workman to Pete Stinchcomb pass, but miss the extra point, then win, 13 to 7, when the same combination clicked on a 50-yard pass with less than 30 seconds left.

Then and there Camp reserved a place for the 144-pound Stinchcomb at halfback on his All-America team.

Stinchcomb, admitting that what he said might be construed as a lame attempt to alibi, declared decades after the Buckeyes' defeat, "Why we were beaten only 28-0, I'll never know. It was our bad luck to catch one of the hottest New Year's Days in Pasadena history.

"It was 85 degrees at 10:30 in the morning. People watching the parade were fainting all along Colorado Boulevard. It was a dry heat that affected our reflexes and made us listless. We called time out early in the game and talked it over. Everybody knew what was wrong. Yet we could do nothing about it. We just weren't able to play to the top of our ability."

The *New York Times* pulled out all stops in reporting: "Coupled with the phenomenal California display of passing was an offense as varied as any ever seen in the West."

The famous pass from Muller to left end Brodie Stephens was erroneously listed for many years as traveling 70 yards in the air. And some writers charged Stinchcomb with not bothering to cover

Stephens, saying the Buckeye back thought it impossible a ball could be hurled that far—that is, from past midfield.

"It is true I had been playing safety most of the time but for a few downs I went to halfback in our 7–1–2–1 defense, covering an end," Stinchcomb related. "On the play before Muller's pass, Workman had been hurt in the kidneys. I noticed him back there bent down and obviously in a lot of pain. I shouted: 'You go up; I'll come back and protect things.' It was too late. The play was off. Workman was still bent over when Stephens went by him."

California had carefully rehearsed the play.

Fullback Archie Nisbet bucked three yards to Ohio State's 37. There he faked an injury. The Buckeyes relaxed. Muller strolled nonchalantly into the backfield. Center George Latham sauntered to an end position, Muller's. Suddenly Nisbet sprang into action and centered the ball to halfback Pesky Sprott. Muller circled wide to his right and took a lateral pass from Sprott. Then Muller drifted back to his own 47. He rifled a long, low, beeline spiral pass. Stephens caught it on the goal line. The ball traveled 53 yards in the air.

That was the second touchdown. Earlier, Sprott rammed home

1921—Pesky Sprott (10) plunges for a California touchdown. No. 19 is Ohio State All-America Pete Stinchcomb.

six points from close range and, just before the half ended, when the Golden Bears led, 21 to 0, he got the third touchdown on a five-yard tour of left end.

Ohio State wasted three scoring opportunities in the first 20 minutes on penetrations within California's 10. That finished the Buckeyes. They never launched another serious threat.

Tournament Park swelled with 42,000 spectators that sunny day. Gross receipts amounted to a record $93,314.

It would be 26 years before another Big Ten team would play in Pasadena.

SATURDAY, JANUARY 1, 1921

California	7	14	0	7	28
Ohio State	0	0	0	0	0

California—Touchdowns: Sprott 2 (1, center plunge; 5, left end), Stephens (37, pass from Muller), Deeds (1, right tackle). Points after touchdown: Toomey 3, Erb.

STATISTICS

California		Ohio State	California		Ohio State
Stephens	LE	Myers	17	First downs	11
Dean	LT	Huffman	234	Net yards rushing	85
Majors (c)	LG	J. Taylor	12	Passes attempted	27
Latham	C	Nemecek	8	Passes completed	10
Cranmer	RG	Wieche	1	Passes had intercepted	4
McMillan	RT	Trott	134	Net yards passing	121
Muller	RE	N. Workman	368	Total net yards	206
Erb	QB	H. Workman	10	Number of punts	7
Sprott	LH	Stinchcomb	38.3	Punting average	41.2
Toomey	RH	Blair	0	Fumbles lost	3
Nisbet	FB	C. Taylor	45	Yards penalized	0

Substitutes—California: Hall, end; Barnes, tackle; Clark, guard; Deeds, Eells, halfbacks; Morrison, fullback. Ohio State: Slyker, end; Spiers, guard; Bliss, Cott, Wiper, Isabel, Henderson, Wilder, halfbacks; Willaman, fullback.

– 1922 –

ROSE

"The only thing I know about Washington and Jefferson is that both are dead."

Tongue in cheek, a Pacific Coast sports editor wrote that after the surprising announcement on December 2, 1921, that the team from the small all-male college in Washington, Pa., founded in 1781, had been selected to play in the Tournament of Roses game.

Unbeaten California didn't accept its rightful invitation until a week later because, an announcement from the Berkeley school said, there was a feeling Washington and Jefferson might have committed itself to play the Texas Aggies in Dallas on New Year's Day. Washington and Jefferson replied it had considered such an offer but took no action.

While Washington and Jefferson was unknown in the West, its credentials in the East were impressive. Victories over Pop Warner's Pittsburgh Panthers, Syracuse, and West Virginia sparkled on a perfect ten-game record.

Coach of the Presidents was a 28-year-old young man with six years as a major league outfielder behind him. As rightfielder for Cincinnati in the 1919 World Series with the Chicago White Sox, he obtained ten hits and led both teams in batting with a .357 batting average. The outfielder was Alfred Earle (Greasy) Neale.

Greasy Neale played in 768 major league games. He came up to the Reds in 1916. On September 4 of that year he caught a routine fly in Chicago for the last out in a game in which Cincinnati defeated the Cubs, 10 to 8. It was significant because the putout was made on the last pitch ever thrown by Christy Mathewson and it sealed the great hurler's 373rd triumph.

In a third phase of his remarkable career in sports, Neale rose to the top when his Philadelphia Eagles won the professional football championship in 1948 and 1949.

Neale had plenty of fight talk ammunition. Aroused by numerous slurs, aware that the West expected them to furnish more cannon fodder for the unbeaten, untied Golden Bears, reveling in their underdog role, the Washington and Jefferson Presidents battled California to a scoreless draw.

The statistics indicated a considerable edge to the doughty men from the East. An apparent Washington and Jefferson touchdown was called back.

From the California 36 early in the game, a pass from right halfback Wayne Brenkert to left end Herb Kopf, lightest but one of the scrappiest W&J players at 153 pounds, was called by Captain Russell Stein, 210-pound All-America left tackle. Stein directed his team on offense as well as defensively.

Brenkert was rushed hard. Kopf was covered. So Brenkert burst by his tormentors, headed left, cut back, and crossed the California goal line. The touchdown run was nullified, though. Stein was off-side.

California Coach Andy Smith held out the great Brick Muller, now a full-fledged All-America end, until the second quarter, hoping for an advantageous time to insert him. Muller had been injured in the 1921 season and was not fully recovered.

The Presidents were well rehearsed on how to greet the famous Bear.

Chester Widerquist, right tackle, one of the eleven Presidents who played without relief, remembers a terrific roar.

"I asked a California man what all the shouting was about," Widerquist said. "He looked at me a little annoyed and answered, 'Why, Brick Muller is coming in.' 'Is that so?' I said. 'Well, a bunch of us boys want to give him the sort of welcome he's entitled to.' We walked over to Muller. Our hands were very muddy because of a heavy rain which had converted the field to a quagmire. We all wiped our hands on his clean jersey and someone said, 'So this is the wonder man. Why, he's got only two arms and two legs like the rest of us.' I don't know how it affected him but he didn't complete a pass all afternoon. And California made only two first downs and less than 50 yards against us."

Muller played commendably but the Presidents fenced him in successfully.

Forty years afterward Dr. Muller laughed at the memory of the mud-smearing and related:

"I remember the W&J players had a lot of fun wiping their hands on me when I came in and saying, 'Goody, goody. Now we can go home and say we touched an All-American.' Actually, I didn't get very mad about the razzing. It was kind of funny to me.

"I think I made a few friends in both games in Pasadena. I think

that is one of the greatest rewards in football—the friends you make
while you play."

It was the last New Year's Day game at Tournament Park. With
standing room for 5,000 spectators to be sold in the last few hours
before the kickoff, a crowd of 50,000 was in prospect. The 12-hour
downpour which began the night before the game sliced 10,000
from the estimate.

MONDAY, JANUARY 2, 1922

California	0	0	0	0	0
Washington and Jefferson	0	0	0	0	0

STATISTICS

California		Washington and Jefferson	California		Washington and Jefferson
Stephens	LE	Kopf	2	First downs	8
Barnes	LT	Stein (c)	49	Net yards rushing	114
Clark	LG	Neal	6	Passes attempted	4
Latham (c)	C	Crook	2	Passes completed	1
Cranmer	RG	Vince	1	Passes had intercepted	1
McMillan	RT	Widerquist	0	Net yards passing	23
Berkey	RE	Konvolinka	49	Total net yards	137
Erb	QB	West	13	Number of punts	15
Toomey	LH	Ericksen	39.1	Punting average	32.4
Nichols	RH	Brenkert	2	Fumbles lost	3
Nisbet	FB	Basista	30	Yards penalized	25

Substitutes—California: Muller, end; Dean, tackle; Schuur, guard; Dunn, halfback; Morrison, fullback. Washington and Jefferson: none.

– 1923 –

ROSE

Now the game had shifted, henceforth to be played in the handsome concrete stadium located in the bed of the Arroyo Seco.

The new stadium, begun in early 1922 and finished in the fall, remained a horseshoe in shape until five years later when it became an oval. However, it was immediately named the Rose Bowl by Harlan W. Hall, a Pasadena newspaperman. It was one of the most happily chosen, catchy designations in the history of sport.

A quarrel for supervision of the annual event between the Tournament of Roses Association and the Pacific Coast Conference preceded the 1923 game between Southern California and Penn State.

But Max Colwell, manager of the Tournament of Roses Association, said it would be wrong to place overemphasis on the differences.

"You must remember that in early days when the Tournament of Roses was pioneering the idea of a post-season football game, it had to use its own initiative and row its own boat," Colwell said.

"It was, however, our own people who first realized and suggested that the Rose Bowl game be operated under college control. It is true that there were a few rough times during this transition period before agreement was made wherein the colleges would not only run the Rose Bowl but would choose their own opponents.

"I truly believe this formula not only preserved the Rose Bowl game but saved all other bowl games which followed from being legislated out of business by the N.C.A.A."

Generally, the champion or co-champion of the Pacific Coast Conference—and later the Athletic Association of Western Universities —would be the designated western representative. After the 1924 game the only years it wasn't were 1929, when Southern California refused the invitation, and 1955, when UCLA was unable to play because of the no-repeat rule then in effect.

Thus, after a few verbal conflicts, the Tournament of Roses Association placed selection in the hands of the conference and the western team then picked its opponent from another section of the country—until the marriage with the Big Ten.

Southern California was named to face Penn State in 1923, although conference champion California would have been preferred. The Golden Bears beat the Trojans 12 to 0 and battered eight other teams into submission. But after two straight Pasadena visits, California was disenchanted.

The Trojans were to win eight consecutive games in the Rose Bowl, then drop three of their next four.

Southern California lost only to California. Penn State had played 30 games without defeat until a late-season 14 to 0 loss to Navy. After that, Pennsylvania and Pittsburgh beat them.

In the Rose Bowl, their coach, Hugo Bezdek, who switched from Oregon to Penn State in 1918, and Elmer (Gloomy Gus) Henderson, Southern California coach, assailed each other verbally before 43,000 fans. They almost came to blows. The argument was caused by Penn State's late arrival at the stadium.

Game time was 2:15 P.M., but only the Trojans were primed to play. The Nittany Lions left the Raymond Hotel at 11 A.M. in cars bound for the bowl but minus a police escort. An almost hopeless traffic jam developed. They were right in the thick of it.

Joe Bedenk, who became an All-America guard in 1923 and would have started in the Rose Bowl but for three broken ribs sustained on the first day of practice for Southern California, said, "I was in the car with Bezdek and Neil Fleming, our graduate manager, when they gave an individual $10 to drive across his lawn in an attempt to get to the stadium in time. Because of the crush of cars and the unpaved roads at the time, this was impossible. We walked the last mile down the gorge. Henderson believed we arrived late on purpose so we wouldn't have to play in the extreme early afternoon heat. That wasn't true. At the end of the first half people were still trying to reach the stadium. The traffic tie-up was that bad."

The Penn State party didn't enter the gates until almost 20 minutes after the scheduled kickoff time.

Henderson was burning about Penn State's tardiness, concerned lest his Trojans lose their edge. He flatly accused Bezdek of stalling. Hugo, already inflamed by the unpreventable delay in reaching the bowl, denied it vehemently. Those nearby heard him say, "You're a liar."

Henderson did not withdraw the charge. He was invited to remove his glasses forthwith. But with Henderson, discretion proved the better part of valor. He was well aware of the powerful Bezdek's ability with his fists.

The game was finished in semidarkness. It started with the Easterners in command. However, after Mike Palm's dropkick for a field goal from the 20, the Trojans kept the Lions caged in their own territory almost constantly, permitting only a couple of escapes. The Trojans won, 14 to 3.

Leader of that first quarter assault was "Lighthorse Harry" Wilson, who later played for Army. Wilson ripped through apertures at right guard and left tackle as fast-rushing Trojan defenders were mousetrapped.

"Penn State's early score actually was the turning point because we changed our defense following Palm's field goal," said Leo Calland, guard, captain, and also line coach for Southern California. In his unique position as player-coach, he issued commands on the spot.

"Immediately after their opening drive, I pulled the tackles and ends in and drifted wide myself," he explained. "We found that

Penn State's main power was inside from a shift either way. So we switched from a seven-diamond defense to a six-man line with myself playing a sliding center. I filled in when a hole opened or drifted with wide stuff."

A short punt of 16 yards by Palm to Penn State's 35 set up Troy's first touchdown well into the second period. Just before fullback Gordon Campbell hacked out the final yard, tiny quarterback Harold Galloway made one of the most brilliant of all pass catches in the Rose Bowl.

From the Lions' 8, halfback Roy (Bullet) Baker shot a short, hard pass. Galloway lunged, rolled, and grabbed the ball while sliding on his back. The referee took it from an unconscious man's hands on the 2. Helped from the field, Galloway received a mighty ovation.

Baker personally recorded most of the yardage on the second touchdown drive that began on Southern California's 45 as the second half got under way. The hard-hitting Bullet put up the six points on a one-yard slash. Baker hot-footed 107 yards in 27 totes for the afternoon.

A month before the game Bezdek had announced he would refuse an offer to manage the Philadelphia club of the National League.

"Financially, this means the sacrifice of several thousand dollars a year," Bezdek said. "Ideals cost money, and I find that my ideals can best be worked out in college ranks."

MONDAY, JANUARY 1, 1923

Southern California	0	7	7	0	14
Penn State	3	0	0	0	3

Southern California—Touchdowns: Campbell (1, center plunge), Baker (1, right guard). Points after touchdown: Hawkins 2.

Penn State—Field goal: Palm (20, drop kick).

STATISTICS

Southern California		Penn State	Southern California		Penn State
Pythian	LE	Frank	14	First downs	6
N. Anderson	LT	Johnson	260	Net yards rushing	100
Calland (c)	LG	Prevost	11	Passes attempted	6
Lindley	C	Hamilton	3	Passes completed	2
Hawkins	RG	Elwood	1	Passes had intercepted	3
Newman	RT	McMahan	36	Net yards passing	5
Milton	RE	Artelte	296	Total net yards	105
Galloway	QB	Palm	8	Number of punts	14
Baker	LH	Wentz	33	Punting average	35.9
Kincaid	RH	Patton	3	Fumbles lost	1
Campbell	FB	Wilson	35	Yards penalized	10

Substitutes—Southern California: Boice, Emmons, ends; Cummings, tackle; Dolley, quarterback; Riddle, Wayahn, halfbacks; Leahy, O. Anderson, fullbacks. Penn State: McCoy, end; Logue, tackle; Flock, Hamilton, guards; Bentz (c), center; Hufford, W. Anderson, Lafferty, halfbacks.

– 1924 –

ROSE

The Rose Bowl game's reputation for singular happenings grew in 1924.

Marty Burke, sports writer for the *Los Angeles Examiner,* was tossed out of the Washington dressing room bodily by Coach Enoch Bagshaw after the 14 to 14 tie with Navy.

Referee George Varnell was refused admittance to the stadium when he attempted to enter without a ticket. He was finally rescued. But the game was again late in starting.

Commander Byron McCandless, Navy's director of athletics, slid into a tub of cold water fully clothed during a bathroom conference with Washington officials the night before the game.

R. C. (Torchy) Torrance, Washington's assistant graduate manager, recalled that "Commander McCandless was determined at that time that each school participating would handle its own ticket sales. We put our tickets on sale through the regular channels and had pretty good luck.

"However, Commander McCandless felt the Navy should have all of the tickets in their section and had planned on selling nearly all of their quota to the San Pedro Naval Base. About four days before the game the Navy decided to have special maneuvers, which eliminated any possibility of a sizable number of boys coming from the base.

"So McCandless walked into my room one evening about 6 o'clock with all of his tickets in a suitcase. We set up a program of advertising and rushed tickets to all parts of Los Angeles and ultimately were successful in selling the greater portion of his remaining tickets. It was a nightmare, to say the least."

The touchdown that enabled Washington to get a deadlock was scored on a pass to the left guard.

Navy's invitation was issued in early September and accepted September 27, 1923—before the 1923 season began. California, Pacific Coast Conference champion for the fourth straight year, wasn't interested. Washington, beaten only by California, 9 to 0, became the logical choice.

Navy quickly asserted itself in its first bowl appearance. In the first quarter the Midshipmen drove from their 20 to the Washington one-foot line but were thwarted there.

They were back in a jiffy, scoring when quarterback Ira McKee, on a running pass, pegged the ball 17 yards to halfback Carl Cullen, who scattered Huskies to either side five more yards to the goal line.

An abortive onside kick attempt by Navy gave Washington possession at midfield. Four plays later the score was tied. Fred Abel passed 27 yards to Kinsley DuBois. On the next play, the 40,000 fans saw one of the Rose Bowl's all-time greats at his best. The player was George Wilson, Washington's All-America halfback (1925). Propelling through right tackle, he twisted free from grasping arms and drove 23 yards to score.

Dorset V. Graves, then assistant Washington coach, said, "I coached 35 years and it is my honest opinion that George Wilson easily surpassed any back these eyes ever beheld. He hurt everyone he hit, offensively and defensively. He was a bullet passer for 40 to 50 yards and a tremendous kicker. To have seen him would have been to agree with those who think he had no equal."

It was 14 to 7, Navy, at halftime. The Middies, navigating mostly by air, steered a 78-yard touchdown course just before the intermission. The big strike was a 57-yard pass play from McKee to Cullen.

That put Navy on the 8. A pair of underhand tosses shoveled from fullback Alan Shapley to McKee netted the score. Navy played a wide-open style against the beefier Huskies. Short screen passes were particularly effective. The Midshipmen completed 11 successive passes in the first half and three more in the third quarter, and for the game, 16 of 20.

The final period had scarcely started when Washington got its biggest break. Navy had the ball on its 30.

As Rear Admiral William D. Brown (retired), who played right end, related years later, "Robert Matthews, our center, had been kneed or kicked in the head. He became so dazed he lined up with Washington. After calling time and walking him around, we thought he was all right. But on the next play he passed the ball to the wrong back. It scooted past the deep man, Steve Barchet. Washington (right tackle Roy Petrie) fell on it."

With the Huskies ten yards from a touchdown, Navy's line toughened and repulsed three straight assaults. It was fourth down, 12 to go. Obviously, something special was needed by Washington in that crisis.

Instead of deploying as usual with an unbalanced line, left end DuBois on the weak side dropped back two yards on the shift and the halfback on the right side, Leonard Ziel, slipped into position between the right tackle and right end. That made left guard Jim Bryan the flankman on his side.

Bryan blocked the tackle, then swung out to his left. There wasn't a Navy player within ten yards of him when he received the ball from Abel over his left shoulder and trotted the last four yards.

"Unknown to most fans, that wasn't the critical play," Graves said. "It was the conversion which followed.

"Les Sherman, our placekicker, had a broken bone in his right foot. The trainer and I fixed a splint and taped felt around his instep for protection. He played wearing a size eight left shoe and size ten right shoe. As Bagshaw and I looked up after the touchdown, the ball was about to be snapped to the holder with Sherman in kicking position.

"Bagshaw roared like a lion and yours truly put his hands over his eyes. Sherman glanced over when he heard Bagshaw and with a grin yelled, 'Don't worry, Baggie, I'm a cinch.' Then he kicked it perfectly."

Navy, outgaining Washington, 362 yards to 202, deserved nothing worse than a tie at the least but came within two feet of defeat late in the game. Ziel's placekick from the 33 sailed that far to the left of the post.

TUESDAY, JANUARY 1, 1924

Navy	0	14	0	0	14
Washington	0	7	0	7	14

Navy—Touchdowns: Cullen (22, pass from McKee of 17, run of 5), McKee (2, shovel pass from Shapley). Points after touchdown: McKee 2.

Washington—Touchdowns: Wilson (23, right tackle), Bryan (12, pass from Abel of 8, run of 4). Points after touchdown: Sherman 2.

STATISTICS

Navy		*Washington*	*Navy*		*Washington*
Taylor	LE	DuBois	15	First downs	9
Schreiner	LT	Kuhn	187	Net yards rushing	137

Navy		Washington	Navy		Washington
Carney (c)	LG	Bryan	20	Passes attempted	8
Matthews	C	Walters	16	Passes completed	3
Levensky	RG	Bellman	2	Passes had intercepted	2
Shewell	RT	Petrie	175	Net yards passing	65
Brown	RE	Hall (c)	362	Total net yards	202
McKee	QB	Abel	5	Number of punts	9
Devens	LH	G. Wilson	32.8	Punting average	33.9
Cullen	RH	Ziel	1	Fumbles lost	1
Shapley	FB	Tesreau	5	Yards penalized	20

Substitutes—Navy: Clyde, Vieweg, tackles; Swart, Ballinger, halfbacks; Barchet, fullback. Washington: Westrom, Cole, ends; A. Wilson, tackle; Sherman, quarterback; Beck, fullback.

– 1925 –

ROSE

The decade in sport that began in the early twenties, known as the Golden Age, was a time of champions who combined color with their greatness, of record crowds, and of writers whose inspired work produced lasting American literature.

Midway in the decade the Tournament of Roses Association captured the fancy of the entire nation as never before by presenting on January 1, 1925, Notre Dame and Stanford.

Grantland Rice made Notre Dame's Four Horsemen unforgettable in sport when he started his story after seeing Notre Dame defeat Army in 1923: "Outlined against a blue-gray October sky, the Four Horsemen rode again. In dramatic lore they are known as Famine, Pestilence, Destruction and Death. These are only aliases. Their real names are Stuhldreher, Miller, Crowley and Layden."

Notre Dame, with its Four Horsemen and Seven Mules, achieved a perfect season in 1924. The Four Horsemen met defeat only twice, as sophomores and juniors at Nebraska's hands.

That backfield was unusually light, averaging 160 pounds, and very fast. The Fighting Irish, under the dynamic Knute Rockne, dazzled spectators from one side of the country to the other with their precise shift. The backfield and line worked in flawless cadence, always striving for the perfect play.

In the fall of 1921 the Four Horsemen entered Notre Dame—Harry Stuhldreher from Massillon, Ohio; Jim Crowley from Green Bay, Wis.; Don Miller from Defiance, Ohio, and Elmer Layden from Davenport, Iowa.

Stuhldreher displayed leadership qualities. He was intelligent and utterly fearless. He was at his best on crucial third-down plays. He never has known a peer as an offensive tactician.

Layden was a remarkable punter and could stay even with ten-second men on the cinder track. Miller had excellent speed, too. Crowley was nifty, although not exceptionally fast or shifty. His sleepy appearance completely belied his nimble wit.

"Not so hot" was Rockne's first impression of them in practice as freshmen. But this backfield became marvelously synchronized, its members complementing each other in temperament, physique, and instinctive pacing.

Unusual speed, deception, and devotion to attaining perfection were characteristics of Rockne's teams.

Glenn S. (Pop) Warner was then in his first year at Stanford after varying periods of service at Iowa State, Georgia, Cornell, Carlisle, and Pittsburgh. "You wear out your welcome and lose your initiative staying too long at one place," he once said. "It's good to move around and get a fresh start now and then."

Warner was a great innovator. His teams were meticulously trained in dexterous ball handling, faking, and timing. He popularized the single wingback offense and introduced the double wing.

Warner's best back was Ernie Nevers, a big blond Wisconsin native who was placed at fullback by Rice on his first All-America team in 1925. Nevers' forte was his bull-like plunges. This was enhanced by his fierce determination to thrust ahead. He was also a good passer and punter. Against Notre Dame, Nevers gave a magnificent all-around exhibition.

Rockne started the game with his so-called "shock troops" as he almost invariably did in the 1924 season. This was the second team. Its objective was to wear down the enemy as much as possible and perhaps present the ball to the varsity in an advantageous position when it appeared on the field.

The strategy was quicky disrupted as Stanford from the opening kickoff stabbed tellingly at the Irish defense. After penetrating 43 yards to the Notre Dame 37, the Indians were fended off. A long field-goal attempt by halfback Murray Cuddeback failed.

Miller fumbled on Notre Dame's first play and Charles Johnston,

Stanford's right tackle, recovered on the 17.   On fourth down Cuddeback toed the ball over the crossbar for three points.

Horsemen and Mules got their second chance from their 20 after
Cuddeback's punt a few plays afterward.   This time they brought the
spectators to their feet with a reverberating roar of admiration as
their famed hippety-hop plays began to tear at the Stanford flanks
and middle.   Notre Dame reached the Indians' 4 before the blows
were parried.

"On our last play on that drive (an incomplete pass), I got my
leg twisted under me, resulting in what we thought was a bad sprain,"
Stuhldreher related.   "It was taped up tightly to cut off circulation.
I got along on it fairly well the rest of the game.   When the tape was
taken off in the dressing room, it ballooned to a size all out of propor-
tion.   Pictures later showed the outer leg bone had been broken."

Nevers had sustained an ankle fracture early in the season.   He
recovered but late in the year suffered a bone break in the other
ankle.   He played with both legs tightly wrapped.   After certain
plays, Nevers' teammates had to lift him to his feet, but he never
stopped hammering the Notre Dame line.

At the start of the second quarter Notre Dame was on Stanford's
7, having capitalized on Cuddeback's side-footed punt out of bounds
on his 32.

Crowley hit right tackle for four yards.   Layden, weighing only
162 and quite unlike the popular conception of what a fullback's
build ought to be, rocketed through the line with his distinctive low
charge for the first touchdown.   It was the only touchdown Notre
Dame made by straight football and the only one of an unspectacular
nature.

Nevers, only a minor factor up to now, soon made his presence
keenly felt.   During the afternoon he rammed 114 yards in 34 mostly
pulverizing slams.

But after reaching Notre Dame's 31 on a march originating 49
yards to their rear, Warner's men faced an emergency.   It was fourth
down, six yards to go.   Quarterback Fred Solomon called for Nevers
to flick a flat zone pass to his right where an end would be waiting.

"As a result of careful scouting, we well knew Nevers was accustomed to throw passes into the right flat," Stuhldreher explained.
"Layden backed up on his side, watching carefully for this.   Twice
he intercepted and ran the ball all the way for touchdowns.   The
interesting thing was that the intended receivers were taller than
Elmer and he purposely jumped high and tapped the ball, basketball-
like, to a spot where he would be clear to complete the interception.

"Another important role in these interceptions for touchdowns was played by Crowley. He reacted quickly on each and cleared defensive men out of the way so Layden had a free lane."

Right end Ed Hunsinger also gave Layden fine protection as he streaked 78 yards to score his second touchdown on Nevers' pass.

Alert play enabled Notre Dame to make another defensive touchdown in the third period. Safetyman Solomon lost a high punt by Layden in the sun. He fumbled the ball, then tried to snap it up hastily. Without losing a stride, Hunsinger scooped up the rolling ball while brushing Solomon aside and ran 20 yards across the Stanford goal line.

Solomon beat his hands in a frenzy on the ground shouting all the while, "What a butter-fingered dope I am!" Chancing by at the time, Crowley overheard and remarked, "All right, Solly, nobody disagrees with you."

Stanford also scored in that quarter on a seven-yard end zone pass from Ed Walker to Ted Shipkey. When Cuddeback converted, it was 20 to 10.

As the last quarter began, Stanford center George Baker intercepted Crowley's third-down pass on the Irish 39 and ran to the 31. Shipkey on an end-around battled for five. Nevers banged ahead for eight more with a mighty effort. He had to fight harder for every yard but soon it was first down on the 6. Two more jabs moved the ball three yards.

Harry Mehre, Rockne's center of a few years earlier and a wonderful banquet speaker as well as humorous syndicated football analyst, usually included the story of what happened next in his talks.

"Here John McMullan replaced Rip Miller at right tackle and the Notre Dame players were sure he had an important message from the bench," Mehre would say. "Because of the existent rule, the Irish had to wait until after the next play before they could communicate with John.

"On fourth down they all rushed to him and asked anxiously, 'What did Rock say?' McMullan replied, 'Rock said, Hold 'em.' "

Hold 'em they did. On fourth down they piled up the nearly exhausted Nevers just short of the goal line. Stanford partisans, Warner among them, insisted Ernie's dive carried him across.

In fact, Pop made much of the fact that Stanford held a topheavy margin in first downs and net yardage. But the scoreboard read 27 to 10 late in the game—and didn't change—when Nevers attempted the same flat pass to the right on which Layden scored in the second quarter. Elmer picked it off and beelined 70 yards.

Rockne removed Layden from the game after his long run. The crowd of 53,000 gave him a tremendous ovation.

"I know why you're taking me out, coach," Layden said. "You saw it."

"Saw what?" Rockne demanded. "Are you out of your head?"

"Why, on that last run I carried the ball under the wrong arm," explained Elmer, ever the perfectionist.

Some time before his death in an airplane crash in 1931, Rockne said, "This quartet of backs, destined to be immortal in football, caused me labor, sometimes caused me pain, but mostly brought great joy, not only to their coach but to the spectators. By accident they were brought together. But it was no accident that made them collectively and individually fine players. That was design and hard work. The Four Horsemen have the right to ride with the gridiron great."

THURSDAY, JANUARY 1, 1925

Notre Dame	0	13	7	7	27
Stanford	3	0	7	0	10

Notre Dame—Touchdowns: Layden 3 (3, center plunge; 78, intercepted pass by Nevers; 70, intercepted pass by Nevers), Hunsinger (20, recovery of fumble by Solomon). Points after touchdown: Crowley 3.

Stanford—Touchdown: T. Shipkey (7, pass from Walker). Field goal: Cuddeback (17, placekick). Point after touchdown: Cuddeback.

STATISTICS

Notre Dame		Stanford		Notre Dame	Stanford
Crowe	LE	T. Shipkey	7	First downs	17
Boland	LT	H. Shipkey	127	Net yards rushing	172
Eggert	LG	Swan	8	Passes attempted	21
Harmon	C	Baker	3	Passes completed	11
Maxwell	RG	Neill	2	Passes had intercepted	5
McManmon	RT	Johnston	52	Net yards passing	126
Eaton	RE	Lawson (c)	179	Total net yards	298
Scharer	QB	Solomon	8	Number of punts	2
Hearden	LH	Cuddeback	36.8	Punting average	28.5
O'Boyle	RH	Walker	1	Fumbles lost	2
Cerney	FB	Nevers	30	Yards penalized	15

Substitutes—Notre Dame: Collins, Hunsinger, ends; Bach, E. Miller, McMullan, tackles; Weibel, Kizer, Glueckert, Hanousek, Harrington, guards; Walsh (c), center; Stuhldreher, Edwards, quarterbacks; Crowley, D. Miller, halfbacks; Layden, Livergood, fullbacks. Stanford: Hunt, guard; Mitchell, quarterback; Kelly, halfback.

– 1926 –

ROSE

If asked to list the ten or twenty greatest football games of all time, most fans wouldn't hesitate in the choice of one: the 1926 Rose Bowler in which Alabama won over Washington, 20 to 19.

Returning to the field for the second half trailing, 12 to 0, the Crimson Tide staged the most exciting rally the Pasadena crowd ever witnessed.

There had been great teams in Dixie before—at Georgia Tech, Vanderbilt, Centre, Sewanee, Tulane. But the South was considered a Johnny-come-lately in big time football.

Alabama's victory at Pasadena gained new and permanent respect from all sections, especially the West, for Southern football. In succeeding years, Alabama was to return five times to the Rose Bowl. Duke, Tennessee, Georgia, Tulane, and Georgia Tech were to be invited, too, as the Pacific Coast cottoned to schools south of the Mason and Dixon line.

Under Coach Wallace Wade's command, Alabama earned national recognition for the first time. His 1925 team won the second of three consecutive Southern Conference titles. It allowed only one touchdown.

Washington piled up 459 points in winning the Pacific Coast Conference championship. Several inferior opponents were manhandled. California was beaten, 7 to 0. It was the first loss by the Golden Bears to a college team since 1919.

Wade's men arrived in California to find Washington had been made a 2 to 1 choice mainly because of the presence of the Huskies' all-around halfback ace, George Wilson.

During the first half those odds seemed to be about right. Alabama was unable to contain Wilson and his cohorts after an early Tide threat reached the Washington 15 before petering out.

The marvelous Wilson intercepted a pass by Wu Winslett and raced 36 yards to his own 46. That served to end Alabama's touchdown bid and launch Washington's. Capping the drive, Wilson legged it around left end for nine yards to the 1, scattering Alabama folks along the way. Halfback Harold Patton plowed over. Quarterback George Guttormsen, a leftfooted punter and drop kicker, missed the extra point attempt.

The second quarter had hardly gotten under way when Wilson bolted off right tackle and into the clear for 36 yards to the Tide 20. The fleet Johnny Mack Brown tackled him from the rear. Expected to run again, Wilson crossed up Alabama by throwing a pass over the goal line to reserve left end Johnny Cole. Guttormsen's conversion try hit the bar and bounced back. But the score was 12 to 0 and Washington rooters, roaring a tribute to their team as it came up the field, weren't worried about the two misses—not then.

Wilson, already knocked out once making a tackle, fell unconscious again halfway through the second period when gang-flattened.

Brown, still rated the shiftiest halfback Alabama ever had, discussed the incident thirty years later in Nashville where he was top-billed on an all-western program for the entertainment of underprivileged children. A cowboy movie star of long standing, Johnny Mack gave an amazing demonstration of pistol twirling with a pearl-handled six-shooter.

"Naturally, we concentrated on Wilson," Brown said. "And we were a hard hitting team. In fact, I'll take that team over any I've ever seen before or since and I've seen some great ones. Wilson was hurt and had to leave the game—oh, it was all legitimate, mind you. Nothing dirty. But I'll say this: we put plenty in our tackles when he had the ball.

"George Wilson was probably the greatest player I have ever seen. Everything centered around him, offensively and defensively. Big, powerful and fast he was. And he could take it."

In his book on the Rose Bowl series, Rube Samuelsen pointed out that during the time Wilson was in the game, which was 38 minutes, his team scored three touchdowns and gained 300 yards (of its total of 314). Wilson was out of the game 22 minutes, injured. In seven minutes of the third quarter, with him on the bench, Alabama got all of its points.

Wilson carried the ball for 134 yards against the Crimson Tide and completed five passes for 77 yards and two touchdowns.

Bama quarterback Pooley Hubert battled forward 26 yards to the Washington 15 the second time the Southerners went on offense in the second half. Enraged because he thought he had been roughed, Hubert called his own signal four straight times. He cleaved his opposition for a yard on the final thrust. Bill Buckler, the left guard, placekicked the extra point—and a mighty important one it was.

Washington received the kickoff, couldn't move, and punted to Alabama's 22. In three whacks fullback Emile Barnes punctured the Husky line for a first down on the 39. Brown added two.

"On the next play Grant Gillis went back to pass and spotted me tearing down the field," Brown related. "He floated a long one. I grabbed it on the dead run on the Washington 25. All I had to do was sidestep one man and I was across. We were ahead now but weren't through scoring.

"A fumble gave us another chance on their 30. On first down Hubert told me to run as fast as I could to the goal. When I reached the three, I looked around. Sure enough, the ball was coming down over my shoulder. I took it in stride, used my stiff arm on one man and went over carrying somebody. The place was really in an uproar."

In that third quarter Alabama gained 173 yards. Incidentally, Barnes and Gillis both became major league baseball players.

Washington, with Wilson revived and back in the fray, resolutely slashed 88 yards to its third touchdown in the fourth period. A 27-yard pass play on which Wilson and Guttormsen collaborated polished off the drive. This time Gene Cook converted, but the Huskies were one point shy.

Johnny Mack Brown, Alabama's shifty halfback, on the loose against Washington in one of the most exciting Rose Bowl games.

The game was broadcast for the first time by a Pasadena radio station.

Brown returned to the campus, married his college sweetheart, Cornelia Foster, and became an assistant coach under Wade in 1926. He fully intended to make coaching his profession.

"It was at a game in Birmingham that fall that an actor, George Faucett, became interested in me for some reason," Johnny Mack said. "He and Milton Sills, Doris Kenyon and Victor McLaglen were there making a picture called 'Men of Steel.' They were using the steel mills in Bessemer for background. The Alabama coaches met these actors. Faucett told me he would like for me to take some tests in Hollywood.

"The opportunity arose when we went out to play Stanford in the 1927 Rose Bowl game. I signed with Metro Goldwyn Mayer and played opposite Greta Garbo, Mary Pickford, Marion Davies, Norma Shearer, and Joan Crawford in my early years there. Later, I was the first 'Billy the Kid.'"

FRIDAY, JANUARY 1, 1926

Alabama	0	0	20	0	20
Washington	6	6	0	7	19

Alabama—Touchdowns: Hubert (1, right guard), J. M. Brown 2 (59, pass from Gillis of 34, run of 25; 30, pass from Hubert of 27, run of 3). Points after touchdown: Buckler 2.

Washington—Touchdowns: Patton (1, left tackle), Cole (20, pass from Wilson), Guttormsen (27, pass from Wilson of 17, run of 10). Point after touchdown: Cook.

STATISTICS

Alabama		Washington	Alabama		Washington
Winslett	LE	Schuh	15	First downs	13
Pickhard	LT	E. Wilson	220	Net yards rushing	220
Buckler	LG	E. Brix	14	Passes attempted	16
Holmes	C	Bonamy	4	Passes completed	7
Jones (c)	RG	Wright	3	Passes had intercepted	2
Perry	RT	Erickson	141	Net yards passing	94
T. Brown	RE	Cutting	361	Total net yards	314
Hubert	QB	Guttormsen	5	Number of punts	6
J. M. Brown	LH	G. Wilson	40.8	Punting average	37.5
Gillis	RH	Patton	0	Fumbles lost	1
Barnes	FB	E. Tesreau (c)	0	Yards penalized	15

Substitutes—Alabama: Ennis, Hudson, ends; Camp, Bowdoin, tackles; Caldwell, Johnson, fullbacks. Washington: Cole, Douglass, ends; H. Brix, tackle; Thompson, Cook, guards; L. Tesreau, halfback.

– 1927 –

ROSE

It had been the Tournament of Roses Association's remarkably good fortune to present three straight pulse-accelerating games. Such a run couldn't last. While fine games mechanically, the Rose Bowl offerings in 1927 and 1928 were not particularly disquieting to fans with high blood pressure.

They were close, fiercely waged, and not totally devoid of thrills. Yet they couldn't begin to approach the 1924–25–26 contests in rich drama and suspenseful action.

Wallace Wade was invited to return with Alabama for the 1927 renewal after another perfect season. His great backs of 1925 were gone and he was not wealthy in reserves. It was, nevertheless, a skillful, plucky, tricky combination.

It was also a team with some unusually colorful nicknames: for example, Lovely Barnes, Goofy Bowdoin, Snake Vines, and Rosy Caldwell.

Stanford, rising steadily under Pop Warner, conquered ten successive foes, scoring 261 points with its baffling now-you-see-it, now-you-don't double wingback offense.

His wingback formations, single and double, were copied by hundreds of coaches. The wingback craze swept the country after Warner's Indians of 1928 paralyzed Army 26 to 0 in New York with a bewildering assortment of spinners and reverses, fake reverses, and power plays in which massed interference in front of the ball carrier was almost terrifying.

The bowl was packed, including temporary seats enlarging its capacity to 57,417. Gross receipts of $218,047 were the highest yet. Approximately $100,000 was refunded, so great was the ticket demand. The game was carried by the National Broadcasting Company for the first time with Graham McNamee describing the details —and the surrounding scenery.

Stanford lost no time in impressing on the Alabama boys the fact they were meeting a rugged, well-coordinated group of athletes. Full-back Biff Hoffman passed to halfback "Tricky Dick" Hyland on the first play. It was good for 38 yards to Alabama's 27.

Stanford invaded the last 20 yards of Crimson Tide-defended territory then and three more times. But there was only one payoff and that was just before the first quarter ended.

Aerials accounted for most of the 63 yards on the touchdown sortie. A screen toss from Hoffman to left end Ted Shipkey gobbled up 22 yards. Another netted 11 yards. On a reverse Hyland got 11. A few sundry gains and losses coupled with a five-yard penalty against Stanford left the ball on the Alabama 20. Whereupon halfback George Bogue passed five yards to right end Ed Walker, who ran 15 more for a touchdown.

With four minutes to go in the fourth quarter, the Tide swiftly capitalized on an unexpected harvest from a blocked kick against the Indians, who more than tripled the Southerners' total yardage gained.

Back to punt on fourth down from his 47, Frankie Wilton, 157-pound sophomore substitute for Hyland, who was knocked groggy in the third quarter, toed the ball. As he did so, Alabama center Clarke (Babe) Pearce, a linebacker, leaped in front of him, deflecting the ball.

The Tide's two middle men wedged Stanford's left guard and center. Pearce perfectly timed his drive through the hole. He was right on top of Wilton. It was a well-executed, well-planned stratagem. And the inexperienced Wilton was standing too close, only eight yards behind his center.

The ball rebounded toward the Stanford goal line pursued by Wilton, Pearce, and others behind them.

"My recovery of my own blocked kick was the best individual play of the game," said Wilton, jestingly. He recovered on his 14, but the ball belonged to Alabama.

Into the game went 170-pound Jimmy Johnson at halfback. A dislocated shoulder had prevented him from playing much. He was dependable in the clutch. Wade felt the team would respond to Johnson's presence.

First, it was right end Wu Winslett, at left half on offense, battering straight ahead for three yards, then Johnson knifing forward for seven. Winslett smashed to the 1, next to within inches of the goal line. Now it was Johnson's turn. When he banged over right guard, resistance crumpled under his charge.

It was 7 to 6 now. A ruse was coming up next.

As the teams lined up for the crucial extra point attempt with the crowd respectfully hushed, Captain Barnes barked signals. Suddenly someone shouted, "Signals off." Stanford's forewall stood at ease in anticipation of another signal sequence. At that moment center Gordon Holmes snapped the ball to Winslett who touched it down. Unrushed and with plenty of time, Caldwell smoothly kicked it through the posts and over the bar.

The 7 to 7 game ended three plays later.

It was the second time Alabama had thrilled the Rose Bowl crowd with a last half comeback and the second time Warner had left the field unvictorious despite an imposing statistical advantage.

A year later the Warner-Wilton success story was to unfold, providing an elderly coach with an enriching memory and instilling in the younger man a measure of confidence and self-esteem he might otherwise not have known.

SATURDAY, JANUARY 1, 1927

Alabama	0	0	0	7	7
Stanford	7	0	0	0	7

Alabama—Touchdown: Johnson (1, right guard). Point after touchdown: Caldwell.

Stanford—Touchdown: Walker (20, pass from Bogue of 5, run of 15). Point after touchdown: Bogue.

STATISTICS

Alabama		*Stanford*	*Alabama*		*Stanford*
Ennis	LE	Shipkey	6	First downs	12
Perry	LT	Poulson	87	Net yards rushing	139
Hagler	LG	Swan (c)	7	Passes attempted	16
Pearce	C	McCreery	1	Passes completed	12
Bowdoin	RG	Robesky	2	Passes had intercepted	1
Pickhard	RT	Harris	9	Net yards passing	174
Winslett	RE	Walker	96	Total net yards	313
Barnes (c)	QB	Lewis	8	Number of punts	7
Brown	LH	Hyland	31.7	Punting average	30.3
Taylor	RH	Bogue	2	Fumbles lost	3
Caldwell	FB	Hoffman	5	Yards penalized	60

Substitutes—Alabama: Payne, tackle; Pearce, Pepper, guards; Holmes, center; Smith, Johnson, Vines, halfbacks. Stanford: Freeman, Sellman, tackles; Post, quarterback; Wilton, halfback.

– 1928 –

ROSE

It is an uncommon fact that three of football's greatest coaches, Glenn S. (Pop) Warner, Dr. John B. (Jock) Sutherland, and General Robert R. Neyland, had losing bowl records. Warner's was 1–2–1, Sutherland's 1–3, and Neyland's was 2–5.

Warner's only triumph was in 1928 when Stanford shaded Pittsburgh, 7 to 6, the first of the Panthers' three ill-fated journeys to southern California and the Rose Bowl within a five-year span.

The stadium had now been enlarged to meet ticket demands. It accommodated 72,000 with construction of 20,000 new seats closing in the south end. But the game did not arouse the ardent interest needed to fill the bowl. Attendance was 65,000, slightly disappointing.

It wasn't a spectacular contest, but it was furiously fought. Warner pronounced it "the hardest game I have ever watched." He had done a lot of watching—and was to see much more before retiring from coaching after the 1938 season. In 44 years his teams won 312 games.

The scoring consisted of two recovered fumbles run over for touchdowns within a period of seven minutes in the third quarter.

Taking the play away from his fancy-footed brethren, a Stanford guard, Seraphim Post, pounded 24 yards for the longest run. The guard-around maneuver was characteristic of Warner's inventive genius.

There was an element of drama in the touchdowns that escaped most of the spectators.

The story really began when Alabama capitalized on Frankie Wilton's blocked punt to tie Stanford the year before. His Rose Bowl luck continued, all bad, against Pittsburgh. In the third quarter he fumbled trying to turn left end. Jimmy Hagan, the Panthers' right half who had come up to meet Wilton, picked up the ball with the loss of scarcely a stride and dashed 17 yards to score.

Southern Baptist College
BRUST
LIBRARY
Walnut Ridge, Ark.

During the 1927 season Wilton had committed a fateful fumble enabling Southern California to tie the Indians.

With this latest mishap, Warner rose from the bench and glanced along it. But he didn't pick a replacement.

"Pop's confidence in me, his willingness to stay with me until I delivered is one of the high spots of my life," Wilton said 34 years later at his home in Neenah, Wis.

How he did it is one of the golden moments in bowl history.

Trailing 6 to 0, tackle Walt Heinecke having blocked Allan Booth's extra point attempt, Stanford received the kickoff and put the ball in play on its 37. Twice before the Cardinals had been thwarted within Pittsburgh's 5. Now, after determinedly driving 61 yards, Stanford again was faced with a momentous fourth-down play as the Panthers took root on the 2.

The crucial play evolved from the double wingback formation with unbalanced line (four men to the right of the center).

Wilton lined up four yards behind the center, took Hal McCreery's snap, and faded slightly to his left. Right halfback Bob Sims, running parallel to the scrimmage line to his left, received a pass from Wilton just about the time he (Sims) reached the other side of the line. Preceded by his right guard and right tackle, who pulled out, Sims darted for a hole between Pittsburgh's right end and tackle. The gap closed quickly, however. Sims lost possession when hit hard by rugged Panthers. The ball rolled to his left, and, said Wilton, "I who had shoveled it to him picked it up and ran for a touchdown."

Wilton encountered competition from three Panthers in the scramble for the scooting ball but not only beat all of them to it but then ran away from them. Biff Hoffman kicked the game-deciding extra point.

A father roved the sidelines carrying a large camera. He was Frank Wilton, Sr., a commercial photographer assigned to the game. No father was ever closer to his son during a game. Or was any prouder.

Twenty-seven years afterward a dentist from Sharon, Pa., was on hand to see his son play in the Rose Bowl. The dentist was Pittsburgh's starting fullback against Stanford, Dr. Allan Booth, whose conversion try had been blocked. His boy, Bill, was reserve quarterback for Ohio State against Southern California in 1955.

Dr. Booth probably was watching one game and "playing" another that day.

MONDAY, JANUARY 2, 1928

Stanford	0	0	7	0	7
Pittsburgh	0	0	6	0	6

Stanford—Touchdown: Wilton (5, recovery of fumble by Sims). Point after touchdown: Hoffman.

Pittsburgh—Touchdown: Hagan (17, recovery of fumble by Wilton).

STATISTICS

Stanford		Pittsburgh	Stanford		Pittsburgh
Preston	LE	Donchess	14	First downs	11
Sellman	LT	Kern	200	Net yards rushing	118
Post	LG	Fox	14	Passes attempted	12
McCreery (c)	C	Cutler	3	Passes completed	2
Robesky	RG	Roberts	3	Passes had intercepted	2
Freeman	RT	Wasmuth	35	Net yards passing	22
Harder	RE	Guarino	235	Total net yards	140
Murphy	QB	Fisher	6	Number of punts	9
Hyland	LH	Welch (c)	43.8	Punting average	45.6
Hill	RH	Hagan	1	Fumbles lost	1
Hoffman	FB	Booth	53	Yards penalized	82

Substitutes—Stanford: Muller, Worden, ends; Heinecke, tackle; Driscoll, guard; Lewis, quarterback; Sims, Wilton, Frentrup, halfbacks; Smalling, fullback. Pittsburgh: DeMoise, Fyock, Sargeant, ends; Salata, Getto, tackles; Montgomery, Doverspike, guards; Goldberg, center; Edwards, quarterback; Uansa, Hoban, halfbacks; Parkinson, Fyock, fullbacks.

– 1929 –

ROSE

The game that immortalized Roy Riegels also made famous from coast to coast the name of Bill Munday, a drawling Georgian with a colorful vocabulary and a quaint way of expressing himself.

One story had it that when California center Riegels picked up that fumble by Stumpy Thomason, Georgia Tech halfback, and sped madly toward his own goal line, Graham McNamee, who was broadcasting the Rose Bowl game to millions of listeners, was dumfounded and could not continue. And that Munday, equal to the emergency, carried on and that his depiction of the strangest of all runs made history.

It was a good story but not the case at all.

Munday was indeed in the booth with McNamee. But a third announcer, Carl Haverlin, was on the air when Riegels galloped the wrong way to an undying, if an afflictive kind of fame. Munday and Haverlin each handled two quarters alternately. McNamee stuck strictly to color. Munday, having reported the first quarter, had just handed the microphone to Haverlin a few plays before Riegels' extraordinary run.

Munday was in New York in 1951 to be interviewed by veteran announcer Ben Grauer on the occasion of the National Broadcasting Company's twenty-fifth anniversary. With the aid of appropriate sound effects, Bill breathlessly recreated the historic dash in a broadcast that surely must have been the most realistic and thrilling of its kind ever done.

It went like this:

And the battle rages. It's Georgia Tech's ball on her own 20-yard ribbon, the oval resting 17 yards in from the western boundary with the Engineers headed north. Second quarter just under way. Score: Georgia Tech 0, California 0. The Southerners drop back into their crapshooting formation (center and quarterback stationed back to back). Quarterback Bob Durham has the dice and he might throw a natural. Now they come out of it, cool as firemen playing checkers on a rainy day. Cool, yes, but determined.

Short punt formation, unbalanced line, strong side to the right. Stumpy Thomason back in the tail. Peter Pund snaps the ball to Thomason. He swings wide to his left. He's following good interference. He cuts back off tackle and is through for three, four, five, six, seven yards. Bam! He fumbles when hit around the ankle in an open field.

There's a mad scramble for the pigskin. Center Roy Riegels of California catches it on the bounce and heads for the Tech goal. He's swerving, he's fighting, he's squirming, Tech tacklers all around him. He can't get away. He pivots and—whoa! Wait a minute! What is this! Why, he's turned completely around and he's heading for his own goal, 65 yards away.

Halfback Benny Lom pops out of nowhere and tries to stop him but he can't! He can't! He's hollering and hollering and hollering! But Riegels doesn't hear him! Now everybody is after him, both teams helter-skelter all over the field! Everybody, including me, is going crazy! Now he passes his own 25, the 20! Lom is closing up to nail him but he doesn't! Oh, me!

Riegels crosses the 10! Lom grabs him by the arm! They're at the three and Lom is turning him around! He's trying to get him to run the right way! Blooey! One hundred and eighty-two Tech tacklers hit 'em both in a big pile! The ball catapults over the goal line! The referee dives in and picks up the ball! He's signaling it's dead on the one-yard line! California's ball there.

Thus was history made in the 1929 game.

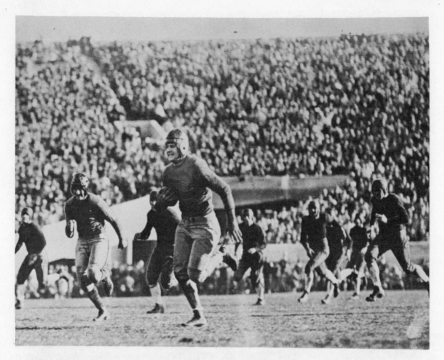

1929—Roy Riegels of California racing toward his own goal line pursued by teammate Benny Lom: football's most startling play.

After his astonishing run, Riegels, crushed, sat on the ground in the end zone holding his hand to his head. Captain Irvine Phillips bent over him solicitously. Some of the Tech players patted Riegels sympathetically on the shoulders. The stadium buzzed as 66,604 spectators jabbered excitedly.

Nibs Price, the California coach, allowed Riegels to remain in the game. It was a considerate decision. Riegels centered the ball accurately to Lom who stood deep in his end zone. But the ball got no more than two feet off his right foot. Vance Maree, Tech's right tackle, led a charge into the backfield, leaped high and blocked the punt. In the ensuing scramble, Stan Barr, California halfback, was the last to touch the ball before it bounced out of the end zone. Referee Herb Dana ruled it a safety.

Those two points were decisive. Tech won, 8 to 7.

Riegels' run was not the first in the wrong direction, nor the last. Yet, because of the fact so many saw it and so many heard it described and because it was the turning point, the amazing dash has become a living legend.

1929—A newsreel sequence of Riegels' unforgettable wrong-way run after picking up a Georgia Tech fumble. Note Lom overtaking him and swinging him around. Tech tacklers flattened Riegels in the next instant.

This Tech team that California, runnerup in the Pacific Coast Conference (champion Southern California was at odds with the Tournament of Roses at the time) met was the best ever coached by William A. Alexander. It swept aside nine straight teams, including Notre Dame. That game had moved Notre Dame coach Knute Rockne, in tribute to Tech's All-America center, Peter Pund, to declare: "We were hopelessly beaten but I had the thrill of my life to see great fighters go down in defeat before a greater fighter."

The first quarter between Tech and California had rocked along evenly. Lom, a fine little halfback, had gotten away for 37 yards but nothing came of that. Warner Mizell, Tech's left half, had raced 32 yards to midfield, but a fumble ruined the subsequent penetration.

There is no doubt about how the next memorable play unfolded and finished. Football movies then were in their infancy. But Munday had a segment of the game film, the Riegels run. He used it to augment speech appearances.

It shows Thomason circling left. A Golden Bear tries a flying tackle but Stumpy gives him a straight arm. Between the 25 and 30 he is hit. Getting away, he reaches the 30 before he is cracked by Phillips and Charlie Schmidt. The ball squirts out of Thomason's grasp and bounces along the turf.

Let Riegels pick up the description here.

"I was playing roving center on defense and drifted with the play. After the tackle, as the ball fell away from Thomason, I picked it up and ran. The defense could do that in those days. I started in the right direction but made a complete horseshoe turn after going four or five yards when I saw two players coming at me from the right. In pivoting to get away I completely lost my bearings. I wasn't out of my head at all and I hadn't been hurt. I just headed the wrong way."

The quick-thinking Lom was the first man on the gridiron to comprehend the situation and first to react. He took after the fleeing Riegels. Ordinarily, the fleet Benny might have overtaken the center within 30 or 40 yards. But Riegels was running with super speed. He was on the left side of the field and was so determined to score that he shifted the ball from his right armpit to his left, apparently so he could use his right as a straight-arm if needed.

As Lom gained on Riegels, he shouted frantically, "Stop, stop! You're going the wrong way!"

At first, the din of the crowd drowned out Lom's voice. But Riegels said, "As I neared the goal line I could hear Benny yelling for me to throw him the ball. Shucks, I wasn't going to throw it to him after that run."

By the time Lom finally grabbed Riegels' right hand and swung him around, they were on the one-yard line. The movie here shows a poignant scene. There stand Lom and Riegels looking upfield at the distant Tech goal line. Riegels at last realizes something is terribly wrong. But before he can make the slightest move to undo any part of his monumental mistake, a Tech man (end Frank Waddey) plows into him. Then a wave of Engineers rolls over him, driving him into the end zone as Lom steps aside.

Referee Dana ruled the ball dead on the 1.

The Golden Tornado (as Tech was known then) scored in two plays from the California 45 in the third quarter. Mizell broke outside right end and beat a 30-yard path down the sidelines behind a four-man wall of interference until forced out of bounds. On the next play, the squatty Thomason bounded off left tackle, reversed his field, and went for a touchdown.

California scored on a pass of ten yards from Lom to Phillips with two minutes left.

To his everlasting credit, Riegels never let his blunder get him down.

Rival center Pund said, "He played a whale of a game. Some would have folded after what he did. Roy was a battler who never quit."

Riegels was elected captain of his team in 1929, made the All-Coast selection, even gained All-America mention. He became a successful high school coach and businessman after his graduation.

TUESDAY, JANUARY 1, 1929

Georgia Tech	0	2	6	0	8
California	0	0	0	7	7

Georgia Tech—Touchdown: Thomason (15, left tackle). Safety: Maree blocked punt by Lom from California 1, ball rolled out of end zone last touched by Barr.

California—Touchdown: Phillips (10, pass from Lom). Point after touchdown: Barr.

STATISTICS

Georgia Tech		California	Georgia Tech		California
Jones	LE	Avery	5	First downs	11
Thrash	LT	Fitz	156	Net yards rushing	135
Westbrook	LG	Gill	3	Passes attempted	15
Pund (c)	C	Riegels	1	Passes completed	7
Drennon	RG	Schwartz	0	Passes had intercepted	1
Maree	RT	Bancroft	22	Net yards passing	103
Waddey	RE	Phillips (c)	178	Total net yards	238
Schulman	QB	Breakenridge	12	Number of punts	12
Mizell	LH	Lom	31.1	Punting average	35.7
Thomason	RH	Barr	3	Fumbles lost	2
Lumpkin	FB	Schmidt	35	Yards penalized	10

Substitutes—Georgia Tech: Holland, end; Watkins, tackle; Brooke, guard; Durant, quarterback; Dunlap, halfback. California: Norton, end; Beckett, Handy, guards; Miller, center; Eisan, quarterback; Schlichtling, Rice, halfbacks; Cockburn, fullback.

– 1930 –

ROSE

Howard Harding Jones created four of the Pacific Coast's most powerful teams in 1929–30–31–32.

His Southern California Trojans demolished Pittsburgh 47 to 14, in the 1930 Rose Bowl game. The next fall they lost only to Washington State in their conference although thrashed by Notre Dame. They beat Tulane 21 to 12 in the New Year's Day game at Pasadena in 1932. And in 1933, also in the Rose Bowl, they walloped Pitt 35 to 0.

The Trojans' lopsided conquest of the Panthers in 1930 started the Pacific Coast's most successful decade (six triumphs in the ten games) of Rose Bowl competition.

Jones, who died of a heart attack on July 27, 1941, was a man who lived largely within himself, containing emotions and masking feelings. His energy for, dedication to, and concentration in his profession were virtually boundless. He was ever considerate and a man who put sportsmanship above everything.

His 1929 team scored a whopping total of 445 points. It was one of his seven conference championship clubs in 16 years at Southern California.

The same season Jock Sutherland turned out a typically tough Pittsburgh machine. It emphasized sledgehammer ground tactics but also a sensational breakaway artist with a collection of dazzling long touchdown runs. The shifty, speedy operative was Octavius G. (Toby) Uansa, born in Germany, March 4, 1908, of Roumanian emigrants.

This Pittsburgh outfit was extolled by some experts as the strongest in the school's history. Various All-America selections honored end Joe Donchess, guard Ray Montgomery, fullback Tom Parkinson, and Uansa.

"Stories of dissension spread after our defeat by such a whopping score," Ernie Lewis, a Pittsburgh guard, told the authors thirty years later. "We were all confident and the result was totally unexpected, difficult to swallow, hard to believe."

To Lewis' way of thinking, "the loss can be attributed to the type of defense we used.

"All year we employed a basic 6–2–2–1 defense. Charley Bowser, backfield coach, was sent to scout Southern California in its final game with Carnegie Tech. When we reached Tucson by train on our way to the coast, Mr. Bowser met the squad. The defense was changed to 7–2–2 with man-for-man against passes.

"After Southern California scored twice on long passes in the first quarter, we were given the word to change our defense to a seven-diamond. We were more vulnerable to short flat passes then.

"The scouting report indicated that USC was a terrific ground club with Russ Saunders and Marshall Duffield capable, fast tailbacks and Gus Shaver and Jim Musick, piledriving fullbacks. Their passing attack was said to be mediocre. They used it as a last resort. Notre Dame, which had whipped them, 27–0, used a 7–2–2 to good advantage. In the face of such information, the defense Pitt would adopt seemed obvious.

"We were outsmarted, however. Southern California was keen, resourceful and aroused. Those Trojans exploited our weakness to the utmost and the scores kept coming."

On the very first play from scrimmage, Uansa, on a reverse to the right, slanted inside the Trojans' All-America left end, Francis Tappaan, and ran over the featherbed turf 69 yards from his own 17 to Southern California's 14. It was one of the most electrifying, longest remembered runs in the annals of the football classic.

"The decision was to bring up the kickoff to the left," said Lewis. "All year we had been springing Uansa loose on the first or second play of the game for a touchdown.

"According to our scouting reports, they used a 6–3–2 defense with ends smashing and converging into the backfield. Their linebackers were wide to take care of sweeps. Our strategy was to run around the ends and drive the wide linebacker in or out, whichever could be accomplished.

"Therefore, our thinking was to line up in left formation and reverse deep with Uansa carrying. This we did, and Uansa was off for touchdown-land 83 yards away. However, Saunders picked himself up and caught Toby at the 14. But we failed to score. A fourth down pass was grounded in the end zone."

As Garrett Arbelbide, Southern California's right end, explained, "The run went away from me between Bob Hall (left tackle) and Tappaan. I was trailing Uansa on the reverse, but I was about a stride away from making the tackle behind the line when I got cut off. All I could do was watch him run and yell like the devil for Saunders to catch him, which he did."

The Trojans struck for a 55-yard touchdown on their first pass. Saunders threw straight down the middle to halfback Harry Edelson. He caught it in the clear on the 30 and scored.

Within a few minutes Pittsburgh halfback Bill Walinchus fumbled on a reverse. Hall recovered on the Panthers' 31. On fourth down from the 25, Saunders fired his second pass. It was good for the distance, too. Halfback Ernie Pinckert, blocker extraordinary, grabbed the ball for the touchdown.

The score was 26 to 0 at halftime. By then the Trojans had used the pass only four times but had completed every one for a total of 136 yards.

Give Pittsburgh credit. Down 33 to 0 in the third quarter, Pitt didn't quit. Walinchus made a magnificent running catch of a 28-yard pass from quarterback Eddie Baker for a touchdown. But the deluge continued. Saunders pitched his third touchdown pass, a 39-yard play with Edelson on the receiving end.

Southern California's fourth scoring pass spanned 57 yards with Duffield flinging the ball to Ralph Wilcox.

The total of six touchdowns on aerials, the 282 yards gained by that method, were Rose Bowl marks. The crowd itself constituted still another record: 72,000. And the receipts, $306,421, yet another.

The Tournament of Roses Association presented miniature gold footballs to all of the 55 players in the game.

One of them went to Ward Bond, a reserve Trojan tackle who went into the movies and became the star of a popular television western, "Wagon Train," in the late fifties. He died of a heart attack November 5, 1960.

One of the little footballs is still worn by Toby Uansa's daughter, Carolie.

WEDNESDAY, JANUARY 1, 1930

Southern California	13	13	14	7	47
Pittsburgh	0	0	7	7	14

Southern California—Touchdowns: Edelson 2 (55, pass from Saunders of 25, run of 30; 39, pass from Saunders of 19, run of 20), Duffield 2 (3, right end; 2, center spinner), Pinckert (25, Saunders pass), Saunders (16, left end), Wilcox (57, pass from Duffield of 37, run of 22). Points after touchdown: Shaver 2, Baker 2, Duffield.

Pittsburgh—Touchdowns: Walinchus (28, pass from Baker), Collins (36, pass from Williams). Points after touchdown: Parkinson 2.

STATISTICS

Southern California		Pittsburgh		Southern California	Pittsburgh
Tappaan	LE	Donchess	10	First downs	8
Hall	LT	Tully	145	Net yards rushing	187
Barrager (c)	LG	Montgomery	13	Passes attempted	19
Dye	C	Daugherty	8	Passes completed	4
Galloway	RG	DiMeolo (c)	3	Passes had intercepted	3
Anthony	RT	MacMurdo	282	Net yards passing	89
Arbelbide	RE	Collins	427	Total net yards	276
Saunders	QB	Baker	4	Number of punts	7
Edelson	LH	Uansa	49.5	Punting average	33.6
Pinckert	RH	Walinchus	2	Fumbles lost	2
Shaver	FB	Parkinson	65	Yards penalized	65

Substitutes—Southern California: Wilcox, Jurich, Steponovich, Joslin, ends; Seitz, Hoff, Ward, Templeton, Bond, tackles; Baker, Shaw, guards; Williamson, center; Duffield, Chambers, quarterbacks; Mortensen, Apsit, Brown, Stephens, halfbacks; Hill, Musick, Moses, fullbacks. Pittsburgh: Loehr, Hirschberg, ends; Quatse, Babic, tackles; Morris, Lewis, Milligan, guards; Barnes, center; Edwards, quarterback; Williams, Murphy, Rooney, halfbacks; Clark, fullback.

– 1931 –

ROSE

To Orin E. (Babe) Hollingbery, "the memory is still a nightmare."

The day was Monday, January 1, 1931. The site was the Rose Bowl. The contestants were two of the nation's strongest teams, Washington State and Alabama, both unbeaten and untied.

Washington State caused the biggest pregame sensation in bowl history by appearing for its warmup attired completely in red—shoes, pants, helmets, jerseys. "They looked like 11 bottles of strawberry pop," one reporter wrote.

But it was the Red Elephants from Tuscaloosa who captured the fancy of the crowd of 60,000 (capacity now was 85,000) once the whistle blew and the game began. It was a Wallace Wade creation, his last at Alabama before becoming head coach at Duke, and it typified the personality of the coldly efficient strategist.

It was tough. It was thorough and all-business. It made few crucial blunders. It bruised its foes and tricked them. It was well stocked with capable reserves. It carried out his maxim that there are more ways to win on defense than on offense. It proceeded to destroy Washington State 24 to 0.

"We had a much stronger team than the score indicated," said Coach Hollingbery. "It was a calamity to us when we lost our regular quarterback-safety man in the early part of the game. Perhaps if the game could have been replayed, with him in there, the outcome might have been different.

"It is the same today as it was then—sometimes you win, sometimes you lose. When two outstanding teams meet, the outcome depends on mental and physical condition on that particular day."

Glen (Turk) Edwards, Washington State's 235-pound All-America tackle, agreed that the loss of Bill Tonkin due to injury in the first two minutes was the turning point.

"He had to leave when tackled as he caught a high punt," Edwards said. "With him gone, our pass defense was wrecked."

On New Year's Eve, Wade announced to a group of sports writers that he planned to open with his second team. Some were incredulous. But Wade, who felt Alabama was two touchdowns better, meant it.

The Cougars held the upper hand most of the first period although they didn't come close to scoring. Late in the period Wade inserted his first string and things began to pop.

Alabama's first 13 plays from scrimmage were on the ground. Suddenly, from Bama's 39, with the Cougars drawn in and unsuspecting, left end Jimmy Moore turned and sped into his own backfield. He received the ball from fullback John Cain, took a few more steps and spiraled a long pass downfield. Left halfback John (Flash) Suther, galloping at high speed, gathered it in smoothly on the Washington State 22. In a flash he was in the end zone.

Within a few minutes, Tuffy Ellingsen, triple-threat Cougar halfback, tried a short pass. Crimson Tide center Jess Eberdt intercepted it and was downed on the Washington State 47. Monk Campbell picked up six yards. Here came Moore again, into the backfield to throw another long pass. End Ben Smith was surrounded by three defenders but came down with the ball on the 1. Campbell powered over right guard for the touchdown.

Crimson lightning struck in another direction the third time. The bolt wasn't long delayed. Washington State went nowhere after the kickoff, punted, and on third down Campbell, on a beautifully set-up fake to Moore, shot through left guard. He wriggled free of fullback Elmer Schwartz's clutches and continued 43 yards to score.

Elements of surprise and deception combined with superb passing, running, and play execution left the Cougars dazed and whipped. They were 21 points behind within a stretch of six minutes of the second quarter.

Wade's second team was on the field in the third quarter when the final points were registered. Guard J. B. (Ears) Whitworth, later head coach at his alma mater, kicked a field goal from the 30.

Hollingbery coached seventeen Washington State teams. His 1930 production was the last with a perfect record. Mel Hein, his brilliant center of that season, insists no other coach ever got more out of less material or gave a more inspirational fight talk before a game.

"He was unsurpassed as a colorful coach, too," said Hein. "He was a real crowd pleaser. He played the game on the sideline, kicking water buckets, stomping his hat and all that. Once he tackled a player coming off the field, telling him, 'Here's the way to tackle.' "

THURSDAY, JANUARY 1, 1931

Alabama	0	21	3	0	24
Washington State	0	0	0	0	0

Alabama—Touchdowns: Campbell 2 (1, right guard; 43, left guard), Suther (61, pass from Moore of 39, run of 22). Field goal: Whitworth (30, placekick). Point after touchdown: Campbell 3.

STATISTICS

Alabama		*Washington State*	*Alabama*		*Washington State*
Dobbs	LE	Hansen	6	First downs	11
Clement (c)	LT	Ahlskog	213	Net yards rushing	140
Sanford	LG	G. Hurley	8	Passes attempted	18
Sharpe	C	M. Hein	2	Passes completed	6
Whitworth	RG	Parodi	0	Passes had intercepted	3
Godfrey	RT	Edwards	103	Net yards passing	65
Elmore	RE	Maskell	316	Total net yards	205
Holley	QB	Tonkin	12	Number of punts	10
Long	LH	Ellingsen	37.2	Punting average	37.5
Tucker	RH	Lainhart	2	Fumbles lost	3
Boykin	FB	Schwartz (c)	55	Yards penalized	30

Substitutes—Alabama: Smith, Dotherow, Moore, Hood, Taylor, ends; Sington, Barker, Jackson, tackles; Miller, Howard, Laslie, Sims, Frey, guards; Houston, Eberdt, centers; McRight, Hansen, quarterbacks; Suther, Campbell, Bellini, Causey, halfbacks; Cain, Brown, fullbacks. Washington State: J. Hurley, Hill, Shaw, H. Hein, ends; Wallulis, tackle; Senn, Yap, guards; Morgan, center; Dahlen, Luft, quarterbacks; Jones, Sander, halfbacks.

- 1932 -

ROSE

Which of the four wondrous Southern California teams coached by Howard Jones between 1929 and 1932 was the best?

"It's hard for a player to say," said Garrett Arbelbide, one of Jones's boys, "but I've checked over material written and said by Mr. Jones about his teams. He definitely favored his '31 team which defeated Tulane in the Rose Bowl, 21–12.

"He called it his finest. I would say it was the better of the two bowl teams I played on. Either the '29 or '31 team was superior to the '32 team which crushed Pitt in the 1933 bowl game."

Yet the 1931 club started on a low note, losing to St. Mary's 13 to 7. Nine straight victories followed. Along the way, the Trojans ended Notre Dame's 26-game unbeaten streak 16 to 14. Despite the one setback, Southern California was generally acknowledged to be the No. 1 team in the country. It was big and quick, closely knit and boyishly enthusiastic about the game.

Tulane was the only major team to win all its games. The Green Wave, coached by Bernie Bierman, defeated eleven foes. Seven victims were shut out.

Bierman's coaching career began at Montana. Lacking material, he enjoyed little success. He left with a bitter memory. In later years, when Bierman was coach of powerful teams at Minnesota, games were scheduled with Washington at Seattle. On the way, he would arrange stopovers at Missoula, Montana, where the university is located. It was his way of reminding Montana what it had lost and what Minnesota had gained.

It was at Missoula that one of football's most famous stories is said to have originated. One night Bierman returned to the hotel where the Gophers were staying and discovered it was on fire. He ran into the lobby, yelling, "Regulars take the fire escape; reserves jump!" Rarely did he ever become excited. This was one of those times, according to the tale.

"One of the reasons our '31 team was so good was that it could think on the field," resumed Arbelbide, one of the Trojans' superb ends of that period.

"In the early part of the Tulane game we were using a crashing type of six-man line. They ran my end a couple of times. So I asked our captain, Stan Williamson, to call time.

"We knew little about Tulane's attack. Howard had told us, if things went wrong, to call time and change strategy. We sat down to think over the situation and decided to go the rest of the way with a 7–1–2–1 defense."

On the last play of the scoreless first quarter, Trojan quarterback Orv Mohler punted to Tulane's 5.

The crowd relaxed, expecting another kick thumped out of the danger zone. But it arose, electrified, when Harry (Wop) Glover, Green Wave right half, escaped on a cutback over left tackle and threaded his way upfield. Maneuvering almost miraculously, Glover sped 59 yards to the USC 36, where Ernie Pinckert pounced on him from behind. It was there the crashing six-man line was abandoned.

Tulane was unable to press on. A punt was forced. And now the Trojans advanced relentlessly to their first touchdown. Operating at fullback—he also played quarterback—Gus Shaver led a drive from the 35 that culminated when Ray Sparling slanted through right tackle on an end-around play that covered the last five yards.

Shaver was on the prowl again in the third quarter, probing his favorite right tackle opening for 12 and then 14 yards more to the Tulane 30.

Pinckert was blocking destructively for Shaver. The Wave expected another foray by that terrifying twosome. Gus crossed up the Greenies by handing the ball to Ernie on a reverse over left tackle. It went for a touchdown.

Don Zimmerman fumbled when hit joltingly by three Trojans as he returned the kickoff. Three plays later the score was 21 to 0 after Pinckert, untouched again, ran 23 yards on the identical call.

It was a complex, elaborate play with a shift. Three Tulane players, including All-America end Jerry Dalrymple, were tricked into thinking Shaver was heading into the line on a spinner. Southern California's blocking left nothing to be desired. The result was perfection.

The Trojans didn't make another first down—in fact, gained only 16 more yards, while the Green Wave rolled across the field twice on touchdown-climaxed sweeps of 76 and 63 yards. Tulane won the heart of the West, if not the game, by refusing to admit it was beaten and fighting back courageously.

Perhaps in no other bowl game were there so many splendid individual performances—by Pinckert, Arbelbide, Shaver, Sparling, Johnny Baker, Ernie Smith, Bob Hall, Larry Stevens, and Captain Williamson of USC and Dalrymple (playing despite an injured kidney), Glover, Zimmerman, Winnie Lodrigues, Nollie Felts, Frances Payne, and John Scafide, a thick-chested, robust guard for Tulane. Many consider Scafide as great a guard as ever rode a runner to earth on the Arroyo Seco field.

As for Arbelbide, he had his own idea of who deserved the laurel sprig.

"I got my thrills seeing and hearing Hal Hammack," he said. "He had been our regular right halfback as a freshman. He had hurt his shoulder early in his sophomore year. He subbed at both halves as a senior. When both Tom Mallory and Gordon Clark left with injuries, Hal took over and you could hear him tackle and block from the top row of seats. He was the best player on the field."

It was a struggle that none of the record throng of 75,562 would forget. No team ever lost, as Tulane did, and gained as much glory. But Southern California convincingly demonstrated the speed, power, and deception that deservedly had brought the national title.

FRIDAY, JANUARY 1, 1932

Southern California	0	7	14	0	21
Tulane	0	0	6	6	12

Southern California—Touchdowns: Sparling (5, right tackle), Pinckert 2 (30, left tackle; 23, left tackle). Points after touchdown: Baker 3.

Tulane—Touchdowns: Haynes (11, 10-yard pass from Zimmerman), Glover (2, left end).

STATISTICS

Southern California		Tulane	Southern California	Tulane
Sparling	LE	Haynes	7	First downs	16
Brown	LT	DeColigny	188	Net yards rushing	255
Baker	LG	Scafide	6	Passes attempted	21
Williamson (c)	C	Lodrigues	1	Passes completed	5
Stevens	RG	McCormick	2	Passes had intercepted	2
Smith	RT	Upton	23	Net yards passing	63
Arbelbide	RE	Dalrymple (c)	211	Total net yards	318
Shaver	QB	Dawson	8	Number of punts	8
Mallory	LH	Zimmerman	41.5	Punting average	38.8
Pinckert	RH	Glover	1	Fumbles lost	2
Musick	FB	Felts	15	Yards penalized	20

Substitutes—Southern California: E. Clarke, end; Hall, Erskine, tackles; Rosenberg, Dye, guards; Mohler, quarterback; Hammack, G. Clark, halfbacks; Shaver, fullback. Tulane: Bankston, tackle; Schroeder, guard; Payne, halfback and fullback.

– 1933 –

ROSE

For the second time in a four-year period a Pittsburgh team, respected and dangerous in its own section, flopped on Pasadena sod in the nineteenth Rose Bowl game on January 2, 1933.

Two years after being graduated at Yale, Ohio-born Howard Jones coached his alma mater's football team to an undefeated, untied, unscored on season. The year was 1909.

His Iowa teams made history. Their 1921–22 records were perfect. In 1921 his Hawkeyes beat Notre Dame 10 to 7, ending a winning streak extending through 20 games.

Now, in 1932, this intense perfectionist whose shifts and multiple alignments created one of the hardest-to-halt attacks in football brought Southern California a flawless season.

Jones rebuilt his backfield but his line was essentially the same as that of the year before. In 1931 his Trojans yielded only 40 points but in 1932, a mere 13.

He introduced, as a sophomore, a flashy tailback (listed as quarterback because he called signals) named Irvine Warburton and called Cotton because of his curly platinum hair. Weighing only 148 pounds and five feet, six inches tall, Warburton looked out of place among the giants on the biggest college team to appear in the Rose Bowl up to that time.

The tricky towhead thrilled the throng of 74,874 on a bright, velvety day with his speedy, low-to-the-ground running in the open. He carried the ball twenty-two times for 87 yards, far more than anyone else.

Warburton scored two of the touchdowns as Southern California's large but mercurial men wore down Pittsburgh and won easily, 35 to 0. It was 7 to 0 at halftime. The good big team poured it on the good little team in the fourth quarter with 21 points.

The victory was Troy's twentieth in succession on the way to its lengthiest string, twenty-five straight.

The Trojans scored the first time that they undertook the offense. The touchdown play was a beauty. Homer Griffith fell back 17 yards to midfield and arched a long pass over the goal line directly between the posts. Right end Ford Palmer, six feet tall, leaped with defending halfback Mike Sebastian (five feet, 10 inches). Although Sebastian seemed for a split second to have the ball in possession, Palmer wrested it away and fell with a six-pointer. It was a superlative effort.

Both of Warburton's touchdowns highlighted the fourth quarter. The crowd, looking for a humorous touch with the game in the bag, found it when the Panthers ripped most of the shirt from Cotton's bag as they clawed at him on a 15-yard run.

Like a number of Southern California football players, including Jesse Hibbs, Russ Saunders, Aaron Rosenberg, and Ward Bond, Warburton became successful in the motion picture industry after graduation.

After Warburton's first touchdown, Pitt's All-America left halfback, Warren Heller, departed and received a standing ovation for the never-say-die quality of his performance.

The galling loss cut Coach Jock Sutherland deeply, coming as it did after frustration in 1928 and humiliation in 1930. But four years hence, things would change.

MONDAY, JANUARY 2, 1933

Southern California	7	0	7	21	35
Pittsburgh	0	0	0	0	0

Southern California—Touchdowns: Palmer (33, pass from Griffith), Griffith (2, pass from Bright of 1), Warburton 2 (1, right tackle; 10, right end), Barber (2, right guard). Points after touchdown: Smith 4, Lady.

STATISTICS

Southern California		Pittsburgh	Southern California		Pittsburgh
Sparling	LE	Dailey	17	First downs	8
Brown (c)	LT	Cuba	202	Net yards rushing	65
Rosenberg	LG	Hartwig	5	Passes attempted	12
Youel	C	Tormey	2	Passes completed	3
Stevens	RG	Onder	0	Passes had intercepted	2
Smith	RT	Walton	35	Net yards passing	39
Palmer	RE	Skladany	237	Total net yards	104
Griffith	QB	Hogan	8	Number of punts	7
Erskine	LH	Heller (c)	31.5	Punting average	32.6
Bright	RH	Sebastian	0	Fumbles lost	3
Clark	FB	Weinstock	31	Yards penalized	26

Substitutes—Southern California: Bescos, Browning, Biggs, Seixas, ends; Harper, Lady, tackles; Dye, Tipton, guards; Jorgensen, center; Warburton, Reboin, Matthews, quarterbacks; McNeish, Clemens, halfbacks; Getz, Griffith, Barber, Beard, fullbacks. Pittsburgh: Rooker, Wojihovski, ends; Meredith, Hoel, tackles; Ormiston, guard; Shotwell, center; Munjas, quarterback; Nicksick, Reider, halfbacks; Weisenbaugh, fullback.

– 1934 –

ROSE

When Stanford invited Columbia to be its opponent in the Rose Bowl in 1934, a wave of pity for the New York City team swept the country. Almost nobody gave the undermanned Lions half a chance against the rugged westerners, champions of the Pacific Coast Conference.

One California sports writer called Columbia: "Pomona High (a suburb of Los Angeles) in blue jerseys." Coach Lou Little's men were ridiculed and Stanford was soundly denounced by press and public alike.

So for Little and his athletes in light blue and white, it became a crusade.

Little was no stranger to Pasadena. As a tackle, he played for Pennsylvania when it lost to Oregon in 1917.

"At that time the Rose Bowl game was in its infancy," he recalled. "Too much emphasis was not placed on the importance of the contest. As a player, I can say that Penn didn't view the game with great seriousness. We enjoyed the trip, had a wonderful time attending social activities and the result was we were not mentally and physically ready for a hard game of football.

"When it was decided Columbia would appear in the 1934 game, I was determined this team would be physically and mentally ready for 60 minutes of all-out action. I would not make the same mistake that was made by the players of that Penn team.

"I decided that for the last 10 days prior to the game, the Columbia squad would do its training and preparation for the game far removed from Pasadena where it would not be distracted by social obligations."

Little declared before Columbia gave Stanford the surprise spanking in all bowl history, 7 to 0, "We expect to win. We did not come
here to fail."

Little kept telling his players they could win if they exerted to the
utmost and concentrated solely on football. On warm afternoons at
Tucson, Ariz., during the week before the game, the Lions drilled
assiduously with particular attention to their pet KF–79 play, one of
a series in which each began the same way. KF–79, evolving from a
spin by the tailback, Cliff Montgomery, was rehearsed endlessly in
the desert until even Little himself could not pick out the ball carrier.

When Little and his team arrived in California the day before the
game, they were drenched by one of the hardest rainstorms in years
in southern California. The Arroyo Seco valley gushed with turbu-
lent waters after more than 18 inches of rain in a three-day period.

The bowl floor was a solid sea of water 48 hours before the kickoff.
Hundreds of thousands of gallons were pumped from the big saucer
by equipment furnished by the Pasadena Fire Department.

Tournament of Roses officials wondered if it wouldn't be an excellent idea to postpone the game from Monday, the first, to Wednesday. Stanford Coach Claude (Tiny) Thornhill favored such a plan.
Little would have none of that, however.

The Columbia coach had brought his team along gradually with
the feeling that precisely at 2 P.M. on Monday, January 1, it would
be at its highest pitch.

A light rain fell on the day of the game. The weather factor,
creating travel problems, plus the natural hesitation many fans felt
about witnessing a probable massacre held the turnout to 35,000.

Within three minutes after the opening kickoff, Stanford halfback
Bob Maentz ran 25 yards to Columbia's 26. Those prognosticating
the Lions' doom awaited the first of the expected deluge of touchdowns.

Here, though, the tide of battle changed abruptly. Stanford was
thrown back and forced to punt. Columbia kicked out of its own
territory and Maentz fumbled on his return (Stanford fumbles were
frequent). Now the Lions had the ball on Stanford's 37.

Montgomery called for KF–79. Columbia deployed with an unbalanced line, strong to the right, two men to the left of the center,
Newt Wilder. Al Barabas flanked Montgomery in the fullback's normal spot with wingback Ed Brominski outside the right end.

Wilder snapped the ball to Montgomery, who spun halfway and
handed it to Barabas, who immediately concealed it behind his left
hip. Continuing to spin as Brominski approached, Montgomery
cleverly faked to him. The wingback headed, as if with the ball,

1934—Al Barabas of Columbia heads for the goal line 17 yards away. This was KF-79, the perfect play that beat Stanford in the biggest bowl stunner of all time.

toward a hole between Stanford's right tackle and end. Meanwhile, Montgomery whirled around and headed low, pretending to have the ball, into the right side of the line.

Barabas paused, watching the two fakes, Brominski's to the left and Montgomery's to the right, draw the perplexed Indians to opposite sides. Then, to complete this unique version of the naked reverse, he began to pick his way, almost gingerly, around the Stanford right end. Once past the scrimmage line, he shifted into high gear. But Maentz, playing safety, cut across and nailed Barabas on the 12. Columbia went no farther that time because Barabas fumbled on the next play and lost the ball.

However, by the time Montgomery signaled for the play again, which was in the second quarter after a successful 24-yard pass to right end Tony Matal, Columbia knew that it must eliminate the speedy Maentz and knew how as well.

Left guard Larry Pinckney told left end Owen McDowell to ignore the right defensive halfback, Bones Hamilton (McDowell's customary assignment on the play), and to concentrate on erasing Maentz, the safety man whose swiftness made it necessary for Columbia to give him personal attention.

"I'll handle Hamilton this time," Pinckney said.

Both executed good blocks. In a flash Barabas streaked 17 yards over the emerald turf and entered the end zone untouched. Wilder place-kicked the extra point and that was the ball game.

Late in the third period Stanford smashed to a first down on the Columbia 3 after three savage thrusts by fullback Bobby Grayson from the Lions' 35. A bunch of photographers gathered at the edge of the end zone. Turning to the cameramen, Matal asked them what they thought they were doing there.

"We're here to get the touchdown," was the consensus reply.

"Forget it," said Tony. "There ain't gonna be any touchdown made here."

The ball was fed to Grayson four straight times. It was still a yard short of the goal line after his fourth carry.

Columbia arrested a fourth-quarter march that reached the seven. The Indians gained 264 yards net to 101 for the Lions and out-first-downed them, 16 to five. But the painstaking hours of practice paid off for Little's underrated men in a colossal upheaval of form.

Thornhill, who succeeded Pop Warner at Stanford in 1933, was the victim of one of the biggest psychological handicaps in Rose Bowl annals.

His were the "Vow Boys," so titled because after their defeat by Southern California as freshmen in 1932, they swore never to lose to the Trojans during their varsity years. And they didn't. In fact, they lost only two games in three regular seasons. But they were beaten twice in the Rose Bowl before closing their careers at Pasadena in triumphant style.

These were—in the 1934 game—the classy sophomores, Grayson (who gained 152 yards against Columbia), Hamilton, tackle Bob Reynolds (who saw 180 minutes of Rose Bowl action), Frank Alustiza, Keith Topping, Wes Muller, Monk Moscrip, Woodward Adams, and others.

Thornhill fought hard to overcome the poisonous seeds of over-confidence sown by newspaper reports and fan reaction, but he couldn't convince his boys Columbia was a good, experienced, brilliantly coached team that would fight them without letup every instant.

In 1954 the Columbia Rose Bowlers met for their 20-year reunion.

"They showed the pictures of the 1934 game," Montgomery said recently. "When the first half ended, Barabas spoke up, 'Lou' (Little was running the projector), 'let's not show the second half. They might beat us.' I guess that's the way we all felt. Even after 20 years we still couldn't quite believe we did it."

MONDAY, JANUARY 1, 1934

Columbia	0	7	0	0	7
Stanford	0	0	0	0	0

Columbia—Touchdown: Barabas (17, left end). Point after touchdown: Wilder.

STATISTICS

Columbia		Stanford	Columbia		Stanford
McDowell	LE	Moscrip	5	First downs	16
Jackel	LT	Reynolds	77	Net yards rushing	240
Pinckney	LG	O'Connor	2	Passes attempted	11
Wilder	C	Muller	1	Passes completed	2
Dzamba	RG	Corbus (c)	0	Passes had intercepted	1
Richavich	RT	Callaway	24	Net yards passing	24
Matal	RE	Smith	101	Total net yards	264
Montgomery (c)	QB	Alustiza	14	Number of punts	9
Barabas	LH	Maentz	32.1	Punting average	26.7
Brominski	RH	Hamilton	2	Fumbles lost	5
Nevel	FB	Grayson	20	Yards penalized	69

Substitutes—Columbia: Chase, end; Demshar, guard; Ciampa, center; Tomb, quarterback; Linehan, halfback; Linehan, Chippendale, fullbacks. Stanford: Topping, Trompas, ends; Drown, tackle; Adams, guard; Bates, center; Hillman, quarterback; Sim, Van Dellen, halfbacks.

– 1935 –

The Orange and Sugar Bowls Arrive

ORANGE BOWL

The Orange Bowl game began as a huge publicity scheme to attract winter tourists to Miami a month sooner than they had been in the habit of coming.

In the early depression-marked thirties, northern folks rarely went south until late January. Pasadena had been doing bowl business for years, ultra-successfully. Why not Miami where the temperature is equally mild in the wintertime? An intersectional football game was the obvious magnet to draw visitors to Florida earlier.

Envisioning a healthier economy, the Chamber of Commerce, businessmen, and Miami and Miami Beach hotelmen eagerly embraced the plan. It would be good for the University of Miami, too, then a struggling newcomer in the field of higher learning.

They called it the Palm Festival and they invited Manhattan University to meet the Miami Hurricanes on January 2, 1933. The game was played at Moore Park, now a playground, before an assemblage of 3,500.

The Hurricanes had a squad of only sixteen players, little equipment, not even a coach for their postseason game. The stricken coach, Tom McCann, a sinusitis victim, persuaded his old mentor at Illinois, the illustrious Bob Zuppke, to help prepare his team.

Meanwhile, George E. Hussey, chairman of the Greater Miami Athletic Club, went to Manhattan Coach Chick Meehan and prevailed on him to hold down the score so as not to duplicate the rout that ruined the first Tournament of Roses game in 1902. Meehan assured Hussey and other civic leaders attending the secret meeting of his cooperation. The night before the game, Hussey informed Zuppke, "I've asked Meehan to take it easy after he gets a two or three touchdown lead and he's agreed."

That was all the psychological fuel Zuppke needed. He relayed the message to "his team" as it took the field. The charged-up Hurricanes repulsed the favored New Yorkers time and again, once stopping them three inches from a touchdown. In the fourth quarter Miami drove from its own 44 to the 2. There the Hurricanes executed perfectly the one play Zup had taught them, a simple wide end run, and scored to win, 7 to 0.

The halftime show at the Orange Bowl is one of the most stupendous, imaginative, colorful outdoor productions in the world. No other bowl comes close to equaling it. The guiding genius of this extravaganza is Ernie Seiler, executive vice-president of the Orange Bowl Committee, a group of civic-minded Miamians working without compensaton. In fact, the Orange Bowl charter rules out private profit.

Seiler was director of the City of Miami recreation department when that forerunner to the Orange Bowl game was played. Even then his creative mind wrought a unique show.

Shortly before the kickoff, a car was driven on the field. On the roof was a giant football, resting on a miniature gridiron. A cannon boomed at 2 P.M., the football opened, and dozens of pigeons fluttered into the blue sky.

Seiler, business manager and then general manager of the Orange Bowl before receiving his present title, smiles when recalling the half-time show. The queen, Marguerite Sweat, was brought to the center of the gridiron in a cellophane football. Inadvertently, the air vents had been sealed. Fortunately, her shouts were heard. They got her out, wilted and shaken. The show went on.

Duquesne, coached by Elmer Layden, was invited to Miami to meet the Hurricanes in the 1934 Palm Festival renewal. The Dukes poured it on in the fourth quarter, winning 33 to 7.

The 1935 game between Bucknell and Miami was the first to be played on the present site of the Orange Bowl stadium. Now the game was part of what was to be called the Orange Bowl Festival. Through the years it would swell to take in a sumptuous parade complete with floats, musicians, and marching units, a tennis tournament, powerboat regatta, basketball tournament, and pyrotechnics show among the festivities and diversions.

The 5,134 fans who watched the first recognized Orange Bowl game sat in wooden bleachers. The lumber was secondhand. It was purchased by Seiler for $1,000 from the American Legion, which had constructed 4,000 grandstand seats for its Miami convention parade the year before.

In a decidedly unspectacular contest, Miami was unable to muster the faintest resemblance to a sustained offense. The Hurricanes bowed, 26 to 0. They were held to 33 yards on the ground.

That game was the exception. And seven years later Ed Danforth, an Atlanta sports editor, wrote, "None of the games is quite like the Miami show. The Orange Bowl picks up where the others leave off and goes on from there."

TUESDAY, JANUARY 1, 1935

Bucknell	0	7	6	13	26
Miami	0	0	0	0	0

Bucknell—Touchdowns: Smith 2 (23, pass from Jenkins; 19, right tackle), Miller (4, center), Reznichak (10, right end). Points after touchdown: Dobber 2 (dropkicks).

STATISTICS

Bucknell		Miami	Bucknell		Miami
Wilkinson	LE	Sissan	12	First downs	4
Bergkamp	LT	Beary	231	Net yards rushing	33
Drayton	LG	W. Dansky	13	Passes attempted	14
McGaughey	C	Glogowski	3	Passes completed	3

Bucknell		Miami		Bucknell	Miami
Green	RG	Brion	1	Passes had intercepted	5
Boiston	RT	Mastro	65	Net yards passing	18
Filer	RE	Wilson	296	Total net yards	51
Sitarsky	QB	Baker	6	Number of punts	13
Reznichak	LH	Panker	41.7	Punting average	29.6
Ramaley	RH	Petrowski	1	Fumbles lost	3
Smith	FB	Rose	30	Yards penalized	15

Substitutes—Bucknell: Pethick, Delaney, ends; Pocius, tackle; Dobber, Crouse, guards; Zanarini, center; Whipkey, quarterback; Miller, Jenkins, halfbacks; Walesky, fullback. Miami: Wolcuff, Shin, guards; Leonard, center; Cook, H. Dansky, halfbacks.

SUGAR BOWL

New Orleans, that remarkably lively Mississippi River port city steeped in history and famous for its gay, cosmopolitan atmosphere, became the scene of yet another outstanding tourist attraction on January 1, 1935.

This, of course, was the Sugar Bowl football game. The project was a success from the start.

It was conceived in 1927 by Colonel James M. Thomson, publisher of the *New Orleans Item*. The public was somewhat cool to Thomson's proposed venture, but *Item* sports editor Fred Digby wouldn't let the idea perish.

Digby constantly campaigned in his column for the establishment of a New Year's Day football classic to rival, in time, the Rose Bowl game, not to overlook enhancing the prestige of New Orleans as a winter tourist capital.

Digby's scheme went beyond football alone. He envisioned a program of varied sports competition. The enthusiasm and persistence of this man won over many of his fellow citizens. In 1947 he became full-time general manager of the New Orleans Mid-Winter Sports Association, which was formed in early 1934 and which sponsors the football game as well as the basketball and tennis tournaments, track meet, and regatta. It was organized as a nonprofit civic enterprise with 39 charter members representing many clubs in the city.

From the beginning the Sugar Bowl people have been neither controlled by nor connected with any commercial interests or professional sports. The charter specifically prohibits private profit. Any surplus above the required operating expenses and reserve fund must be used for charitable, religious, or educational purposes.

With the raising of $30,000 by subscription of 300 guarantors to finance the game, consent of Tulane University to use its stadium without rental fee, and approval of the Southeastern Conference, the promoters staged their first production.

The Sugar Bowl has no affiliation with the Southeastern Conference, of which Tulane is a member, and is bound by no obligation to invite its champion. However, a conference team usually receives a bid.

On October 9, 1953, a civic Appreciation Dinner, attended by 1,000 and tendered by the citizens, honored the founders of the Sugar Bowl game "on the beginning of their twentieth season for their memorable contributions to their community and the world of intercollegiate athletics."

In a speech at the banquet, I. Newman II, then president of the Chamber of Commerce, declared:

The Sugar Bowl group worked for seven years before figuring out how to raise the $30,000 necessary to launch the program. Within a decade after that, this community generously, gladly and quickly produced a half million dollars in voluntary gifts to establish International House, raised over a million dollars for the International Trade Mart, contributed several hundred thousand dollars to Greater New Orleans, spent almost two million dollars enlarging the Tulane-Sugar Bowl stadium, reorganized and extended its chamber of commerce, brought the world's largest aluminum plant here, made this the cordage city of the world, launched construction work costing several hundred million dollars, including new schools, new hospitals, created a great symphony orchestra and expanded all of its cultural activities and produced a remarkable civic spirit that has attracted the attention of the whole nation.

I do not for a moment think we would have undertaken as many projects and done it as successfully if we had not had the inspiration of the Sugar Bowlers, and their experiences and enthusiasm to guide us. They were the pathfinders, and they blazed a trail that became a highroad.

When Tulane defeated Temple 20 to 14 in the first game, Tulane Stadium, built in 1926, seated 24,000. Within two years a need for expansion was evident. Gradually, the size of the huge steel oval was increased, and eventually double-decked.

Sugar Bowlers closed one end of the stadium at a cost of $171,592 in 1937, boosting capacity to 37,000. Citizens eagerly purchased $100 bonds to finance subsequent enlargements—69,000 for the 1940 game and 81,000 in 1949. The 1939 bond issue was for $550,000. The later issue was for $500,000. Bond purchasers were offered two per cent interest and the privilege of buying two tickets to the game.

In 1942, when large outdoor sports gatherings were prohibited on the Pacific Coast, the East-West game was shifted from San Francisco to New Orleans on invitation of the Sugar Bowl.

No bowl was more appropriately named. The site of the game

The Sugar Bowl in New Orleans with seating capacity of 80,985.

was once a plantation owned by Etienne de Bore, a planter who raised sugar cane and founded a national industry.

In the opening game of the series, Tulane, coached by Ted Cox, fell behind by 14 points in the first half but seized the initiative after that.

The Green Wave scored its first touchdown on a second-quarter kickoff. Claude (Monk) Simons, Jr., took a lateral from John Mc-Daniel and didn't stop until he had crossed the Temple goal line 85 yards distant. In later years Simons became an associate director of the Association, president, and after Digby died on November 3, 1958, he served, in effect, as general manager.

The third quarter was well along before Tulane tied the score on an 11-yard pass from Bucky Bryan to end Dick Hardy. Tulane was aflame now and wouldn't be denied. No sooner had Temple punted, unable to move the ball after the kickoff, than the Greenies rolled down the field again from their 39.

From Temple's 43, Barney Mintz threw a pass in the direction of Hardy on the 15. Temple halfback Rocco Mowrey tipped the ball. Hardy grabbed it, whirled, and raced for the end zone. He planted it an inch across the goal line with quarterback Glenn Frey hanging onto his legs.

The Green Wave made a determined stand to protect its lead in the last four minutes. The Owls, with powerful fullback Dave Smukler and Mowrey smashing through the Tulane defense, stormed from their 36 to the 5. An offside penalty hurt them badly at that point.

Two downs later Smukler, who handled the ball almost as a magician would have, tossed his only poor lateral pass of the game and Mowrey was tackled on the 17. Tulane took the ball on downs on the 13 and marched 65 yards before time expired.

Each school received $27,800 from gate receipts provided by the crowd of 22,026. Twenty-six years later shares amounted to $165,000 apiece.

| Tulane | 0 | 7 | 7 | 6 | 20 |
| Temple | 7 | 7 | 0 | 0 | 14 |

Tulane—Touchdowns: Simons (85, lateral from McDaniel on kickoff), Hardy 2 (11, pass from Bryan; 43, pass from Mintz of 28, run of 15). Points after touchdown: Mintz 2.

Temple—Touchdowns: Testa (7, pass from Smukler), Smukler (1, center plunge). Points after touchdown: Testa, Smukler.

STATISTICS

Tulane		*Temple*	*Tulane*		*Temple*
Hardy	LE	Wise	8	First downs	12
Moss	LT	Docherty	146	Net yards rushing	179
Evans	LG	Boyd	13	Passes attempted	12
Robinson	C	Stevens	4	Passes completed	2
Smither	RG	Gurzynski	1	Passes had intercepted	2
Ary	RT	Russell	78	Net yards passing	21
Kyle	RE	Anderson	224	Total net yards	200
Brownson	QB	Frey	10	Number of punts	12
Mintz	LH	Testa	34.3	Punting average	30.3
Simons	RH	Stonik	2	Fumbles lost	0
J. Loftin	FB	Smukler	20	Yards penalized	5

Substitutions—Tulane: Memtsas, Preisser, ends; Stroble, tackle; Tessier, Monk, guards; N. Loftin, center; McDaniel, quarterback; Bryan, Thomas, halfbacks; Lodrigues, fullback. Temple: Zanin, end; Miller, guard; Longsderff, Mowrey, halfbacks.

ROSE

Grantland Rice never quite forgave himself for not putting Dixie Howell on his 1934 All-America team.

After watching Alabama vanquish Stanford, 29 to 13, in the Rose

Bowl, the matchless sports writer from Tennessee knocked out this lead from the press box: "Dixie Howell, the human howitzer from Hartford, Ala., blasted the Rose Bowl dreams of Stanford today with one of the greatest all-around exhibitions football has ever known."

Howell, teaming with the incomparable pass catching end, Don Hutson, electrified the crowd of 84,474 with a 22-point second quarter. In those 15 minutes Alabama amassed 150 yards on passes and 106 on the ground. Howell himself gained 96 yards in the air on four completions to Hutson and three more to Paul Bryant, the other end. Dixie also ran 96 yards, including a sensational 67-yard sprint for a touchdown.

The first quarter offered no hint of coming events. Alabama was held to four yards net and had the ball for only four plays.

When Stanford end Keith Topping recovered Tide fullback Joe Demyanovich's fumble, the Indians were only 27 yards from the Bama goal line. They got there in five irresistible smashes. Bobby Grayson pounded right tackle for the final foot.

Came the second period and the complexion of the game changed abruptly, thrillingly, and decisively.

"Your only chance is through the air," Alabama Coach Frank Thomas told his boys before the game. They took him at his word.

Before the half ended, nine Tide passes were thrown and eight were completed. It was a wonderful display of timing, accuracy, and mechanical perfection.

The first series of three passes set up Howell's first touchdown, which he scored from the 5. Bouncing off a wall of humanity that jammed the designated point of attack, Dixie corkscrewed from right to left and went over the final line.

Determined to prove this a fluke, Stanford chose to kick off. Four more pass connections merged with a 17-yard run by Howell brought Alabama to the Indians' 6. On fourth down, Howell knelt and held the ball for quarterback Riley Smith, whose toe swung through and lofted it over the crossbar.

Now it was 9 to 6 and still Stanford refused to believe the mounting evidence. Big Bob Reynolds, 25 years later to become president of the new Los Angeles Angels baseball club in the American League, kicked off again.

Two plays after that Howell swung to his right around Monk Moscrip. Smith leveled Grayson with a hard block. As the Stanford secondary closed in, Dixie swerved from the sidelines and cut across the field diagonally. He ran 67 yards. The crowd was on its feet, agog at this masterly piece of speed and maneuvering.

Trailing 16 to 7, and not so cocksure now, Stanford sought the ball but had it for only two plays. On second down Smith intercepted Stan Anderson's long pass on the Alabama 46.

Thomas inserted Tilden (Happy) Campbell, a conservative quarterback, to replace the daring Smith with orders to play it safe and stick to the ground. Only eight seconds were left in the half. What Thomas didn't know was that Smith told his teammates, just before going to the sidelines, "I've called the play. Make it good."

They did. Joe Riley, who took Howell's place after his long run, flung a long pass to Hutson, who was in the clear and scored easily on making the catch.

Hutson, later to become even more celebrated as a pass-catching marvel with the Green Bay Packers, could all but fake defenders out of their shoes with his varying speeds and change of pace. He could feint so expertly that he shook many defenders just by moving his head or shoulders.

"What made me a football player was the time I realized I was catching passes only when I was pulling the defensive man out of position," Hutson once said. "And for every pass I caught in a game, I caught a thousand in practice."

The Howell-to-Hutson battery was quiescent until the early part of the fourth quarter. From the Alabama 41 it struck. Don caught Dixie's long spiral on the Stanford 30 and whizzed for his second touchdown.

Howell left the field late in the game after a 52-yard punt with his ears ringing to the noisiest ovation ever given a visiting player on a California gridiron. He had gained 111 yards running, 160 yards passing (nine completions in 12 attempts) and had punted six times for an average of 43.8 yards.

"No team in the history of football, anywhere, anytime, has passed the ball as Alabama passed it today," read the story filed by sports editor Ralph McGill to the *Atlanta Constitution*. "And no man ever passed as did Dixie Howell, the swift sword of the Crimson attack."

Alabama	0	22	0	7	29
Stanford	7	0	6	0	13

Alabama—Touchdowns: Howell 2 (5, left guard; 67, right end), Hutson 2 (54, pass from Riley of 24, run of 30; 59, pass from Howell of 29, run of 30). Field goal: Smith (22, placekick). Points after touchdown: Smith 2.

Stanford—Touchdowns: Grayson (1, right tackle), Van Dellen (12, right end). Point after touchdown: Moscrip.

STATISTICS

Alabama		Stanford	Alabama		Stanford
Hutson	LE	Moscrip	11	First downs	15
Lee (c)	LT	Reynolds	145	Net yards rushing	180
Marr	LG	Adams	13	Passes attempted	23
Francis	C	Muller	10	Passes completed	5
Morrow	RG	Rouble	1	Passes had intercepted	4
Whatley	RT	Callaway	215	Net yards passing	89
Bryant	RE	Topping	360	Total net yards	269
Smith	QB	Alustiza	6	Number of punts	5
Howell	LH	Van Dellen	42.5	Punting average	36
Angelich	RH	Hamilton (c)	2	Fumbles lost	0
Demyanovich	FB	Grayson	40	Yards penalized	40

Substitutes—Alabama: H. Walker, J. Walker, Gandy, ends; McGahey, Baswell, tackles; Danuletti, Peters, Dahlkamp, A. White, guards; Dildy, Moye, centers; Campbell, Goldberg, quarterbacks; R. White, Stapp, Riley, Boozer, halfbacks. Stanford: Monsalve, Smith, Schott, Trompas, ends; Lettunich, tackle; Callaghan, Walton, Black, guards; Brandin, center; Anderson, Maentz, quarterbacks; Reisner, White, halfbacks; Anderson, fullback.

– 1936 –

SUGAR

The 1936 Sugar Bowl program, printed well in advance of game day, took an unusually optimistic stand.

"This second Sugar Bowl football classic is an unprecedented success," it stated. And so it was.

The New Orleans Mid-Winter Sports Association had a powerful magnet in Texas Christian, admirably well balanced and replete with standout individuals. Most famous of the Horned Frogs was Sammy Baugh, a phenomenal passer. They had lost one game in 12, a 20 to 14 defeat by Southern Methodist. In that game Baugh threw 45 passes.

Louisiana State whipped every team it faced after losing its opener to Rice 10 to 7. Over a three-year period the Tigers, coached by

Bernie Moore, lost to only one team in the South, to Vanderbilt in 1937, 7 to 6.

Although he did not pass for a touchdown in TCU's 3 to 2 "pitchers' duel" victory over LSU in the Sugar Bowl, some writers believe Baugh played what may have been the greatest all-around game of his collegiate career.

Sammy proved he could do considerably more than pass the football with speed, accuracy, timing, and calmness. His punting (for a 44.6 average), blocking, ball-carrying (he sloshed 52 yards through the mud to the LSU 1 late in the game), and defensive work were something to see and remember.

Rain started to fall heavily on a gloomy, raw day soon after the opening kickoff. TCU punted fourteen times and LSU thirteen. All the points went up on the scoreboard in the second quarter. Through it all the tall, sinewy Baugh was a mighty mudder.

The Tigers were repulsed midway in the second period after making a first down on the Frogs' 2. On Bill Crass' final plunge, center Darrell Lester prevented a touchdown. He suffered an injured shoulder crashing into Crass and was forced to leave the game. But he had saved it for his team.

As Texas Christian took possession of the ball on its one-foot line, Baugh faked a punt, then daringly passed. LSU's All-America end, Gaynell Tinsley, rushed him hard. In a hurry to turn the ball loose, Sammy threw off balance and it slipped off his fingers onto the ground behind his own goal line. It was an automatic safety.

Crass fumbled on the first play after the ensuing kick. Left end Will Walls recovered for TCU on the LSU 40. Continuing his heroics, Walls hastened downfield in time to catch a 23-yard pass from Jimmy Lawrence. Three line jabs were blunted whereupon fullback Talden Manton kicked a field goal from the 26.

Interceptions by Baugh halted two penetrations in the third quarter. However, a fumbled punt by the peerless passer gave the Bayou Bengals one last chance from the TCU 31 in the fourth period. They chewed up 27 yards before their claws were clipped.

Baugh and Tinsley were teammates in the College All-Star game in Chicago the next year. Tinsley caught a pass from Baugh for a touchdown in one of the collegians' rare triumphs over the National Football League champions. The Green Bay Packers went down 6 to 0.

Sammy signed for $500 to play pro football for the Washington Redskins. He led the Redskins to the world's championship in his "freshman" season. In 16 years as a pro, he completed 1,693 passes for an efficiency rating of 56.5 per cent.

Baugh always patted his linemen and blockers on the back whenever he could publicly. He would always room with a lineman or blocking back.

Once a huge, muscular youngster trying out with the Redskins was introduced to the Texan. Considerably awed, the big boy said, "Gee, I dreamed of playing with the great Sammy Baugh and now it's gonna come true."

"What's your position?" Baugh asked.

"Tackle," answered the kid.

"Well, you knock the dickens out of some of those linemen and I'll dream of you," Sammy responded.

WEDNESDAY, JANUARY 1, 1936

Texas Christian	0	3	0	0	3
Louisiana State	0	2	0	0	2

Texas Christian—Field goal: Manton (36, placekick).
Louisiana State—Safety: (incomplete pass by Baugh in own end zone).

STATISTICS

Texas Christian		Louisiana State	Texas Christian		Louisiana State
Meyer	LE	Tinsley	6	First downs	9
Ellis	LT	Carroll	114	Net yards rushing	108
Harrison	LG	Brown	8	Passes attempted	20
Lester	C	Stewart	3	Passes completed	3
Kellow	RG	Helveston	1	Passes had intercepted	3
Groseclose	RT	Rukas	53	Net yards passing	60
Roach	RE	Barrett	167	Total net yards	168
Baugh	QB	Seago	14	Number of punts	13
Kline	LH	Mickal	44.6	Punting average	42.2
Lawrence	RH	Fatheree	1	Fumbles lost	2
Manton	FB	Reed	15	Yards penalized	15

Substitutions—Texas Christian: Walls, Needham, Diggs, ends; Godwin, Holt, Linne, tackles; Rogers, Dunlap, Mayne, guards; Tittle, center; Harrell, Montgomery, McCall, Clark, McClanahan, McClure, halfbacks; Roberts, fullback. Louisiana State: Mihalich, Dumas, ends; Leisk, Baldwin, guards; Lawrie, quarterback; Crass, Coffee, Rohm, halfbacks; Bowman, fullback.

ORANGE

Although there were really only three major games on New Year's Day now, the distinguished Damon Runyon wrote, "Only a finger bowl is lacking to give us enough football dishes to cover a sideboard this first day of 1936.

"There is enough larceny of ideas in this world as it is, without our municipalities joining in the theft. We hold that the other cities are displaying plenty of gall, and a singular lack of imagination, in stealing Pasadena's 'Bowl' title, morally copyrighted, so to speak, by long custom and tradition."

Runyon must have been shocked by the bowl craze that swept the country in the forties.

Doing nothing by halves, the Orange Bowl Committee also sponsored a $40,000 parade complete with floats, thirty of them. Its theme was a tribute to Florida's citrus industry. On the lead float drawn by a mechanized seahorse rode the Orange Bowl queen.

The game between Catholic University and Mississippi, won by the team from Washington. D. C., 20 to 19, was a crowd-pleaser. But there were only 6,568 who saw it. The Orange Bowl had not come of age.

Ole Miss never was ahead but made it a tingler by scoring twice in the fourth quarter, which started with the Rebels trailing 20 to 6.

Right halfback Ned Peters ran 67 yards for Mississippi's first touchdown to earn a long-standing place in the Orange Bowl record book. The last 27 yards were made possible when Bruiser Kinard, the Rebels' great tackle, obliterated safetyman Stuart Foley.

It was a bowl debut for Arthur J. (Dutch) Bergman, Catholic coach who was a backfield teammate of Notre Dame's immortal George Gipp on Knute Rockne's perfect record 1919 machine. But Ole Miss Coach Ed Walker was no bowl stranger. He passed for a touchdown against Notre Dame in the Rose Bowl 11 years before and scored for Stanford against Alabama in the 1927 classic at Pasadena.

Catholic	7	6	7	0	20
Mississippi	0	6	0	13	19

Catholic—Touchdowns: Adamaitis (2, right end), Foley (48, pass from Adamaitis of 28, run of 20), Rydzewski (blocked punt by Bernard from Mississippi 24, run of 20). Points after touchdown: Mulligan, Makofske.

Mississippi—Touchdowns: Peters (67, left end), Bernard (1, right tackle), Poole (24, pass from Baumsten). Point after touchdown: Richardson.

STATISTICS

Catholic		Mississippi	Catholic		Mississippi
Schmarr	LE	Poole	7	First downs	15
Karpowich	LT	Kinard	124	Net yards rushing	201

Catholic		Mississippi		Catholic	Mississippi
Anthonavage	LG	Bilbo	3	Passes attempted	15
Yanchulis	C	Nelson	1	Passes completed	4
Lajousky	RG	Breyer	2	Passes had intercepted	4
Clements	RT	Dickens	48	Net yards passing	56
Mulligan	RE	Jackson	172	Total net yards	257
Dranginis	QB	Bernard	13	Number of punts	11
Adamaitis	LH	Hapes	41	Punting average	34
Carroll	RH	Peters	0	Fumbles lost	2
Makofske	FB	Rodgers	30	Yards penalized	15

Substitutes—Catholic: McGann, Brown, Dunne, Rydzewski, ends; Chludenski, Katalinas, tackles; Sochon, Perron, Arnold, guards; Orth, Gemlo, centers; Foley, quarterback; Walker, Munhall, Glodeck, halfbacks; Greco, fullback. Mississippi: Bogard, Kincade, ends; Richardson, tackle; Wilson, Madre, guards; Hutson, Aston, centers; Kelly, quarterback; Baumsten, halfback.

ROSE

And so there was joy in Palo Alto on New Year's Day after all. And the Vow Boys of Stanford, who had disappointed their followers and themselves twice in the Rose Bowl, won the game they had to win, with Southern Methodist the victim, 7 to 0.

This was a contest so drab, in complete contrast to the expectations of the crowd of 84,784, that one spectator, Bob Zuppke, the esteemed Illinois coach, commented: "Neither line could open a hole that a sparrow could fly through. Blocking was poor. Tackling was ragged in many spots. Forward passing was about as bad as I've seen all year. One good play was wiped out by three bad ones."

Coach Matty Bell's Mustangs won more regular season games— twelve—than any bowl team in history. Smart and poised and spectacular, they were the talk of the country. Their 20 to 14 victory over Texas Christian, with Bobby Wilson, their skittering little, 155-pound halfback, leaping for an almost impossible pass grab and scoring the winning touchdown, was the thrill of the year.

They had played in the Los Angeles area once before. They had beaten UCLA 21 to 0. California fans so loved their flashy, deceptive attack, which included all sorts of laterals off forward passes, that they all but demanded a return appearance in the Rose Bowl.

SMU brought thousands of rip-roaring, kiyi-yipping, supremely confident Texans with them. They found seats, but possibly 150,000 other fans were turned down so intense was interest in the game.

It was an aroused group of Stanford seniors who took the field. They who had vowed three years before never to lose to Southern California were determined not to fail again in the Rose Bowl.

Although there was every prospect that the game would furnish high scoring action and offensive frills, it did precisely the opposite.

Late in the first quarter Stanford quarterback Bill Paulman sent a 62-yard punt into the sky. The ball was downed on the 10. Bob Finley zoomed one back 51 yards that Jimmy Coffis returned to the SMU 42. On the seventh play of the advance from there, Paulman rammed right guard for one yard and the touchdown as the Mustangs braced for a plunge by Bobby Grayson.

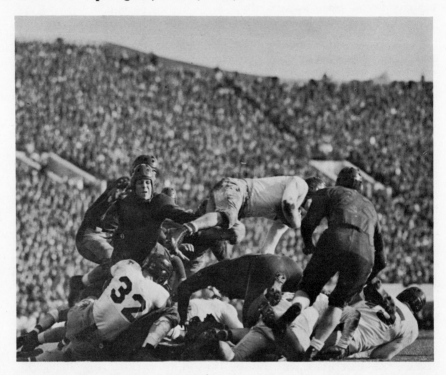

1936—Bobby Grayson, Stanford's All-America fullback of the mid-thirties, cracks the Southern Methodist line. On the ground at the right is Bob Reynolds, Stanford tackle who played every minute of three straight Rose Bowl games.

Closest SMU came to scoring was in the second period. Passes carried the Texans most of the distance from their 25 to the Stanford 5. The 35-yard play on which they almost scored left the crowd gasping. It was a series of beautifully executed laterals after a pass from John Sprague to Bill Tipton.

But with first down and a touchdown in sight, SMU called for another complicated ball-tossing maneuver instead of a smash or sweep. By the time the ball reached Finley after a prior flip from

Sprague to Harry Shuford, several Indians were waiting to nail him. The ball was fumbled. Stanford center Wes Muller recovered on the 8.

Stanford's exceedingly aggressive defense held SMU to 40 yards rushing. Right end Keith Topping smothered play after play. The other end, Monk Moscrip, was almost as good.

But the most ballyhooed of all Rose Bowl games was disappointingly ordinary and unspectacular.

Stanford	7	0	0	0	7
Southern Methodist	0	0	0	0	0

Stanford—Touchdowns: Paulman (1, right guard). Point after touchdown: Moscrip.

STATISTICS

Stanford		Southern Methodist	Stanford		Southern Methodist
Moscrip	LE	Tipton	5	First downs	9
Reynolds	LT	Spain	75	Net yards rushing	40
Adams	LG	Wetzel (c-c)	5	Passes attempted	30
Muller	C	Johnson	2	Passes completed	9
Rouble	RG	Stamps	1	Passes had intercepted	6
Beedle	RT	Orr	43	Net yards passing	98
Topping	RE	Stewart (c-c)	118	Total net yards	138
Paulman	QB	Sprague	16	Number of punts	10
Coffis	LH	Wilson	35.5	Punting average	35.9
Hamilton (c)	RH	Burt	0	Fumbles lost	1
Grayson	FB	Shuford (c-c)	25	Yards penalized	20

Substitutes—Stanford: Schott, end; Carlson, tackle; Black, Matthews, guards; Williams, fullback. Southern Methodist: Sanders, Weant, tackles; Scottino, Baker, guards; Raborn, center; Smith, Finley, halfbacks; Finley, fullback.

– 1937 –

Cotton Joins the Ranks

COTTON BOWL

The 1940 Cotton Bowl program described J. Curtis Sanford as "a genial, smilin' fellow, a marvelous asset to Dallas because he sponsors the Cotton Bowl classic each New Year's Day.

"Not only does Dallas reap splendid, heavy publicity and tremendous financial benefits from the Cotton Bowl game, but also the entire State of Texas. Visitors come from many states and enroute to and from Dallas they see much of this state of which we are so proud, visit many cities and spend much money, for sports loving people are liberal people."

The introduction concluded: "He (Sanford) never has and never intends to gain any personal profits from staging the Cotton Bowl game."

Dallas oil man Sanford conceived the idea of putting on his own bowl game on a trip to the Rose Bowl. He undertook the promotion, first as a football fan with the private funds to afford it, and secondly as an advertising scheme for his city and the Lone Star State.

The oil magnate went $8,000 in the red on his first independent venture. Less than half of the 45,500 seats were occupied on January 1, 1937, when Texas Christian outclassed Marquette 16 to 6. Each school received $10,000, although it would have been less except for Sanford's certified check guarantee.

Twice in the first four years of the Cotton Bowl's existence, the wealthy sportsman turned over sponsorship to Dallas civic organizations. Each time he was asked to re-assume full responsibility and did. The game has been operated on a paying basis since 1938.

After the 1940 game a group of Dallas citizens acquired from Sanford the right to stage it. That same year these men, constituting a so-called Custodian Committee, offered a plan which would make the Cotton Bowl Athletic Association an agency of the Southwest Conference. The conference adopted the plan.

The Southwest Conference champion played in the bowl for only the second time in five years in 1941. After that the conference voted officially to send its champion to the game each year.

In the 1951 program, Bill Rives, *Dallas Morning News* sports editor, wrote: "The Cotton Bowl is unique, because it is the only game of its kind which is controlled and operated by an athletic conference. When the National Collegiate Athletic Association became alarmed over the growing number of bowl games and over charges that some of them were operated for private benefit, it looked about for a model which other bowls could emulate. The Cotton Bowl was that model."

Actual operation and management are handled by the Cotton Bowl Athletic Association, a nonstock, nonprofit organization. Its board of directors includes alumni representatives from the eight conference schools (three from each institution), past Association presidents, the executive secretary of the conference, and members of the civic group that turned the game over in 1940.

As in all the big bowls, the competing teams' shares of the gates have multiplied through the years, especially since the signing of lucrative television contracts running in excess of $100,000. At the silver anniversary game in 1961, Duke and Arkansas received $173,-402 apiece. Some schools before that got even more.

They don't pocket the entire amount. The Southwest Conference, in common with other major conferences, long has had a rule providing for equitable distribution among all members. The host school receives the lion's share. But it is never a huge sum.

At present the first seven per cent of the gross receipts is taken off the top to help retire bonded indebtedness on the stadium. Thirty-nine per cent of the remainder goes to each school. Twenty-two per cent is used by the Association to defray expenses of staging the game. When the Association has money left over, it is presented to the conference.

The original football stadium was a wooden structure. In 1930 the present framework of the Cotton Bowl, owned and operated by the State Fair of Texas, was erected with a seating capacity of 45,500 at a cost of $400,000. The stadium was double-decked on the west side for the 1949 game. This cost $1,280,000. It increased the number of seats to 67,431 and was financed by a sale of $100 bonds. Each bond gave the holder a priority to buy one ticket to all bowl sporting events for twenty years from that time.

The east side was double-decked before the 1950 game at a cost of $400,000. Fifty-dollar ticket options were sold. Capacity was 75,-504 for subsequent games.

It has become customary at the site of the major bowls for other events, mostly athletic, to revolve around the pièce de résistance. The sports festival plan is popular in Dallas at the year's end and succeeds in drawing many visitors several days earlier than they might have ordinarily arrived. There's basketball, bowling, tennis, rodeo, and, inevitably, a parade.

The annual meeting of the Southwest Conference Sportsmanship Committee is held during Cotton Bowl Week. Delegates from each school discuss methods for implementing good sportsmanship on the field and in the stands. They also select the conference student body that has distinguished itself at varsity sports events during the year. The award is part of pregame ceremonies at the Cotton Bowl game.

Identical twins, quarterback Art and halfback Al Guepe, played for Marquette in Sanford's introductory private enterprise. Art caught a punt by Sammy Baugh in the first quarter and ran 60 yards for the bowl game's first touchdown.

Just before making that dash, Guepe, playing in the safetyman role, yelled to the TCU bench, "Watch me this time, boys; I'm going all the way." Guepe was like that as a player, and as a coach—full of confidence, optimism, and frankness.

The rest of the afternoon belonged to the Horned Frogs, quarterback Baugh, center Ki Aldrich, end L. D. Meyer (nephew of Coach Dutch Meyer), and a fine cast.

Meyer, later a major league baseball player, scored all of his team's points. He caught two passes for touchdowns, kicked a field goal that covered 40 yards, and added an extra point.

FRIDAY, JANUARY 1, 1937

Texas Christian	10	6	0	0	16
Marquette	6	0	0	0	6

Texas Christian—Touchdowns: Meyer (50, pass from Baugh of 20, run of 30; 18, pass from Montgomery). Field goal: Meyer (40, placekick). Point after touchdown: Meyer.
Marquette—Touchdown: Art Guepe (60, punt return).

STATISTICS

Texas Christian		Marquette	Texas Christian		Marquette
Meyer	LE	Anderson	16	First downs	10
Hale	LT	Siefert	178	Net yards rushing	95

Texas Christian		Marquette		Texas Christian	Marquette
Holt	LG	Czernecki	20	Passes attempted	21
Aldrich	C	Schoemann	9	Passes completed	10
Harrison	RG	Reif	3	Passes had intercepted	3
Ellis	RT	Hansen	151	Net yards passing	130
Roach	RE	Muth	329	Total net yards	225
Baugh	QB	Art Guepe		Number of punts	
McCall	LH	Buivid	32.5	Punting average	39.3
Montgomery	RH	Sonnenberg	0	Fumbles lost	0
Roberts	FB	Cuff	35	Yards penalized	25

Substitutes—Texas Christian: Needham, end; Linne, Hensch, White, tackles; Kline, Rogers, Dunlap, Mayne, guards; Tittle, center; O'Brien, quarterback; Clifford, McClure, Hall, Harrell, Wilkinson, halfbacks. Marquette: Cooper, Higgins, ends; Lumb, Kuhn, tackles: Mosovsky, Jennings, Lauterbach, guards; Al Guepe, halfback.

SUGAR

Here was Harry Borba's lead on the Sugar Bowl game in the *San Francisco Examiner* on January 2, 1937:

"These boys from the West have just torn down the north goal posts, and quite appropriately, too.

"Now the south goal posts are falling prey to small, joy-crazed bands of Santa Clara rooters all the way from northern California.

"Their Bronco heroes have just beaten Louisiana State, 21–14, in the major upset of the post season."

Santa Clara made two straight triumphant expeditions to New Orleans. Louisiana State was the victim both times.

The Broncos were coached by Lawrence T. (Buck) Shaw, a strikingly handsome, silver haired man. He played tackle on three great Notre Dame teams in 1919–20–21. While he was with the Irish, they lost only one game in three years and had a streak of twenty successive victories.

Santa Clara's fortunes soared to the zenith in 1936 and 1937 under Shaw. In 1960 he hit the top as a professional team coach. He retired after his Philadelphia Eagles won the National Football League championship.

LSU was a pronounced favorite, but the first quarter was an absolute denial of the odds. The Broncos were in front 14 to 0.

Four minutes after the opening kickoff Santa Clara took the lead. A 27-yard pass play with Nello Falaschi pitching and Manny Gomez catching clicked for a touchdown. Seven minutes later Bruno Pellegrini uncoiled a 30-yard throw to Norman Finney, who crossed the goal in two strides.

The Tigers sliced the handicap to seven points in the last minute of the first half. From midfield Bill Crass lobbed a 23-yard pass to All-America end Gaynell Tinsley. Reversing his field, Tinsley bounced off several Broncos on his way to the end zone.

Santa Clara struck early again in the second half. Gomez intercepted a pass by Pat Coffee and ran 35 yards to the LSU 15. On reaching the 5, an end-around was called. Carrying the ball was Frank (Mississippi) Smith, whose home was in Picayune, Miss., hardly more than a whoop and a holler from the Sugar Bowl.

Pinned by two large Tigers on the 2, Smith did an unusual thing. He played a long shot since it was fourth down. Falling in a whirl of figures, he tossed the ball in the air with a take-it-or-leave-it gesture. Falaschi grabbed it in full stride. Don DeRosa knocked out the props from a potential tackler. Nello continued across the goal line for the touchdown.

Second-string Broncos were on the field when LSU made its second and last touchdown in the fourth period.

The ball changed hands ten times on fumbles. It was a record for all the bowls.

| Santa Clara | 14 | 0 | 7 | 0 | 21 |
| Louisiana State | 0 | 7 | 0 | 7 | 14 |

Santa Clara—Touchdowns: Gomez (27, pass from Falaschi of 22, run of 5), Finney (30, pass from Pellegrini of 28, run of 2), Falaschi (1, recovery of fumble by Smith). Points after touchdown: Pellegrini 2 (placekicks), Smith (pass from Falaschi).

Louisiana State—Touchdowns: Tinsley (50, pass from Crass of 23, run of 27), Reed (17, pass from Crass of 9, run of 8). Points after touchdown: Crass, Milner.

STATISTICS

Santa Clara		Louisiana State	Santa Clara		Louisiana State
Smith	LE	Tinsley	10	First downs	7
McGee	LT	Strange	108	Net yards rushing	44
Rodgers	LG	Leisk	12	Passes attempted	21
Dougherty	C	Stewart	6	Passes completed	7
Bassi	RG	Baldwin	2	Passes had intercepted	4
Wolff	RT	Carroll	74	Net yards passing	125
Finney	RE	Dumas	182	Total net yards	169
Falaschi	QB	May	12	Number of punts	13
Gomez	LH	Milner	42	Punting average	36
DeRosa	RH	Morton	4	Fumbles lost	6
Pavelko	FB	Coffee	42	Yards penalized	0

Substitutions—Santa Clara: Coughlan, Foley, Misegades, ends; Cope, Locke, Artoe, tackles; Farasyn, Ginney, Cook, guards; Kelly, center; Perrin, quarterback; Seramin, Pellegrini, Gilbert, halfbacks; Fisher, fullback. Louisiana State: Myrick, Mihalich, ends; Lester, Gatto, Farmer, tackles; Matlock, Clark, guards; Gormley, center; Booth, quarterback; Rohm, Coffee, Crass, Reed, halfbacks; Crass, Reed, fullbacks.

ORANGE

The Orange Bowl game of 1937 was notable for several reasons. One quality was the sheer excitement of the game itself.

Another was an 82-yard punt by Mississippi State's Ike Pickle, a bowl record.

No two teams were more rule conscious than Mississippi State and Duquesne. Their combined penalty yardage, only ten, is another Orange Bowl mark.

Then there was that 72-yard touchdown pass, from Boyd Brumbaugh to Ernie Hefferle, that stood as an Orange Bowl record until 1959.

With three minutes to play, Duquesne, behind 12 to 7, was desperate—a "far piece" to go and time running out.

The fateful play was obvious. Brumbaugh, the passer, was to dodge Maroon linemen as best he could. Hefferle, the end, was to get downfield as quickly as possible.

At the instant Ernie got the jump on Pickle and burst into an undefended sector, Boyd, free momentarily of annoying Mississippi State pass rushers, flung the ball with all his might. Brumbaugh was far behind the scrimmage line by then, almost 20 yards. His pass traveled 60 yards in the air to Hefferle. Ernie caught it on the State 30 and traveled unhindered for the touchdown that beat the Maroons, 13 to 12.

Brumbaugh, who had undergone a tonsillectomy a few days before the game and whose availability was questionable until shortly before the kickoff, made all thirteen of the Dukes' points. Until he trained his sights on the State goal line, however, the eastern team that had conquered mighty Pittsburgh 7 to 0 was trailing by 12 points.

Ground for new Roddey Burdine Stadium, which would seat 22,-000 and cost $325,000, was broken at a ceremony held a week before the game. Conducting the ceremony was Colonel Horatio B. Hackett, an Army engineer who lettered in football for West Point in 1904. Colonel Hackett had been sent to Miami to decide if the city would get a new much needed stadium and, more specifically, if a Public Works Administration appropriation could be justified.

What did Orange Bowl Committee members do but invite Colonel

Hackett to serve as field judge at their next New Year's Day game. They got their new stadium.

Duquesne	0	7	0	6	13
Mississippi State	6	6	0	0	12

Duquesne—Touchdowns: Hefferle (72, pass from Brumbaugh of 42, run of 30), Brumbaugh (1, right tackle). Point after touchdown: Brumbaugh.

Mississippi State—Touchdowns: Pickle (8, left end), Walters (47, pass from Armstrong of 15, run of 32).

STATISTICS

Duquesne		*Mississippi State*	*Duquesne*	*Mississippi State*
Platukis	LE	Gelatka	14 First downs	12
Maras	LT	Lott	199 Net yards rushing	111
Amann	LG	Reagh	15 Passes attempted	23
Basrak	C	Price	5 Passes completed	8
Barko	RG	Moak	0 Passes had intercepted	4
Critchfield	RT	Pittman	110 Net yards passing	159
Hefferle	RE	Keenan	309 Total net yards	270
Zopetti	QB	Cross	9 Number of punts	6
Dillon	LH	Armstrong	26 Punting average	34
Vairo	RH	Pickle	0 Fumbles lost	0
Bechtloff	FB	Steadman	5 Yards penalized	5

Substitutes—Duquesne: Kirschling, Serangelli, ends; Goodman, Laputka, Manuel, Minnick, tackles; Horn, Faziola, guards; Grabinski, Sussano, centers; Terrone, Barron, quarterbacks; Onder, Brumbaugh, Matsik, Casillo, McKeeta, halfbacks; Karrs, fullback. Mississippi State: Walters, Reddock, Edwards, ends; Meigs, Musselwhite, tackles; Weed, Carroll, guards; Mollere, Burch, centers; Stubbs, quarterback; Ward, Hight, halfbacks; Hardison, fullback.

ROSE

Dr. John Bain (Jock) Sutherland spoke to his football players in a calm, professional manner, much like his lectures in dentistry at the University of Pittsburgh.

His teams never heard emotional speeches from him before a big game or between halves. His type of football called for precision and clear thinking, straight-ahead power and soft-pedaled passing. He never yelled or pleaded or raved.

However, the Scotchman was not above applying a psychological touch to his preparations, especially when such ammunition was so handy in the weeks preceding Pittsburgh's fourth appearance in the Rose Bowl.

Although Pittsburgh, in 1936, had proved itself one of the strongest teams in the country, Washington's choice of the Panthers as its Rose Bowl foe was not popular.

Well remembered on the Pacific Coast were Pittsburgh's flops in 1930 and 1933, its three defeats in Pasadena. When the invitation was issued to Pittsburgh, sports writers dwelled on the Panthers' dreary Rose Bowl record. Sutherland made sure his players digested every critical clipping.

Pittsburgh's sensation was an 18-year-old sophomore halfback named Marshall Goldberg. He gained 1,000 yards in 1936 and was to be an All-American in 1937–38. Sutherland rarely used sophomores. "They are likely to be undependable," he said, "and they are likely to get tired of football by the time they reach their last year of competition." In the case of Goldberg, though, Sutherland had to use him because of early season injuries to experienced backs. Then he had to keep him in the lineup because he was so good.

For all the apathy evinced toward the selection of the Eastern team, the game drew 87,196 fans, largest Rose Bowl crowd up to that time.

The second time the Panthers moved the ball they didn't stop until it had been planted behind Washington's goal line 55 yards away. It was the first of their three touchdowns in a 21 to 0 victory.

Pittsburgh scored again the second time it went on offense in the second half, traveling 75 yards. Bobby LaRue, 164-pound halfback, got 44 of those yards in one chunk. That put Pitt on Washington's 30. Fullback Frank Patrick was given the ball for five successive slams. He scored from the 3 on his fifth smash. Patrick had made the first touchdown, too, on a one-yard plunge.

The fourth quarter was young when ambidextrous Byron Haines of the Huskies tried to pitch a lefthanded lateral over his head. Bill Daddio, Pitt's redoubtable left end, stole it and fled unimpeded 71 yards for a touchdown.

After the game Sutherland engaged in an altercation with athletic director Don Harrison over the amount of spending money the triumphant players should receive. This was the beginning of the end for the great coach at Pittsburgh. The school was on the way to "purifying" its football program.

Sutherland resigned on March 5, 1939, saying, "My resignation has nothing to do with the ideals and objectives of the code for the conduct of good athletics. I am in favor of good standards. However, the present system of athletic administration has resulted in conditions which, for me, are intolerable."

| Pittsburgh | 7 | 0 | 7 | 7 | 21 |
| Washington | 0 | 0 | 0 | 0 | 0 |

Pittsburgh—Touchdowns: Patrick 2 (1, center plunge; 3, right guard). Daddio (71, intercepted lateral pass by Haines). Points after touchdown: Daddio 3.

STATISTICS

Pittsburgh		Washington	Pittsburgh		Washington
Daddio	LE	Johnson	11	First downs	8
Matisi	LT	Markov	254	Net yards rushing	57
Glassford	LG	Starcevich	4	Passes attempted	18
Hensley	C	Wiatrak	2	Passes completed	7
Petro	RG	Slivinski	2	Passes had intercepted	4
Daniell	RT	Bond (c)	46	Net yards passing	96
Hoffman	RE	Peters	300	Total net yards	153
Michelosen	QB	Newton	5	Number of punts	6
Goldberg	LH	Cain	41.2	Punting average	30.7
LaRue	RH	Johnston	1	Fumbles lost	1
Patrick	FB	Nowogroski	20	Yards penalized	0

Substitutes—Pittsburgh: Souchak, Spotovich, Miller, ends; Delich, Lezauski, Merkovsky, tackles; Raskowski, Dalle Tezze, guards; Adams, Dannies, centers; Chickerneo, McClure, quarterbacks; Stebbins, Urban, Malarkey, Wood, halfbacks; Stapulis, Greene, fullbacks. Washington: Wise, Sheldrake, ends; McKenzie, Kindred, Worthington, Zemeck, tackles; Means, Mattes, guards; Ericksen, center; Logg, quarterback; Waskowitz, Haines, halfbacks; Miller, fullback.

– 1938 –

ROSE

Edwin Camp, known as the "Ole Timer" when he wrote sports for the *Atlanta Journal,* was an "innocent bystander" when Frank Thomas became head coach at Alabama.

Dr. George H. Denny, elderly president of the university, who loved football, was speaking. Camp was listening.

"Now, Mr. Thomas," said Dr. Denny, "now that you have accepted our proposition, I will give you the benefit of my views, based on many years of observation.

"It is my conviction that success in football derives from two factors. These are, one, material; two, coaching ability.

"It is my conviction that material is 90 per cent, coaching ability, 10 per cent.

"I desire further to say that you will be provided with the 90 per cent, and that you will be held to strict accountability for delivering the remaining 10 per cent."

The stubby former Notre Dame quarterback succeeded Wallace Wade under chilling circumstances. But he was not dismayed. Thomas installed the Rockne shift out of the T into the box formation, replacing Wade's single wing attack with unbalanced line. He came up with a 9–1 record in his first season as head coach.

Recalling Dr. Denny's observations many years later, long after Thomas was forced to retire from coaching because of ill health, Ole Timer wrote in the magazine *Coach & Athlete*:

"He gave a genius to coaching, without which Alabama could not have achieved the remarkable record (115–24–7) made during his tenure.

"Furthermore, the mere possession of a large squad of able athletes is no assurance of championships. It takes a keen and experienced eye, a deep knowledge of boy psychology and an unflagging zeal of leadership to pick from 100 or more scholarship athletes the 18 or 24 to be fitted, welded and bolted into a team which operates like a piece of precision machinery."

Thomas' 1937 team, which California invited to play in the Rose Bowl, was not one of his best. But none was better coached or accomplished quite so much with what it had.

The Crimson Tide experienced several close calls. Sandy Sanford literally kicked his team to Pasadena. In the game with Tulane, Sanford booted a late fourth-quarter field goal of 32 yards when Alabama had only six men on the line of scrimmage. The illegal formation was undetected by officials. The Tide won, 9 to 6. Sanford beat Vanderbilt 9 to 7 with another late-game field goal.

In the Rose Bowl, there was no opportunity for Sanford's heroics. Alabama was subdued 13 to 0.

California, coached by Leonard B. (Stub) Allison, demonstrated too much power and speed, better balance, and some exceptionally skilled and rugged players in center Bob Herwig, end Perry Schwartz, quarterback Johnny Meek, guard Vard Stockton, and halfback Sam Chapman, the latter soon to become a major league outfielder.

But the star of the game was Vic Bottari, a junior tailback who started his career as a virtual nonentity on the Golden Bear squad. Bottari scored both touchdowns against Alabama on almost identical plays in the second and third quarters, quick, well-escorted trips around right end of three and five yards, respectively.

California punched over touchdown No. 1 to culminate a 63-yard, 12-play land march. Alabama couldn't check driving, brutal power smashes accompanied by paralyzing blocking. The Bears hammered out No. 2, pushing the Tide 48 yards in nine whacks in much the same fashion. No passes were thrown on this scoring sweep as well.

Alabama lost the ball on fumbles four times and suffered four pass interceptions. One scoring opportunity was muffed on the California 1 and another on the 6, both on fumbles. The Bears tackled with crunching, stunning force.

"It was a heartbreaker," said Alabama captain Leroy Monsky. "I still try to blank it from my mind."

A check for $104,129.94 from gross receipts of $293,372.61 helped to ease some of the grief felt by the Alabama party.

SATURDAY, JANUARY 1, 1938

| California | 0 | 7 | 6 | 0 | 13 |
| Alabama | 0 | 0 | 0 | 0 | 0 |

California—Touchdowns: Bottari 2 (3, right end; 5, right end). Point after touchdown: Chapman.

STATISTICS

California		*Alabama*	*California*		*Alabama*
Dolman	LE	Warren	11	First downs	10
De Varona	LT	Tipton	192	Net yards rushing	140
Evans	LG	Monsky (c)	9	Passes attempted	13
Herwig	C	Cox	2	Passes completed	3
Stockton	RG	Bostick	2	Passes had intercepted	4
Stoll	RT	Ryba	16	Net yards passing	40
Schwartz	RE	Shoemaker	208	Total net yards	180
Meek	QB	Hughes	10	Number of punts	8
Bottari	LH	Kilgrow	39.2	Punting average	37.8
Chapman	RH	Zivich	0	Fumbles lost	4
Anderson	FB	Holm	30	Yards penalized	5

Substitutes—California: Callaghan, L. Smith, ends; J. Smith, Pollack, tackles; Wheeler, guard. Alabama: Blackwell, Sanford, ends; Merrill, Woods, tackles; Foshee, Redden, Harkins, guards; Machtolff, center; Cochrane, Bradford, quarterbacks; Mosley, Slemmons, halfbacks; Roberts, fullback.

COTTON

Byron (Whizzer) White, a gifted halfback who was a Phi Beta Kappa student and became a Rhodes scholar, led undefeated, untied

Colorado into the Cotton Bowl in 1938 against Rice, best in the always tough Southwest Conference.

Colorado, coached by Bunny Oakes, a teammate of Red Grange at Illinois, was given little chance. This was due to the lack of a rigorous schedule in the Rocky Mountain conference, which could not compare in strength to the one drawing the Texas powers.

White had gained 1,121 yards rushing, scored 16 touchdowns, and punted for a 43.3 yard average as well as passing brilliantly and performing excellently on defense. Yet there were skeptics who wondered if he were not perhaps overrated.

Quite quickly Whizzer converted doubting Thomases.

Whizzer White, All-America halfback at Colorado who scored a touchdown in the 1938 Cotton Bowl game. He became a United States Supreme Court justice in 1962.

Four first downs and 63 yards after the beginning of a Colorado drive, White shot an eight-yard scoring pass to halfback Joe Antonio.

Rice received the kickoff and began a downfield march. After the Owls reached their 42 and tried two incomplete passes, Coach Jimmy Kitts inserted 215-pound quarterback Ernie Lain, a talented sophomore.

Lain was to stand out like an oil derrick on an east Texas prairie before the game ended. But his first pass turned out badly for the Owls. White intercepted it and swiftly moved 47 yards for a touchdown. At the quarter it was 14 to 0, Colorado.

That was the end of the scoring for the Buffaloes.

Fifteen minutes later it was 21 to 14, Rice. Touchdown advances measured 72, 57, and 91 yards in order. Each was generously spiced by Lain's passes. So was the fourth scoring push in the third quarter.

Rice, with its superior manpower and Lain's three-touchdown aerial skill, prevailed, 28 to 14. And Whizzer White proved beyond doubt that he belonged with the greatest backs of his decade.

Rice	0	21	7	0	28
Colorado	14	0	0	0	14

Rice—Touchdowns: Schuehle (7, pass from Lain of 5), Lain (3, right tackle), Cordill (43, pass from Lain of 35, run of 8), Steen (9, pass from Lain). Points after touchdown: Vestal 4.

Colorado—Touchdowns: Antonio (8, pass from White), White (47, intercepted pass by Lain). Points after touchdown: White 2.

STATISTICS

Rice		Colorado	Rice		Colorado
Nance	LE	Davies	20	First downs	6
Hines	LT	Brill	257	Net yards rushing	87
Moore	LG	Stevens	20	Passes attempted	6
Arthur	C	Moore	11	Passes completed	1
Landry	RG	Smith	2	Passes had intercepted	2
Stanzel	RT	Brown	158	Net yards passing	8
Steen	RE	Lavington	415	Total net yards	95
Hancock	QB	White	38	Punting average	41
Vickers	LH	Antonio	1	Fumbles lost	0
Cordill	RH	Rooney	65	Yards penalized	15
Schuehle	FB	Cheney			

Substitutes—Rice: Williams, Palmer, Hager, ends; Green, Singletary, Hughes, tackles; Hairston, McBrayer, Haner, Stern, guards; Husbands, Flowers, Price, centers; Vestal, Rogers, Mechler, quarterbacks; Lain, Sullivan, Neece, Coffee, Parker, halfbacks; Brandon, fullback. Colorado: Liley, Grove, Quarnberg, ends; Kreager, Lowen, Levine, tackles; Davidson, Smart, Card, guards; Thompson, center; Rocchio, quarterback; Reeves, Heeb, halfbacks; Hickey, Hill, fullbacks.

SUGAR

Trips to the Sugar Bowl in 1936, 1937, and 1938—short, boring bus expeditions from the campus at Baton Rouge to New Orleans—were unrewarding for Louisiana State. The Tigers dropped their third successive bowl game 6 to 0 to Santa Clara, before 40,000.

It was a particularly galling defeat for LSU coach Bernie Moore. He moaned once: "How can I get my boys steamed up for it? It's just a 90-mile bus trip to them. But to the boys on the other team it's the thrill of a lifetime."

A 6 to 0 score suggests a somewhat dull affair. This, however, was anything but a humdrum punting duel. Yet it couldn't be proved by a glance at the statistics.

Coach Buck Shaw's Broncos achieved the goal of all football teams —a perfect season capped by a bowl triumph. They were clever, defensively stout, and strong in reserves.

Shaw's second unit divided time almost equally with the starting eleven. In fact, it was the second string that not only won the game with a first-quarter touchdown but also saved it in the fourth period by staving off the Tigers when they were within three yards of tying the score.

The game had barely begun when Santa Clara got in deep trouble on a fumbled punt by Orv Hanners 28 yards from his own goal line. LSU was finally subdued but not until the ball rested one yard from the end zone.

The tide changed.

A familiar Santa Clara trick, running to one side and throwing to the other, was the decisive stroke. Halfback Jim Barlow sped far to his left, wheeled, and fired diagonally 50 yards to the right. Quarterback Ray McCarthy made the reception on the LSU 12. He ran three more yards. The play gained 20 yards.

Fullback Jimmy Smith stormed over right tackle for four yards, then added another at the same spot. On third down, Bruno Pellegrini took the snap and immediately whipped the ball to left end Jimmy Coughlan. The wingman sidled into the flat zone, caught the pass over his right shoulder, and in one bound reached the end zone.

LSU's big chance came in the fourth quarter. It was set up by a 56-yard punt off the toe of Pinky Rohm. The punt went out of bounds on the Broncos' 9. Jack Roche, attempting to skirt right end, was forced deep and finally smeared by left end Ogden Baur. Roche tumbled over the goal line but the play was ruled dead on the 1.

Barlow boomed a beautiful 54-yard clutch spiral, but Rohm nullified much of the distance with a 23-yard return. Three plays availed the Tigers six yards. Here they staked everything on a reverse that followed a fake punt by Rohm. Cotton Milner wasn't stopped until he'd gone 23 yards to the 3. LSU tossed away its last-gasp opportunity with unsuccessful passes.

Never has a more spirited band invaded New Orleans than the 23 Santa Clara Broncos who defeated LSU.

Santa Clara	6	0	0	0	6
Louisiana State	0	0	0	0	0

Santa Clara—Touchdown: Coughlin (4, pass from Pellegrini of 3, run of 1).

STATISTICS

Santa Clara		Louisiana State	Santa Clara		Louisiana State
Coffer	LE	Baur	4	First downs	10
Cope	LT	Friend	34	Net yards rushing	106
Farasyn	LG	Clark	13	Passes attempted	21
Dougherty	C	Gormley	5	Passes completed	8
Cook	RG	Smith	0	Passes had intercepted	3
Wolff	RT	Gatto	67	Net yards passing	95
Brown	RE	King	101	Total net yards	201
Pavelko	QB	Booth	14	Number of punts	14
Roche	LH	Rohm	36	Punting average	32
Gilbert	RH	Milner	3	Fumbles lost	0
Gunther	FB	Morton	30	Yards penalized	55

Substitutions—Santa Clara: Coughlan, Anahu, ends; Locke, W. Smith, tackles; Ginney, Clarke, guards; Schiechl, center; McCarthy, quarterback; Pellegrini, Hanners, Barlow, halfbacks; J. Smith, fullback. Louisiana State: Kavanaugh, Dumas, ends; Farmer, Campbell, tackles; Lester, Cunningham, Messina, guards; Warmbrod, center; Cajoleas, quarterback; Bussey, Stell, halfbacks; Anderson, Staples, fullbacks.

ORANGE

The score was misleading, no true indicator of the trend. Auburn smothered Michigan State in the first Orange Bowl game played in Miami's new 22,000-capacity, $325,000 stadium.

But the score was close, 6 to 0.

The Spartans from the Midwest made only two first downs—to 12—and were held to 65 yards running and passing—to 278. Johnny Pingel, their wheel horse, was able to pick up only 12 yards rushing.

Auburn got its points in the second quarter and sat tight on them. A pass from George Kenmore to Ralph O'Gwynne covered 29 yards to Michigan State's 1. O'Gwynne swept left end for the touchdown.

Jimmy Fenton and Spec Kelly, with 71 and 61 yards net, respectively, helped to keep pressure on the Spartans throughout the game.

Halftime pageantry, soon to be unexcelled anywhere, delighted a crowd of 18,972. More than 1,000 musicians marched across the gridiron and blared forth.

The contest was a particular treat for devotees of the Notre Dame shift. Both coaches, Jack Meagher of Auburn and Charlie Bachman of Michigan State, were schooled under Knute Rockne. In fact, they were teammates in 1916.

One of the great sport broadcasters, Ted Husing, dramatized the game for the Columbia Broadcasting System over a national hookup.

| Auburn | 0 | 6 | 0 | 0 | 6 |
| Michigan State | 0 | 0 | 0 | 0 | 0 |

Auburn—Touchdown: O'Gwynne (1, left end).

STATISTICS

Auburn		Michigan State	Auburn		Michigan State
McKissick	LE	Bremer	12	First downs	2
Russell	LT	Speelman	197	Net yards rushing	40
Sivell	LG	Rockenbach	10	Passes attempted	12
Antley	C	McShannock	4	Passes completed	2
Howell	RG	Lueck	2	Passes had intercepted	3
Holman	RT	Swartz	81	Net yards passing	25
Whatley	RE	Gaines	278	Total net yards	65
Smith	QB	Diebold	10	Number of punts	12
Kelly	LH	Pingel	33.7	Punting average	35.2
Fenton	RH	Szasz	0	Fumbles lost	0
Heath	FB	Haney	50	Yards penalized	40

Substitutes—Auburn: Harrison, Burford, ends; Wolff, Nichols, tackles; Gillam, Burns, Thorpe, guards; Morgan, center; Walker, quarterback; Kenmore, Mims, O'Gwynne, halfbacks; Sitz, fullback. Michigan State: Nelson, Diehl, Kinek, ends; Schroeder, Pearson, Ketzko, tackles; Pogor, Dudley, Olman, guards; Alling, Miknavich, centers; Bruckner, Pearce, Ciolek, Harris, halfbacks; Kovacich, fullback.

– 1939 –

ORANGE

Damon Runyon described it as "a regular old-fashioned pier 6 sort of brawl."

To Wirt Gammon of the *Chattanooga Times* it was "a savage battle that resembled two streamlined trains crashing head on. A coatless crowd of 32,191 at the Orange Bowl, enlarged by the addition of end zone bleachers, was alternately thrilled and horrified."

Never before, never since has there been a bowl game as violent as the one played in Miami, January 2, 1939, when Tennessee overpowered, outclassed, and out-toughed Oklahoma, 17 to 0.

Twenty-five penalties were called, nine for unnecessary roughness. Tennessee was set back 130 yards for rules infractions. Oklahoma was assessed 91 yards. The total of 221 yards set a bowl record.

The opening kickoff fixed the tempo. The teams clashed vehemently with a series of chilling thuds. It was surely one of the most vicious kickoff collisions in football. Many a gladiator did not exactly bounce to his feet after the flattening contact. Oklahoma lost Cliff Speegle, its center.

On Tennessee's first play from its balanced-line single wingback formation, blocking back Sam Bartholomew took some of the starch out of the Sooners' All-America end, Waddy Young, who was killed in action in World War II. Young was belted so hard he seemed to bound along the ground several yards.

Oklahoma never had a chance. The Volunteers limited the Sooners to 25 yards rushing and 69 yards passing and only six first downs.

Bowled over by fierce gang tackling—a trademark of General Bob Neyland's teams—and staggered by vigorous blocking—another Tennessee characteristic—Oklahoma threatened only once to score. That was late in the game.

An illegal shift put Oklahoma in a hole early. Hugh McCullough kicked out. George Cafego, a tailback who ran with abandon, returned 16 yards to the Sooners' 27. Tennessee scored in five plays.

The telling thrust was an eight-yard run by wingback Bob Foxx on a reverse.

All-America end Bowden Wyatt kicked a field goal shortly before the half with the ball placed on the 22. The opportunity was made possible by Bob Seymour's fumble, recovered by Bob (Breezer) Andridge on Oklahoma's 27.

Walter (Babe) Wood galloped 19 yards for the final touchdown in the third period. Tailback Wood started right on a pass or run option play, a Tennessee favorite. He cut in and made excellent use of natural open field talent to outsmart the Sooner secondary.

The Volunteers had been forewarned that the big, chesty Oklahoma team, which held a decided weight advantage, would go into the contest with the idea of trying to intimidate them, hoping to cool their ardor for combat in a hurry. Tennessee was determined to give blow for blow—and then some. And that's just what happened.

It was a rough-and-tumble duel, right enough. Even a Tennessee cheer leader, Thelma Guinn, was knocked unconscious when she went down in an out-of-bounds pileup.

This was generally conceded to be the best of West Point-educated Neyland's many outstanding teams at Tennessee where he enjoyed tremendous success. During the 1938–39–40 seasons the Volunteers were neither beaten nor tied and had a 23-game winning streak until defeated by Southern California in the 1940 Rose Bowl game.

MONDAY, JANUARY 2, 1939

| Tennessee | 7 | 3 | 0 | 7 | 17 |
| Oklahoma | 0 | 0 | 0 | 0 | 0 |

Tennessee—Touchdowns: Foxx (8, right tackle), Wood (19, right end). Field goal: Wyatt (32, placekick). Points after touchdown: Wyatt (run), Foxx (placekick).

STATISTICS

Tennessee		*Oklahoma*	*Tennessee*		*Oklahoma*
Wyatt	LE	Shirk	15	First downs	6
Shires	LT	Duggan	205	Net yards rushing	25
Molinski	LG	Thomas	13	Passes attempted	27
Rike	C	Speegle	4	Passes completed	10
Suffridge	RG	Stevenson	0	Passes had intercepted	1
Woodruff	RT	Bowers	64	Net yards passing	69
Hunter	RE	Young	269	Total net yards	94
Bartholomew	QB	Favor	13	Number of punts	13
Cafego	LH	Rogers	35.8	Punting average	40.3
Foxx	RH	Corrotto	1	Fumbles lost	3
Coffman	FB	McCullough	130	Yards penalized	91

Substitutes—Tennessee: Hendricks, Coleman, Cifers, Eldred, ends; Luttrell, Cowan, West, Clay, Melton, tackles; Smith, Steiner, Thomas, Hubbuck, Lampley, Sellers, guards; Ackerman, Little, centers; McCarren, Weber, Bailey, quarterbacks; Duncan, Wood, Andridge, Warren, Barnes, halfbacks; Wallen, Broome, fullbacks. Oklahoma: Ivy, Kitchens, Hotchkiss, Coppage, ends; Phebus, Edgeman, Lahar, Manley, tackles; LaRue, Locke, Bolton, Potter, guards; Wood, Wilhelm, centers; Crowder, Spottswood, quarterbacks; Clark, Seymour, halfbacks; Martin, West, fullbacks.

ROSE

With the seconds in the last minute dwindling, Duke leading by three points and the Rose Bowl in a tumult, Braven Dyer of the *Los Angeles Times* sports staff was leaving the stadium bound for his office.

"Somebody had to get out the paper," he said. "I was just pulling out when over the radio came this:

" 'Nave is back . . . he's going to pass . . . he's throwing the ball . . . it's in the end zone and it's complete to Krueger for a touchdown.'

"And still there are people who say a sports writer leads an ideal existence."

Dyer never quite got over not seeing the finish in 1939.

A devoted admirer of Howard Jones, ever a close follower of Southern California football and a man who thought very highly personally of Doyle Nave, Dyer departed from the press box with four minutes remaining to get the jump on the crowd of 89,452.

The Trojans won, 7 to 3. They sullied Duke's perfect record and became the first team to cross its goal line. And they did it with 40 seconds to play at Pasadena.

"It took four teams to beat us," Coach Wallace Wade observed. "We played three teams to a standstill and had them beaten. But their reserve strength was too much."

An organization of Blue Devil partisans known as the Duke Vigilantes in Durham, N. C., site of the university, lightened its grief somewhat with a warrant for the arrest of Doyle Nave and Al Krueger telegraphed to Charles W. Kelley, Los Angeles chief of police. The message read: "Hold Nave and Krueger of Southern California football. Both charged with grand larceny, viz., stealing game from Duke University. Truly two great opportunists."

Kelley, a man with a sense of humor, sent this return wire: "Your order has been duly obeyed. Krueger and Nave in dungeon guarded by squad with machine guns. New Year's greetings to supporters of most gentlemanly and scrappiest football team ever to appear in Rose Bowl."

Neither team was able to probe beyond the other's 35 until Eric Tipton connected on a 24-yard pass to George McAfee three plays before the third quarter ended. That put Duke on the Southern California 25. The Trojans toughened. On fourth down with one yard to go, tackle Tony Ruffa kicked a field goal from the 23.

Six minutes were left when the Trojans got a break but didn't capitalize. Bob Spangler fumbled a punt by Ollie Day. Tackle Phil Gaspar recovered on the Duke 10. Southern California couldn't penetrate any deeper and Gaspar's try for a field goal was wide.

The final charge began from Troy's 39. Fourth-stringer Nave, a junior who had played less than 30 minutes during the previous season and wasn't expecting to get a letter, went in for triple-threat ace Granny Lansdell when the Trojans reached the Duke 34. There were two minutes, 20 seconds left now.

Maxwell Stiles, a Los Angeles newspaperman who wrote the first book on the Rose Bowl in 1946, revealed the inside story of how Nave actually entered the game.

Stiles reported that Nave was sent in by Joe Wilensky, an assistant freshman coach, on a fake telephone call from the press box. Only recently Wilensky said the story is true as written in Stiles' book and Nick Pappas, also an assistant freshman coach at the time, verified it, too.

Wilensky had been taking calls from the press box and relaying the advice of assistant coaches sitting there, Sam Barry, Bob McNeish, and Julie Bescos, to Jones. With time running out, the assistants started down the stadium steps to the bench.

Aware that the press box phone was on the hook, Wilensky pretended to acknowledge instructions.

"Yes, yes—I get it—I'll tell him right away!" He put the instrument down and shouted: "The word is to send in Nave and have him throw passes to Krueger!"

Wilensky had often watched Nave throw to Krueger in practice and marveled at their skill. He was convinced that if the Trojans were somehow to pull the game out of the embers, this pair could do it.

The extra timeout caused by Nave's arrival cost the Trojans five yards. Nave passed to Krueger, successively, for 13, nine, then minus two yards. On each play, the second-string sophomore left end broke across the scrimmage line, cut to his right, and took Nave's cast.

On the fourth pass, Krueger tricked the Blue Devils. He slanted

1939—With 40 seconds left, Southern California end Al Krueger catches Doyle Nave's pass behind Eric Tipton.

back sharply to his left, away from the tired Tipton in the secondary. Trojan blockers checked Duke's weary linemen. Nave faded back, calmly waiting for the proper moment. As Krueger crossed the goal, he was several yards in the clear. The ball floated down over his left shoulder and nestled into his big hands. The play covered 19 yards.

Turning to Jones in the jubilant Trojans' dressing room, Nave said, "Thanks for the opportunity of getting into the game, coach."

"Don't thank me," said Jones. "Let me thank you."

As he was being patched up for a forehead cut, Doyle asked the team physician, "I wonder if I'll get a letter."

"I'm in favor of giving you the whole alphabet," said the doctor.

Southern California	0	0	0	7	7
Duke	0	0	0	3	3

Southern California—Touchdown: Krueger (19, pass from Nave). Point after touchdown: Gaspar.

Duke—Field goal: Ruffa (33, placekick).

STATISTICS

Southern California		Duke		Southern California	Duke
Fisk	LE	Darnell	13	First downs	5
Stoecker	LT	Maloney	128	Net yards rushing	84
Smith	LG	Johnson	31	Passes attempted	13
McNeil (c)	C	Hill (c)	12	Passes completed	5
Tonelli	RG	Yorke	3	Passes had intercepted	2
George	RT	Haas	81	Net yards passing	59
Stanley	RE	Perdue	209	Total net yards	143
Lansdell	QB	Spangler	17	Number of punts	17
Hoffman	LH	Eaves	32.5	Punting average	35.7
Morgan	RH	Tipton (c)	0	Fumbles lost	1
Sangster	FB	O'Mara	35	Yards penalized	30

Substitutes—Southern California: Winslow, Krueger, Stonebraker, ends; Thomassin, Gaspar, tackles; Fisher, Phillips, guards; Dempsey, center; Anderson, Day, Nave, quarterbacks; Shell, Jones, Jesse, halfbacks; Banta, Peoples, Peccianti, fullbacks. Duke: Bailey, Marion, ends; Winterson, Ribar, tackles; Baskervill, Alabaster, Ruffa, guards; Burns, Robb, centers; G. McAfee, quarterback; Davis, Deane, W. McAfee, halfbacks; Robinson, fullback.

COTTON

What had the aspect of a lopsided triumph for St. Mary's suddenly became a close contest in the final 11 minutes of the third Cotton Bowl game staged as a one-man promotion by J. Curtis Sanford.

A three-touchdown lead melted quickly, but the Galloping Gaels coached by Slip Madigan hung on to overcome Texas Tech, 20 to 13. Sustained power and defensive diligence prevailed over a late flash of aerial razzle-dazzle.

At the outset of the fourth quarter, Tech's Red Raiders had made only two first downs. Reviving a passing offense that earlier had boomeranged discouragingly, the undefeated team from the Border Conference bombed the Gaels repeatedly.

Gene Barnett dropped the projectiles and the Texans, striving for an eleventh straight victory, gained more passing yards, 190, in one quarter than any other Cotton Bowl team ever did.

Elmer Tarbox, the Raiders' outstanding back, legged it 23 yards for the first touchdown after receiving a ten-yard pass. With three minutes remaining, end E. J. McKnight took a 31-yard strike. Barnett pitched in each instance.

After McKnight's touchdown, however, Texas Tech never touched the ball again.

The power smashes of Ed (Hellzapoppin) Heffernan and Mike Klotovich—both scored—pierced the Raiders' defense in the first half.

Herb Smith hurried 24 yards for a gift touchdown in the third quarter after he intercepted a pass thrown by Bobby Holmes.

Years later, the crowd of 40,000 would still remember Texas Tech's late-game shower of passes, long and short, screen and lateral—and probably forget that no other center, playing in a bowl, ever punted as far as Jerry Dowd, St. Mary's captain. He booted one 73 yards, another 64, and his average on all kicks was 47.5.

St. Mary's	7	7	6	0	20
Texas Tech	0	0	0	13	13

St. Mary's—Touchdowns: Heffernan (9, right end), Klotovich (1, left end), Smith (24, intercepted pass by Holmes). Points after touchdown: Perrie, Marefos.

Texas Tech—Touchdowns: Tarbox (33, pass from Barnett of 10, run of 23), McKnight (31, pass from Barnett). Point after touchdown: Marek.

STATISTICS

St. Mary's		Texas Tech	St. Mary's		Texas Tech
Crampton	LE	Webb	11	First downs	10
Cantwell	LT	Latch	200	Net yards rushing	99
Mesak	LG	Waldrep	15	Passes attempted	31
Dowd	C	Williams	1	Passes completed	11
Jack	RG	White	2	Passes had intercepted	5
Katzemayer	RT	Murphy	15	Net yards passing	193
Bettencourt	RE	Scott	215	Total net yards	292
Perrie	QB	Flusche	47.5	Punting average	34.3
Heffernan	LH	Akins	2	Fumbles lost	2
Rimassa	RH	Tarbox	65	Yards penalized	30
Smith	FB	Calhoun			

Substitutes—St. Mary's: Pivarof, Brusati, Aguirre, ends; Garard, Jones, tackles; Ruddell, guard; Milicevich, center; Nichols, Mazaika, Guthrie, quarterbacks; Klotovich, Magnani, Aronson, halfbacks; Marefos, fullback. Texas Tech: McKnight, Philbrick, ends; Overton, Davis, tackles; Harmon, Greene, McCurry, guards; Balfanz, quarterback; Barnett, Holmes, Hill, halfbacks; Marek, Rankin, fullbacks.

SUGAR

Carnegie Tech, strongest team in the East, and Notre Dame were locked in a furious duel at South Bend, Ind., on October 22, 1938.

In the fourth quarter of the scoreless game, Carnegie Tech had the ball at midfield. The quarterback asked Referee John Getchell what down it was. He was informed it was third down. He tried a run.

It failed to make a first down. Getchell then discovered he was in error and that it was fourth down. He rushed in and awarded the ball to Notre Dame. The Irish pressed on, scored, and won, 7 to 0. It was the Tartans' only defeat.

Bill Kern, Carnegie Tech coach, said, "It was the biggest bonehead I ever saw pulled by any official. I don't know if he will quit or not, but I know what I'd do if I were in his place."

Yet when Carnegie Tech was picked to play Texas Christian in the Sugar Bowl, "Wrong Down" Getchell was the team's choice as referee.

After that match in New Orleans, Getchell said, "The mistake I made will always be a regret to me, of course. But it was a lucky error. It allowed me to see the greatest football game I ever saw, to officiate in the cleanest game I ever worked in, played between two of the finest sets of boys America ever produced."

Texas Christian won 15 to 7. Davey O'Brien, the Horned Frogs' 150-pound All-America quarterback, set a Sugar Bowl record with 17 pass completions in 27 attempts for 225 yards.

Bill Keefe, veteran *New Orleans Times-Picayune* sports editor, was so smitten by the diminutive O'Brien, he wrote, "If I am ever to see a player better than he, I expect to be crowding old Horace Methuselah's record for staying around."

TCU Coach Leo (Dutch) Meyer preached the passing game. Even so, it was remarkable he could turn out two such superb aerialists as Sammy Baugh and Davey O'Brien within such a short span of years.

Allie White, a tackle teammate of O'Brien's, recalled how as a 12-year-old boy in Fort Worth he had scoffed when someone enthused about the possibility Davey would come to TCU.

A quarter of a century later White said, "I doubt if there'll ever be another his equal."

O'Brien was a back of multiple talents with the heart and head for football. Only once in his career did he require a timeout. He was fearless, never flinching when rushed by merciless giant linemen. He had complete confidence in his ability to pass accurately and would fire unhesitatingly if his target had no more than a one-step lead.

A Carnegie Tech player was asked why the Tartans didn't try to wear down O'Brien with crashing linemen. He replied, "We'd rather lose than to have won that way. After all, we do not feel a bit disgraced, losing to a great little boy like that."

Referee Getchell was right. These were two unusual teams.

TCU fullback Connie Sparks stormed through center for the first touchdown from the one in the first quarter. O'Brien's passes ac-

1939—Davey O'Brien, Texas Christian's 150-pound All-America quarterback, throws a pass. He completed seventeen against Carnegie Tech.

counted for most of the distance from the Tartans' 48. Davey, usually a reliable placekicker, missed the extra point try.

Carnegie Tech took the lead in the last minute of the first half. Pete Moroz, a lightweight back, threw a long high pass from the Frogs' 44. George Muha made a spectacular grab on the 1 and scored. Then he toed the ball between the upright posts to put his team ahead, 7 to 6.

TCU lost little time asserting its supremacy in the third quarter. O'Brien led his team 80 yards in five plays. Two lengthy passes, one from Davey to Earl Clark for 35 yards and another three plays later to Durwood Horner for 44 yards and a touchdown, highlighted that sally-forth.

In the last period O'Brien kicked a field goal with the ball placed down on the 10.

The victorious Texas Christian team had size, speed, strength, topnotch reserves, spirit, and confidence. There may not have been a better team ever produced in the Southwest Conference.

Of the 44 Carnegie Tech squad members, 42 were recruited.

They received free tuition, books, room, and board. All but six of the 42 earned degrees, mainly in engineering and science. Twenty years later their average salary was better than $15,000 a year.

Mel Cratsley of the 1938 squad, later his alma mater's athletic director, said, "They weren't afraid of hard work and they had an ability to bounce back. That's what made them so successful.

"I think any school can have a good football team and still maintain good academic standards provided it insures getting the right kind of boys interested in obtaining an education.

"They had good common sense and guts. They were hustlers then and they're still hustlers."

Texas Christian	6	0	6	3	15
Carnegie Tech	0	7	0	0	7

Texas Christian—Touchdowns: Sparks (1, center plunge), Horner (44, pass from O'Brien of 14, run of 30). Field goal: O'Brien (20, placekick).

Carnegie Tech—Touchdown: Muha (44, pass from Moroz of 43, run of 1). Point after touchdown: Muha.

STATISTICS

Texas Christian		Carnegie Tech	Texas Christian		Carnegie Tech
Looney	LE	Striegel	17	First downs	10
Hale	LT	Dobrus	142	Net yards rushing	129
Kline	LG	Pyzynski	28	Passes attempted	8
Aldrich	C	Schmidt	17	Passes completed	3
Taylor	RG	Reith	0	Passes had intercepted	2
White	RT	Campbell	225	Net yards passing	59
Horner	RE	Fisher	367	Total net yards	188
O'Brien	QB	Carnelly	1	Number of punts	6
Clark	LH	Condit	40	Punting average	40
Hall	RH	Muha	0	Fumbles lost	0
Sparks	FB	Lee	5	Yards penalized	20

Substitutions—Texas Christian: Snow, Ehlers, Hensch, Williams, ends; Cook, Kerlee, tackles; Shook, Sherrod, guards; Alexander, center; Odle, quarterback; Clifford, Ware, halfbacks; McClanahan, Wilkinson, fullbacks. Carnegie Tech: Betz, Kuenzli, Howarth, Church, ends; Forsythe, Gumbert, Yeknik, tackles; Dominy, Wolfarth, Henrion, Senchuk, guards; Guffrey, center; Moersch, Friedlander, Tammaro, quarterbacks; Jordano, Moroz, Fouse, Zawacki, halfbacks; Ingalls, Laposki, fullbacks.

– 1940 –

SUGAR

A Texas A&M team rated one of the most powerful ever produced in the Southwest Conference came from behind to earn a 14 to 13 victory over Tulane in the 1940 Sugar Bowl extravaganza.

It was the first game played in the enlarged stadium. Double decking of the east and west sides boosted seating capacity and the place was packed with 73,000 fans. Concrete was poured only four days before the game.

Homer Norton, who coached the nationally top-ranked Aggies, put Jarrin' John Kimbrough, his six-foot, two-inch, 212-pound fullback, in his personally chosen all-time backfield with Bronko Nagurski, Red Grange, and Jim Thorpe.

"He could run the ends just as well as he could crash through the line," Norton said. "He had big legs, an inextinguishable will to win and he was never down until they had every inch of him down."

Norton didn't stop there. He thought his right halfback, Jim Thomason (Texas A&M used the double wing attack), deserved to be mentioned with the finest blocking backs in history. He unhesitatingly applied the adjective "great" to a tackle, Joe Boyd, and a guard, Marshall Foch Robnett. He considered several others terrific in certain departments.

The Aggies' defense was almost fabulous. Its feat in limiting opponents to an average of 1.71 yards per play is still a major college record.

One of the remarkable features of the game was that four Aggies —Kimbrough, Thomason, Robnett, and 173-pound left end Herb Smith—played 60 minutes. Smith, one of the two starters who lost their lives in World War II—left halfback Derace Moser was the other —blocked Johnny Thibaut's placekick after Tulane's second touch-

1940—Jarrin' John Kimbrough of Texas A & M slams into the Tulane line.

down. He also tossed the lateral pass to Kimbrough resulting in his team's winning touchdown.

Tulane rose up mightily to stop Kimbrough and his cohorts on the 1 in the first quarter. But the Aggies successfully pressed a 32-yard attack following a punt. When they reached the 16, Green Wave center Pete Mandich was charged with unnecessary roughness in throwing Moser out of bounds. The penalty moved the ball to the 1. This time Jarrin' John wouldn't be denied as he crashed over right guard for the touchdown.

Near the end of the third quarter fleet Bobby Kellogg grabbed Moser's quick kick and flashed 75 yards for a touchdown. It was 7 to 7 now. Near hysteria gripped the crowd a few moments later when Tulane took a 13 to 7 lead.

Moser pitched a wild lateral pass in Thomason's direction that Mandich recovered on the A&M 39. Soon after the fourth period began Monette Butler rammed two yards for a touchdown.

Aroused, the Aggies went to work with a vengeance. Kimbrough splintered Tulane's defense in a series of crunching whacks from the A&M 31 to the Green Wave 18. At that point Walemon Price passed to Smith, who flipped the ball back to Kimbrough. Little Herbie blocked the defensive left halfback. The big man bowed his neck, stomped a pair of would-be tacklers, and scored standing. Price added the vital extra point.

Kimbrough was handed the ball 26 times. He responded for 152 yards.

Tulane halfback Buddy Banker said, "I never thought I'd ever have the honor of tackling a truck but that's just what it was like to hit Kimbrough."

Reporters, surrounding a bench where the Aggie fullback stripped off his uniform, heard him say, "These 10 boys with me did the work, and this boy did it especially—he's the best blocking back in the country."

And Kimbrough patted Thomason's knee.

MONDAY, JANUARY 1, 1940

Texas A&M	7	0	0	7	14
Tulane	0	0	7	6	13

Texas A&M—Touchdowns: Kimbrough 2 (1, right guard; 18, lateral from Smith, run of 10 after pass from Price to Smith of 8). Points after touchdown: Price 2.

Tulane—Touchdowns: Kellogg (75, punt return), Butler (2, left guard). Point after touchdown: Thibaut.

STATISTICS

Texas A&M		*Tulane*	*Texas A&M*		*Tulane*
Smith	LE	Bodney	18	First downs	8
Pannell	LT	White	244	Net yards rushing	193
Robnett	LG	O'Boyle	15	Passes attempted	4
Vaughn	C	Mandich	8	Passes completed	0
Henke	RG	Groves	1	Passes had intercepted	0
Boyd	RT	McCollum	62	Net yards passing	0
Dawson	RE	Wenzel	306	Total net yards	193
Price	QB	Nyhan	8	Number of punts	11
Moser	LH	Kellogg	44	Punting average	34
Thomason	RH	Banker	1	Fumbles lost	0
Kimbrough	FB	Gloden	30	Yards penalized	20

Substitutions—Texas A&M: Sterling, Buchanan, ends; Wesson, Routt, tackles; Browder, Rahn, guards; Hauser, Herman, centers; Pugh, Jeffrey, quarterbacks; Conatser, halfback. Tulane: Golomb, DeFraites, Mullin, ends; Kirchem, Blandin, DuFour, tackles; Clay, Dailey, guards; Flower, center; Krueger, quarterback; Hays, Cassibry, halfbacks; Butler, Thibaut, fullbacks.

ORANGE

George Tech overcame Missouri in the Orange Bowl in 1940 with one of the most bewildering hidden ball offensives ever unveiled on a football field.

C. E. McBride of the *Kansas City Star,* who covered the game, wrote: "How can I criticize the Missouri team for its defensive play? I had powerful glasses on Tech and couldn't find the ball. It was the finest handling I ever saw."

Missouri's All-America quarterback, Paul Christman, whose passes gained 803 yards in 1939, said: "I still can't figure out where they hid that ball. They had a big end named Bob Ison, about six-four. It's hard to hide a guy that big. But I'll tell you he ran right by me to score and I didn't even see him."

Frequently, a Tech runner was far along his way before the Tigers succeeded in finding the ball.

The Engineers' speed and deception resulted in a 21 to 7 victory.

During the previous fall, a widely circulated picture showed a defensive halfback for one of Tech's opponents directing a teammate on the other side of the field to stop a certain player pretending to have the ball when at that very moment the actual carrier was running within arm's length.

These magical concoctions were products of the imaginative brain of Tech backfield coach Bobby Dodd. Under his teaching, the Engineers, or Yellow Jackets, became a national sensation of the "now-you-see-it, now-you-don't" school.

As quarterback at Tennessee, under General Bob Neyland, Dodd was what Ralph McGill, publisher of the *Atlanta Constitution* and a former sports writer, called "the most valuable football player any team, anywhere, ever had. He was the greatest in only one department, and that the most important—the thinking end of it. He could upset and outguess another team better than any other man I've ever seen or heard about."

In later years Bobby forsook his tendency to make prestidigitators of his players and taught basically conservative football. And as head coach at Georgia Tech, starting in 1945, he enjoyed remarkable success, particularly in the bowls. He took six straight teams to the bowls, beginning in 1952. All of them won.

Double and triple reverses and end-around plays off fake reverses were a part of the "who has the ball?" technique of the Yellow Jackets.

The end-around operated by fullback Howard Ector and left end Ison was a pet maneuver. Ector would fake handing the ball to the right halfback, then spin toward the line. As the opposition concentrated on the halfback or fullback, Ison would be thundering around the other side after taking the ball from Ector and putting it against his hip.

It was this play that Tech used to score its second touchdown in the first half. Ison broke away for 59 yards. Describing the trickery, Morgan Blake wrote in the *Atlanta Journal*: "Missouri was murdered in cold blood with a combination of sound football and black magic the like of which these old eyes never beheld before."

On a double reverse also involving Ector and the 140-pound Johnny Bosch, halfback Earl Wheby started around left end and sped 34 yards for the final touchdown in the third quarter. He ran into a pack of Tigers at the 15 but somehow escaped. One writer explained: "The only thing we can say is that Mr. Wheby just vanished temporarily and appeared again in a clear field."

Georgia Tech	7	7	7	0	21
Missouri	7	0	0	0	7

Georgia Tech—Touchdowns: Ector (1, right guard), Ison (59, end around), Wheby (34, left end). Points after touchdown: Goree 3.

Missouri—Touchdown: Christman (1, right tackle). Point after touchdown: Cunningham.

STATISTICS

Georgia Tech		Missouri	Georgia Tech		Missouri
Ison	LE	R. A. Orf	12	First downs	14
Wood	LT	Wetzel	210	Net yards rushing	151
Cavette	LG	Waldorf	14	Passes attempted	26
Wright	C	Moser	8	Passes completed	8
Aderhold	RG	Crocker	1	Passes had intercepted	1
Lackey	RT	Haas	91	Net yards passing	76
Webb	RE	Currence	301	Total net yards	227
Murphy	QB	Notowicz	35	Punting average	33
Bosch	LH	Christman	3	Fumbles lost	1
Pair	RH	Starmer	36	Yards penalized	15
Ector	FB	Cunningham			

Substitutes—Georgia Tech: Arthur, Sprayberry, Clay, Bartlett, ends; Muerth, Perkinson, Wild, Fain, tackles; Richards, Sanders, Dyke, guards; Beard, Sutton, Wilkins, Quigg, centers; Shaw, quarterback; Beers, Bates, Nettles, Wheby, halfbacks; Goree, fullback. Missouri: R. C. Orf, Rouse, Amelung, Wallach, ends; Landers, Gordon, Dodd, tackles; Schultz, Pickett, Ellis, guards; Duckeck, center; Faurot, King, quarterbacks; Leech, Cooper, Gale, Meyers, Brinton, halfbacks; Counsil, Hydron, fullbacks.

ROSE

It was unusual that in two successive winning appearances in the Rose Bowl, Southern California would be pitted against teams that went through the season with goal line uncrossed.

Tennessee, which had not allowed a point to be scored by the opposition in ten regular season games, was turned back, 14 to 0, in the 1940 spectacle. The Volunteers advanced beyond midfield only once as their 23-game winning streak ended.

General Bob Neyland never considered his 1939 team his best. But he said, "I don't believe it ever reached its peak."

His trickiest runner was Johnny Butler, second-string tailback whose spectacular, will-o'-the-wisp dashes broke up the Alabama and Auburn games that year.

Edwin Camp of the *Atlanta Journal* described his swerving, cut-back, 56-yard touchdown run against Alabama as "an S curve, thrice extended." The movie of the run was shown for years. Comedian Eddie Foy used to say, "Don't miss it, if you can."

Butler carried the ball only five times against the powerful Southern California line, gaining 40 yards.

While Butler was the breakaway specialist, Tennessee's "bread and butter" man in 1938–39 was tailback George Cafego. This West Virginia youth, not quite 180, ran with fearsome drive. Not exceptionally fast, he ripped off yardage with fiery determination. He was a twisting, fighting type who operated on each play as if the outcome depended on his personal contribution.

But Cafego's knee was injured in an early November skirmish. Although he started against Southern California, he was far below his normal form.

The tailback who really had himself a day in the Rose Bowl was the Trojans' No. 3 quarterback, Ambrose Schindler.

Starting from Tennessee's 47 in the second quarter, Schindler personally conducted an advance that resulted in the first touchdown surrendered by the Vols in 15 games. Amby handled the ball on seven of the eight plays. A 15-yard penalty for unnecessary roughness eased the way through the hotly defended zone and brought a first down on the 3. Schindler scored on his second plunge.

Near the end of the third period a startling event occurred. Traditionally conservative Tennessee passed from its own 1. Butler completed an 18-yard flip to Mike Balitsaris. But after traveling 84 yards, the Vols gave up the ball on a fumble by fullback Fred Newman.

Howard Jones, whose Southern California teams won five Rose Bowl games and lost none.

Southern California marched back 85 yards forthwith. Again, Schindler was the big ball of fire as he charged through the lighter Tennessee line with knees high. On reaching the 1, Amby tossed a fourth-down scoring pass to Al Krueger, the end whose catch beat Duke the year before.

"The better team won and won decisively," wrote Grantland Rice. "But with all its superior manpower, Southern California needed all the breaks of the game."

His 1938–39 teams were among Howard Jones' best. He coached one more before his death on July 27, 1941.

Jones beat Jock Sutherland (twice), Bernie Bierman, Wallace Wade, and Bob Neyland in the Rose Bowl—five triumphs. He never lost. He stands at the top of the list.

Bob Suffridge, great Tennessee guard who played in the Orange, Rose, and Sugar Bowls consecutively in 1939–40–41.

| Southern California | 0 | 7 | 0 | 7 | 14 |
| Tennessee | 0 | 0 | 0 | 0 | 0 |

Southern California—Touchdowns: Schindler (1, right guard), Krueger (1, pass from Schindler). Points after touchdown: Jones, Gaspar.

STATISTICS

Southern California		Tennessee	Southern California		Tennessee
Fisk	LE	Coleman	17	First downs	8
Stoecker	LT	Shires	227	Net yards rushing	71
Smith	LG	Suffridge	14	Passes attempted	12
Dempsey	C	Rike	7	Passes completed	6

Southern California		Tennessee		Southern California	Tennessee
Sohn	RG	Molinski	1	Passes had intercepted	1
Gaspar	RT	Clay	44	Net yards passing	76
Winslow	RE	Cifers	271	Total net yards	147
Lansdell	QB	Bartholomew (c)	8	Number of punts	11
Hoffman	LH	Cafego	40.1	Punting average	39.2
Robertson	RH	Foxx	0	Fumbles lost	1
Peoples	FB	Coffman	40	Yards penalized	25

Substitutes—Southern California: Jones, Krueger, Stonebraker, Mena, Galvin, ends; Thomassin, de Lauer, tackles; Phillips, Benson, guards; Morrill, Atanasoff, centers; Nave, Schindler, quarterbacks; Engle, Shell (c), halfbacks; Banta, fullback. Tennessee: Disspayne, Balitsaris, Hust, ends; Luttrell, Edmiston, West, tackles; Thomas, Steiner, Smith, guards; Ackerman, center; Peel, quarterback; Warren, Butler, Andridge, halfbacks; Newman, Wallen, fullbacks.

COTTON

"They did everything except pull rabbits out of their headgears and carve the referee in half as they entertained 20,000 shivering and pop-eyed spectators with a bruising, bewildering spectacle."

So wrote Jake Wade in the *Charlotte Observer* on January 2, 1940, the day after Clemson defeated Boston College, 6 to 3, in the Cotton Bowl.

All of the scoring was compressed into a six-minute segment of the second quarter. And it was a captivating game, despite the 54 minutes devoid of goal-line crossing.

Near the end of the first period, Clemson found itself on the one-yard line following a clipping penalty. Bru Trexler got off a 49-yard punt, but 155-pound Charlie O'Rourke, the Eagles' wiry, gritty left halfback, slithered 37 yards with the runback.

Boston College couldn't budge the Tiger line. On fourth down Alex Lukachik, a substitute end, kicked a field goal with the ball placed on the 25.

After the next kickoff and a subsequent punt exchange, Clemson charged 57 yards for its touchdown scored by sophomore fullback Charlie Timmons on a one-yard plunge.

O'Rourke's aerial markmanship was a constant worry to Clemson Coach Jess Neely in the last half. Into the final minute the Tiger secondary was kept busy batting down his touchdown-labeled passes.

The game climaxed Frank Leahy's first year as a head coach and resulted in one of only five losses inflicted on his teams in his first nine years.

It also marked the last time J. Curtis Sanford would be individual promoter.

Clemson	0	6 0	0	6
Boston College	0	3 0	0	3

Clemson—Touchdown: Timmons (1, right tackle).
Boston College—Field goal: Lukachik (35, placekick).

STATISTICS

Clemson		Boston College		Clemson		Boston College
Blalock	LE	Harrison	11	First downs		9
Fritts	LT	Manzo	210	Net yards rushing		184
Moorer	LG	Schwotzer	4	Passes attempted		23
Sharpe	C	Gladchuck	2	Passes completed		4
Tisdale	RG	Kerr	1	Passes had intercepted		1
Hall	RT	Yauckoes	31	Net yards passing		73
Black	RE	Goodreault	241	Total net yards		257
Payne	QB	Toczylowski	42.6	Punting average		39.3
McFadden	LH	O'Rourke	0	Fumbles lost		0
Bryant	RH	Ananis	63	Yards penalized		90
Timmons	FB	Cignetti				

Substitutes—Clemson: Jackson, Blessing, Pasley, ends; McLendon, Hamer, Jameson, tackles; Deitz, Padgett, guards; Pearce, quarterback; Rion, Floyd, halfbacks; Trexler, fullback. Boston College: Lukachik, E. Zabilski, ends; Levanitis, Morro, tackles; Galvani, White, J. Zabilski, guards; Dubzinski, center; Cowhig, Powers, Lucey, quarterbacks; McCarthy, Maznicki, McGowan, Jauron, halfbacks; Davis, fullback.

– 1941 –

COTTON

It was pretty generally agreed that the Cotton Bowl was the scene of a miscarriage of justice in 1941 when Texas A&M beat Fordham, 13 to 12.

"The Rams were definitely the better team," Grantland Rice wrote. He said they were "victims of incredibly bad luck as even the most rabid supporters from this great sporting state were more than willing to admit."

On one occasion, Fordham fullback Steve Filipowicz threw a touchdown-labeled pass, but it was caught by end Jim Lansing a yard beyond the end zone. On another, Fordham drove to the Aggies' 4 where a substitute quarterback fumbled.

The Rams' misfortunes took a turn for the worse in the third quarter. Texas A&M revived the ancient sleeper play to score its first touchdown.

Fordham had kicked off out of bounds. On the second play from the 38, halfback Earl (Bama) Smith sauntered toward the sideline. Suddenly the ball was snapped. Smith, unnoticed near the edge of the field, bolted down the gridiron. On the Fordham 30 he caught a pass from Marion Pugh. He was then 20 yards past the last Ram defender. It was an easy touchdown, of course.

Overzealous use of the elbows by a keyed up Fordham man resulted in a virtual gift touchdown in the same period. The penalty moved Texas A&M to the Rams' 1. All-America fullback John Kimbrough headed for right tackle, swerved away from a congested situation, and turned the corner to score. Pugh's placement was true—and decisive.

As if all of this were not enough, when Fordham registered its last touchdown in the final quarter on Jim Blumenstock's 15-yard run through a gap at left tackle, Steve Hudacek's extra point attempt hit the crossbar after being partially blocked by Aggie tackle Martin Ruby and bounced back.

Kimbrough pounded the Rams shatteringly. But he was never grabbed more fiercely by any opponent. Actually, Blumenstock was rated the standout all-around back on the field that day. The Aggies were held to a mere 52 yards on the ground.

It was the first game held under the joint sponsorship of the Cotton Bowl Athletic Association and the Southwest Conference, which cooperated by sending its representative.

A record crowd of 45,500 watched. Each school received a check for $52,700.

WEDNESDAY, JANUARY 1, 1941

Texas A&M	0	0	13	0	13
Fordham	0	6	0	6	12

Texas A&M—Touchdowns: Smith (62, pass from Pugh of 32, run of 30), Kimbrough (1, right end). Point after touchdown: Pugh.

Fordham—Touchdowns: Filipowicz (1, right tackle), Blumenstock (15, left tackle).

STATISTICS

Texas A&M		Fordham		Texas A&M	Fordham
Sterling	LE	Dennery	8	First downs	13
Pannell	LT	Kuzman	52	Net yards rushing	118
Robnett	LG	Bennett	18	Passes attempted	23
Vaughn	C	De Filippo	6	Passes completed	5
Henke	RG	Sartori	1	Passes had intercepted	3
Routt	RT	Ungerer	101	Net yards passing	62
Simmons	RE	Lansing	153	Total net yards	180
Pugh	QB	Noble	10	Number of punts	8
Smith	LH	Eshmont	32.9	Punting average	30.4
Thomason	RH	Blumenstock	3	Fumbles lost	1
Kimbrough	FB	Filipowicz	25	Yards penalized	29

Substitutes—Texas A&M: Henderson, Buchanan, ends; Hauser, Ruby, tackles; Rahn, Richardson, guards; Herman, center; Jeffrey, Spivey, quarterbacks; Conatser, Moser, Rothe, halfbacks; Webster, fullback. Fordham: Ritinski, end; Hudacek, Santilli, tackles; Pierce, Lucas, guards; Pieculewicz, Hearn, quarterbacks; Lewcyzk, halfback.

SUGAR

"The greatest Cinderella story in the history of American college football roared on into and through its super sunburst finale in this magnificent Sugar Bowl saucer this hot and humid New Year's afternoon when the Boston College Eagles met and literally strangled the mighty Volunteers from the University of Tennessee by the margin of 19 to 13."

That was the enthusiastic lead to Bill Cunningham's story in the *Boston Post,* January 2, 1941.

Slim, 158-pound Charlie O'Rourke, Boston College's left halfback, had faked a pass and threaded his way 24 yards to score the touchdown that broke a 13 to 13 tie with two and a half minutes to play.

Here is more of what Cunningham wrote:

"O'Rourke rolled into and out of at least a half dozen pairs of clutching arms. It was a magnificent run to close a great career and it was O'Rourke who, after all, won the Sugar Bowl game for Boston College.

"The Cinderella epic is now complete. The team from the day school is now national champion, from regional renown to national fame in the swift upswing of two years is the breath-stopping pace of the suddenly singing story. The kid coach (Frank Leahy) is now a titan, rating front rank in the seats of the mighty."

It was the last game Leahy, former Notre Dame tackle, ever coached at Boston College. In 1941 he returned to his alma mater,

1941—Charlie O'Rourke of Boston College on his late-game 24-yard touchdown run against Tennessee.

there to produce some of the hardest-to-beat teams in modern football. He was called a genius, and properly, too.

"I think people are inclined to confuse genius with hard work," Leahy said. "If they're not, then anyone can become a 'genius' who is willing to pay the price."

Perfectionist Leahy, who switched to the T formation at Notre Dame, built the single wing to a high state of efficiency at Boston College. To spruce it up, he used as many as three flankers on one side, a man in motion, and the line charging from an upright stance.

General Bob Neyland's Vols went into the bowl game, their third in three years, unbeaten and untied for the third straight regular season. In those three years Tennessee made 807 points to 42, yet was outscored, 33 to 30, in successive bowl appearances.

Leahy's Eagles were outplayed in the first half. They trailed 7 to 0 early in the third quarter. Then something utterly unexpected occurred. A Tennessee punt was blocked. It hadn't happened for seven years. It was a demoralizing blow.

Henry Woronicz, Boston College end, threw his body in front of Bob Foxx's kick. The Eagles recovered, guard Joe Zabilski capturing the ball, on the Vols' 17. They scored quickly. Tennessee cracked out another touchdown. But Boston College tied it again before the third period ended.

With six minutes left Boston College took possession on its 20 following a missed field goal by Foxx. The Eagles were unwilling to settle for a moral victory tie. O'Rourke began passing. After running plays picked up ten yards, three consecutive completed pitches of 20, 19, and seven yards moved the ball to Tennessee's 24.

"The thin man lifted his arm as if to pass again," Cunningham wrote, "but instead, he ran straight through the Tennessee right flank, picking his path just inside their right tackle. Knifing through the line of scrimmage, he cut back sharply to his right. With one of the fanciest pieces of broken field running of his career, he traveled virtually untouched through the Tennessee secondary to score the winning touchdown."

The fake pass and run—an old Tennessee favorite—had been installed by Leahy at a secret practice in the Bay St. Louis, Miss., High School gymnasium a few days before the game.

Boston College	0	0	13	6	19
Tennessee	7	0	6	0	13

Boston College—Touchdowns: Connolly (12, right end), Holovak (1, center plunge), O'Rourke (24, left tackle). Point after touchdown: Maznicki.

Tennessee—Touchdowns: Thompson (4, left tackle), Warren (3, left guard). Point after touchdown: Foxx.

STATISTICS

Boston College		*Tennessee*	*Boston College*		*Tennessee*
Woronicz	LE	Coleman	11	First downs	13
Manzo	LT	Shires	142	Net yards rushing	124
J. Zabilski	LG	Molinski	14	Passes attempted	22
Gladchuck	C	Ackerman	6	Passes completed	9
Kerr	RG	Suffridge	3	Passes had intercepted	2
Morro	RT	West	106	Net yards passing	121
Goodreault	RE	Cifers	248	Total net yards	245
Toczylowski	QB	Peel	6	Number of punts	7
O'Rourke	LH	Thompson	35	Punting average	36
Maznicki	RH	Foxx	1	Fumbles lost	1
Holovak	FB	Nowling	25	Yards penalized	36

Substitutions—Boston College: Naumetz, Lukachik, Currivan, E. Zabilski, ends; Levanitis, Yauckoes, Strumski, tackles; Repko, White, Fiorentino, Galvani, guards; Dubzinski, center; Nash, quarterback; Connolly, Williams, halfbacks; Kissell, fullback. Tennessee: Hust, Balitsaris, ends; Edmiston, Hubbell, Luttrell, Simonetti, tackles; Steiner, Noel, guards; Graves, center; Weber, quarterback; Butler, Warren, Andridge, halfbacks; Newman, Broome, fullbacks.

ORANGE

In January of 1959 the *Nashville Banner* brought back for a big sports banquet the winners of its Southeastern Conference Player of the Year awards for a silver anniversary reunion. Among the honored guests was Buddy Elrod, who earned the accolade in 1940 when he was an outstanding end at Mississippi State.

Each of the players was asked to describe his most unforgettable experience. Elrod replied:

"We were about to come on the field for the Alabama game our senior year knowing that we would be selected to play in the Orange Bowl if we won. In fact, it had been announced to both teams. The pressure was really on. It was evident that our coaches—Allyn Mc-Keen, Murray Warmath and Bowden Wyatt—felt it, too.

"As we came out of the dressing room, our old freshman coach and athletic director at State, Dudy Noble, was standing there, chewing tobacco. 'Come over here,' he said. 'I've got something I want to say. You goats go out there and have some fun. Don't worry about a thing. Just hit them where they bend.'

"The effect was like a cold drink of water on a hot day. We scored on the fourth play after receiving the kickoff. It was our day all the way; we didn't make a mistake, won the game [13 to 0], went to the Orange Bowl and won that game, too. I'll always credit Dudy Noble for that victory, which was my finest football experience."

At Miami the Maroons conquered a Georgetown team, coached by Jack Hagerty, which had lost only to Boston College, 19 to 18, in one of the greatest college games of the first half century. Mississippi State was a 14 to 7 winner.

Georgetown was down by two "touches" at the half. The Hoyas gave up one on a blocked punt by Captain Hunter Corhern, another when a pass interference penalty put the Maroons in an advantageous position to score. It was a fourth-down pass which had gone awry.

Between these touchdowns another stroke of misfortune befell the easterners.

With the ball on its own 34, Georgetown deployed in a spread formation. Julius Koshlap, deep, faded and then ran wide and forward. Finally, he threw far downfield. Arthur Lemke received the pass after it had sailed 46 yards. He was tackled on the 4.

But the play was nullified. Referee Emil Heintz ruled that Koshlap had not passed from a point five yards behind the line of scrimmage, as required by the rules at that time. Motion pictures seemed to show otherwise.

Mississippi State   7   7   0   0   14
Georgetown   0   0   7   0   7

Mississippi State—Touchdowns: Tripson (recovered ball in end zone after Corhern blocked Daniels' punt from Georgetown 12), Jefferson (2, right tackle). Points after touchdown: Dees, Bruce.

Georgetown—Touchdown: Castiglia (2, right guard). Point after touchdown: Lio.

STATISTICS

Mississippi State		Georgetown	Mississippi State	Georgetown
Elrod	LE	Wixted	7	First downs	14
Tripson	LT	Fullilove	78	Net yards rushing	118
Corhern	LG	Ostinato	11	Passes attempted	22
Griffin	C	Matuza	6	Passes completed	11
McDowell	RG	Lio	0	Passes had intercepted	3
Arnold	RT	Daniels	51	Net yards passing	112
Moore	RE	Lascari	129	Total net yards	230
Dees	QB	McFadden	11	Number of punts	8
Johnson	LH	Koshlap	34	Punting average	32
Craig	RH	Ghecas	2	Fumbles lost	1
Tullos	FB	Castiglia	82	Yards penalized	88

Substitutes—Mississippi State: Varnado, Harrison, ends; White, Jones, tackles; R. Ray, Grove, guards; Price, E. Ray, centers; Campbell, quarterback; Black, Jefferson, Bruce, Wohner, halfbacks; Yancey, Neal, fullbacks. Georgetown: Wiley, Lemke, Jujack, Pavich, ends; Perpich, Blozis, Nealon, tackles; Mickey, Paternoster, McMahon, guards; Reichey, Erickson, centers; Falcone, quarterback; Bulvin, Dornfeld, Doolan, Kull, halfbacks; McLaughlin, fullback.

ROSE

The keen-minded coach who popularized the modernized T formation was Clark Daniel Shaughnessy. He taught football at the University of Chicago for seven years through 1939. Chicago had very little outstanding material and was short on manpower. His record there was 17–34–4.

After the 1939 season, Chicago's worst (0–8), the university dropped intercollegiate football.

In early January of 1940, Shaughnessy was in Los Angeles representing the University of Chicago at the National Collegiate Athletic Association convention. Stanford at the time was in the market for a new coach. The Indians under Tiny Thornhill had lost all of their Pacific Coast Conference games in 1939.

When someone suggested to Shaughnessy that he try to sell himself to Stanford officials, he replied, "Why, they wouldn't want me. I'm the losingest coach in the country."

Nevertheless, the union took place. It occasioned no prolonged rejoicing among Stanford alumni, players, or students. After all, virtually the same team was to return in 1940—to be coached by a man to whom victory certainly had been a stranger in recent years.

Under Shaughnessy, Stanford reversed its 1939 showing and finished with a perfect season.

The new coach discovered in quarterback Frankie Albert, fullback Norman Standlee, right halfback Hugh Gallarneau, and left halfback Pete Kmetovic the elements for a backfield that he has always maintained was as proficient as any ever assembled. He stated just that in his book, *Football In War And Peace,* published in 1943.

Albert, not fast enough to prosper as a double wing halfback the year before, was a daring little fellow who loved to trick opponents with unorthodox football and take calculated risks.

Standlee at 220 was a plunger with crunching power. Kmetovic was graceful and swift. He could start with jet speed. Gallarneau, bigger than Kmetovic, also was extremely fast and a superb blocker.

Albert once told Prescott Sullivan of the *San Francisco Examiner* that Stanford players disbelieved Shaughnessy at first when he would diagram a play and tell them it was sure to score a touchdown. He had to sell his men on two counts—on himself and on themselves. He succeeded. Suddenly, football became fun. Stanford defeated nine straight foes.

Then on January 1, 1941, in a game of far-reaching significance, Stanford outsmarted and outplayed Nebraska, 21 to 13, in the Rose Bowl.

The Stanford T was an up-to-date, wide open, spectacular version of the offense in vogue in football's early days and earlier in the century when Shaughnessy was the man-in-motion fullback at Minnesota.

Long after Shaughnessy had left Stanford, Dick Hyland wrote in the *Los Angeles Times*: "None has been superior to Clark Shaughnessy as a football analyst. None has had a greater impact on the game. It was while Shaughnessy was coach at Chicago and helping George Halas with the Bears that the modern T formation was first used in 1939."

Stanford in 1940 was the first college team to employ the T in a long, long time. In its intricacies, men in motion, spreads, and emphasis on deception, the revitalized Stanford T was the standard immediately copied by a majority of schools.

Stanford's success against Nebraska, less than a month after Halas'

Chicago Bears, using a similar method of attack, crushed the Washington Redskins 73 to 0 in the National Football League title game, convinced almost everyone that the modern T was terrific.

Nebraska, coached by Major Lawrence (Biff) Jones, a former Army player, had lost only its first game, 13 to 7, to Minnesota. The Cornhuskers, so nicknamed in 1900 by Charles S. (Cy) Sherman, one-time sports editor of the *Lincoln Star,* delighted the thousands of rooters who followed them to California with the ease in which they chewed up 53 yards in seven bites for a quick 7 to 0 lead.

Shaughnessy in his book said he feared most the reverse runs of wingback Butch Luther. The defense he concocted probably would have been effective against Nebraska's pet play. But his guards neglected to split wider to compensate for the tackle moving out to help the weak side end toward which Luther would head.

Thus, huge holes yawned invitingly. After fullback Vike Francis, cracking through these gaps on spinners (faking the reverses to Luther), had scored, Shaughnessy rushed in orders to make adjustments. Francis did little gaining thereafter.

"My team was at its best when it was behind," Shaughnessy said. "Put them on the spot and the boys really felt at home."

Late in the first quarter Stanford tied the score. The touchdown play was ingenious. After a magically masked bit of Albertian fakery, Gallarneau took the ball from Frankie, shot through right guard and tackle, and was in the end zone, nine yards away, before anyone knew he had it.

Herman Rohrig thumped a 44-yard punt that Kmetovic fumbled over his shoulder in the second quarter. Allen Zikmund recovered for the Cornhuskers on Stanford's 33. Rohrig threw a long pass. Zikmund, breaking free behind Gallarneau, caught it a yard from the goal line. Center Vic Lindskog blocked the extra point try. But Nebraska was in front, 13 to 7.

It wasn't long before Gallarneau retaliated. From Nebraska's 41, Albert passed straight ahead. Hugh took it on the 20 between Zikmund and Rohrig, the deep defensive backs. Eluding them, he sped for a touchdown.

Albert added the extra point, putting Stanford on top, 14 to 13. The lead almost vanished on the next kickoff. Zikmund nearly escaped from the Indians but was bumped out of bounds on Stanford's 39 after a run of 46 yards.

In the third quarter Stanford drove from its 24 to Nebraska's 1. The Cornhuskers gamely hurled back the Indians four successive times.

Harry Hopp punted to his 39. Kmetovic returned it all the way, breaking the backs of the midwestern team. Kmetovic started left, then cut to his right as a force of blockers mowed down menacing Nebraskans.

Late in the game, with victory certain, Shaughnessy permitted himself to relax and reflect. He glanced toward a section high in the Pasadena stadium jammed with 92,000 fans. Twelve months ago he had sat there, an unnoticed spectator.

What a difference a year had made.

Stanford	7	7	7	0	21
Nebraska	7	6	0	0	13

Stanford—Touchdowns: Gallarneau 2 (9, right tackle; 41, pass from Albert of 21, run of 20), Kmetovic (39, punt return). Points after touchdown: Albert 3.

Nebraska—Touchdowns: Francis (2, center plunge), Zikmund (33, pass from Rohrig of 32, run of 1). Point after touchdown: Francis.

STATISTICS

Stanford		Nebraska	Stanford		Nebraska
Graff (c)	LE	Preston	16	First downs	9
Stamm	LT	R. J. Kahler	277	Net yards rushing	68
Taylor	LG	Schwartzkopf	13	Passes attempted	14
Lindskog	C	Burruss	6	Passes completed	4
Palmer	RG	Alfson	0	Passes had intercepted	2
Banducci	RT	Herndon	68	Net yards passing	85
Meyer	RE	Prochaska	345	Total net yards	153
Albert	QB	Petsch (c)	6	Number of punts	7
Kmetovic	LH	Hopp	34.0	Punting average	36.6
Gallarneau	RH	Luther	1	Fumbles lost	0
Standlee (c)	FB	Francis	45	Yards penalized	20

Substitutes—Stanford: Tomerlin, Meiners, ends; Purkitt, Burford, Warnecke, Mannon, tackles; Robesky, guard; Stahle, Verdieck, Thompson, centers; Peterson, Crane, quarterbacks; Armstrong, Cole, South, Casey, halfbacks; Parker, fullback. Nebraska: Ludwick, Bunker, ends; Schleich, Behm, tackles; Abel, Myers, guards; Meier, center; Knight (c), Thompson, quarterbacks; Rohrig, Zikmund, R. W. Kahler, Bradley, Rubottom, halfbacks.

– 1942 –

ROSE

A young Portland insurance salesman who lost both arms after the crash of his Air Force jet plane in 1946 saw his first Rose Bowl game in Pasadena in 1957. He watched Oregon State, his alma mater, lose to Iowa.

His name? Gene Gray. He was a reserve right halfback on a twice-beaten team given little chance against undefeated, untied Duke in the transplanted Rose Bowl game at Durham, N. C., January 1, 1942. During World War II, he flew many missions in the European Theater.

Gray and his wife were staked to the trip to Pasadena through a fund-raising campaign started by *Oregon Journal* (Portland) sports editor George Pasero. The money was contributed quickly by Oregon State football followers who remembered the day Gene helped the Beavers shock Duke 20 to 16.

As he sat there in the Rose Bowl, invigorated no doubt by the atmosphere of the occasion, Gray must have been thinking of a New Year's Day in North Carolina long past.

Pacific Coast cities were blacked out after the disaster at Pearl Harbor, December 7, 1941. The Army wished to avoid large gatherings as a precaution growing out of the belief the coast might be in danger of a Japanese attack. At the request of Lieut. Gen. John L. DeWitt, head of the Western Defense Command, Tournament of Roses officials agreed not to hold their game in Pasadena. The Rose Bowl game would have been suspended except for the efforts of Durham citizens.

Wallace Wade, Duke athletic director and football coach, offered the use of his school's stadium.

Between December 15, 1941, and January 1, 1942, Duke and Durham enlarged a stadium ordinarily seating 35,000 to 56,000 capacity.

Jack Guenther of the United Press, who spent the week before the game in Durham writing about the preparations, was deeply moved.

"The people of Durham haven't merely salvaged a great sporting event," Guenther wrote. "They have added to its prestige and increased its stature.

"The game is going on and it will be one remembered when the hair on the players' heads has grown white or vanished altogether. It will remain a symbol of all that the word sportsmanship means long after the score has been forgotten. That's because thousands of folks have put their shoulder to the wheel.

"I have seen a city of 80,000 put on in three weeks a show which usually involves a year of solid effort."

The game itself didn't turn out to the satisfaction of the partisan Durham crowd. The Beavers from Corvallis, champions of the Pacific Coast Conference for the first time, mastered firmly favored (four to one) Duke in the rain. But the result didn't dim the throng's appreciation of superb performance.

When the game ended, Oregon State halfback Don Durdan, who played ahead of Gray, was mobbed by a large, swirling body of fans eager to congratulate him. It took him almost half an hour to reach his dressing room.

Durdan scored the first touchdown on a 15-yard fake pass and run after setting up the opportunity with a 70-yard kick out of bounds on Duke's one. He passed to George Zellick, a 32-yard play, for the second touchdown.

Two plays after the Blue Devils tied the score at 14 to 14 late in the third quarter it was Oregon State's ball, second down and eight yards to go on its 32. Bob Dethman hurled a long, accurately aimed pass, 40 yards beyond the scrimmage line. On the Duke 28, Gray received the ball. He tricked Moffat Storer, Duke's deep defender, with a nifty feint, then took off for the touchdown that won the game.

Duke halfback Steve Lach was his team's brightest figure. He ran eleven times for 129 yards and averaged 47.1 yards on eight punts.

On November 29, 1943, Lach had a different role. Playing for Great Lakes Naval Training Station against unbeaten, untied Notre Dame only 28 seconds from a perfect season under Coach Frank Leahy, Lach threw a pass good for 46 yards, a touchdown, and a 19 to 14 victory.

"It was one of the greatest thrills I've had," Steve said. "In a way, though, I was sorry it had to happen that way. I know what it's like to have an undefeated season in your hand, then lose it in the final game."

THURSDAY, JANUARY 1, 1942

Oregon State	7	0	13	0	20
Duke	0	7	7	2	16

Oregon State—Touchdowns: Durdan (15, left tackle), Zellick (32, pass from Durdan of 24, run of 8), Gray (68, pass from Dethman of 40, run of 28). Points after touchdown: Simas 2.

Duke—Touchdowns: Lach (4, right tackle), Siegfried (1, center plunge). Points after touchdown: Gantt, Prothro. Safety: Burns and Karmazin tackled Durdan in end zone on play from Oregon State 2.

STATISTICS

Oregon State		Duke	Oregon State		Duke
Zellick	LE	Smith	12	First downs	15
Bain	LT	Karmazin	166	Net yards rushing	199
Halverson	LG	Burns	14	Passes attempted	16
Greenough	C	Barnett (c)	6	Passes completed	6
Chaves (c)	RG	Goddard	2	Passes had intercepted	3
Saunders	RT	McDonough	159	Net yards passing	144
N. Peters	RE	Piasecky	325	Total net yards	343
G. Peters	QB	Prothro	9	Number of punts	8
Dethman	LH	Davis	44.3	Punting yardage	47.1
Durdan	RH	Lach	1	Fumbles lost	3
Day	FB	Siegfried	20	Yards penalized	25

Substitutes—Oregon State: Perryman, Gustafson, ends; Bain, Czeck, tackles; Parker, Zielaskowski, guards; Clement, center; Gray, Smith, Libbee, Simas, halfbacks; Shelton, fullback. Duke: Dempsey, Gantt, ends; Nanni, Redding, tackles; Poole, Lipscomb, Fawcett, guards; Beatty, center; Bokinsky, quarterback; Rute, Storer, halfbacks; Long, fullback.

COTTON

A world's record was set in Dallas on January 1, 1942.

Alabama was held to one first down by Texas A&M, gained only 75 yards to 309, completed one pass against 13, and ran only 32 plays to 79.

Yet the Crimson Tide led the Aggies, 29 to 7, midway in the fourth quarter and won, 29 to 21, in the Cotton Bowl.

The significant statistics were seven Alabama pass interceptions—of 42 thrown by Texas A&M—and five ball-losing Aggie fumbles.

Alabama broke a 7 to 7 tie in the third quarter. Jimmy Nelson, one of the finest in a long line of talented Tide tailbacks, took Derace Moser's 33-yard punt, momentarily fumbled, darted to his left, and began a 72-yard run for a touchdown.

Aggie mistakes made three more Bama scores easy. The last eight minutes belonged to the Southwest Conference champions. But it was much too late to catch up.

"Well, it was just another ball game," said Moser to Daniels as they packed their uniforms. "We've got a bigger game now. And if you lose in that one, you don't get another chance."

Alabama	0	7	13	9	29
Texas A&M	0	7	0	14	21

Alabama—Touchdowns: Craft (8, left end), Nelson 2 (72, punt return; 21, right end), Rast (10, intercepted pass by Moser, tipped by Webster). Field goal: Hecht (31, placekick). Points after touchdown: Hecht 2.

Texas A&M—Touchdowns: Cowley (18, pass from Daniels of 15, run of 8), Webster (1, right tackle), Sterling (43, pass from Moser, tipped by Nelson). Points after touchdown: Webster 3.

STATISTICS

Alabama		Texas A&M	Alabama		Texas A&M
Rast	LE	Sterling	1	First downs	13
Olenski	LT	Wesson	59	Net yards rushing	115
Hecht	LG	R. Bucek	7	Passes attempted	42
Domnanovich	C	Sibley	1	Passes completed	13
Wyhonic	RG	Maples	0	Passes had intercepted	7
Langdale	RT	Ruby	16	Net yards passing	194
Weeks	RE	Simmons	75	Total net yards	309
Sabo	QB	Spivey	36.3	Punting average	36.6
Nelson	LH	Moser	1	Fumbles lost	5
Brown	RH	Zapalac	81	Yards penalized	5
Salls	FB	Webster			

Substitutes—Alabama: Sharp, Bires, Roberts, Leeth, ends; McAllister, Richeson, Whitmire, Fichman, McKewen, tackles; Kimball, Baughman, Hargrove, Leon, guards; Wesley, center; Blackmon, Harrell, Gammon, quarterbacks; Papais, Tollett, Craft, McCoy, Martin, Mims, Hughes, Mosley, halfbacks; Scales, Spencer, fullbacks. Texas A&M: Cowley, Cox, Slaughter, Henderson, ends; Luethy, Motley, Tulis, Dickey, tackles; Richardson, Mulhollan, F. Bucek, Cure, guards; Holder, Mercer, centers; Rogers, quarterback; Daniels, Williams, halfbacks; Andricks, fullback.

SUGAR

Torrents of rain converted the Sugar Bowl gridiron into an ooze only a pig could revel in on January 1, 1942.

A safety settled the issue, Fordham winning over Missouri, 2 to 0.

"At the end of the game, the field was ready for stocking with trout and bream and tarpon were reported to be leaping in the end zone."

That's how Henry McLemore, United Press writer, described the scene.

The downpour ruined what had been predicted to be a spectacular show of offensive pyrotechnics. However, even in the mud the teams displayed enough sparkle to make the 73,000 fans constantly aware of what might have been on a firm turf.

This was the first Missouri team to be taught Coach Don Faurot's split T offense, a system that reached the height of its popularity in the early fifties. It was used with remarkable success by Oklahoma, Maryland, Michigan State, Navy, and Mississippi.

The basic difference between this form and the modernized T formation re-introduced to college football by Stanford in 1940 was that in the Faurot system, a sliding, rather than a spinning, quarterback was the hub of the offense and the linemen were split wider.

Faurot devised a variation of the straight T that made use of the quarterback as something more than a ball-feeder and passer. He wanted a man who could run in that position.

Faurot conceived the quarterback option keep or pitch-out, which is the soul of the split T. He foresaw that a deft-fingered, shifty quarterback, running laterally along the scrimmage line, could exert tremendous pressure on opposing ends and tackles by cleverly mixing keep and pitch-out plays.

Inventor Faurot preferred the split T version because he maintained it gained more ground, propelled backs into the open oftener, and put a greater burden on the defense.

Employing this offense for the first time, Missouri led the country in rushing in 1941 with an average of 307.7 yards per contest. The Tigers lost their opener against Ohio State, 12 to 7, with All-America center Darold Jenkins unable to play because of an injury. But they won all the others.

"The Ohio State game sold me on the split T," Faurot said. "We ran 30 single wing plays and averaged 1.8 yards per try. We ran 10 split T plays and averaged 10 yards per carry."

Early in the first quarter at New Orleans, Missouri was forced to punt from its own 10. The center snap was low. End Don Greenwood momentarily fumbled the slippery ball. Just then Alex Santilli, Fordham's right tackle, burst into the Tigers' backfield unchecked. Greenwood's kick bounced off Santilli's chest into the end zone. Stan Ritinski, Rams' left end, reached the ball first and pounced on it. Ritinski slid out of the end zone. Officials ruled it a safety, saying Ritinski didn't have control before going out.

After that neither team sloshed within the other's 20, although fleet Missouri quarterback Harry Ice almost got away twice on runs of 32 and 34 yards.

With three minutes to play, Missouri halfback Bob Steuber attempted a field goal from Fordham's 35. The soggy ball fell a few yards short of the cross bar into a puddle.

In the swirling rain, the Rams never had a chance to unveil their famed passing attack. Uncertain footing handicapped both teams.

To acknowledge Faurot's contributions to football, Arthur Daley, *New York Times* sports columnist, suggested changing the name of the split T to the Faurot T.

Fordham	2	0	0	0	2
Missouri	0	0	0	0	0

Fordham—Safety: Santilli blocked Greenwood's punt from Missouri 10, ball rolled through end zone.

STATISTICS

Fordham		Missouri	Fordham		Missouri
Ritinski	LE	Lister	10	First downs	7
Hudacek	LT	Brenton	137	Net yards rushing	148
Bennett	LG	Jeffries	4	Passes attempted	5
Sabasteanski	C	Jenkins	0	Passes completed	2
Sartori	RG	Fitzgerald	0	Passes had intercepted	2
Santilli	RT	Wallach	0	Net yards rushing	21
Lansing	RE	Ekern	137	Total net yards	169
Pieculewicz	QB	Ice	9	Number of punts	6
Blumenstock	LH	Adams	34	Punting average	36
Cheverko	RH	Steuber	1	Fumbles lost	2
Filipowicz	FB	Reece	30	Yards penalized	10

Substitutions—Fordham: Tepo, end; Yackanich, tackle; Pierce, guard; Kovach, center; Noble, Hearn, quarterbacks; Andrejco, Ososki, halfbacks. Missouri: Shurnas, Greenwood, ends; Hodges, Lightfoot, tackles; Abrams, Keith, Tarpoff, guards; Davis, center; Wade, quarterback; Pitts, Bowen, Carter, halfbacks; Bouldin, fullback.

ORANGE

In his third year as Georgia coach, Wally Butts led his Bulldogs into the Orange Bowl where they defeated Texas Christian, 40 to 26, in 1942.

All sorts of records were set. Four Georgia touchdowns on forward passes was one. Seven touchdowns by both teams through the air was another.

A sports writer described Butts as "a little round fellow with a kewpie's build, the countenance of a choir boy and the heart of a game rooster."

As a coach, his principles were, in order of importance: discipline, conditioning, fundamentals, and pass patterns.

Butts was one of the foremost experts on the pass. However, when a girl reporter asked him once to explain the basis for his teams' success, he answered: "It's the color system. We just try to knock down everybody not wearing our color."

While not precisely a martinet, Butts was a stern disciplinarian.

After his sophomore season, Frank Sinkwich had had enough and quit the squad. Butts wasn't in the least perturbed, at least outwardly, although he was fully aware of Sinkwich's tremendous potential.

Sinkwich had a change of heart, approached Butts, and requested

1942—Fireball Frank Sinkwich of Georgia gallops for a gain against Texas Christian. Note his special protection for a broken jaw. Sinkwich gained 382 yards running and passing in this game, an Orange Bowl record.

permission to return. Butts said he doubted if it would be fair to
the players who had already gone through four weeks of spring practice. He promised he would find out what the players thought. He
accepted their vote that Sinkwich be taken back.

As fourth-string tailback, immediately after his return, Sinkwich
worked harder than anybody. In the season of 1941 he gained 1,816
yards running and passing despite a jaw fracture suffered early in the
season. Frankie's rushing total of 1,103 yards led the nation.

Eighteen years later another prominent Georgia player left the
team abruptly. The young man was halfback Fred Brown, nephew
of Alabama's Johnny Mack Brown. When Brown came back a week
later, Sinkwich asked for and received permission from Butts to talk
to him.

"I wanted to talk to Fred," Sinkwich said, "because I made the
same mistake myself. I was all mixed up. Now I know I would have
regretted it forever had I not returned to school and football."

Butts' teams were models of perfect physical condition. In his
first eleven years at Georgia they didn't lose a game in the fourth
quarter. Yet if the Bulldogs hadn't built up a comfortable 40 to 7
lead in the second half of the Orange Bowl game, they could have
come to grief.

"We left our first team in too long," Butts admitted. "In Miami,
when you get tired, you don't snap back. TCU scored and kept
scoring. I thought they were going to run us all the way to Miami
Beach. The only defense we had was the clock. It finally saved us.
We won but it was a moral defeat by the time we got through."

The Horned Frogs came within a step or two of two more touchdowns. Once, Lamar Davis tackled Jim Woodfin at midfield after
the latter had intercepted a pass on his 15 and appeared to be free.
With a minute to play Beecher Montgomery ran 56 yards to the
Georgia 8 on a punt return.

This was the day Sinkwich put on one of the most dazzling shows
in bowl history.

He was the spearhead on five of Georgia's six touchdowns. He
ran 22 times for 139 yards.

In his own words, "I threw 13 passes and completed all 13—nine
to my own receivers and four to TCU."

He scored one touchdown on a 43-yard run and passed for three
others on plays covering 61, 60, and 15 yards.

"The record book shows that as a coach, I won so many games—
but they were won by boys who paid the price," said Butts.

One of those who learned how, the hard way, was Frank Sinkwich.

Georgia	19	14	7	0	40
Texas Christian	7	0	7	12	26

Georgia—Touchdowns: Keuper 2 (2, left guard; 15, pass from Sinkwich of 10, run of 5), Conger (61, pass from Sinkwich of 24, run of 37), Kimsey (60, pass from Sinkwich of 11, run of 49), L. Davis (23, pass from Todd of 12, run of 11), Sinkwich (43, fake pass, run through center). Points after touchdown: Costa 4.

Texas Christian—Touchdowns: Gillespie (4, left tackle), Alford 2 (20, pass from Nix; 15, pass from Gillespie), Kring (54, pass from Gillespie of 1, run of 53). Points after touchdown: Medanich, Roach.

STATISTICS

Georgia		*Texas Christian*	*Georgia*		*Texas Christian*
Poschner	LE	Alford	12	First downs	8
Greene	LT	Palmer	223	Net yards rushing	101
Ruark	LG	Crawford	23	Passes attempted	23
Godwin	C	Woodfin	12	Passes completed	9
Kuniansky	RG	Pugh	4	Passes had intercepted	6
Keltner	RT	Adams	288	Net yards passing	176
V. Davis	RE	Roach	511	Total net yards	277
Kimsey	QB	Gillespie	4	Number of punts	7
Sinkwich	LH	Sparks	19.2	Punting average	36.9
L. Davis	RH	Medanich	2	Fumbles lost	0
Keuper	FB	Kring	60	Yards penalized	31

Substitutes—Georgia: Conger, Marshall, Phelps, ends; Ellenson, Posey, Williams, Lewis, tackles; Miller, Burt, guards; Ehrhardt, Costa, centers; Polak, quarterback; Dudish, Todd, halfbacks; Bray, fullback. Texas Christian: Brumbaugh, Slover, Taylor, ends; Hampton, Flowers, tackles; Harter, Moss, Rogers, guards; Blackstone, center; Bagley, Nix, Montgomery, quarterbacks; Conway, Ramsey, Hall, Bierman, halfbacks.

– 1943 –

ORANGE

"The people gathered in the Orange Bowl on this New Year's Day are a cross-section of a unified America determined to carry the war to an ultimate and final victory over our enemies in all parts of the globe . . . and to do it the American way, enthusiastically and with a balanced regard for the necessity of recreation and wholesome sport.

"Most of the players will soon be wearing different uniforms in the Greatest Game of all . . . bucking the line to the roar of guns . . . carrying the Flag to the goal posts of victory."

So it said on page 24 of the 1943 Orange Bowl program.

The people gathered there saw a spectator's delight—eight touchdowns, a field goal, and a safety plus five extra points.

In the early moments, Boston College stunned and bewildered Alabama. The Eagles led 14 to 0. The Crimson Tide was on the brink of disaster.

All-America center Joe Domnanovich, Alabama's captain, called his men into a huddle as they awaited the next kickoff.

"Don't give up," he said, simply but firmly. "We haven't had a chance to go with that ball yet. We're going to receive and we're going to run them into the ground."

Twenty minutes later, at halftime, Alabama was in front, 22 to 21, and won the game, 37 to 21.

Three plays following the opening kickoff, Mike Holovak, the Eagles' swift-striding right halfback, broke free around left end and ran 65 yards for a touchdown. Moments later he was loose again, this time for 35 yards around the same side.

The Crimson scored thrice in the second quarter as Russ Craft, Dave Brown, Johnny August, and Russ Mosley tore off big chunks of turf and the Boston College defense caved in. Bobby Tom Jenkins raced 40 yards for one of the touchdowns.

The Eagles bounced back to recapture the lead. Fullback Carl

Lucas, who was to suffer a broken leg, passed to Holovak for 45 yards to the Bama 12. Holovak plowed the last two yards for his third touchdown.

That made it 21 to 19 when Mickey Connolly kicked the extra point. But the Boston College advantage was brief. With 30 seconds remaining in the first half, guard George Hecht booted a field goal from the 15. And it was 22 to 21.

Against the Eagles' porous defense—Alabama's was none too stout —the Southeastern Conference team added two more touchdowns and a safety in the second half.

Boston College sustained an almost unbelievable series of misfortunes. A few minutes before the game started the water cooler in the dressing room fell and regular tackle Joe Repko was injured. Lucas was lost in the second quarter. Quarterback Eddie (The Brain) Doherty suffered an injured shoulder and couldn't play the last half. End Don Currivan retired early because of an ailing hand.

The Boston press treated the game from an unbiased standpoint.

Bill Cunningham, widely respected columnist for the *Boston Post,* wrote, "When you're beaten as clearly and as splendidly as was Boston College today, the only thing to do is stand and salute as the victors go by. It was a fine game, played in the truest tradition of sportsmanship, brilliantly won and gallantly lost in a magnificent setting, so in taste with the times that none who saw it will ever forget it."

FRIDAY, JANUARY 1, 1943

Alabama	0	22	6	9	37
Boston College	14	7	0	0	21

Alabama—Touchdowns: Leeth (14, pass from Mosley of 9, run of 5), Cook (17, pass from August), Jenkins 2 (40, left end; 1, left guard), August (15, fake pass, right end). Field goal: Hecht (25, placekick). Points after touchdown: Hecht 2. Safety: Domnanovich tackled Connolly in end zone on play from Boston College 7.

Boston College—Touchdowns: Holovak 3 (65, left end, lateral from Doherty; 35, left end; 2, right guard). Points after touchdown: Connolly 3.

STATISTICS

Alabama		Boston College	Alabama		Boston College
Sharp	LE	Currivan	13	First downs	13
Whitmire	LT	Furey	244	Net yards rushing	202
Hecht	LG	Canale	14	Passes attempted	17
Domnanovich	C	Naumetz	9	Passes completed	11
Leon	RG	Darone	1	Passes had intercepted	2
Olenski	RT	Bouley	96	Net yards passing	167

Alabama		Boston College	Alabama		Boston College
Roberts	RE	Furbush	340	Total net yards	369
Sabo	QB	Doherty	5	Number of punts	4
August	LH	Mangene	39	Punting average	33.1
Brown	RH	Holovak	0	Fumbles lost	1
Salls	FB	Lucas	20	Yards penalized	20

Substitutes—Alabama: Leeth, Cook, Bires, Grantham, ends; Compton, Fichman, McKewen, Aland, tackles; Staples, McKosky, Chorba, Killian, guards; Baughman, Chapman, centers; McWhorter, Avery, Cain, quarterbacks; Mosley, Craft, Reese, Gammon, halfbacks; Jenkins, Rodgers, Scales, fullbacks. Boston College: Lipka, E. Fiorentino, ends; Kissell, Repko, tackles; A. Fiorentino, Palladine, guards; Zissis, center; Boudreau, quarterback; Lanoue, Commane, Killelea, halfbacks; Boyce, Connolly, fullbacks.

ROSE

"We're in to Win" was the title of the 1943 Tournament of Roses parade. The Association asked communities and organizations traditionally entering floats in the competition to turn their efforts to selling war bonds. Instead of flower-covered vehicles, bands paraded in downtown Pasadena on New Year's Day morning.

After Georgia defeated UCLA, 9 to 0, in the Rose Bowl, officials of the universities joined with the Tournament and the Pacific Coast Conference in announcing a gift of $50,000 to the Red Cross.

A fierce defense and sheer determination prevented the Bruins, champions of the Coast Conference for the first time, from being beaten worse. Even with the leading ground gainer since the beginning of national collegiate statistics, "Fireball Frankie" Sinkwich, hobbled by two sprained ankles, Georgia completely dominated the game. The Bulldogs squandered several scoring opportunities, however, before concentrating their goal-line punch in the final quarter.

Sinkwich set a total offense record of 2,187 yards in 1942 in earning the Heisman Trophy as the country's outstanding player. His career figure of 4,610 yards topped Red Grange's 4,280, Glenn Davis' 4,024, and Tom Harmon's 3,592.

But without Sinkwich in the pink in the Rose Bowl, Georgia was still able to claim a commanding bulge in first downs (24 to 5) and yardage (379 to 158). The Bulldogs controlled the ball for 96 plays to 47 for the Bruins.

This superiority was due chiefly to the crackerjack performance of sophomore Charlie Trippi. He gained more rushing yardage, 130 in 25 carries, than all the Uclans and he threw passes good for 96 additional yards.

Two other Bulldogs in the spotlight were halfback Lamar Davis, who almost ran for a touchdown on the opening kickoff, and end George Poschner. Two years later Poschner was wounded in the Battle of the Bulge. He received the Distinguished Service Cross for gallantry in action. Frostbite, suffered as he lay helpless on the battlefield more than 48 hours after being shot in the head, forced Army surgeons to amputate both legs and part of his right hand.

Georgia was checked on the UCLA 2 and again on the 10 in the second quarter. As the third quarter ended Sinkwich fumbled, trying to score from the 1. Bruin halfback Al Izmirian recovered on the 3. But in another moment the Southeastern Conference champions had all they needed, two points. Right tackle Red Boyd blocked Bob Waterfield's punt from behind the goal line. The ball bounced out of the end zone for a safety.

On the morning of the game Boyd found a hairpin in Georgia's hotel. "I told my roommate, Lamar Davis, something good would happen to me after I found that hairpin," Boyd said.

Something good happened to center Clyde Ehrhardt, too. He picked off a Waterfield pass and ran 20 yards to the UCLA 25. Georgia scored in six plays. Sinkwich, who made spasmodic appearances in the offensive lineup, crashed over from the 1.

Georgia Coach Wally Butts said, "I knew Sinkwich would not be in shape to play, although I also knew we could tape his ankles so no further injury would result. But I felt a responsibility beyond even our winning the game.

"In the first place all those people were entitled to see Frank in action. They had read about him and wanted to see him play. And Sinkwich himself was entitled to compete. His whole athletic career had been built on the hope that one day he could play in the Rose Bowl."

Frankie's pretty wife, Adeline, and her sister, Dorothy, had a wonderful time on a visit to Universal Studios in Hollywood. Talented as a dance team, the sisters put on an act that interested movie people there.

But when Sinkwich heard of it, he promptly put down both feet and that was the end of that.

Georgia	0	0	0	9	9
UCLA	0	0	0	0	0

Georgia—Touchdown: Sinkwich (1, right tackle). Point after touchdown: Costa. Safety: Boyd blocked Waterfeld's punt from UCLA 3, ball bounced out of end zone.

STATISTICS

Georgia		UCLA	Georgia		UCLA
Poschner	LE	M. Smith	24	First downs	5
Ellenson	LT	Finlay	212	Net yards rushing	97
Kuniansky	LG	Lescoulie	30	Passes attempted	14
Godwin	C	Dougherty	13	Passes completed	5
Ruark	RG	Sparlis	2	Passes had intercepted	4
Williams	RT	Fears (c)	167	Net yards passing	61
V. Davis	RE	Wiener	379	Total net yards	158
Keuper	QB	Waterfield	5	Number of punts	7
Trippi	LH	Solari	34	Punting average	34.6
L. Davis	RH	Riddle	1	Fumbles lost	1
McPhee	FB	Snelling	40	Yards penalized	43

Substitutes—Georgia: Tereshinski, Strother, King, Vickery, ends; Boyd, Pierce, Poss, Richardson, McClure, tackles; Miller, Lee, Heyn, guards; Costa, Ehrhardt, centers; Maguire, Polak, quarterbacks; Dudish, Nunnally, Sinkwich, halfbacks; Todd, Lloyd, fullbacks. UCLA: Baldwin, Robotham, Breeding, ends; Obidine, Griswold, tackles; Compton, Harrison, Marienthal, Woelfle, guards; Spielman, center; V. Smith, Izmirian, Kurrasch, Tyler, halfbacks; Phillips, Pierson, fullbacks.

COTTON

Coaching a bowl team was a new experience for Dana Xenophon Bible of Texas, but he had been exposed to the extracurricular responsibility of preparing a team for a New Year's Day football game before 1943.

On January 1, 1922, Texas A&M, coached by Bible, defeated Centre's Praying Colonels (who had upset Harvard), 22 to 14.

The Aggies were playing a breather opponent that season of 1921. Overconfident and listless, they trailed at halftime and expected the worst from Bible.

He entered the dressing room, sat down, and remained silent. An official tapped on the door, reminding him that in three minutes the second half would start. He still said nothing.

A minute later Bible walked slowly to the door. He stopped and turned. "Well," he inquired in tones of frigid politeness, "shall we go, girls?" Texas A&M won.

His 1942 Texas team was less spectacular and less talented than the high scoring Longhorns of 1941. But Texas won its first Southwest Conference title in twelve years and went into its first bowl game.

No coach ever deserved the accolade of "Coach of the Year," which he received, more than W. A. Alexander of Georgia Tech did in 1942. This was a coach's team. Alexander started with the leftovers from a losing team in 1941. He faced a cruel schedule. His young men played with a fervid resolve few teams have equaled.

His most remarkable player was Clint Castleberry, 155-pound freshman tailback. Castleberry threw a touchdown pass that beat powerful Notre Dame at South Bend. He ran back a punt 95 yards for a touchdown in the conquest of Navy. He was the spark of a team that played inspired football and won nine of its ten games.

Castleberry enlisted in the Air Force after his dazzling freshman season. He was never again to wear a mustard-colored Tech jersey. On November 7, 1944, as the Allied forces pushed closer to victory and the end of World War II, Lieutenant Castleberry flew on a B-26 bomber mission—he was co-pilot—from which he did not return.

"He was a great player," said Bobby Dodd, Tech's backfield coach under Alexander. "He might have been the best of them all. But what is more important is this: he was a great boy—gentle, brave, manly, yet sweet."

The story of Texas' 14 to 7 triumph in the Cotton Bowl was somewhat prosaic. The Longhorns' heavy, sinewy line won the day, halting Georgia Tech at crucial stages, paving the way for hard running backs—and stopping the slippery Castleman.

Texas scored in the first quarter on a 52-yard drive, again in the third period on Jackie Field's beautiful dodging, twisting 60-yard punt return, then held on.

Castleberry had the bad luck to bat Roy Dale McKay's three-yard flat pass into the air at the goal line and wingback Max Minor grabbed it for touchdown No. 1.

Tech's score marked the consummation of a 67-yard surge. The Engineers resurrected the Statue of Liberty play with little Davey Eldridge taking the ball from Eddie Prokop and flying the last three yards around left end in the fourth quarter. They pounded back from their 46 with four minutes left and reached the Texas 3 again before the attack came a cropper.

The game was dedicated to Cotton Bowl players who "have died the death of a hero."

Texas	7	0	7	0	14
Georgia Tech	0	0	0	7	7

Texas—Touchdowns: Minor (3, pass from McKay), Field (60, punt return). Points after touchdown: Field, McKay.

Georgia Tech—Touchdown: Eldredge (3, left end). Point after touchdown: R. Jordan.

STATISTICS

Texas		Georgia Tech	Texas		Georgia Tech
Schwarting	LE	Marshall	15	First downs	10
Mauldin	LT	Anderson	201	Net yards rushing	57
Fisher	LG	Hardy	9	Passes attempted	20
Gill	C	Manning	5	Passes completed	8
Freeman	RG	J. Jordan	1	Passes had intercepted	1
Conoly	RT	West	23	Net yards passing	138
Scott	RE	Helms	224	Total net yards	195
Collins	QB	Kuhn	30	Punting average	31
Field	LH	Sheldon	2	Fumbles lost	2
Minor	RH	McHugh	20	Yards penalized	20
McKay	FB	Dodd			

Substitutes—Texas: Bumgardner, West, ends; Harris, Morries, tackles; Heap, Lobpries, Coltharp, guards; Sachse, Patterson, centers; Fambrough, Magliolo, quarterbacks; Matthews, Park, Raven, Roberts, Guess, halfbacks; Petrovich, Mayne, Jones, fullbacks. Georgia Tech: R. Jordan, Richter, ends; Healy, West, Slaten, Eaves, tackles; Beall, guard; Castleberry, Luck, Prokop, Eldridge, halfbacks; Plaster, fullback.

SUGAR

"Neither team, no matter what the score, stopped trying," said Tennessee Coach John Barnhill after the Sugar Bowl game of 1943. "That's the stuff that insures victory against Germans and Japanese."

His Volunteers wore down and overpowered deft, daring Tulsa, 14 to 7. The Hurricane, coached by Henry Frnka, was repelled repeatedly on the ground and wound up with minus 39 yards. Yet Tennessee had to battle hard to the last few seconds to avert a tie.

Tulsa's 46-yard air lift in the eleventh hour dropped the Hurricane on the Vols' 12. Freshman end Jim Powell intercepted a pass on his 3. One play later the game ended.

The light, plucky Tulsans learned early their only chance was in the air. A highly effective battery took to the gridiron late in the first quarter—the combination of tailback-passer Glenn Dobbs to end-receiver Saxon Judd.

From Tulsa's 40, Dobbs rifled six completed passes in sequence, four to Judd. When the quarter ended, the ball was on the 2. Dobbs chucked to wingback Cal Purdin for the touchdown on the first play of the second period.

The Tulsa sharpshooter completed two more passes in succession to make it nine altogether before misfiring.

Tennessee lashed back and matched the touchdown shortly before the intermission. Fullback Bill Gold's two-yard plunge climaxed a nine-play drive of 60 yards. But Charlie Mitchell missed the extra point. Minutes later tailback Walt Slater passed 12 yards to end Al Hust for an apparent touchdown. However, the play had begun a second after the horn sounded at halftime.

Tennessee went in front in the third quarter when sophomore tackle Denver Crawford blocked a Dobbs punt. The ball bounced out of the end zone for a safety.

Incautious now, the Hurricane passed from deep in its own territory. One behind-his-goal-line attempt by Dobbs was batted in the air by Powell and intercepted by Dick Jordan on the 19. Jordan ran to the 13. Fullback Ig Fuson smashed the last three yards.

N. A. Keithley was pitching in the fourth quarter when Tulsa threatened to tie the Vols. Dobbs begged Frnka to let him return but permission was refused.

Kicking was sensational throughout the game. Ten Tennessee punts averaged 41 yards. Fourteen Tulsa punts averaged 43 yards. One, by Dobbs, traveled 76 yards.

Frnka had probably the widest acquaintance among college coaches of any high school coach in history when he was at Greenville, Tex., in the early thirties.

The manager of the Greenville telephone company, an ardent team supporter, allowed Frnka to use long distance facilities whenever he pleased free of charge. It was nothing for Henry to call famous coaches such as Lou Little, Fritz Crisler, or W. A. Alexander and consult for as long as half an hour on technical situations.

No coach during World War II had as much success with 4-Fs (selective service rejectees) or recruited them so extensively.

Tennessee	0	6	2	6	14
Tulsa	0	7	0	0	7

Tennessee—Touchdowns: Gold (2, center plunge), Fuson (3, center plunge). Safety: Crawford blocked G. Dobbs' punt from Tulsa 10.

Tulsa—Touchdown: Purdin (2, pass from G. Dobbs). Point after touchdown: LeForce.

STATISTICS

Tennessee		Tulsa	Tennessee		Tulsa
Hust	LE	Green	14	First downs	10
Crawford	LT	Paine	208	Net yards rushing	−39
Myers	LG	Hail	17	Passes attempted	27
Fisher	C	Spilman	7	Passes completed	17

Tennessee		*Tulsa*	*Tennessee*	*Tulsa*
Price	RG	Jones	0	Passes had intercepted	2
Huffman	RT	Cooper	88	Net yards passing	168
Lloyd	RE	Judd	296	Total net yards	129
Mitchell	QB	Ericksen	10	Number of punts	14
Cifers	LH	G. Dobbs	41	Punting average	43
Gaffney	RH	Purdin	2	Fumbles lost	0
Nowling	FB	B. Dobbs	100	Yards penalized	44

Substitutions—Tennessee: Jordan, Hubbell, Powell, ends; Rotella, Chadwell, tackles; Drost, Dobelstein, Klarer, guards; Brandau, center; Meek, quarterback; Slater, Hillman, Zontini, halfbacks; Fuson, Gold, fullbacks. Tulsa: Herriman, Goodnight, ends; Greene, Winfrey, Hedrick, tackles; Bland, Goerner, Burgeis, Burris, guards; D'Arcy, center; LeForce, quarterback; Keithley, Spangler, half-backs; Taylor, fullback.

— 1944 —

SUGAR

Until the last, Tulsa was as dangerous as dynamite.

Georgia Tech had rallied from apparent halftime doom, 18 to 7, to go ahead 20 to 18.

Near the end, with most of the 69,000 Sugar Bowl patrons standing and shouting, Clyde LeForce fired a long shot in a final bid for victory. Frank Broyles intercepted on his 10. Thus Tech was able to get the ball in the last three minutes, control it, and protect its two-point lead.

Tulsa's all-civilian military-rejected or undrafted players—Coach Henry Frnka said how he collected them was his secret—jumped in front by two touchdowns before Tech pulled itself together and marched 72 yards to score.

Jimmy Ford, 17, five feet and seven inches tall and weighing 145, made the Hurricane's second touchdown. He dashed off tackle, wriggled away from a Yellow Jacket, and ran 76 yards. LeForce missed the second of three bungled conversions. These were, in the last analysis, fatal to Tulsa.

Just before halftime Tulsa received a gift touchdown that seemed to all but clinch it. A Tech back lined up too close to center Bob Cummings. His hand misguided the snapback to Broyles. Tulsa end Barney White recovered on the 1. LeForce, who had passed to Ed Shedlosky for the first touchdown, went over from the 6 after a five-yard penalty.

Coach W. A. Alexander's Navy trainees swung back with two dynamic drives, one in the third and another in the fourth quarter. Halfback Eddie Prokop spearheaded both offensives with important help from Broyles, Ed Scharfschwerdt, and Malcolm Logan.

Although eschewing the pass for the most part, on Alexander's orders, Tech capped an 89-yard sortie early in the second half with a 49-yard aerial scoring play. Prokop caught Tulsa with its defense drawn in too close. He passed to end Phil Tinsley for the touchdown.

Scharfschwerdt whacked inside right tackle from the 2, rolled off the jam-up, and fought into the end zone for the winning points. The push began on the Jackets' 22 five minutes after the fourth quarter began.

Prokop set Sugar Bowl records with 199 yards running, 29 carries, and 256 yards total offense.

Tulsa Coach Henry Frnka said it wouldn't have been justice for his team to have won by extra points since a Tech fumble made the third touchdown possible.

"It was the toughest game to lose I've ever known," he added, "but I must hand it to Coach Alex and his grand team. More than anything now, I want to wish good luck to these boys in the service at Tech who will soon be going into action."

Said Coach Alex: "I consider the game a tie. Each team scored three touchdowns. That's glory enough for both."

"If those Tulsans were 4-F, then the Army has been sound asleep," wrote Ed Danforth of Atlanta. "They would make ideal commando troops. The Yellow Jackets will swear to that."

By playing in this game, Georgia Tech became the first school to participate in four major bowls. In the fifties Georgia Tech was the most successful bowl school of the decade, carrying out the have-fun policy introduced at New Orleans.

The Jackets practiced in the morning. Entertainment was arranged in the afternoon and evening. The players were asked to observe a sensible curfew. There was no chance for them to go stale or become overly tense.

SATURDAY, JANUARY 1, 1944

Georgia Tech	0	7	6	7	20
Tulsa	6	12	0	0	18

Georgia Tech—Touchdowns: Broyles (1, left guard), Tinsley (49, pass from Prokop of 19, run of 30), Scharfschwerdt (2, center plunge). Points after touchdown: Prokop 2.

Tulsa—Touchdowns: Shedlosky (15, pass from LeForce of 5, run of 10), Ford (76, right tackle), LeForce (6, right tackle).

STATISTICS

Georgia Tech		Tulsa	Georgia Tech		Tulsa
Tinsley	LE	Goodnight	25	First downs	8
Chambers	LT	Stanley	373	Net yards rushing	211
Steber	LG	Buda	16	Passes attempted	15
Cummings	C	Prewitt	4	Passes completed	6
Hoover	RG	E. Jones	1	Passes had intercepted	1
Phillips	RT	Burgeis	83	Net yards passing	87
Kilzer	RE	Herriman	456	Total net yards	298
Faulkner	QB	Taylor	6	Number of punts	7
Prokop	LH	Shedlosky	38	Punting average	34
Logan	RH	LeForce	3	Fumbles lost	1
Broyles	FB	Wilson	60	Yards penalized	50

Substitutions—Georgia Tech: Dorough, Daniel, ends; Bourne, Mills, tackles; Beall, Furchgott, guards; Wakefield, quarterback; Broyles, Scharfschwerdt, Gaston, halfbacks; Scharfschwerdt, fullback. Tulsa: Luhn, White, Stegman, ends; Stegman, Butterworth, LaGreca, White, Gray, tackles; R. Jones, Minarik, guards; Malone, center; Kowalski, quarterback; Walker, Ford, Wade, Smith, halfbacks; Taylor, Smith, LeForce, fullbacks.

ORANGE

Because of the military's call on the services of America's strapping young football players, big colleges that did not benefit from on-campus training units were stripped of their usual talent. A large number gave up the sport entirely.

Freshmen, 16- and 17-year-olds many of them, were the salvation of some schools who carried on during wartime seasons. They supplied a contagious spark of enthusiasm and eagerness that amazed coaches and helped to offset inexperience.

The Orange Bowl game of 1944 was played by the youngest men ever to appear in a New Year's Day contest. A sprinkling were only 16. Most were 17. Texas A&M didn't have a player not in his teens. LSU had just six in their twenties.

"Oldsters" were tackle Charles Hartley, 23, and halfback Steve

Van Buren, 22. With Van Buren as the spearhead, LSU defeated
the pass-dependent Aggies 19 to 14 and avenged a 28 to 13 setback
at their hands in the regular season.

The Office of Defense Transportation restricted sale of tickets to
the Miami area to discourage unnecessary travel. Shortly before the
game started a thousand servicemen outside the gates were admitted
to sit on the grass behind the end zones. But Orange Bowl business
manager Ernie Seiler, an Air Force captain, was forced to miss his
first game in the series. He was stationed in Sioux Falls, S. D.

The game was young when Van Buren swung and swayed to score
from 11 yards away on a double reverse around right end.

It continued only a few more minutes before Bing Turner of
Texas A&M fumbled Van Buren's quick kick and Charlie Webb recovered on the Aggies' 22. Van Buren passed to end Burton Goode
for another touchdown.

In the second period Van Buren raced into the clear on a fake
punt and scurried 45 yards to the A&M 25 only to stumble and fall
with a touchdown in sight. The youngsters from Texas stopped the
Tigers on the 2.

However, in the third quarter Steve retained his footing all the
way on a 63-yard run for a touchdown.

The Aggies were licked but wouldn't admit it. They kept battling. They had scored a touchdown on a pass in the first period
and they made their second touchdown by air in the third quarter.
They struggled desperately for a winning aerial strike in the final
period. But interceptions killed them.

They attempted 32 passes, completing 14 for 199 yards. But five
were stolen by the Tigers. Thus, in their two bowl games within a
two-year stretch (Cotton in 1942), the Aggies tried 74 passes. Twelve
were intercepted.

A pulled muscle prevented A&M's ace pass receiver, Marion Flana-
gan, from playing. He was also a talented runner. Without him, the
Aggies lost 15 yards net rushing.

Two years and nine and a half months later, the head linesman
in this Orange Bowl game would manage the St. Louis Cardinals, as
a freshman big league pilot, to victory over the Boston Red Sox in
the World Series.

He was Eddie Dyer, a former Rice football player.

Louisiana State	12	0	7	0	19
Texas A&M	7	0	7	0	14

Louisiana State—Touchdowns: Van Buren 2 (11, right end, double reverse;

63, left tackle), Goode (20, pass from Van Buren). Point after touchdown: Van Buren.

Texas A&M—Touchdowns: Burditt (21, pass from Hallmark), Settegast (19, pass from Hallmark of 12, run of 7). Points after touchdown: Turner 2.

STATISTICS

Louisiana State		Texas A&M	Louisiana State		Texas A&M
Webb	LE	Geer	7	First downs	7
Tullos	LT	Bryant	201	Net yards rushing	−15
Lewis	LG	Turley	10	Passes attempted	32
C. Schroll	C	R. Wright	4	Passes completed	14
Trapani	RG	Tassos	0	Passes had intercepted	5
Hartley	RT	Moncrief	100	Net yards passing	199
Goode	RE	Settegast	301	Total net yards	184
Nagata	QB	Burditt	10	Number of punts	9
Van Buren	LH	Hallmark	38	Punting average	42.1
Griffith	RH	Butchofsky	3	Fumbles lost	1
W. Schroll	FB	Turner	75	Yards penalized	35

Substitutes—Louisiana State: Walker, McClelland, Casanova, ends; Miller, Bernhard, tackles; Janneck, Polozola, Reeder, Weimar, guards; Claunch, center; Barney, quarterback; Knight, Pardo, Bryan, Payne, halfbacks; Corgan, fullback. Texas A&M: Darnell, McCurry, Gibson, Wiley, C. Wright, ends; Eberle, tackle; Brown, Overly, Hohn, guards; Gary, center; Deere, quarterback; Beesley, Muehlhause, halfbacks; McAllister, fullback.

ROSE

War caused strange bowl happenings.

In 1944, for the first time, a conference championship was decided in the Rose Bowl. For the first time the intersectional aspect was missing. Wartime travel restrictions deprived the game of that flavor.

Extending its perfect Pasadena record, Southern California, a 13-point underdog, swatted Washington 29 to 0.

The magic numbers were three, seven, and one.

Quarterback Jim Hardy threw three touchdown passes. That tied the former Rose Bowl record set 14 years before by Russ Saunders.

It was Southern California's seventh straight bowl victory and its first under Coach Jeff Cravath, who played under Howard Jones in the mid-twenties. In Cravath's three varsity seasons the Trojans lost six games but by a combined score of only 22 points.

Washington was favored in the game that decided the Pacific Coast Conference championship. The reason for that was found in a comparison of scores against a common opponent.

The Huskies, sweeping a four-game schedule that ended October

30, trimmed the Fourth Air Force Flyers of March Field of California, 27 to 7. The airmen walloped the Trojans, 35 to 0.

What the odds-makers seemed to overlook was that Washington would play Southern California without fullback Pete Susick, its leading ground gainer, starting halfback Jay Stoves, and first string tackle Tony Balchunas. All had been sent to the marine base at Parris Island, S. C.

Hardy's scoring passes capped drives of 72, 41, and 31 yards.

Writers covering the game credited Norman Verry, Trojan guard and captain, with one of the finest line performances in Rose Bowl annals.

Southern California	0	7	13	9	29
Washington	0	0	0	0	0

Southern California—Touchdowns: G. Callanan 2 (11, pass from J. Hardy of 7, run of 4; 10, pass from J. Hardy), G. Gray 2 (21, pass from J. Hardy; 15, pass from Bell of 10, run of 5). Points after touchdown: Jamison 3. Safety: Planck blocked Austin's punt from Washington 15, ball recovered in end zone by Kramer, Washington.

STATISTICS

Southern California		Washington	Southern California		Washington
G. Gray	LE	Tracy	8	First downs	7
Ferraro	LT	Deeks	117	Net yards rushing	134
Jamison	LG	Saksa	16	Passes attempted	22
W. Gray	C	Berlin	9	Passes completed	5
Verry (c)	RG	Ward	0	Passes had intercepted	3
Ossowski	RT	Christensen	113	Net yards passing	51
J. Callanan	RE	Hagen	230	Total net yards	185
Bell	QB	Austin	10	Number of punts	7
Saenz	LH	Robinson	37.5	Punting average	35.9
G. Callanan	RH	Akins	0	Fumbles lost	2
Whitehead	FB	Kramer	25	Yards penalized	10

Substitutes—Southern California: Dominis, D. Hardy, Welker, Webb, ends; Gelker, Romer, Stall, tackles; Planck, Marincovich, Garzoni, Curtis, Patapoff, Ingle, guards; Wolf, Fortney, Alden, centers; J. Hardy, Miller, Pattee, quarterbacks; Evans, Parsons, Dreblow, Dunne, McFadden, halfbacks; Page, Shipkey, Curry, Antles, Worden, fullbacks. Washington: Buck, Roark, Clinton, ends; McGovern, tackle; Johnson, Coles, Meyers, guards; McCurdy, Oliver, centers; Zech, quarterback; Wren, Bruce, halfbacks; DeCourcey, Smith, fullbacks.

COTTON

"The West Point of the Air," Randolph Field, where young men were trained for Air Force duty, was the only service team, among many powerful outfits, to play in a major bowl game during World War II.

Two-thirds of Dana Bible's Texas Longhorns who won the Southwest Conference title for the second straight year were Naval trainees.

These once-beaten teams met in Dallas and fought to a 7 to 7 tie. It was the first of three Cotton Bowl deadlocks in a five-year period.

The flyers' bombardier was Glenn Dobbs of Tulsa fame, also an excellent punter. Passing and running, Dobbs had accounted for 1,823 yards and had thrown for 20 of his team's 39 touchdowns.

Dobb's favorite target was halfback Tex Aulds, who scored 55 points, most of them on passes. This pair teamed up for the first touchdown. Fullback J. R. Calahan, a smashing Longhorn fullback who had proved the difference between a mediocre and a championship season, fumbled on the Texas 26 in the first quarter. Halfback Walter Parker recovered. Dobbs ran 11 yards, then tossed the scoring aerial.

In the second quarter Dobbs dropped the ball on his 41. Texas took possession and scored on the third play thereafter when Ralph Ellsworth connected with George McCall. The pass covered 35 yards.

One of Dobbs' punts traveled 68 yards in the rain that held the crowd to 15,000, although more than twice that number bought tickets.

Dan D. Rogers, chairman of the board of the Cotton Bowl Athletic Association, wrote in the 1944 game program:

"Athletics have meant much to the nation's war effort . . . When men all over the world—in the foxholes of the Solomons or in the hilly boot of Italy—ask to hear football and other sports broadcasts in preference to any other type of entertainment, we realize the really great morale value of this home activity for the men at the front."

| Randolph Field | 7 | 0 | 0 | 0 | 7 |
| Texas | 0 | 7 | 0 | 0 | 7 |

Randolph Field—Touchdown: Aulds (15, pass from Dobbs). Point after touchdown: West.

Texas—Touchdown: McCall (35, pass from Ellsworth of 32, run of 3). Point after touchdown: Calahan.

STATISTICS

Randolph Field		Texas	Randolph Field		Texas
Morse	LE	Parker	7	First downs	3
Ruby	LT	Phillips	99	Net yards rushing	73

Randolph Field		Texas	Randolph Field		Texas
Vaughn	LG	Butler	16	Passes attempted	10
Killian	C	Marshall	3	Passes completed	3
Davis	RG	Simons	3	Passes had intercepted	1
Harpring	RT	Plyler	51	Net yards passing	37
Leinweber	RE	McCall	150	Total net yards	110
Yaremko	QB	Magliolo	39.9	Punting average	33.1
Dobbs	LH	Ellsworth	1	Fumbles lost	1
Parker	RH	Park	20	Yards penalized	0
West	FB	Calahan			

Substitutes—Randolph Field: Pickens, Keeton, ends; Drucker, guard; Aulds, Fixx, halfbacks; Wright, fullback. Texas: Harville, Maurer, ends; Kishi, tackle; Bolin, Wetz, Mayfield, guards; Canady, Schutze, quarterbacks.

– 1945 –

COTTON

Twenty years after the jersey number 77 was made famous by Red Grange, another wearer of double numerals achieved All-America recognition.

He was blond, 188-pound (18 pounds heavier than Grange; players were growing larger) Bob Fenimore. He wore No. 55. He scored 77 points during Oklahoma A&M's eight-game season. He led the nation in total offense with 1,758 yards, an average of 219.8 per game.

Fenimore had been rejected for military duty because of a calcium deposit on his left knee. It developed after a heavy thigh bruise which he sustained as a freshman in 1943. Whenever he got a hard hit on his left leg, it caused him to limp slightly.

The big tailback was one of three starting Oklahoma A&M backs who could run 100 yards in 10 seconds or less. The Aggies' speed was more than Texas Christian could cope with. TCU was routed in the Cotton Bowl 34 to 0.

The Horned Frogs never threatened to score as Oklahoma A&M reaped 295 yards running and 199 more passing. Fenimore made two touchdowns in a typical applause-worthy demonstration of multiple skills. Fleet freshman fullback Jim Spavital scooted 52 yards on the longest scoring run.

This was on the first day of 1945, a year which brought peace to a war-torn world.

MONDAY, JANUARY 1, 1945

Oklahoma A&M	14	0	7	13	34
Texas Christian	0	0	0	0	0

Oklahoma A&M—Touchdowns: Fenimore 2 (1, right tackle; 8, right end), Spavital (52, center), Thomas (1, right guard), Creager (1, right guard). Points after touchdown: Creager 4.

STATISTICS

Oklahoma A&M		Texas Christian	Oklahoma A&M		Texas Christian
Armstrong	LE	Gibson	20	First downs	5
Foster	LT	Rose	295	Net yards rushing	74
Colhouer	LG	Cooke	17	Passes attempted	10
Gattis	C	Cooper	9	Passes completed	3
Fulk	RG	Smith	1	Passes had intercepted	1
Riddle	RT	Flowers	199	Net yards passing	31
G. Moore	RE	Mullins	494	Total net yards	105
Watson	QB	Hadaway	34	Punting average	31
Fenimore	LH	Rogers	1	Fumbles lost	1
Hankins	RH	Ruff	75	Yards penalized	25
Spavital	FB	Cox			

Substitutes—Oklahoma A&M: Patton, Brewton, Lipe, Rhodes, Griffin, R. Moore, ends; Tait, Grissom, Hodges, Oaks, Barger, Karraker, tackles; Weaver, Duckett, Lynch, Fowler, Gay, DeMoss, guards; Wilkerson, Foran, Peterson, centers; Conner, Walker, quarterbacks; Stafford, Thomas, Rozell, Creager, Cope, halfbacks; Cohlmia, Bradford, fullbacks. Texas Christian: Buschman, Garren, Ifland, ends; Smalley, Cohagan, tackles; Kohler, Gallagher, guards; Pannell, center; Busby, quarterback; Jackson, Mason, Harrelson, halfbacks.

SUGAR

If you said the 1945 Sugar Bowl game was charged with drama every minute, it wouldn't be much of an exaggeration.

The lead changed hands four times. The outcome was uncertain until the last second. The heart-throbbing finish pulled 72,000 people out of their seats.

In the last analysis, it was the power and experience of Duke's Navy trainees that prevailed over Alabama's inspired wartime civilian group, 29 to 26.

After watching Harry Gilmer, Alabama's 18-year-old freshman

tailback, complete eight out of eight passes despite the rushing of a hard-charging line, Grantland Rice called him "the greatest college passer I ever saw."

Gilmer hit the tough Duke line hard for important gains and made many tackles, personally downing the Blue Devil ball carrier after every kickoff.

One pass in particular stood out. Forced far back, Harry tripped over one Duke man. Two more Blue Devils got a piece of him. Suddenly, he broke loose for an instant, leaped high, and whipped the ball 41 yards to Ralph Jones, a big end.

In bowl history never has one so young performed so brilliantly.

On the last play he fired another long pass to Jones, who just missed going for a touchdown on a 33-yard gainer to Duke's 25.

Duke led early, 7 to 0. Halfback George Clark ran 52 yards on the first play from scrimmage. He scored on a 14-yard bolt up the middle.

Gilmer's aerial craft set up three Crimson Tide touchdowns before Duke could score again, making it 19 to 13 at halftime.

Duke fullback Tom Davis carried ten straight times on a 64-yard thrust in the third quarter. It wound up with Davis scoring his second touchdown. Now it was 20 to 19, Duke.

Alabama threw back the Blue Devils on the Tide 12 early in the fourth period. But they surged forward again. This time Hugh Morrow stepped in front of Gordon Carver and intercepted Cliff Lewis' pass. Morrow moved 75 yards at top speed. With his conversion it became 26 to 20, Alabama.

Duke took the kickoff and wasn't stopped until the goal line was a yard away.

Three minutes remained. Coach Frank Thomas decided on a calculated risk. He sent in orders to give up two points through an intentional safety. Thomas hoped for a long high punt from the 20 by John Wade, who would have plenty of time. He hoped also for good coverage and a resolute defense.

The strategy backfired. The punt sailed 40 yards. Clark returned it 20 yards to Alabama's 40. The Blue Devils cracked the Tide defense for the touchdown in two inspired runs. First, wingback Jim LaRue gained 20 on a reverse after which Clark rushed through right tackle in a furious charge and scored.

"I'd say that last run LaRue made won the game," Rice wrote. "He fought his way for 20 yards where he might have been thrown for a loss. He carried two red shirts on his back for the last seven yards and it was this terrific determination to win that saved the day for Duke. I've never seen a more thrilling game."

Duke	7	6	7	9	29
Alabama	12	7	0	7	26

Duke—Touchdowns: Clark 2 (14, fake pass, through the middle; 20, right tackle), Davis 2 (1, center plunge; 1, center plunge). Points after touchdown: Raether 3. Safety: Gilmer knelt in end zone intentionally on play from Alabama 1.

Alabama—Touchdowns: Hodges 2 (1, plunge; 1, plunge), Jones (10, pass from Gilmer), Morrow (75, intercepted pass by Lewis). Points after touchdown: Morrow 2.

STATISTICS

Duke		Alabama	Duke		Alabama
Jones	LE	Jones	19	First downs	8
Hardison	LT	Whitley	319	Net yards rushing	107
Sink	LG	Wozniak	8	Passes attempted	8
Crowder	C	Mancha	5	Passes completed	8
Knotts	RG	Green	1	Passes had intercepted	0
Irwin	RT	Edwards	47	Net yards passing	142
Harry	RE	McConnville	366	Total net yards	249
Kriza	QB	Self	4	Number of punts	5
Carver	LH	Gilmer	34	Punting average	35
Clark	RH	Tew	1	Fumbles lost	1
Davis	FB	Hodges	5	Yards penalized	6

Substitutions—Duke: Raether, end; Eisenberg, Leitheiser, tackles; Perini, guard; Sharkey, center; Lewis, quarterback; Stephanz, Smith, LaRue, Haggerty, halfbacks; Spears, fullback. Alabama: Fields, end; Cassidy, tackle; Filippini, Conway, guards; Morrow, quarterback; Wade, Robertson, Albright, halfbacks; Grant, fullback.

ORANGE

The bowl program was prophetic.

Van C. Kussrow, president of the Orange Bowl Committee, welcomed spectators in 1945 "with the sincere hope that next New Year's Day and the 1946 Orange Bowl game will find the enemy whipped in both Europe and Asia—and fathers, husbands, sons and brothers will be here with you to witness the game and festival."

Georgia Tech, playing for the last time under W. A. Alexander, fell to revenge-minded Tulsa, 26 to 12.

Tulsa led the nation in total offense in 1944 with an average of 434.7 yards per game, one of the highest in history.

When the Orange Bowl contest ended, Tech had netted more yards than Tulsa. But the Hurricane had clearly demonstrated superiority in running, line strength, speed, and manpower.

Bent on reversing the outcome of the Sugar Bowl game of the year before, Tulsa wasted few plays and little time in taking positive steps.

It was 14 to 0 at the quarter. And after a point-empty period, three touchdowns within five minutes of the start of the third quarter kept the scoreboard lights flashing.

Tulsa got two of those touchdowns, spectacularly achieved.

Fullback Camp Wilson raced 90 yards on a kickoff return. The other came on a razzle-dazzle forward-lateral from Perry Moss to Clyde Goodnight, who flipped back to Barney White as the ends crisscrossed. The play covered 65 yards.

Tech inserted its first scoring effort between them and it was another eye-opener.

Frank Broyles lobbed a 31-yard pass to Johnny McIntosh, who took it on the 20 and ran over the goal line.

Broyles threw twenty passes on the hot afternoon. He completed 17 for 276 yards. It was a remarkable percentage of success and until 1963 an all-time record for all the bowls in total yardage through the air.

In the final period Tech, although hopelessly beaten, worked out a 76-yard touchdown march in fourteen Broyles-led plays. It caused Ed Danforth, *Atlanta Journal* sports editor, to observe, "Your reporter thinks that last drive made by a battered, gasping team with key men out of the game or out on their feet was the finest exhibition he has seen on a football field in many a day." Rumsey Taylor rammed over for the touchdown with a minute to play.

It was Broyles' leadership, Danforth wrote, that kept the young Tech team together when "it might have been routed by 40 or 50 points."

Frank survived a somewhat risky encounter late in the contest. Forrest Grigg, 300-pound Tulsa lineman, fell on him making a tackle. The hardy Broyles arose as if nothing heavier than a building cornerstone had been dropped on him.

Tulsa	14	0	12	0	26
Georgia Tech	0	0	6	6	12

Tulsa—Touchdowns: Shedlosky 2 (14, pass from Moss; 4, left end reverse), White (65, pass from Moss to Goodnight of 5, lateral to White, run of 38), Wilson (90, kickoff return). Points after touchdown: Moss 2.

Georgia Tech—Touchdowns: McIntosh (51, pass from Broyles of 12, run of 39), Taylor (2, right guard).

STATISTICS

Tulsa		Georgia Tech	Tulsa		Georgia Tech
Goodnight	LE	Daniel	14	First downs	17
Stanley	LT	Glenn	182	Net yards rushing	43
Buda	LG	Phillips	15	Passes attempted	35
Prewitt	C	Duke	6	Passes completed	20
E. Jones	RG	Hills	0	Passes had intercepted	2
Burgeis	RT	Gaines	137	Net yards passing	319
White	RE	Tinsley	319	Total net yards	362
Kowalski	QB	McIntosh	6	Number of punts	4
Moss	LH	Broyles	35.2	Punting average	38
Shedlosky	RH	Mathews	1	Fumbles lost	3
Wilson	FB	Williams	10	Yards penalized	15

Substitutes—Tulsa: Luhn, Gray, Jarrett, Field, Swaney, ends; LaGreca, Collins, Grigg, tackles; Bloom, R. Jones, Morgan, Thomas, guards; Schmidt, center; Mitchell, quarterback; Verkins, Stuart, Wade, Boone, Walker, Toler, halfbacks; Smith, Moseley, fullbacks. Georgia Tech: Wilson, Enders, Murdock, ends; Dombach, Davis, tackles; Furchgott, J. Bowen, guards; Holtsinger, center; Helzer, quarterback; A. Bowen, Logan, Ritter, halfbacks; Taylor, fullback.

ROSE

There was never any doubt in the minds of Southern California players that they would handle Tennessee with ease in the Rose Bowl game of 1945.

The day before, in fact, Bob Rule, then writing for the *Nashville Banner,* reported from Pasadena that a Trojan whom he didn't identify told Tennessee captain Bill Bevis that Southern California would score the first time it got the ball. The anonymous Trojan made good the boast.

On the third play Buster Stephens, Tennessee's freshman tailback and a fine one, attempted to punt from his 43. End Jim Callanan blocked it, chased it, scooped it up while facing his own goal line, whirled, and sprinted 24 yards for a touchdown.

Jim Hardy, captain and versatile quarterback of the Trojans, glittered grandly. He threw two touchdown passes (making five in two years in the Rose Bowl). He slanted three punts out of bounds inside the Vounteers' 10. He scored a touchdown on a nine-yard bootleg play. Throughout, he directed his team almost flawlessly.

Tennessee fought fiercely in the first half. The Vols, with mostly a freshman lineup, gave an inspired performance. But they didn't have the physical qualifications, or get the breaks, and succumbed 25 to 0. They never advanced beyond their conquerors' 40.

Southern California Coach Jeff Cravath lashed his men verbally
during the intermission.

"We had been messing things up," said Hardy. "Jeff gave us the
dickens. He woke us up."

Still, the fourth quarter was under way before the Trojan offense
rolled down the field with any sustained force. Then it tore off 73
yards to score in ten plays. The gun had been fired ending the game
when Hardy shot a six-yard pass to end Doug MacLachlan for the
fourth touchdown.

It was Southern California's eighth successive Rose Bowl victory.
There were several oddities.

Three pairs of brothers took part, Jim and Don Hardy and Jim
and George Callanan of Southern California and Russ and Bob
Dobelstein of Tennessee.

Two Trojans, Blake Headley and Ben Schlegel, had never played
in a college game before this, an unusual situation in a bowl perhaps,
but characteristic of the wartime years in football.

One of the Tennessee centers, George Kelley (he didn't get into
the game), later transferred to Vanderbilt, Tennessee's ancient intra-
state rival. He captained the Commodores' basketball team that upset Kentucky's 1951 national champions in the finals of the Southeastern Conference tournament.

| Southern California | 6 | 6 | 0 | 13 | 25 |
| Tennessee | 0 | 0 | 0 | 0 | 0 |

Southern California—Touchdowns: J. Callanan (blocked punt by Stephens
from Tennessee 43, recovered on 24), Salata (22, pass from J. Hardy), J. Hardy
(9, right end), MacLachlan (6, pass from J. Hardy). Point after touchdown:
West.

STATISTICS

Southern California		Tennessee	Southern California		Tennessee
D. Hardy	LE	Wildman	15	First downs	8
Ferraro	LT	R. H. Dobelstein	258	Net yards rushing	153
Curtis	LG	Asbury	15	Passes attempted	14
Antles	C	Morrow	5	Passes completed	3
Wall	RG	R. E. Dobelstein	0	Passes had intercepted	1
Pehar	RT	Stewart	53	Net yards passing	17
J. Callanan	RE	Pike	311	Total net yards	170
J. Hardy (c)	QB	Bevis (c)	11	Number of punts	13
Morris	LH	Stephens	32.6	Punting average	34.6
Burnside	RH	Stephenson	1	Fumbles lost	1
West	FB	Major	25	Yards penalized	35

Substitutes—Southern California: McKinney, MacLachlan, Salata, ends; Musick, tackle; McGinn, Higgins, guards; Fortney, center; Murphy, quarterback; Gardner, Schlegel, Headley, G. Callanan, Davis, halfbacks; Whitehead, fullback. Tennessee: Blessing, end; Edmonds, Murray, Bailey, Paidousis, tackles; McRee, Steffy, Chadnock, McQuady, guards; Miller, center; Holsclaw, Law, Redding, halfbacks; Manning, fullback.

− 1946 −

Jacksonville's 'Gator

GATOR BOWL

The most colorful, interesting, and original football bowl program ever published came out in 1960 on the occasion of the Gator Bowl's crystal anniversary game between Arkansas and Georgia Tech.

It was produced and edited by Dick Stratton, a Jacksonville sports announcer. In a tribute to the game's development, Bill Kastelz, sports editor of the *Florida Times-Union,* wrote in the program: "Young as major bowl games go, the Gator Bowl nevertheless stands shoulder-to-shoulder beside all the others with a dramatic, star-spangled history."

None of the major established bowls had a humbler beginning than the Gator Bowl. None has a brighter future. Certainly, none of the other fixtures was arranged on such short notice—just three weeks before it was played.

The Gator Bowl burst upon the scene at a time when college football was rebuilding from the manpower drains of World War II. Millions of Americans were hungry to see American athletes display their skills.

Because of the lateness of the hour and suddenness of the decision to stage a bowl game, the Jacksonville folks could hardly be truly selective for their 1946 baby. They chose teams from the same conference, the Southern. Neither won the championship. South Carolina had a losing record. Only 7,362 paid to see Wake Forest, coached by raconteur Douglas (Peahead) Walker, rap the Gamecocks 26 to 14.

The idea originated with Charles Hilty of the Downtown Lions Club in Jacksonville. It seemed to have perished for lack of financial nourishment. But Hilty, later permanent secretary of the Gator Bowl Association until his death in 1960, clung to it. He and three other men—Ray McCarthy, Maurice Cherry, and W. C. Ivey—decided to underwrite the first game. They put up $10,000.

The nonprofit Association openly states its aim in this simple language: "to give the people of Jacksonville and this area a good football game and some place to go during the festive New Year season."

Man-hours devoted to the enterprise, designed also to draw visitors from afar, are given gratis by Jacksonville civic leaders. Executive vice-president George R. Olsen is a permanent paid employee.

As the game's popularity has progressively increased, Municipal Stadium with an original capacity of 20,000 was enlarged several times.

Taking a cue from other successful bowl programs that offer more than football, the Gator Bowl Association in time introduced these additional attractions: basketball and golf tournaments, a regatta, bowling, beauty contest, fireworks, and, of course, a parade.

Wake Forest was clearly superior in the first game. Yet South Carolina led at halftime, 7 to 6. The Deacons asserted their strength when they returned to the field. They were moving toward what would have been their fourth touchdown of the second half when Charlie Brembs, a South Carolina halfback, intercepted Herb Appenzeller's pass late in the game and ran 90 yards to cross the Wake Forest goal line.

The Gator Bowl made friends fast. It drew great coaches, famous players, and fine teams to Jacksonville. Before it was quite ten years old, the Association wisely changed its date from New Year's Day to the Saturday before or the Saturday after to harvest more publicity and a larger television audience.

"The Gator Bowl Association is confident its brainchild will grow into sturdy manhood." So read a prophetic statement by the citizens who promoted the first game.

TUESDAY, JANUARY 1, 1946

Wake Forest	6	0	6	14	26
South Carolina	0	7	0	7	14

Wake Forest—Touchdowns: N. Sacrinty (3, left end), Brinkley 2 (3, right guard; 1, center plunge), Smathers (25, left end). Points after touchdown: B. Sacrinty 2.

South Carolina—Touchdowns: Giles (1, plunge), Brembs (90, intercepted pass by Appenzeller). Points after touchdown: Brembs 2.

STATISTICS

Wake Forest		*South Carolina*	*Wake Forest*		*South Carolina*
Bruno	LE	Schmidt	24	First downs	7
Ratteree	LT	Strobel	378	Net yards rushing	88
J. Harris	LG	Lane	6	Passes attempted	11
Foreman	C	Meeks	1	Passes completed	4
Garrison	RG	Huffman	2	Passes had intercepted	1
Hobbs	RT	McDonald	18	Net yards passing	68
D. Harris	RE	Riggs	396	Total net yards	156
Ognovich	QB	Hanson	3	Number of punts	7
N. Sacrinty	LH	Carr	35	Punting average	35
B. Sacrinty	RH	Brembs	1	Fumbles lost	1
Brinkley	FB	Giles	70	Yards penalized	5

Substitutes—Wake Forest: Marney, Kensic, Parrish, Worthington, ends; Martin, Rhodes, Berman, tackles; Dochinez, Liggon, Colivata, Alford, guards; Dawson, Kelly, centers; Jayne, quarterback; Smathers, Demetriou, Appenzeller, Grandy, Bullard, halfbacks; Garry, Jones, fullbacks. South Carolina: Farris, Radenz, Scruby, ends; Helmly, Spivey, tackles; Botkins, Daniels, guards; Bedgood, center; Haralson, quarterback; McMillan, Smith, Maginn, Isom, halfbacks; Sideman, fullback.

COTTON

Sixty-seven points . . . 980 yards gained . . . 11 completed passes in 12 throws by Bobby Layne . . . Texas touchdown marches of 80, 75, 74, 69, and 60 (two) yards . . . Missouri scoring expeditions of 93, 80 (two), and 62 yards.

All of this made the 1946 Cotton Bowl game the most spectacular two-team point-making orgy ever played in Dallas. Texas won, 40 to 27.

Missouri led in first downs, 22 to 19, and also amassed the astonishing total of 408 yards rushing. The Tigers, whose lineup included contrasting physical specimens Jim Kekeris, 295, and Leonard Brown, 139, outgained Texas, 514 to 466.

Layne's passing, with Hub Bechtol his principal receiver—eight catches—proved to be the difference. Missouri's zone defense only once solved the Longhorn patterns.

Texas completed nine straight passes. The tenth was broken up. Four more successful passes in a row brought the day's aerial harvest to 13 out of 14.

As C. E. McBride of the *Kansas City Star* wrote, "You can't beat that kind of passing and Missouri didn't."

Layne, brilliant as a freshman in 1944, returned from service in the Merchant Marine to play in the Longhorns' seventh game in 1945. Texas had a 5–1 record then and finished 9–1.

Against Missouri, Bobby figured in the scoring of every point. He ran for three touchdowns, caught a long pass from Ralph Ellsworth for a fourth; he flicked the ball to Joe Baumgardner for two more touchdowns; and he kicked four extra points.

Texas	14	7	6	13	40
Missouri	7	7	0	13	27

Texas—Touchdowns: Baumgardner 2 (48, pass from Layne of 35, run of 13; 15, pass from Layne), Layne 4 (1, center plunge; 1, plunge; 50, pass from Ellsworth of 35, run of 15; 2, right end). Points after touchdown: Layne 4.

Missouri—Touchdowns: Oakes (65, pass from Dellastatious of 25, run of 40), Dellastatious (3, left tackle), Bonnett (21, center), Hopkins (1, left tackle). Points after touchdown: Kekeris 3.

STATISTICS

Texas		Missouri	Texas		Missouri
Bechtol	LE	Whitaker	19	First downs	22
Wetz	LT	Kekeris	202	Net yards rushing	408
Green	LG	Eigelberger	14	Passes attempted	17
Harris	C	Stewart	13	Passes completed	4
Callan	RG	Croak	0	Passes had intercepted	1
McCauley	RT	Burk	264	Net yards passing	106
Schwartzkopf	RE	Oakes	466	Total net yards	514
Halfpenny	QB	Brown	41.5	Punting average	37
Ellsworth	LH	Hopkins	1	Fumbles lost	1
Baumgardner	RH	Brinkman	35	Yards penalized	30
Layne	FB	O'Connell			

Substitutes—Texas: Tatom, Blount, ends; Plyler, Mitchell, Ring, tackles; Harrell, Heap, guards; Musselwhite, center; Nunnelly, Buxkemper, quarterbacks; Gillory, Jackson, halfbacks; Graham, Sweet, fullbacks. Missouri: Nickell, Lindley, Chase, ends; Riddle, Glauser, Piepmeier, tackles; Cliffe, guard; Henderson, Cox, centers; Howard, Ihm, Mills, quarterbacks; Whitacre, Dellastatious, Bonnett, halfbacks; Clodfelter, fullback.

SUGAR

The Sugar Bowl people were reasonably confident they had engaged two teams for their 1946 game that would insure a spectacular.

They were never more correct.

It was supposed to be an exciting duel between two of the leading personalities on the 1945 collegiate stage, Bob Fenimore of Oklahoma A&M and Herman Wedemeyer of St. Mary's. And it was.

It was expected to pit the deception and finesse of St. Mary's against the sledge hammer power of Oklahoma A&M with sensation-filled action. And it did.

Fenimore led the nation in total offense for the second straight year. His two-season average per game, 212.4 yards, was even better than Frank Sinkwich's performance in that respect for the same span, or Tom Harmon's, or Glenn Davis's.

The sizable, hard hitting Aggies under Coach Jim Lookabaugh climaxed an all-victorious season by trouncing Oklahoma, 47 to 0, worst defeat in Sooner annals. It would be the last Oklahoma "white meat" the Aggies, or any other team, would taste for many and many a year.

Coach Jim Phelan's Gaels of Moraga, Calif., were the rage of the Pacific Coast. They conquered Southern California, champion of the Pacific Coast Conference, 26 to 0. UCLA beat them, 13 to 7, in the last second of the last game, their only defeat.

St. Mary's dazzled opponents with a variety of audacious, fancy maneuvers accenting the lateral pass. They overcame foes with more heft, manpower, and experience by their gridiron legerdemain and captivated crowds wherever they played.

But in the Sugar Bowl the rugged Cowboys of Oklahoma A&M wore down and finally flattened the ball-handling magicians from the West, 33 to 13.

It was that flair for trickery that kept the game close until well into the last half. Eventually the burly Aggie forewall prevailed and the score mounted. But until the final five minutes the Oklahoma team held an insecure one-touchdown lead.

Offensive didoes began early, St. Mary's getting the jump.

Wedemeyer took a Fenimore punt on his 25 and sped 10 yards before lateraling to Wes Busch, who was headed for a touchdown when he slipped on the A&M 46. The Hawaiian-born Wedemeyer yanked the throng to its feet again on the very next play. He passed to Dennis O'Connor, who had sneaked behind Fenimore. O'Connor rank for an easy touchdown.

In five plays following the next kickoff the Aggies tied the score at 7 to 7. Tailback Fenimore passed down the middle for 29 yards to halfback Cecil Hankins for the equalizer.

Fenimore's team never trailed after that. The Aggies seized the lead in the second quarter on Fenimore's smash through right tackle.

The tricky Gaels brought another roar of admiration from 75,000 throats before the half ended with a free lance display centering around Wedemeyer.   From the Aggies' 44, Squirmin' Herman ran to his right, cut back, and lateraled to Carl DeSalvo on the 20.   DeSalvo sprinted the rest of the way.   But Wedemeyer failed to make the extra point, leaving the score 14 to 13.

In the third period Fenimore, who stormed 125 yards on 25 carries, scored his second touchdown.   He did it on a fourth-down plunge after returning a Wedemeyer punt from midfield all the way to the 6.

Now the Aggies were in command, 20 to 13.   It might have remained that way but for an unusual occurrence in the fourth quarter. In the act of punting, Wedemeyer's foot slipped.   He missed the ball completely.   Oklahoma A&M recovered on the St. Mary's 35.   On the seventh play thereafter fullback Jim Reynolds plunged a yard across the goal line.

With the clock whirling toward zero in the last minute, Reynolds aimed a final fling toward end Neill Armstrong.   Gael halfback Paul Crowe tipped the ball.   As he did, the game ended.   But the ball was still in the air.   Halfback Joe Thomas grabbed it on the 10 and darted into the end zone.

It was a million to one chance.   An hour earlier, in Miami, another touchdown had been scored, that one winning the game, after time had officially expired.

Oklahoma A&M	7	7	6	13	33
St. Mary's	7	6	0	0	13

Oklahoma A&M—Touchdowns: Hankins (29, pass from Fenimore of 28, run of 1), Fenimore 2 (1, right tackle; 1, right guard), Reynolds (1, center plunge), Thomas (20, pass from Reynolds of 10, deflected by Crowe, run of 10).   Points after touchdown: Reynolds 3.

St. Mary's—Touchdowns: O'Connor (46, pass from Wedemeyer of 36, run of 10), DeSalvo (44, run of 24 around right end by Wedemeyer, lateral to DeSalvo, run of 20).   Point after touchdown: Wedemeyer.

STATISTICS

Oklahoma A&M		St. Mary's	Oklahoma A&M		St. Mary's
Armstrong	LE	Schultz	15	First downs	8
Cheek	LT	Beasley	217	Net yards rushing	61
Colhouer	LG	DeSalvo	13	Passes attempted	24
Wilkerson	C	Cuccia	6	Passes completed	11
Gay	RG	Bland	4	Passes had intercepted	2
Cole	RT	Van Gieson	112	Net yards passing	177
Moore	RE	Ryan	329	Total net yards	238

Oklahoma				*Oklahoma*	
A&M		*St. Mary's*		*A&M*	*St. Mary's*
Watson	QB	O'Connor	4	Number of punts	6
Fenimore	LH	Wedemeyer	48.7	Punting average	38
Hankins	RH	Cordeiro	0	Fumbles lost	2
Parmer	FB	Busch	45	Yards penalized	35

*Substitutions—*Oklahoma A&M: Van Pool, Long, ends; Monroe, Howell, tackles; Duckett, Faucette, guards; Schellstede, center; Loyd, quarterback; Thomas, Grimes, halfbacks; Reynolds, fullback. St. Mary's: Adkins, Basich, ends; Murphy, Adair, tackles; Bryant, Zakarian, guards; Farleigh, center; Crowe, halfback; Adams, fullback.

ORANGE

Only a few seconds were left now. The score was tied, 6 to 6. Settling for a deadlock, many in the Orange Bowl crowd had already departed.

Holy Cross had the ball in Miami territory. The Crusaders were trying to beat the clock's last sweep with a touchdown pass, unwilling to accept a stalemate.

From the 26, fullback Gene De Filippo twirled a pass diagonally in the direction of end Fran Parker. The wingman leaped but could only touch the ball with his finger tips. It was deflected upward and goalward, apparently out of reach of everybody.

Suddenly, from his deep defending spot, substitute Miami halfback Al Hudson, a sprint ace in track, flashed into the scene. He jumped and his left hand sent the ball spinning crazily. After juggling it momentarily, he gained control and was off for the nearer sideline.

A roar went up. Hundreds in the exit tunnels hurried back, thinking Holy Cross must have shaken someone into the open in the last second or so.

With every stride Hudson seemed to accelerate. It wasn't clear sailing immediately. But Al flew with whippet-like speed the last 50 unobstructed yards of his history-making 89-yard run.

Time officially expired as Hudson crossed the Holy Cross 30. But the game wasn't over until the ball was dead. And that was the split second the Miami speedster arrived in the end zone.

Pandemonium broke out.

"The greatest finish I ever saw in sport," sports writer Henry McLemore said.

The conversion was good and Miami won, 13 to 6.

Here was a touch of irony: Holy Cross, after passing for a first down on the 26 on the play before its fatal pass, had feigned an injury

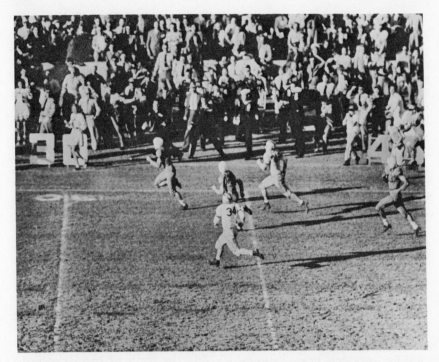

1946—Al Hudson of Miami streaks toward Holy Cross goal line on game-ending 89-yard dash. It won the game. This is the exact moment official time expired.

to stop the clock and work in one more play. Otherwise, the game would have ended before the ball could have been centered.

It was ironic, too, that a team which failed to complete a pass in ten attempts would win the game in the air.

| Miami | 0 | 6 | 0 | 7 | 13 |
| Holy Cross | 0 | 6 | 0 | 0 | 6 |

Miami—Touchdowns: Krull (1, right end), Hudson (89, intercepted pass by De Filippo). Point after touchdown: Ghaul.
Holy Cross—Touchdown: Brennan (16, pass from Koslowski of 14, run of 2).

STATISTICS

Miami		Holy Cross	Miami		Holy Cross
Del Grande	LE	Dieckelman	7	First downs	13
Frantz	LT	Donnalley	185	Net yards rushing	169
Cameron	LG	Kronoff	10	Passes attempted	19

Miami		Holy Cross	Miami		Holy Cross
Levitt	C	Stephenson	0	Passes completed	9
DeMarco	RG	Cregar	2	Passes had intercepted	4
Corrigan	RT	Strojny	0	Net yards passing	70
Mell	RE	Conway	185	Total net yards	239
Mazejka	QB	Lemay	10	Number of punts	9
Krull	LH	Koslowski	37.8	Punting average	38.3
Bowman	RH	Byers	1	Fumbles lost	1
Ghaul	FB	Conroy	42	Yards penalized	5

Substitutes—Miami: Moyer, Hagan, DiBuono, ends; Settembre, Spinelli, tackles; Whittle, Pinckney, guards; Smith, center; Dermigny, Doyle, quarterbacks; Jones, Hancock, Injaychock, Hudson, Angelus, halfbacks; Krasnai, fullback. Holy Cross: Parker, Durand, ends; Sicuranza, Spinelli, DesRoches, DeLisle, tackles; Zuaro, Geopfrich, Kelly, guards; Brennan, quarterback; Bryson, halfback; De Filippo, Godere, fullbacks.

ROSE

Ancient Troy, on the southern shore of the Hellespont, fell sometime in the 1100's B.C.

Modern Troy, better known as the University of Southern California football stronghold, toppled from bowl eminence with a resounding crash 3,000 years later.

The "wooden horse" dragged inside the walls of the Rose Bowl was a speedy, hard hitting, versatile, alert Alabama football team.

The Trojans, victorious in eight straight Pasadena battles since 1923, were put to rout, 34 to 14. They surrendered more points than all their previous eight victims made collectively.

Alabama Coach Frank Thomas was merciful. It could have been much more onesided if he had chosen to play his regulars longer. Southern California was outgained, 351 yards to 41. Troy's pitiful running offense netted just six yards.

Harry Gilmer, the Crimson Tide's extraordinary passer, threw only eleven times, one touchdown resulting. But he ran 116 yards in sixteen totes.

Despite Gilmer's presence, Alabama, operating out of the shift into the Notre Dame box, placed no utter reliance on his arm as its primary weapon. It averaged only thirteen aerial attempts per game in mastering nine opponents to rank second to Army. Gilmer made only eighty-eight pitches but completed fifty-seven for an amazing 64.8 per cent success record.

For Thomas it was his last bowl trip as a coach. His health began to fail in 1946. He was forced to stop coaching in early 1947. He died May 10, 1954.

Thomas was a favorite pupil of Knute Rockne's at Notre Dame.

He played in 1920, 1921, and 1922. Part of that time Elmer Layden, Jimmy Phelan, Harry Mehre, Harry Stuhldreher, Buck Shaw, Tom Lieb, Chet Wynne, Adam Walsh, Jim Crowley, Clipper Smith, Eddie Anderson, Hunk Anderson, Slip Madigan, and Don Miller were also at Notre Dame. All became outstanding coaches. Probably no such large and talented group came from any other school in so short a period.

Thomas belongs in the company of the greatest coaches.

For Coach Jeff Cravath it was his third consecutive Rose Bowl game. Two years later he would return to watch his team cut to pieces by Michigan.

For the Pacific Coast, it was the start of a miserable 14-year showing in the bowl: seven straight defeats by a combined score of 219 to 69; a 7 to 0 triumph by Southern California in 1953; then six more beatings by a cumulative total of 148 to 79—overall, 367 to 155.

In the 1946 Rose Bowl game the Trojans were pathetic.

"Those of us who foolishly predicted Southern California's big linemen would wear down their lighter foes couldn't have guessed worse," admitted Braven Dyer in the Los Angeles Times.

At halftime, when Alabama led, 20 to 0, Troy's 21 plays had resulted in a net loss of 24 yards.

Not until the score was 27 to 0 in the third quarter did Southern California make a first down or invade Tide territory. The crowd yelled derisively when that happened.

Before the fourth period was well advanced, Alabama blew up the field 78 yards. Gilmer ripped off a 36-yard chunk on this trip. Harry ended it with a 24-yard scoring pass to Hal Self.

Halfback Ted Tannehill performed bravely for the Trojans. Tannehill, a talented pianist, made numerous tackles. But he was unable to go anywhere on offense with no faint semblance of blocking.

"Coach Thomas' system would go today," Captain Tom Whitley said 15 years later. "He used an innovation no scout could capture with notes and against which no defense could be securely set."

Thomas called Whitley, 175, "pound for pound, the best tackle Alabama ever had."

Alabama	7	13	7	7	34
Southern California	0	0	0	14	14

Alabama—Touchdowns: Self 2 (1, sneak; 24, pass from Gilmer of 3, run of

21), Gilmer (1, left guard), Tew (2, left guard), Hodges (1, center). Points after touchdown: Morrow 4.

Southern California—Touchdowns: Adelman (20, pass from Lillywhite), Clark (Doornbos blocked Gryszka's punt from Alabama 28, recovered by Clark and run for touchdown). Points after touchdown: Lillywhite 2.

STATISTICS

Alabama		Southern California	Alabama		Southern California
Steiner	LE	Adelman (c)	18	First downs	3
Whitley (c)	LT	Musick	292	Net yards rushing	6
Wozniak	LG	Vasicek	11	Passes attempted	11
Mancha	C	Bradford	4	Passes completed	2
Green	RG	Rea	1	Passes had intercepted	2
Flowers	RT	Aguirre	59	Net yards passing	35
Cain	RE	Willumson	351	Total net yards	41
Self	QB	Bowman	2	Number of punts	6
Gilmer	LH	Morris	19.3	Punting average	47.8
Fedak	RH	Tannehill	1	Fumbles lost	3
Hodges	FB	Cole	35	Yards penalized	15

Substitutes—Alabama: Gibson, Grantham, Dickson, Moorer, ends; Terlizzi, Cassidy, Hood, Collins, tackles; Bush, Filippini, Domanico, Fortunato, guards; Gambrell, Czerkawski, centers; Morrow, Singleton, quarterbacks; Pettus, Corbitt, Tew, Robertson, Gryszka, halfbacks; Grant, Scales, fullbacks. Southern California: Clark, Schimenz, Reed, Schade, Facciola, ends; Perrin, Pehar, Romer, Waddell, Doornbos, tackles; Albee, McGinn, Lardizabal, Heinberg, guards; W. McCormick, Waters, centers; Lillywhite, Peterson, quarterbacks; Scott, Ragan, Lawrence, McElroy, Harvey, fullbacks; Headley, Gee, McNutt, H. McCormick, fullbacks.

– 1947 –

ROSE

As the autumn of 1946 waned, football fans and sports writers on the Pacific Coast all but demanded that mighty Army be invited to play in the Rose Bowl.

The Cadets in three years had scored 1,179 points and had been stopped short of victory only once, a scoreless tie with Notre Dame

in 1946. Glenn Davis, who played high school football in a Los
Angeles suburb, and Doc Blanchard, Mr. Outside and Mr. Inside of
the Army attack, scored 89 touchdowns and ran for 5,169 yards in
these seasons.

"We want Army" was the cry. West Point and the War Department were willing to send the team. But the bid was never extended.

The strong Big Nine had rejected the overtures of the Pacific Coast
Conference and the Tournament of Roses Association on other occasions over the years. After 25 years of opposition to postseason games,
the Big Nine was at last changing its tune.

With the field of Rose Bowl eligibles dwindling somewhat, the
Tournament and the host conference claimed to be motivated in their
negotiations by a desire to protect the game from the risk of mediocrity and second-rate billing. It was also emphasized that the agreement would stimulate competition in other sports between conferences with similar standards and objectives.

Important, no doubt, to the Big Nine was the chance to stop Southern schools from taking home Rose Bowl swag and using part of it
for recruiting widely. Big Nine bigwigs professed to be stressing
amateurism in college football, setting an example for management
of bowl games with the two conferences in full control. The Big
Nine long had criticized recruiting and financial aid practices of other
conferences, particularly the Southeastern—and just as long was coun-
tercharged with hypocrisy.

Under the five-year pact signed in late November of 1946 at Berkeley, Calif., each school received a share of the game proceeds. No one
school could get rich. Illinois, which squelched UCLA, 45 to 14, in
the first game of the series, netted less than $10,000 after deduction
of expenses. Michigan actually lost money the next year.

A group of Los Angeles sports writers suggested the Big Nine
might gracefully withdraw from its part in the agreement until January 1, 1948—in favor of Army. But with the Big Nine it was "now
or never." It was explained that a further delay in fulfilling negotiations, long in progress, might result in their complete collapse.

Los Angeles Times sports editor Paul Zimmerman wrote with im-
passioned conviction and eloquence: "The Pacific Coast Conference
sold the Rose Bowl birthright for a bundle of high-sounding phrases
about athletic respectability.

"Not that there is anything wrong with 'athletic respectability' or
the earnest desire of the two great conference bodies to strive for it.
The pact, as such, has its merits. But the way in which the decision
was reached has irreparably hurt the Rose Bowl classic.

"It would have been so easy for these two groups to do the graceful thing and jointly invite Army. That action would have met with popular approval not only here but across the land.

"After all, it was only a little more than a year ago that the World War ended. Army's appearance in the Rose Bowl would have been a final gesture of appreciation to all the millions who served in the armed forces."

Ordinarily, the teams with the best record in the Big Nine and Pacific Coast Conference would clash. Some detractors pointed out that conceivably the Big Nine's third best team might appear in Pasadena for certain games. The original contract would not permit a Big Nine team to play in the Rose Bowl more than once in three years.

Although greeted cordially in California, Illinois players were stung by the criticism denouncing the timing of the pact. They felt unwanted. Few coaches ever were presented with more explosive psychological fuel than Ray Eliot of Illinois. He made the most of it.

"All I had to do was let the boys read the newspapers," Eliot said. "I didn't have to fire them up myself."

Well noted was the fact that UCLA (and Southern California) favored Army and led a losing battle to bring the Cadets to the Rose Bowl. But the Pacific Coast intended no reflection on the Big Nine or Illinois and wasn't opposed to an alliance. It simply wanted Army then, the Big Nine later.

Illinois was loaded with seasoned war veterans and a few crack transfers. Still, the Illini were disappointing in the first month of the 1946 campaign, losing to Notre Dame and Indiana. During the week after the latter defeat, students chalked Champaign-Urbana sidewalks: "Goodby, Eliot." The veterans righted themselves, jelled, and mowed down their last five foes to win what they were supposed to win, the conference championship.

Keyed up, the Illini, who were doped to lose by one point in the Rose Bowl, dispatched unfortunate UCLA, victor in ten straight games. On the first play, quarterback Perry Moss, transfer from Tulsa, passed to Julie Rykovich for 20 yards and the big right halfback carried the ball 24 yards farther to the Bruins' 16. Left halfback Buddy Young, an elusive speed demon, dashed six yards, then eight. From the 2 it took three thrusts, Rykovich getting the last yard. Don Maechtle missed the conversion attempt.

Illinois fell behind when the Bruins, relying strongly on Ernie Case's throwing arm, traveled 51 yards. Case scored from the 1 on a quarterback sneak. He kicked the extra point to give UCLA a case of false confidence.

Came the second quarter and a shambles. Three Illinois touchdowns were punched over then, after drives of 77, 51, and 49 yards. This splurge was followed by three more touchdowns in the fourth period, two on intercepted passes (64 yards by fullback Russ Steger and 20 yards by substitute tackle Stanley Green).

Rykovich (106 yards net) and Young (89 yards) with their inside-outside running made many Far West football fans wonder if Blanchard and Davis could have made life any more terrifying for the Bruins.

Illinois made 23 first downs and 320 yards rushing.

Only thrill for UCLA rooters, after their team led early, 7 to 6, was 144-pound Al Hoisch's 103-yard run with a second-quarter kick-off.

1947—Little Al Hoisch of UCLA off on his record 103-yard kickoff return against Illinois.

UCLA Coach Bert LaBrucherie left Los Angeles the day after the game for New York. He was scheduled to deliver an address before the American Football Coaches Association. The subject of his speech was to be "Football Defense."

He said, "I think I'll ask to be excused."

WEDNESDAY, JANUARY 1, 1947

Illinois	6	19	0	20	45
UCLA	7	7	0	0	14

Illinois—Touchdowns: Rykovich (1, left guard), Young 2 (2, right tackle; 1, left tackle), Patterson (4, left end), Moss (1, sneak), Steger (64, intercepted pass by Case), Green (20, intercepted pass by Case). Points after touchdown: Maechtle 3.

UCLA—Touchdowns: Case (1, sneak), Hoisch (103, kickoff return). Points after touchdown: Case 2.

STATISTICS

Illinois		UCLA	Illinois		UCLA
Zatkoff	LE	Baldwin (c-c)	23	First downs	12
L. Agase	LT	Malmberg	320	Net yards rushing	72
Wrenn	LG	Dimitro	15	Passes attempted	29
Wenskunas (c)	C	Paul	4	Passes completed	14
A. Agase	RG	Clements	2	Passes had intercepted	4
Genis	RT	Chambers	76	Net yards passing	176
Huber	RE	Fears	396	Total net yards	248
Moss	QB	Case (c-c)	5	Number of punts	8
Rykovich	LH	Rowland	33.8	Punting average	32
Young	RH	Rossi	0	Fumbles lost	0
Steger	FB	Myers	55	Yards penalized	45

Substitutes—Illinois: Owens, Maechtle, Valek, Heiss, Buscemi, Ciszek, ends; Green, Kasap, Bingaman, Franks, tackles; Prymuski, Serpico, Gottfried, Siegert, Martignago, guards; Seliger, Mastrangeli, Cahill, centers; Gallagher, Stewart, quarterbacks; Patterson, Eddleman, Dufelmeier, Kwasniewski, Maggioli, Zaborac, halfbacks; Grierson, Piggott, Dimit, fullbacks. UCLA: Kurrasch, Tinsley, Hoyt, Dobrow, Breeding, Kiefer, ends; Asher, Mathews, Griswold, Mike, Boom, Versen, Pastre, tackles; Nikcevich, Steiner, Russell, Watts, guards; McLaughlin, center; Reiges, quarterback; Hoisch, Shipkey, E. Johnson, Roesch, Brown, Schneider, halfbacks; Steffen, J. Johnson, Hunt, fullbacks.

GATOR

On the fifth play of the 1947 Gator Bowl game Oklahoma fullback Eddy Davis slashed the North Carolina State line for two yards. It was the first of his three touchdowns. And the Sooners were on their way to a 34 to 13 victory and a remarkable 13-year bowl record.

Between 1947 and 1959, inclusive, Oklahoma participated in eight bowl games and won seven times. During that period the Sooners, attacking from the split T with its emphasis on ball control, outscored their bowl opposition, 186 to 65.

In those baker's dozen seasons Oklahoma's football teams were the most successful in the country. Under Coach Charles (Bud) Wil-

kinson they won 114 games, lost 10, and tied 3. He succeeded Jim
Tatum after the Sooners' appearance in the Gator Bowl.

Wilkinson's 1953 to 57 teams won 47 straight games, an all-time
national collegiate record. His 1948 to 1950 teams forged a chain of
31 successive triumphs until upset by Kentucky in the 1951 Sugar
Bowl game. Until beaten by Notre Dame, 7 to 0, in 1957, they
scored in 123 consecutive games, another record.

Counting Tatum's last season at Norman in 1946, Oklahoma's 13-
year record, ending with the Orange Bowl game of 1959, was 122–
13–3. This ranks with the most lustrous in college history over a
comparable stretch.

Wilkinson's teams won national championships in 1950, 1955, and
1956. They were his best. But all were offensively explosive, defensively firm, aggressive, superbly prepared. They were swift, high
scoring, and high spirited.

North Carolina State was no match for Tatum's last team at Oklahoma in the second Gator Bowl contest.

"Our weight advantage was decisive," said Tatum, who returned
to Jacksonville with Maryland twice in the next three years—to tie
and win.

Four players on that Sooner team became prominent head coaches
a decade later. They were Darrell Royal, Jim Owens, Wade Walker,
and Jack Mitchell.

| Oklahoma | 7 | 20 | 0 | 7 | 34 |
| North Carolina State | 7 | 0 | 6 | 0 | 13 |

Oklahoma—Touchdowns: Davis 3 (2, center plunge; 7, center; 2, plunge),
Wallace (5, right end), Owens (15, pass from Sarratt). Points after touchdown:
Wallace 4.

North Carolina State—Touchdowns: Phillips (58, pass from Turner of 28,
run of 30), Palmer (8, right guard). Point after touchdown: Byler.

STATISTICS

Oklahoma		North Carolina State	Oklahoma		North Carolina State
Tyree	LE	Phillips	12	First downs	13
H. Paine	LT	Ramsey	195	Net yards rushing	136
Burris	LG	Watts	9	Passes attempted	18
Rapacz	C	Saunders	3	Passes completed	7
P. Andros	RG	Manning	2	Passes had intercepted	3
Walker	RT	Moser	75	Net yards passing	103
Dinkins	RE	Gibson	270	Total net yards	239

		North Carolina			North Carolina
Oklahoma		State		Oklahoma	State
Mitchell	QB	McLeod	5	Number of punts	4
Sarratt	LH	Turner	31	Punting average	36
Golding	RH	Bozeman	3	Fumbles lost	1
Davis	FB	Palmer	35	Yards penalized	13

Substitutes—Oklahoma: Owens, Goad, Heape, ends; Morris, Trotter, Hale, Wright, McAllister, Hinton, Martin, tackles; McNabb, Husak, D. Andros, West, Jensen, C. Paine, guards; Tillman, Dowell, Pearcy, centers; Royal, Bibb, Parker, quarterbacks; Wallace, Neher, Brewer, Thomas, Allsup, Harp, halfbacks; Fischer, Kreick, fullbacks. North Carolina State: Blomquist, Courts, Miller, Edwards, ends; Gould, W. Smith, Wagoner, Dostanko, tackles; Joyce, Byler, Burnett, Rees, Barksdale, guards; Sykes, P. Gibson, centers; Bowlby, Durant, Richkus, O. Smith, halfbacks; Allen, Johnson, fullbacks.

COTTON

It was a raw afternoon in Dallas that New Year's Day, 1947, and that was the best thing that could be said about the weather.

It was 29 degrees at kickoff time. Sleet and rain fell alternately on 38,000 blanketed fans in the Cotton Bowl.

"The worst football weather I've seen in 35 years of coaching," said Bernie Moore of Louisiana State.

"Terrible playing conditions," agreed John Barnhill of Arkansas.

"Just two hogs in one hole," said one of Moore's slush-soaked boys.

The Tigers and Razorbacks struggled to a 0 to 0 tie in the ice, snow, sleet, and rain. The team from the bayous of Louisiana held an overwhelming advantage in yardage gained, 271 to 54, and a 15 to one margin in first downs. But in view of the score, its statistical superiority was meaningless.

LSU was never in danger of being scored on. Arkansas played a waiting game, punting and praying. But the hoped for break never came.

The Razorbacks' brave defensive troops threw back the Tigers five times within the ten-yard line. It happened twice in the fourth quarter. Once the ball went over to Arkansas on the 2. On the second drive a field goal was attempted. But the ball holder's chilly fingers couldn't control the center snap. When Ray Coates muffed it, the kicker, Holley Heard, recovered on the 15 where the try was to have been made.

Arkansas went home with the trophy which was to have gone to the winner. Barnhill won it in a coin toss at the after-game party.

The Cotton Bowl Athletic Association then ordered a duplicate trophy to be sent to LSU.

Mel McGaha, an Arkansas end, received offers in professional football, basketball, and baseball. He didn't make it to the big leagues as a player. But as a manager he did, being selected in 1962 to handle the Cleveland Indians.

Louisiana State	0	0	0	0	0
Arkansas	0	0	0	0	0

STATISTICS

Louisiana State		Arkansas	Louisiana State		Arkansas
Lindsey	LE	Baldwin	15	First downs	1
Barnes	LT	Lively	255	Net yards rushing	54
Hall	LG	Franklin	17	Passes attempted	4
Ballard	C	Thomas	5	Passes completed	0
Worley	RG	Roberts	0	Passes had intercepted	1
Heard	RT	Minor	16	Net yards passing	0
Wimberly	RE	Canada	271	Total net yards	54
Tittle	QB	Fowler	9	Number of punts	11
Coates	LH	Scott	30.4	Punting average	36
Sandifer	RH	Pipkin	2	Fumbles lost	3
Knight	FB	Campbell	50	Yards penalized	5

Substitutes—Louisiana State: Bullock, Lyle, Adams, Leach, ends; Land, Shurtz, Champagne, tackles; Core, Lewis, Foti, guards; Cason, Heroman, Gray, Landry, halfbacks; Collins, Schroll, Toth, fullbacks. Arkansas: McGaha, Lubker, ends; Thornton, Hager, tackles; White, Counce, guards; Carter, center; Duke, quarterback; Long, Holland, Pritchard, halfbacks; Hoffman, fullback.

SUGAR

The game was over now.

Georgia, twice emerging from behind, had fought off the dynamic Tar Heels of North Carolina to win the thirteenth Sugar Bowl classic 20 to 10. And here was Charlie (Choo Choo) Justice running to Charlie Trippi's side as players sought out opponents to express respects.

"Nice going, Charlie, you're a great back," said the spectacular North Carolina tailback, clasping the senior Georgia halfback's hand.

"Thanks, that's very nice of you, and I really think the same of you," Trippi responded.

Each played terrific football in the foggy, murky atmosphere of the big concrete saucer. The game enthralled 73,000 spectators, uncertain of the outcome until near the finish.

"Carolina completely outplayed us in the first half, but our boys had the stickability, and that's what wins games," Coach Wally Butts said of Georgia's first perfect record team since 1896.

The Tar Heels led 7 to 0 at halftime. They also held the upper hand in the third quarter until a crucial break went against them.

Coach Carl Snavely said, "With just a little better luck in the breaks, we could have upset Georgia."

Two controversial decisions affected the result. On each, Georgia was the beneficiary. The first occurred in the third period. It turned the tide of battle suddenly. The second, in the fourth quarter, wiped out an apparent North Carolina touchdown and prevented an eleventh hour comeback.

Here's how the first huge break developed:

Joe Tereshinski, Georgia end, intercepted fullback Walt Pupa's pass on his 25, interrupting a drive originating on North Carolina's 36. Tereshinski went down almost immediately. A split second before he was tackled by Jim Camp, the intended receiver, he tossed the ball to fullback Dick McPhee.

McPhee ran to the North Carolina 13 before center Dan Stiegman overtook him. Many press box occupants and spectators, too, thought the pass would be ruled a forward, not a lateral, and were surprised a handkerchief hadn't been dropped. Field Judge Gabe Hill ran to the spot of Tereshinski's throw as if to mark an infraction. But he paused there only an instant before hastening downfield to join fellow officials.

"It was an obvious forward pass, we thought, and everybody relaxed," Stiegman said. "When I realized the whistle hadn't blown, I took off and finally caught up to the runner."

That run was the turning point. In three quick thrusts Georgia scored the tying touchdown. Quarterback Johnny Rauch made it on a sneak from a yard away.

Still in the third quarter, Tar Heel end Bob Cox kicked a field goal from the 18. North Carolina was ahead 10 to 7, but this time the lead was brief.

Three plays after the kickoff Trippi, a 60-minute player, displayed his exceptional talent. From his 33, Trippi leaped to throw a short pass to left end Dan Edwards. As he did, he noted Edwards was closely covered. Charlie came down, paused a second or two until Edwards broke into the clear at midfield, then spiraled the slippery ball into his hands. The fleet end ran 50 yards for a touchdown.

Better conditioned, the Bulldog linemen wore down the Carolina forewall as Trippi, Rauch, Rabbit Smith, and Eli Maricich progressed 80 yards in a fourth-quarter attack against the tiring Tar Heels. Rauch faked a pass and scored through right tackle from the 13.

Break No. 2 was soon to come.

Justice's 49-yard kickoff return and a pair of passes from Pupa to Mike Rubish, substitute end, moved the ball to the 20. At that point Justice fired to end Ken Powell. The Tar Heel and the defending halfback, Smith, went into the air simultaneously. Powell came down with the ball, turned, and fell unconscious. He had been knocked out by the contact with Smith. It appeared to be a touchdown but it wasn't.

Linesman George Gardner, following the play, dropped his handkerchief. His ruling was that Powell struck or shoved Smith just before catching the ball. The jig was up for North Carolina.

The game film showed Tereshinski tossed a forward pass and that Powell did not push Smith.

Georgia	0	0	13	7	20
North Carolina	0	7	3	0	10

Georgia—Touchdowns: Rauch 2 (1, sneak; 13, right tackle), Edwards (67, pass from Trippi of 17, run of 50). Points after touchdown: Jernigan 2.

North Carolina—Touchdown: Pupa (4, left guard). Field goal: Cox (28, placekick). Point after touchdown: Cox.

STATISTICS

Georgia		North Carolina	Georgia		North Carolina
Edwards	LE	Romano	12	First downs	17
Bush	LT	Williamson	175	Net yards rushing	166
George	LG	Strayhorn	14	Passes attempted	14
Cooley	C	Weant	3	Passes completed	8
St. John	RG	Varney	1	Passes had intercepted	1
Williams	RT	Szafaryn	81	Net yards passing	99
Tereshinski	RE	Sparger	256	Total net yards	265
Rauch	QB	Wright	7	Number of punts	6
Smith	LH	Justice	32.7	Punting average	38
Trippi	RH	Camp	0	Fumbles lost	1
McPhee	FB	Pupa	30	Yards penalized	50

Substitutions—Georgia: Sellers, Moseley, ends; Jenkins, Perhach, tackles; Payne, Alexander, Jernigan, guards; Chandler, Deavers, centers; Maricich, Donaldson, halfbacks; Geri, fullback. North Carolina: Powell, Tandy, Cox, Rubish, Logue, ends; Fowle, Jarrell, Marczyk, Hazelwood, Plunkett, tackles; Mitten, Cheek, Spurlin, Roberts, guards; Stiegman, center; Hartig, Flamish, quarterbacks; Maceyko, Fitch, Grow, halfbacks; Clements, Rodgers, Sutherland, fullbacks.

ORANGE

"The dullest Orange Bowl game ever played."

That's what most of the sports writers said about the 1947 production.

Rice struck for a 50-yard touchdown and a safety on a blocked punt in the first quarter, conservatively sat on the points, and rode them to an 8 to 0 victory over Tennessee.

Midway in the first period Carl Russ, high-stepping Rice fullback, took a handoff from quarterback Ike Eikenberg and cut between right tackle and end.

Line blocking was effective. Linebackers were bumped aside. Russ pounded to the 23. There, as orange-shirted Volunteers pounced on him, he deftly slipped the ball over his elbow to halfback Huey Keeney. Preceding the center snap, Keeney had been in motion to the right. He veered when Russ started his gallop. Keeney ran for the touchdown without a hand to hinder him.

A few minutes later, after a 15-yard holding penalty, Tennessee put the ball in play from its 13. At that point something unprecedented in performance and embarrassment happened to a General Bob Neyland-coached team. Two successive punts were blocked. One was rare enough.

A low pass from center caused the first. Punter Billy Joe Rowan recovered on the 1 after the ball bounced off the chest of end Froggy Williams. Rowan was simply too slow getting off the next boot. It thudded against the body of tackle Ralph Murphy and bounced through the end zone for a safety and two points.

An unspectacular punting duel ensued. Rice punted 13 times, two less than Tennessee. Keeney's kicking was marvelous. He did it all, for an average of 44.3 yards. Four punts went out of bounds inside the 10.

Tennessee couldn't have gotten a better break to open the second half. Keeney fumbled the kickoff. End Dick Jordan recovered for the Vols on the 18. Freshman tailback Hal Littleford swept left end for ten yards on the first play. But the attack fizzled. That was the only time Tennessee had a chance to operate in Rice territory.

In Neyland's words, the Vols were "outrun, outblocked, outtackled and outplayed."

It was a match of the increasingly popular T formation offense against the nonfrilly single wing.

Rice's Jess Neely, Vanderbilt captain in 1922 when the Commodores won the championship of the old Southern Conference, switched from the single wing to the T during World War II, as so many coaches did.

Neyland, West Point teammate of former president Dwight Eisenhower in 1912, refused to change systems. He stuck to the massed power and precision principles of the single wing. So did his successors at Tennessee following his retirement from coaching.

One of the first spectators to congratulate Neely after the triumph over Tennessee was his nine-year-old daughter, Mary. She kissed him and said over and over, "Daddy, I'm so happy." His 13-year-old daughter Joan hugged him and cried.

Rice	8	0	0	0	8
Tennessee	0	0	0	0	0

Rice—Touchdown: Keeney (50, run of 27 by Russ, lateral to Keeney, run of 23). Safety: Murphy blocked Rowan's punt from Tennessee 1, ball bounced out of end zone.

STATISTICS

Rice		Tennessee	Rice		Tennessee
Williams, D.	LE	Hubbell	9	First downs	5
Armstrong	LT	Huffman	208	Net yards rushing	105
Magee	LG	Myers	4	Passes attempted	19
Watson	C	Stephenson	0	Passes completed	4
Humble	RG	Drost	2	Passes had intercepted	4
Malmberg	RT	Crawford	0	Net yards passing	32
Scruggs	RE	Jordan	208	Total net yards	137
Eikenberg	QB	Mitchell	13	Number of punts	15
Keeney	LH	Slater	44.3	Punting average	38.1
Anderson	RH	Partin	3	Fumbles lost	0
Russ	FB	Major	40	Yards penalized	67

Substitutes—Rice: Taylor, J. Williams, Miner, Lanza, ends; Prichard, Spruill, Noble, Parker, Murphy, tackles; Kwaitkowski, Sultis, Nichols, Nicholson, guards; Jones, center; Easter, Rote, quarterbacks; Ellis, Buckley, Riley, Stockbridge, Walmsley, Pugh, halfbacks; Hoerster, Lantrip, fullbacks. Tennessee: Powell, Pike, Caldwell, Russas, ends; Francis, Gearing, Paidousis, Wildman, Meseroll, tackles; Stapleton, Vugrin, Price, Howard, guards; Kelley, Hueser, centers; Fielden, Armstrong, Milner, quarterbacks; Hillman, Fowler, Lund, Littleford, Rowan, Proctor, halfbacks; Balitsaris, Gold, fullbacks.

— 1948 —

ORANGE

Kansans in the Orange Bowl threw their hats in the air when Ray Evans, All-America halfback, passed to end Otto Schnellbacher, who stepped out of bounds on Georgia Tech's 10. The Yellow Jackets led, 20 to 14. But there were still two minutes to play.

Evans rammed the line for eight yards. Tech was penalized another yard for excessive timeouts. Kansas partisans joyously anticipated the tying touchdown and even had visions of the tie-breaking extra point by guard Don Fambrough.

Time enough left. Enough downs, too. A roar rose as quarterback Lynne McNutt took the snap. It became a moan of disappointment as the ball slipped through his fingers when he was jarred by a wave of Jackets. McNutt dove quickly. He seemed to have it just before a swarm lighted on him heavily.

When the players unpiled, referee Shaky Kain found Tech left guard Rollo Phillips hugging the football. Phillips had wrested it away from the unfortunate McNutt. Kansas, which out-first-downed and outgained Georgia Tech, was beaten.

"Dick Monroe gave me a perfect snapback and I just didn't hang onto it," McNutt said. "A quick whistle would have saved me. I dropped to my knee, temporarily gained possession of the ball, then felt the whole Tech team pile on me. Somebody's shoulder got under me and the ball was gone again."

Tech quarterback Jim Still threw three touchdown passes in completing ten of thirteen throws for 123 yards.

A record crowd of 59,578 occupied the newly double-decked Orange Bowl for the 1948 game. Construction, begun in the summer of 1947, added 22,800 seats. Whether or not the addition would be finished in time for the game was uncertain until mid-December.

Hundreds of tickets were distributed with the following printing on the back: "This ticket valid only if stadium addition completed and seat called for is available; otherwise Orange Bowl committee will refund face value upon return of this ticket."

Miami's Orange Bowl, which now seats 70,029.

THURSDAY, JANUARY 1, 1948

Georgia Tech	0	7	13	0	20
Kansas	0	7	0	7	14

Georgia Tech—Touchdowns: Patton 2 (24, pass from Still; 5, pass from Still), Queen (15, pass from Still of 9, run of 6). Points after touchdown: Bowen 2.

Kansas—Touchdowns: Evans 2 (12, center; 13, pass from Hogan). Points after touchdown: Fambrough 2.

STATISTICS

Georgia Tech		Kansas	Georgia Tech		Kansas
Castleberry	LE	Schmidt	9	First downs	14
Slaten	LT	Ettinger	75	Net yards rushing	117
Phillips	LG	Fambrough	19	Passes attempted	19
Hook	C	D. Monroe	11	Passes completed	10
Healy	RG	Crawford	0	Passes had intercepted	1
Davis	RT	Johnson	129	Net yards passing	158
Brodnax	RE	Schnellbacher	204	Total net yards	275
Southard	QB	Hogan	9	Number of punts	7
Mathews	LH	Evans	39.7	Punting average	34.3
Petit	RH	Bertuzzi	1	Fumbles lost	1
Ziegler	FB	Pattee	70	Yards penalized	37

Substitutes—Georgia Tech: Nolan, Anderson, ends; Coleman, Bradach, tackles; McKinney, guard; Doyal, Smith, Bossons, centers; Brown, Still, quarterbacks; Patton, Jordan, Williams, McCoy, Queen, halfbacks; Bowen, fullback. Kansas:

J. Sperry, Small, ends; Renko, T. Monroe, tackles; K. Sperry, Tomlinson, guards; Brown, center; Scott, McNutt, quarterbacks; French, McDonald, halfbacks; Griffith, fullback.

ROSE

"Them bums! Forty-six years and they ain't improved a bit," a spectator in his cups muttered as he left the Rose Bowl. Michigan, which smashed Stanford, 49 to 0, in 1902, had just overwhelmed Southern California by the same score on its return to Pasadena.

Southern California was served up as a guinea pig to determine whether Notre Dame or Michigan deserved the national championship. That's how most fans regarded the game. The vote of sports writers conducted by the Associated Press after the regular season favored Notre Dame.

Notre Dame thrashed Southern California 38 to 7. When Michigan crushed the Trojans by a bigger score, the late Bill Corum of the *New York Journal-American* wrote: "I hate to see my old pal, Frank Leahy, sitting on a park bench in the snow, but let's face it Frankie, chum, in the public mind this 49–0 trouncing of Southern Cal is going to make Michigan the top college team of 1947."

Red Smith of the *New York Herald Tribune* was similarly inclined and after covering the game reported: "Michigan showed such superlative poise in every department, such a wealth of offensive weapons and the talent to use them, such poise and versatility, that it seemed a sacrilege to mention another college team in the same breath."

Hot arguments arose. Should the national title go to Michigan or Notre Dame? The Associated Press called for another vote but made it clear the outcome wouldn't change the postseason official result. Michigan won this time, easily.

Fritz Crisler, Michigan coach, declared that Notre Dame wasn't mentioned in Rose Bowl game preparations. But when the Wolverines made it 34 to 0 in the fourth quarter, placekick expert Jim Brieske told Watson Spoelstra of the *Detroit News* he heard a voice on the bench.

"I don't know who it was," said Brieske, who kicked seven straight extra points, "but he yelled: 'That ought to take care of the Irish.'"

When the scoreboard showed 42 to 0, quarterback Howard Yerges, whom Crisler referred to as "The Little Master," told teammates, "Let's punch over another one to match that first Rose Bowl score."

Yerges, who directed Crisler's intricate mixture of single wing and T formation plays developing behind an unbalanced line, threw a running pass 28 yards into the end zone where end Dick Rifenburg made a spectacular catch for touchdown No. 7.

Records fell in profusion in the first Rose Bowl game to be televised. The Wolverines' total yardage, 491, was one. Michigan's 17 pass completions, 14 by All-America left halfback Bob Chappuis in 24 throws, was another. Chappuis' total offense, 279 yards, and his passing yardage, 188, broke records. He threw for two touchdowns.

As an aerial gunner in the war, Chappuis was shot down near Brenner Pass. He spent three months in the garret of an Italian home next to German army headquarters in Asulo, Italy. He finally escaped to the British lines.

Chappuis sustained a torn right thigh muscle three days before the game but was able to play superbly. Gaining 91 yards in 13 carries, he shared leadership in that department with tall 175-pound Jack Weisenburger. The spinning, twisting fullback also picked up 91 yards and scored three touchdowns from a yard or less away.

Although Michigan was praised to the skies and Southern California ridiculed in the sports pages in the weeks prior to the game, the psychological advantage availed the Trojans nothing. They were sluggish and bewildered.

Michigan's success was due in a large measure to well-planned platooning. The liberalized substitution rule, which Crisler utilized to the fullest extent, enabled him to place a premium on offensive speed and slick ball handling and rugged tackling on defense.

It was a super showing—deception, play execution, blocking, tackling—by Chappuis, Yerges, Weisenburger, Bump Elliott, Gene Derricotte, Bob Mann, Dominic Tomasi, Alvin Wistert, Dan Dworsky, Bruce Hilkene, Rifenburg, and a number of other Wolverines.

"It was the greatest single game performance by the best team I ever coached," Crisler said.

"We just weren't in the same class with Michigan," said Southern California Coach Jeff Cravath.

A future Southern California head coach, Don Clark, who started at left guard, found the going extremely tough trying to fathom the masterly faking and to keep up with Michigan's speedy backs. But it was nothing, after all, to compare with his experiences of a few years before.

Clark fought in Europe in some of the heaviest action. Bob Smith, who was Southern California's athletic publicity director at one time, said, "I saw him pick up a Browning machine gun, which weighed better than 20 pounds, and spray half a dozen Germans at point blank range. He was absolutely fearless and won a battlefield commission and the Bronze Star."

In 1947 Crisler reached the pinnacle of his profession. He was elected Coach of the Year. When that honor was announced, Les

Etter, Michigan's athletic publicity director, said, "The team held a private celebration. They have a quiet pride in what they've accomplished. There isn't a man on the squad who doesn't think the coach was responsible."

In the spring after his team's Rose Bowl triumph, Crisler, then 49, announced he was resigning as head coach to devote full time to the athletic directorship.

Michigan	7	14	7	21	49
Southern California	0	0	0	0	0

Michigan—Touchdowns: Weisenburger 3 (1, center plunge; 1, plunge; 1, plunge), C. Elliott (11, pass from Chappuis, run of 11), Yerges (18, pass from Chappuis of 13, run of 5), Derricotte (45, pass from Fonde of 24, run of 21), Rifenburg (28, pass from Yerges). Points after touchdown: Brieske 7.

STATISTICS

Michigan		Southern California	Michigan		Southern California
Mann	LE	Tolman	21	First downs	10
Hilkene (c)	LT	Ferraro	219	Net yards rushing	91
Tomasi	LG	Clark (c)	27	Passes attempted	11
White	C	McCormick	17	Passes completed	6
Wilkins	RG	McCall	1	Passes had intercepted	1
Pritula	RT	Bird	272	Net yards passing	42
Rifenburg	RE	Cleary	491	Total net yards	133
Yerges	QB	Murphy	4	Number of punts	8
Chappuis	LH	McCardle	38.2	Punting average	43.7
C. Elliott	RH	Doll	1	Fumbles lost	2
Weisenburger	FB	Lillywhite	40	Yards penalized	10

Substitutes—Michigan: McNeill, Ford, Wisniewski, Hershberger, Andersen, ends; Wistert, Kohl, Johnson, Dendrinos, tackles; Soboleski, Sickels, Kampe, Heneveld, guards; Dworsky, Brieske, centers; P. Elliott, Kiesel, quarterbacks; Derricotte, Teninga, Fonde, Kuick, halfbacks; Kempthorn, Peterson, fullbacks. Southern California: Linehan, Stillwell, Cramer, Salata, Lloyd, Willumson, ends; Schutte, Swope, Perrin, tackles; Bastian, Rea, Colley, Lowell, Monson, guards; Davis, Busch, centers; Powers, Dill, Robertson, quarterbacks; Tannehill, Garlin, Gray, Curry, Kirby, Roundy, Cantor, Craig, Futrell, halfbacks; Betz, Oestreich, Rossetto, Burke, fullbacks.

GATOR

"Maryland, My Maryland's" masterfully executed split T functioned in breathtaking, magical splendor in the 1948 Gator Bowl game.

Georgia's ingenious passing attack, conceived by Coach Wally
Butts, was carried out almost perfectly by Johnny Rauch.

An exciting 20 to 20 tie resulted.

Lu Gambino, 202-pound Maryland right halfback, was devastating. Powerful and fast, he amassed 904 yards during the season.
Against Georgia, Lu ran 165 yards and scored three touchdowns.

1948—Lu Gambino, Maryland's superb runner, off for a gain against Georgia.

Rauch completed 12 of his 20 passes for 187 yards. One of his
throws was a nonscoring 58-yard gainer caught by Bill Henderson.

Georgia was a 13-point favorite. Maryland held a 20 to 7 lead at
three-quarter time, however. But the Bulldogs snapped back with
two-touchdown fury and had driven 45 yards to stand only four from
the game-winner when the gun stopped them.

With four and a half minutes to play, Georgia got its biggest break.
Captain Dan Edwards, right end, rushed in to flatten Earl Roth as
the Maryland fullback, attempting to punt, fumbled the center snap.
Georgia went on offense 33 yards from the Terrapins' goal line. The
Bulldogs made it in four plays, the last a 13-yard pass from Rauch to
John Donaldson. Joe Geri kicked the all-important extra point to
tie the score.

With time fading, Georgia guard Tommy Pope recovered Joe Walston's onside kickoff on the Maryland 49. The Bulldogs hastily chewed up 45 yards. Arriving at the 4, they signaled agitatedly for a timeout to halt the clock. The game ended before they could attract an official's attention.

Although Gambino's sensational running drew rave notices everywhere he played, the Maryland coaching staff headed by Jim Tatum lauded quarterback Vic Turyn, a slick ball handler, as the man who made Lu go places.

Shirley Povich of the *Washington Post* once described Turyn as "deceitful, an audacious swindler, a double-dealer, a colossal faker and owner of all the other larcenous traits that add up to a tremendous T formation quarterback."

Turyn, it was said, would express annoyance when, after faking to other backs and tucking the ball in Gambino's midsection, the big fellow failed to go all the way.

"You big bum," Turyn said once when Lu was tackled 25 yards downfield. "You get 25 lousy yards when you should have had a touchdown."

"Wasn't my fault, Vic," Gambino replied. "I didn't know I had the ball till I was tackled."

Georgia	0	0	7	13	20
Maryland	0	7	13	0	20

Georgia—Touchdowns: Rauch (1, sneak), Geri (6, left tackle), Donaldson (13, pass from Rauch of 11, run of 2). Points after touchdown: Geri 2.

Maryland—Touchdowns: Gambino 3 (35, left end; 1, plunge; 24, pass from Baroni of 23, run of 1). Points after touchdown: McHugh 2.

STATISTICS

Georgia		*Maryland*	*Georgia*		*Maryland*
Sellers	LE	Simler	19	First downs	16
Bush	LT	Krouse	219	Net yards rushing	247
St. John	LG	Phillips	20	Passes attempted	14
Chandler	C	Kinney	12	Passes completed	7
B. Reid	RG	Schwarz	1	Passes had intercepted	1
Payne	RT	Goodman	187	Net yards passing	127
Edwards	RE	Evans	406	Total net yards	374
Walston	QB	Behr	40	Punting average	44.2
Henderson	LH	LaRue	0	Fumbles lost	1
Maricich	RH	Gambino	80	Yards penalized	66
Bodine	FB	Bonk			

Substitutes—Georgia: Lorendo, end; Johnson, Deavers, tackles; George, Hobbs, Pope, guards; Jackura, Bradshaw, Cooley, centers; Prosperi, Rauch, quarterbacks; McCall, Brunson, Nestorak, Donaldson, Geri, Bradberry, F. Reid, halfbacks; Tillitski, Taylor, fullbacks. Maryland: Wingate, Davis, ends; Drach, Gierula, Gayzur, tackles; McHugh, Murphy, Fingar, guards; Bowden, Brasher, centers; Tucker, Targarona, Turyn, quarterbacks; Baroni, Seibert, halfbacks; Roth, fullback.

COTTON

Two handsome 21-year-old youths sparkled like champagne as Penn State and Southern Methodist battled 60 minutes in the 1948 Cotton Bowl game without settling the question of superiority.

SMU was not awed by the eastern team's still-standing record of having allowed opponents an average of only 17 yards per game on the ground. Doak Walker, 170-pound All-America halfback, led the Mustangs to a 13 to 0 advantage near the end of the first half.

But with Elwood Petchel, called by his coach, Bob Higgins, "the best 145-pound back in the nation," as the spearhead, the Nittany Lions charged 65 yards after receiving a late second-quarter kickoff. While SMU starters were resting, they scored on a fourth-down 38-yard pass play with 18 seconds to play. Petchel passed to halfback Larry Cooney, who ran 14 yards after making the catch.

When extra point artist Ed Czekaj (pronounced Check-Eye) made the score 13 to 7, Penn State's lagging spirit seemed to gain the impetus it needed to keep rolling.

Higgins always leaned heavily on Petchel when the situation was difficult. He was an imaginative signal caller, often a gambler who caused his coach to say, "I never know what he's going to do. Even if I did, it wouldn't make any difference."

Penn State's formidable line, headed by All-America guard Steve Suhey, came into its own in the second half. It put a tight checkrein on almost every move Walker and his cohorts made. The Nittany Lions, stronger at the finish than the Mustangs, scored on another pass in the third quarter, a five-yard pitch from Petchel to halfback Wally Triplett. To set it up, Petchel returned a punt by Ed Green 27 yards to the nine. Czekaj missed the conversion that would have won the game but left it tied, 13 to 13.

SMU notched its first touchdown early on a 53-yard pass and run play from Walker to wingback Paul Page. Doak registered the second on a two-yard plunge.

On the last play of the game Dennie Hoggard, a substitute Penn State end, dropped a pass by Petchel in the end zone.

SMU Coach Matty Bell was subjected to a round of second guess-

ing on the allegation he "eased up" with a two-touchdown lead in the
ebbing moments of the first half.

Penn State	0	7	6	0	13
Southern Methodist	7	6	0	0	13

Penn State—Touchdowns: Cooney (38, pass from Petchel of 24, run of 14),
Triplett (5, pass from Petchel). Point after touchdown: Czekaj.
Southern Methodist—Touchdowns: Page (53, pass from Walker of 40, run of
13), Walker (2, left tackle). Point after touchdown: Walker.

STATISTICS

Penn State		Southern Methodist	Penn State		Southern Methodist
Tamburo	LE	Reinking	12	First downs	12
Norton	LT	Ethridge	165	Net yards rushing	92
J. Drazenovich	LG	Lewis	15	Passes attempted	25
Wolosky	C	Baxter	7	Passes completed	11
Suhey	RG	Cook	1	Passes had intercepted	1
Nolan	RT	Hamberger	93	Net yards passing	114
Potsklan	RE	S. Halliday	258	Total net yards	206
G. Drazenovich	QB	Ramsey	33	Punting average	33
Joe	LH	Walker	2	Fumbles lost	1
Durkota	RH	Page	15	Yards penalized	5
Colone	FB	Sullivan			

Substitutes—Penn State: Cze'kaj, Hicks, Hoggard, Bell, ends; Finley, Kyle,
Murray, tackles; Simon, Kelly, Ross, guards; Beatty, center; Ulinsky, LaFleur,
quarterbacks; Triplett, Williams, Petchel, Cooney, Luther, halfbacks; Rogel,
Gorinski, fullbacks. Southern Methodist: Folsom, Blakely, Milam, Wallace,
ends; J. Halliday, King, Hill, tackles; Pechal, Roberds, guards; Sutphin, Goodwin, centers; Parker, Moon, Pulattie, quarterbacks; Green, Payne, Johnson,
halfbacks; McKissick, fullback.

SUGAR

It is a peculiar fact that some of the most celebrated backs in the
Southeastern Conference came to grief in New Orleans in their final
game. Names coming to mind of those so ill-fated are Billy Cannon
(1960), Johnny Majors (1957), Hank Lauricella (1952), and Harry
Gilmer (1948).

Three years before, Gilmer, the Alabama sharpshooter, had heard
the multitude's roar of applause in the Sugar Bowl. It was a far cry
from the reaction of 72,000 fans who saw Texas thwart Gilmer and
the Crimson Tide, 27 to 7, in 1948.

He had blazed so brightly previously in New Orleans and in Pasadena. This time he completed only three of his 11 passes and ran

for a mere five yards. By his own evaluation it was the worst day of his college career.

Loudest cheers went to Texas quarterback Bobby Layne. He sent the ball aloft 24 times and made connections ten times for gains totaling 183 yards.

Layne was an excellent field general, ball handler, and passer. He was also a capable runner.

Ground attacks were virtually non-existent. Alabama was restricted to 41 yards, Texas to 59 rushing.

The Tide was not outplayed to the extent the score would indicate. The difference could have been a touchdown. The first half ended in a 7 to 7 standoff. Texas' last three touchdowns were achieved by defensive alertness. Or, to say it another way, Alabama committed three expensive errors—having a punt blocked, having a pass intercepted and run back for a touchdown, and fumbling deep in its own territory.

The entire left side of the Longhorns' line swarmed into the backfield when Norman Mosley tried to punt from Alabama's 25 in the third quarter. Left tackle George Petrovich blocked the kick and left guard Vic Vasicek recovered in the end zone for a touchdown.

Alabama appeared to wilt after that but displayed the heart to stall Texas drives twice within its 10. Then with six minutes left and the Tide gambling to tie or win, Gilmer was rushed hard and threw almost despairingly over oncoming Longhorns' upraised arms. End Lewis Holder intercepted Harry's soft, short, high pitch. He raced for the red flag at the corner of the field 18 yards away, just making it.

A few plays after that, Holder pounced on a Gilmer fumble five yards from another touchdown. Layne got this one on a sneak.

The result was a shock to Alabama followers who expected the large senior contingent, stars of freshman and sophomore appearances in bowl games, to finish in the grand manner. Texas was faster, more powerful, and deserved to win.

Some years later, Gilmer said, "I wouldn't swap the experiences, the thrills, the friendships and fellowships made in bowl games for anything. Of course, a post-season game means a lot of additional work—practice, training and usually the sacrifice of Christmas vacation—but in the end it's worth even more."

Texas	7	0	7	13	27
Alabama	0	7	0	0	7

Texas—Touchdowns: Blount (5, pass from Layne), Vasicek (recovered ball in end zone after Petrovich blocked Mosley's punt from Alabama 25), Holder (18, intercepted pass by Gilmer), Layne (1, sneak). Points after touchdown: Guess 3.

Alabama—Touchdown: White (8, pass from Gilmer). Point after touchdown: Morrow:

STATISTICS

Texas		Alabama	Texas		Alabama
Bumgardner	LE	Steiner	14	First downs	7
Harris	LT	Whitley	59	Net yards rushing	41
Magliolo	LG	Wozniak	24	Passes attempted	17
Rowan	C	Mancha	10	Passes completed	4
Fry	RG	Richeson	0	Passes had intercepted	2
Kelley	RT	Flowers	183	Net yards passing	62
Schwartzkopf	RE	Cain	242	Total net yards	103
Layne	QB	O'Sullivan	5	Number of punts	9
Pyle	LH	Gilmer	29.3	Punting average	38.6
Canady	RH	Cadenhead	2	Fumbles lost	1
Landry	FB	Tew	5	Yards penalized	15

Substitutions—Texas: Holder, King, Blount, McCall, Watson, ends; Petrovich, Tatom, Edge, tackles; Vasicek, Jungmichel, Wolfe, Mitchell, Heap, Halfpenny, guards; Williams, center; Harris, Guess, Campbell, quarterbacks; Gillory, Guess, Raven, Shands, Landry, Layne, halfbacks; Canady, Jones, Borneman, fullbacks. Alabama: White, Hood, Chambliss, ends; Compton, Cassidy, Hannah, tackles; Franko, Fortunato, guards; Chapman, center; Morrow, Hodges, Cochran, quarterbacks; Mosley, Salem, Tew, Noonan, O'Sullivan, Hodges, halfbacks; Noonan, Cadenhead, Davis, fullbacks.

– 1949 –

SUGAR

Justice never prevailed in the bowls.

The coach, Bud Wilkinson, and the team, Oklahoma, most unaccustomed to losing in the decade following the end of World War II thwarted Justice and North Carolina in the 1949 Sugar Bowl game, 14 to 6.

It was the Sooners' tenth straight triumph. Defeat was not to plague them until two years and 22 games later.

Sugar Bowl photographic coverage included a pathetic picture of a player sitting on a dressing room bench after the game. He was huddled under a blanket covering his back and head.

The picture of dejection was Charlie (Choo Choo) Justice, All-America halfback. Teammates slapped his back as he bent over. He didn't speak for ten minutes and hardly moved. Finally, he lifted his tear-stained face and addressed reporters.

"They've got a great ball club. I lost it—you can say that."

Coach Carl Snavely said, "I don't see how the kid went as far as he did in his condition. He wasn't at his best by far, but he played hard. He's a much better passer than he showed."

Justice played in a somewhat weakened condition caused by an ailing stomach. The only solid food he took in three days was a small piece of steak on the morning of the game.

Myrle Greathouse, Oklahoma's jarring linebacker, intercepted a Justice flat pass and set up his team's first touchdown in the early moments. North Carolina had just made a first down on the Oklahoma 15. Greathouse ran 69 yards to the Tar Heels' 13. From the 1, eight plays later, expert masterminding quarterback Jack Mitchell slid to his left, hooked back, and scored.

Undismayed, North Carolina retaliated before the first quarter ended. Fullback Hosea Rodgers bucked across from the two. A fumble by halfback Lindell Pearson on the Oklahoma 30 presented the Tar Heels with a dividend they quickly cashed in. But Mike Cox's conversion attempt was wide. Les Ming had made his. Oklahoma led 7 to 6.

Just before the intermission, North Carolina reached the Oklahoma 8 and just missed scoring again. Justice floated a pretty pass to end Art Weiner in the end zone, but he dropped it. The Tar Heels didn't emerge from their own territory on offense after that until the last six minutes.

The Sooners hung the clincher on the scoreboard in the third quarter. Pearson cracked over from the 7. A long pass from Darrell Royal to end Frankie Anderson brought Oklahoma from its 47 to the 10. Anderson adroitly snatched the ball away from defender Bill Flamisch.

"The most pleasing feature of the game to me was that we solved their single wing traps," said Wilkinson. "Mitchell was great in his team direction. He was our key man."

SATURDAY, JANUARY 1, 1949

Oklahoma	7	0	7	0	14
North Carolina	6	0	0	0	6

Oklahoma—Touchdowns: Mitchell (1, right tackle), Pearson (7, left guard). Points after touchdown: Ming 2.

North Carolina—Touchdown: Rodgers (2, center).

STATISTICS

Oklahoma		North Carolina		Oklahoma	North Carolina
Tipps	LE	Weiner	15	First downs	12
Paine	LT	Highsmith	186	Net yards rushing	128
Burris	LG	Mitten	4	Passes attempted	21
Tillman	C	Stiegman	1	Passes completed	8
Mayes	RG	Varney	0	Passes had intercepted	2
Walker	RT	Hazelwood	43	Net yards passing	82
Goad	RE	Cox	229	Total net yards	210
Lisak	QB	Knox	5	Number of punts	7
Royal	LH	Justice	36.8	Punting average	38
Jones	RH	Kennedy	1	Fumbles lost	0
Greathouse	FB	Rodgers	40	Yards penalized	30

Substitutions—Oklahoma: Owens (l), Anderson (r), ends; Manley (l), Trotter (r), Wright (r), tackles; McNabb (l), West (r), Andros (r), guards; Dowell, Bodenhamer, centers; Mitchell, quarterback; Pearson (l), Thomas (r), Brewer (r), halfbacks; Heath, Ming, fullbacks. North Carolina: Powell (l), Romano (l), Cooke (l), Marczyk (l), Rubish (r), ends; Fowle (l), Hansen (l), Hazelwood (l), Szafaryn (r), tackles; Wardle (l), Hazelwood (r), Klosterman (r), Mitten (r), guards; Holdash, center; Highsmith, Weant, Rizzo, quarterbacks; Maceyko (l), Purcell (l), Clements (r), Rizzo (r), Neikirk (r), halfbacks; Flamisch, fullback.

ORANGE

The year 1948 was a lean one for the Southeastern Conference in bowl competition. At the finish of the season only Georgia was unbeaten in the league. Only Georgia was invited to a bowl.

Pairing Texas, thrice defeated and tied once, with Georgia in the Orange Bowl pleased few fans. A mismatch was feared. Psychologically, the pregame write-ups redounded to the Longhorns' benefit. Called "third-rate" in some of the newspapers they read, the rugged Texans took out their pique on the Bulldogs. Coach Wally Butts feared as much but was helpless to stop the flow of publicity hurtful to his team.

Between 1941 and 1948, inclusive, Georgia won three conference titles, went to six bowls and didn't lose in one until meeting fired-up Texas. At Miami, the favored Bulldogs led three times and were in front as late as the fifty-fifth minute.

There was enough furious action, eye-pleasing open field sprinting, and lead-changing to make almost everyone in the crowd of 60,523 forget the chilly (for southern Florida) 50 degree weather.

The lead changed five times. Here is how the score mounted (Texas first): 0 to 7, 6 to 7, 13 to 7, 13 to 14, 20 to 14, 27 to 14, 27 to 21, 27 to 28, 34 to 28, 41 to 28.

Tipoff on the game's trend was furnished in the second minute when Georgia fullback Al Bodine intercepted Paul Campbell's flat pass and fled 71 yards for a touchdown.

The Georgia line caved in before the onslaughts of darting, ramming Longhorn backs preceded by quick-charging line blockers creating big holes. Texas backs piled up 332 yards running, an Orange Bowl record.

Scoring plays followed successive advances of 62, 24, 77, 57, 70, and 40 yards.

Most unusual play was a completed pass from Rauch to Rauch. Attempting a short flip over the line, Johnny's fling hit a lanky Texan. The ball rebounded into Rauch's arms. He lost a yard.

"Not only was Texas aroused over being made to feel they weren't good enough for us," Butts said, "but one of their coaches got our starting lineup and went through it, player by player, giving the home state of each—Ohio, Pennsylvania, Indiana, Illinois, Minnesota, etc. Finally, he wound up: 'Boys, it's Texas against the world.' "

Texas	13	7	7	14	41
Georgia	7	7	7	7	28

Texas—Touchdowns: Borneman (4, left tackle), Landry (14, left tackle), Samuels (21, Statue of Liberty, right end), Procter (24, pass from Campbell), Clay 2 (2, right guard; 4, right tackle). Points after touchdown: Clay 5.

Georgia—Touchdowns: Bodine (71, intercepted pass by Campbell), Geri 2 (1, left guard; 6, left guard), Walston (37, pass from Rauch of 29, run of 8). Points after touchdown: Geri 4.

STATISTICS

Texas		*Georgia*	*Texas*		*Georgia*
Holder	LE	Sellers	19	First downs	9
Petrovich	LT	Bush	332	Net yards rushing	56
Vasicek	LG	Hobbs	10	Passes attempted	17
Harris	C	Jackura	5	Passes completed	11
Fry	RG	B. Reid	2	Passes had intercepted	2
Kelley	RT	Payne	70	Net yards passing	161
McCall	RE	Lorendo	402	Total net yards	217
Landry	QB	Field	5	Number of punts	5
Pyle	LH	Geri	40.1	Punting average	41.2
Clay	RH	Maricich	1	Fumbles lost	1
Borneman	FB	Tillitski	55	Yards penalized	50

Substitutions—Texas: Procter (l), Stone (l), Blount (r), Bauman (r), ends; Vykukal (l), Tatom (r), tackles; McFadin (l), Wolfe (r), Myers (r), guards; Rowan, center; Campbell, Lee, quarterbacks; Gillory (l), Samuels (l), Shands (r), halfbacks; Stroman, fullback. Georgia: Walston (l), Chandler (l), Connally (r), Taylor (r), Brunson (r), ends; Feher (l), Yelvington (r), tackles; Pope (l), Johnson (r), guards; Bradshaw, center; Rauch, Prosperi, quarterbacks; Mixon (l), Henderson (l), McCall (l), F. Reid (r), Donaldson (r), Bradberry (r), halfbacks; Bodine, fullback.

ROSE

Pasadena was no place for California to play football. This was shown in 1929. It was proved again in 1949. And in 1950 and 1951, too.

"This just isn't our town," summed up Bob Celeri, quarterback on the 1948 California team that came into the Rose Bowl with the Golden Bears' first perfect record in 26 years.

With time running out in the fourth quarter, darkness coming on and the lights turned on, California led Northwestern, 14 to 13. Northwestern had the ball on its own 12. Earlier in the quarter, California had been stopped eight yards from a touchdown. A punt exchange followed.

Ed Tunnicliff, 165-pound right halfback, attempted to dart through left tackle. He was cracked hard. As he was falling, he dropped the ball and end George Souza of California recovered. However, referee Jimmy Cain said he blew his whistle when Tunnicliff was grabbed, before he turned the ball loose. So Northwestern kept possession and kept going.

Thus encouraged, the Wildcats advanced to near midfield. Now, of all things, on second down with six yards to go from the Northwestern 49, California was penalized five for having twelve men on the field. Frank Van Deren had been replaced, but the weary Bear end hadn't quite reached the sideline when Northwestern ran a play.

Fullback Gaspar Perricone made the first down at the California 45 on a fourth-down plunge that was barely successful. Left half Frank Aschenbrenner got two.

Less than three minutes remained in the game. The crowd of 93,000 was on its feet. The bowl was in an uproar. And now it came, a trick play called by T quarterback Don Burson which the Wildcats had used several times during the season.

Tunnicliff took a direct snap from center Alex Sarkisian as Aschenbrenner went in motion to his right. The Bears were caught unaware. Tunnicliff started off right tackle, backed away, and turned the corner. Under heavy escort, he traveled 43 yards untouched.

That was it, 20 to 14, with two minutes, 15 seconds left.

One California alumnus, listening to Mel Allen's broadcast, clung to a Bible throughout most of the game. When Northwestern reached the California 43, he relaxed his grip on the Bible and it fell to the floor. At that instant, Tunnicliff ran for the touchdown.

On successive plays from scrimmage in the first quarter, Aschenbrenner broke into the clear for 73 yards and fullback Jackie Jensen sped 67 yards for offsetting touchdowns.

Northwestern halfback Tom Worthington raced 40 yards on a punt return in the second period, putting the ball on California's 22. Four plays later fullback Art Murakowski stormed 12 yards to the 2. Next he smashed at the right side and lost possession as he

1949—Here's that controversial touchdown scored by Northwestern's Art Murakowski against California. Frank Brunk is the fumble-causing tackler. Note Tom Worthington blocking Bob Celeri.

plowed ahead with his body crouched. Will Lotter of California fell on the ball in the end zone. California backers insisted a touchback would have been the correct call.

Field judge Jay Berwanger ruled it a touchdown, not a touchback. It was Berwanger's judgment that Murakowski had crossed the goal line or that part of the ball was directly above the line when he fumbled.

On the same play, Worthington, blocking ahead of Murakowski, was suspected of committing a foul when newspaper photographs of the disputed touchdown were viewed. It appeared he may have been guilty of misuse of his forearms in blocking Celeri.

A controversy arose. Pacific Coast writers were inflamed because pictures seemed to prove Murakowski fumbled a few feet short of the goal line.

But he was bent over and referee Cain said: "Berwanger was in a position to see the play. He called Murakowski over the goal line for the touchdown. The rule is explicit on the point that when the ball passes on or over the goal line it is a touchdown. On his decision, which had to be right because he was where he could see, Murakowski had possession of the ball when he crossed the line."

California Coach Lynn (Pappy) Waldorf, never a second guesser and never one to criticize, pointed out, "It's the position of the ball that counts, not the feet. If the officials said he was over the goal line, that's good enough for me."

Kenneth L. (Tug) Wilson, Big Nine commissioner who had an important role in cementing the pact with the Pacific Coast Conference two years before, said he was watching Berwanger at the time. "I saw him give the touchdown signal immediately and emphatically —and he was straddling the goal line," Wilson said.

Murakowski maintained, "I am sure I was across. Somebody tackled me from behind and pulled me back. That's when I fumbled."

As for Worthington, Vincent X. Flaherty wrote in the *Los Angeles Examiner:* "He is flattening this California player (Celeri) with his left arm and has his right fist cocked, ready to follow through as if he meant big business."

Worthington explained he used a high shoulder and arms block. He added that the photograph must have been snapped as he was "following through and starting to fall."

Jensen, who had gained 1,010 yards rushing (7.37 average) in 1948, went down untouched with a leg cramp as he attempted to circle right end the first time he carried the ball in the third quarter. The future major league outfielder never returned. However, Frank Brunk, who replaced Jensen, came through splendidly.

Brunk and the Bears were determined to get the job done without their ace. Brunk did most of the ball-carrying on a 44-yard

touchdown drive shortly after Jensen's removal. From the 4, Jack
Swaner fought through Wildcat defenders to score.

California went ahead, 14 to 13, on Jim Cullom's extra point.
But the lead didn't hold up.

The defeat was additionally galling to the West Coast because
Northwestern, coached by Bob Voights, a former lineman under
Waldorf, was the Big Nine's second best team. Michigan was Big
Nine and national champion but under the rule could not return to
the Rose Bowl, having played in it in 1948.

California partisans left the stadium muttering, "If Murakowski's
touchdown had been called a touchback . . . If Cain hadn't blown
a fast whistle on Tunnicliff's fumble . . . If Jensen hadn't gotten
hurt . . . If Celeri's pass in the last minute had been a foot higher."

But "if's" don't win football games.

Northwestern	7	6	0	7	20
California	7	0	7	0	14

Northwestern—Touchdowns: Aschenbrenner (73, right tackle), Murakowski
(2, right tackle), Tunnicliff (43, right end). Points after touchdown: Farrar 2.

California—Touchdowns: Jensen (67, left end), Swaner (4, left tackle). Points
after touchdown: Cullom 2.

STATISTICS

Northwestern		*California*	*Northwestern*		*California*
Zuravleff	LE	Van Deren	6	First downs	12
Sawle	LT	Cullom	273	Net yards rushing	173
Nemeth	LG	Baker	4	Passes attempted	16
Sarkisian (c)	C	Duncan	1	Passes completed	6
Fatso Day	RG	Franz	0	Passes had intercepted	4
Cernoch	RT	Frassetto (c)	17	Net yards passing	83
Hagmann	RE	Cunningham	290	Total net yards	256
Burson	QB	Erickson	7	Number of punts	4
Aschenbrenner	LH	Main	43	Punting average	33
Tunnicliff	RH	Swaner	2	Fumbles lost	1
Murakowski	FB	Jensen	15	Yards penalized	6

Substitutions—Northwestern: Stonesifer (l), Keddie (r), ends; Maddock (l),
Forman (r), tackles; Anderson (r), guard; Wietecha, Petter, Price, centers; Farrar, Flowers, J. Miller, quarterbacks; PeeWee Day (l), Worthington (r), G. Miller
(r), halfbacks; Sundheim, Perricone, Rossi, fullbacks. California: Souza (l),
Pressley (r), ends; Turner (l), Schmalenberger (l), Borghi (r), Najarian (r),
tackles; DeJong (l), Poddig (r), guards; Hileman, Papais, centers; Celeri, Minahen, Erb, quarterbacks; Keckley (l), Sarver (l), Dal Porto (l), Montagne (r),
Webster (r), halfbacks; Lotter, Brunk, Navarro, fullbacks.

GATOR

Following his graduation from Alabama, Frank Howard went to Clemson in 1931 as line coach. "At least that was my title," he said. "Actually, I also coached track, was ticket manager, recruited players and had charge of football equipment. In my spare time I cut grass, lined tennis courts and operated the canteen while the regular man went to lunch."

In typical Howard fashion Frank seconded his own nomination when put up as head coach by an athletic board member at a meeting held in 1940 to select the successor to Jess Neely, who had left for Rice.

Bald, tobacco-chewing Howard developed his best team in his first decade of coaching in 1948. Clemson beat ten foes, then won a 24 to 23 squeaker over Missouri in the Gator Bowl. Howard called it "the best game I ever saw."

It was the first game played in the enlarged stadium, now seating 36,000. The old concrete stands facing the east-west field became the south end-zone section. The new gridiron ran north and south.

Before sending out his Tigers against Coach Don Faurot's Missourians, Howard admonished them, characteristically: "Boys, keep 'em off the alumni line." It was his way of reminding his players to stop the enemy short of their goal line.

Clemson managed never to get behind although tied at halftime, 14 to 14. Jack Miller, a substitute back, kicked a field goal for what proved to be the decisive points in the fourth quarter. It was made from a difficult angle. The ball was touched down on the 22.

Tailback Bobby Gage said that on the fourth-down play, he was "wondering what to do when Fred Cone came up with the idea of Miller kicking." Howard rated fullback Cone "the best player I ever coached."

Missouri scored late in the fourth period to make it 24 to 23.

"They kicked off to us," Howard related. "We moved inside their territory but had a fourth-and-three situation on their 41. A decision had to be made on whether to run and try to keep the ball or kick and give Missouri another chance to score.

"Gage decided to go for it. I turned to Pop Cohen (then Clemson backfield coach) and said, 'If we make it, I'll be a great coach; if we don't, they might ride me out of Clemson on a rail.'

"Bobby gave the ball to Cone. He hit a stone wall. I thought we'd had it. But he slid off and found a hole to the outside, made six yards and a first down. With less than two minutes to go, I felt we had it made."

Someone asked Gage what had enabled Clemson to win.
"Brains and fortitude," he answered.

Clemson	14	0	7	3	24
Missouri	0	14	2	7	23

Clemson—Touchdowns: Cone 2 (1, center plunge; 1, plunge), Poulos (9, pass from Gage). Field goal: Jack Miller (32, placekick). Points after touchdown: Jack Miller 3.

Missouri—Touchdowns: Entsminger 2 (2, plunge; 1, right guard), Bounds (20, pass from Entsminger). Points after touchdown: Dawson 3. Safety: Gage tackled by Pepper in end zone on play from Clemson 1.

STATISTICS

Clemson		Missouri	Clemson		Missouri
Poulos	LE	Oakes	19	First downs	16
Prince	LT	Fritz	186	Net yards rushing	225
Clanton	LG	Cox	23	Passes attempted	8
Rushton	C	Fuchs	10	Passes completed	4
Gillespie	RG	Pepper	1	Passes had intercepted	0
Salisbury	RT	Scholfield	112	Net yards passing	73
Thompson	RE	Sheehan	298	Total net yards	298
Martin	QB	Entsminger	1	Number of punts	3
Gage	LH	Brinkman	35	Punting average	31
Mathews	RH	Volz	0	Fumbles lost	2
Cone	FB	Carter	10	Yards penalized	42

Substitutions—Clemson: Dyer (l), Carson (l), Hudson (r), ends; Deanhardt (l), Gainer (r), tackles; Davis (l), Cox (r), guards; Moore, center; Wyndham, Carothers, quarterbacks; Calvert (l), Jim Miller (l), Jack Miller (l), Williams (r), halfbacks; Hendley, fullback. Missouri: Bounds (l), Ebinger (l), Dusenbury (l), Sheehan (l), Ebinger (r), Dusenbury (r), Oakes (r), Wren (r), ends; Boyd (l), Donley (l), Keller (l), Bullock (r), Savage (r), tackles; Kadlec (l), Pepper (l), Marusic (l), Cox (r), Marusic (r), guards; Baechle, Hamann, centers; Klein, Robinson, Sauer, quarterbacks; Carras (l), Ghnouly (l), Braznell (r), Carras (r), Dawson (r), Stephens (r), halfbacks; Ashley, Houston, fullbacks.

COTTON

Ewell Doak Walker, Jr., born in Dallas on January 1, 1927, was brought up to be a football player.

Even before he started to elementary school, his father, who once coached football, taught him broken field running. Doak showed an aptitude for the game when he was five. As he grew older and his coordination improved, Mr. Walker would say, "You're good. But so what? Football is just a sport."

So Doak learned the skills but never forgot to practice self-efface-

ment while becoming an All-America halfback, winning the Heisman Trophy in 1948 as a junior, and leading Southern Methodist to
two straight Southwest Conference titles.

A teammate once remarked, "He doesn't seem to give a hoot about
publicity." He got it by the newsprint carload, however, and was
appreciative. He personally answered all fan mail. After he'd written the Associated Press a note of thanks on being named to its All-
America team in 1947, staff writer Harold Ratliff commented, "That
made history. I believe it was the first time we ever got a thank-you
letter from an athlete."

1949—Doak Walker about to escape from Oregon linemen for a Southern
Methodist gain.

Not powerfully built (five feet, 10 inches tall and weighing 170
pounds) and not flashingly fast, Walker had a marvelous sense of timing, a change of pace which seemed to put him a thought ahead of
foes eager to make the tackle.

Abb Curtis, former Southwest Conference official, said of Doak at
the time, "He runs as if he had eyes in the back of his head. And
he's so shifty he'd be hard to catch in a phone booth."

Oregon, with its strongest team since 1919, won seven Pacific Coast Conference games to six for California in 1948. But the Webfoots lost to Michigan's national champions, 14 to 0. California's record was perfect.

A vote of the ten member schools in the conference sent California to the Rose Bowl. Oregon Coach Jim Aiken said Oregon had been slighted. Students paraded around his home shouting "We want a bowl game" again and again. The players concurred. A conference rule prohibited a member team from playing a postseason game anywhere but in Pasadena or Honolulu. In a special vote, the conference gave permission to Oregon to accept an invitation from Cotton Bowl officials.

Southern Methodist had its hands full. The Oregonians gained more yardage running and passing. Yet the Mustangs turned back Oregon, 21 to 13, before a crowd of 69,000 in the Cotton Bowl enlarged by the double decking of the west side.

Walker's performance was typically well rounded. Norm Van Brocklin, the Webfoots' talented passer, engineered two last-quarter touchdowns.

The Cotton Bowl, packed to capacity with 75,504 fans.

A highlight of the game was the prodigious punting of Walker and sophomore SMU halfback Kyle Rote.

In the second quarter Walker quick-kicked 79 yards out of bounds on Oregon's six-inch line. And Rote booted one 84 yards. Later, Rote punted 43 yards. Thus, on their three punts, the Mustangs averaged 68.7 yards.

SMU swept to touchdowns immediately after receiving the kick-offs opening each half. Oregon's first real scoring threat, following Rote's third-quarter touchdown, ended on the SMU 5. One of the ball carriers on the drive was Jim Aiken, Jr.

As a nine-year-old boy, young Doak wrote an essay on "The Greatest Man In America." His subject was Harry Shuford, fullback on the SMU team that went to the Rose Bowl. Shuford wore No. 37. So did Walker when he became a Mustang. But long before that, he pestered his mother until she sewed a "3" and a "7" on the back of a sweatshirt.

Southern Methodist	7	0	7	7	21
Oregon	0	0	0	13	13

Southern Methodist—Touchdowns: Walker (1, right tackle), Rote (36, right tackle), Roberts (8, right end). Points after touchdown: Walker 2, Ethridge.

Oregon—Touchdowns: Wilkins (24, pass from Van Brocklin), Sanders (1, center plunge). Point after touchdown: Daniels.

STATISTICS

Southern Methodist		Oregon	Southern Methodist	Oregon
Payne	LE	Garza	19 First downs	19
Ethridge	LT	Dotur	226 Net yards rushing	242
Lewis	LG	Meland	20 Passes attempted	19
Wood	C	Ecklund	10 Passes completed	8
Halliday	RG	Chrobot	2 Passes had intercepted	0
Hamberger	RT	Stanton	111 Net yards passing	145
Blakely	RE	Wilkins	337 Total net yards	387
Walker	QB	Van Brocklin	3 Number of punts	3
Rote	LH	Lewis	68.7 Punting average	31
Page	RH	Bell	0 Fumbles lost	1
McKissick	FB	Sanders	5 Yards penalized	30

Substitutions—Southern Methodist: Wallace (l), Milam (l), Folsom (r), ends; Vann (l), Collier (r), King (r), tackles; Franklin (l), Roberds (r), Lipke (r), Basham (r), guards; Marion, Davis, centers; Weatherford, Johnson, Grantham, quarterbacks; Roberts (l), Champion (l), Mizell (r), Kendrick (r), halfbacks; Moon, Blackburn, fullbacks. Oregon: D. Robinson (l), Hagen (l), Bartholemy (r), Anderson (r), ends; Roberts (l), L. Robinson (l), Nevills (r), tackles; Berwick (l), Daniels (r), guards; Gibson, center; Johnson, quarterback; McKay (l), Easter (l), Aiken (l), Holcomb (r), halfbacks; Boqua, fullback.

– 1950 –

COTTON

Legislation aimed at limiting the number of bowl games, which mushroomed to ridiculous proportions in the late forties, began to form in early January of 1950 when the National Collegiate Athletic Association held its annual convention in New York.

Sensible regulations to curb promoter abuses, establish definite standards of management, control distribution of receipts, and protect the interests of participating schools had been proposed previously. A special committee investigating the situation reported at the 1949 convention in San Francisco that some bowls spent as much as twenty to thirty per cent of the gross on promotion, publicity, and public relations. Some bowls, it charged, paid as low as 40 per cent to competing schools.

No action was taken in 1949, or in 1950 when a plan under which competing schools would get 80 per cent of gross receipts and one-third of the tickets was referred to a special committee assigned to draft by-laws.

However, at the 1951 N.C.A.A. convention in Dallas a by-law was passed requiring bowl-sponsoring persons or organizations to give not less than 75 per cent of the gross, including concession, radio, television, and movie money, to competing schools.

Starting in 1952, the N.C.A.A. permitted the playing only of bowls certified by its Extra Events Committee. The number of N.C.A.A. approved bowls decreased considerably.

A committee of college presidents, appointed by the American Council on Education, recommended the abolishment of all bowls, athletic scholarships, and out-of-season practice at the N.C.A.A. convention in Cincinnati in 1952. Football coaches were sharply critical. But the N.C.A.A. ordered member schools not to make any bowl commitments beyond January 2, 1953, while a study was made by an investigating group.

A majority of the presidents still opposed bowl games a year later.

However, the committee's study showed that apparently everyone except college presidents approved of them. In a voice vote on the matter at the 1953 N.C.A.A. convention in Washington, D.C., not a "no" was heard.

The only bowl that met the receipt distribution standard adopted in 1951 was the Cotton Bowl. The committee examining the spread of the bowls had informed members at the 1949 meeting that the Cotton Bowl already was setting aside three-fourths of the receipts for competing schools; that the Rose Bowl allotted 70 per cent and the other major bowls less.

In the 1950 Cotton Bowl "model," Rice methodically overwhelmed North Carolina 27 to 13, before a record crowd of 75,347. The Owls rolled up a four-touchdown lead before relaxing.

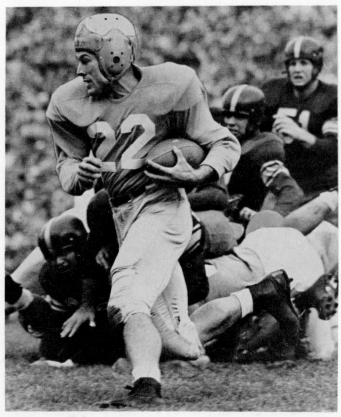

1950—North Carolina's greatest back, Charlie (Choo-Choo) Justice, rips off yardage against Rice.

Rice's swift backs ran for 226 yards. Tobin Rote's passes—he threw for touchdowns on 44- and 17-yard plays to halfback Billy Burkhalter and end James (Froggie) Williams, respectively—produced an additional 152 yards.

As the shadows lengthened Choo Choo Justice, finishing his spectacular four-year career, pulled his teammates together for an exciting windup that roused the fans and resulted in a pair of Tar Heel touchdowns in the last eight minutes. Until then North Carolina hadn't approached within 37 yards of the Rice goal line.

Justice was a player of uncommon skill and fortitude. He gained 5,176 yards running and passing, punted for a 42.5 average, and scored 234 points.

His bowl performances never quite equaled his regular season deeds.

MONDAY, JANUARY 2, 1950

Rice	0	14	7	6	27
North Carolina	0	0	0	13	13

Rice—Touchdowns: Burkhalter 2 (44, pass from Rote of 4, run of 40; 12, left end), Lantrip (3, center), Williams (17, pass from Rote of 6, run of 11). Points after touchdown: Williams 3.

North Carolina—Touchdowns: Rizzo 2 (7, pass from Justice of 4, run of 3; 8, lateral from Justice, left end). Point after touchdown: Williams.

STATISTICS

Rice		North Carolina	Rice		North Carolina
Williams	LE	Weiner	18	First downs	16
Anderson	LT	King	226	Net yards rushing	174
Roberts	LG	Bestwick	19	Passes attempted	22
Watson	C	Holdash	11	Passes completed	9
Schwarz	RG	Augustine	1	Passes had intercepted	1
Murphy	RT	Kuhn	152	Net yards passing	80
Taylor	RE	Powell	378	Total net yards	254
Rote	QB	Knox	4	Number of punts	6
Wyatt	LH	Justice	43	Punting average	38
Riley	RH	Carson	1	Fumbles lost	1
Lantrip	FB	Wiess	26	Yards penalized	30

Substitutions—Rice: Allen (l), Boughton (l), Howton (l), McCurry (r), Pugh (r), ends; Wyman (l), Walls (l), Giroski (r), Winship (r), tackles; Derwood Lee (l), McPhail (l), Neumann (l), Delwood Lee (r), guards; Weatherly, Stonestreet, Price, centers; Glass, Carswell, quarterbacks; Silver (l), Burkhalter (r), Proctor (r), Kelly (r), halfbacks; Glauser, fullback. North Carolina: Nickerson (l), O'Brien (l), Washington (r), Bilpuch (r), Kelso (r), ends; Wiley (l), Rywak (l), Carpenter (l), Ruffin (r), Williams (r), Hendrick (r), tackles; Hansen (l), McDonald (l), Wardle (l), Dudeck (r), Woodell (r), guards; Miketa, center; Rizzo, quarterback; Bunting (l), Gurtis (l), Clements (r), Verchick (r), Norcross (r), Dougherty (r), halfbacks; Gantt, Hayes, Stevens, Hesmer fullbacks.

SUGAR

Three days before Oklahoma mauled Louisiana State 35 to 0 in the Sugar Bowl game of 1950 a man was found who allegedly took motion pictures of the Sooners' secret practice at Biloxi, Miss.

Oklahoma Coach Bud Wilkinson was convinced a spy was afoot. T. P. (Red) Heard, LSU's athletic director, vehemently denied his school was implicated. He suggested it might be a scheme "by some overzealous Oklahoma rooter who wanted to stir things up."

The *New Orleans Times-Picayune* reported that Wilkinson said several persons who looked at a picture of the man he charged with "scouting our drills" identified him as having been a former LSU lineman.

Wilkinson and Heard exchanged hot words at the New Year's Eve press party at Antoine's in New Orleans' French Quarter.

Wilkinson had said, "The interloper saw every card in our hand."

"I naturally resent it when Coach Wilkinson questions the character of our coaching staff and boys, and I told him to his face that the charges were untrue," Heard said after the meeting in the restaurant.

Came the game and the biggest scoring difference in the Sugar Bowl's history as the Sooners won their twenty-first straight with a brilliant demonstration of tricky reverses, forward passes thrown from laterals, and smoothly-timed, unhurried pitch-outs and handoffs.

"Just a strong man spanking a baby," wrote Bill Keefe in the *Times-Picayune*.

The second quarter saw Oklahoma bring big guns to bear on its outplayed Southeastern Conference opponent. Right halfback George Thomas scored on a 34-yard pass from left half Lindell Pearson and again on a six-yard end run.

On the Sooners' first play of the third quarter the long standing record for the longest run in the bowl by Monk Simons of Tulane in 1935 fell. Fullback Leon Heath shot through the center of the line, dodged a Tiger, and ran untouched 86 yards for a touchdown.

Heath, who in three consecutive Sugar Bowl games gained 341 yards, scored midway in the fourth period, too, on a 34-yard scoot around the left side of LSU's tired line. A few plays earlier quarterback Darrell Royal had planted the ball across the goal line on a five-yard smash.

The Tigers, outgained rushing 286 yards to 38, attempted to make headway in the air. But they were frustrated by four pass interceptions in the last half, three in the fourth quarter.

LSU players were paid openly liberal "expense money" for the short trip to New Orleans. Each received $250. Many writers wondered if the National Collegiate Athletic Association would take some sort of action. Nothing was done.

Oklahoma's football team took a vacation in Havana, all expenses paid by the university.

Oklahoma	0	14	7	14	35
Louisiana State	0	0	0	0	0

Oklahoma—Touchdowns: Thomas 2 (34, pass from Pearson of 33, run of 1; 6, left end), Heath 2 (86, center; 34, right end), Royal (5, center). Points after touchdown: Tipps 5.

STATISTICS

Oklahoma		Louisiana State	Oklahoma		Louisiana State
Owens	LE	J. Lyle	10	First downs	8
Manley	LT	Roussos	286	Net yards rushing	38
Andros	LG	Bradley	11	Passes attempted	20
Dowell	C	Cole	2	Passes completed	9
West	RG	Hover	2	Passes had intercepted	4
Walker	RT	Cusimano	74	Net yards passing	121
Goad	RE	Kitto	360	Total net yards	159
Royal	QB	Konz	7	Number of punts	8
Pearson	LH	Hedges	37.4	Punting average	33.6
Thomas	RH	Roshto	4	Fumbles lost	4
Heath	FB	Van Buren	40	Yards penalized	40

Substitutions—Oklahoma: Tipps (l), Hoofnagle (l), Anderson (r), Heape (r), ends; Weatherall (l), Leguenec (l), D. Smith (r), Cole (r), tackles; West (l), McNabb (l), F. Smith (l), McNabb (r), Mayes (r), Marcum (r), guards; Bodenhamer, Moore, Clark, centers; Lisak, Arnold, Lockett, quarterbacks; Parker (l), Heatly (l), Lisak (r), Brewer (r), halfbacks; Jones, Lang, Paine, fullbacks. Louisiana State: S. Lyle (l), Anding (r), Virgets (r), Freeman (r), ends; Potter (l), Coyne (l), Voss (l), Collins (r), tackles; Roussos (l), Shoaf (l), Shoaf (r), Baird (r), guards; Reid, C. Smith, West, centers; Pevey, Baggett, Griffith, quarterbacks; Freeman (l), Konz (l), Barton (l), Baggett (r), Hedges (r), Field (r), halfbacks; Konz, Toth, West, fullbacks.

ORANGE

Paul (Bear) Bryant, who coached Kentucky football teams for eight years starting in 1946, became known as "the great rehabilitator." It was a deserved designation.

In turn he resuscitated the football fortunes of Maryland, then Kentucky, then Texas A&M, and at last, his alma mater, Alabama.

Kentucky changed from mediocrity to national recognition under his guidance. He produced four bowl teams. Three triumphed. One came to grief in the Orange Bowl game of 1950, losing to Santa Clara 21 to 13.

Of Bryant, Zipp Newman wrote in the *Birmingham News:* "He has every qualification of a great grid master. He was the most fearless football player I ever knew. Bryant played his greatest game on a broken leg against Tennessee.

"He has a flair for imparting his know-how to players. He's a tireless worker. He has the patience to rehearse a play 100 times. He not only knows how to handle players on the field but off it. No coach has more personality."

Kentucky struck first in the second quarter. The Wildcats sent halfback Wilbur Jamerson into the end zone from the 2 on the final play of a 49-yard drive. During the first half Kentucky outgained Santa Clara, 185 yards to 50, and out-first-downed the Broncos, 11 to one.

The trend switched abruptly.

Early in the third period Santa Clara's Hawaiian halfback, Abe Dung, smothered a fumble by Bill Leskovar on Kentucky's 11. Four plays later quarterback Johnny Pasco sneaked through the middle to score from only inches away. It was the first of three touchdowns in 30 minutes by the team that completed a 96-hour transcontinental train trip three days before.

With three minutes left in the quarter Santa Clara smashed 41 yards to the 1. A holding penalty checked the Broncos momentarily. Pasco fired a pass intended for end Ellery Williams. It failed but Kentucky was guilty of interference with the wingman on the 3. Halfback Hall Haynes, whose seven punts averaged 44 yards, wriggled over the goal line from the 2.

Santa Clara now led, 14 to 7. But Kentucky had another punch to throw. Babe Parilli, greatest passer in his school's history, flung a 38-yard pass to Emery Clark, who ran 14 more to score. Bob Brooks' extra point try in quest of a tie was wide.

Thirty-one seconds remained in the game when halfback Bernie Vogel crashed through the weary Wildcats for the Broncos' final touchdown on a 16-yard gallop.

"I did more to beat my team than anybody else," Bryant later maintained. "I took them down to Cocoa (Florida) for 10 days and had another spring practice. I've never worked as hard for a bowl game since. But I think that extra scrimmaging helped us to be a great team the next year.

"Yes, I took them too early and I worked them too long. You learn."

Always outspoken and never one to go easy on himself, Bryant also called attention to another mistake he said he made in that game.

Fullback Leskovar had caught a 45-yard pass from Parilli to put the ball on Santa Clara's 3 with 22 seconds to play in the first half.

"I should have called for a pass play, and if that failed, for a field goal," Bryant said. "But I didn't do a thing, just sat there."

Kentucky tried the line twice without avail. The Wildcats were outclassed from that point.

A record crowd of 64,816 watched the contest. The extra seats, added since the 1948 game, were located in the end zone.

Subsequent enlargements boosted seating capacity to 76,561 before the 1956 game. Capacity was later reduced 6,000 to make room for building of a memorial.

Santa Clara	0	0	14	7	21
Kentucky	0	7	0	6	13

Santa Clara—Touchdowns: Pasco (1, sneak), Haynes (2, right tackle), Vogel (16, center). Points after touchdown: Vargas 3.

Kentucky—Touchdowns: Jamerson (2, right guard), Clark (52, pass from Parilli of 38, run of 14). Point after touchdown: Brooks.

STATISTICS

Santa Clara		Kentucky		Santa Clara		Kentucky
White	LE	Yowarsky	8	First downs	18
Hock	LT	Gain	153	Net yards rushing	170
Sterling	LG	Wannamaker	9	Passes attempted	11
Canelo	C	McConnaughey	4	Passes completed	6
Dowling	RG	Holway	1	Passes had intercepted	2
Payne	RT	Ignarski	80	Net yards passing	130
Hennessy	RE	Odlivak	233	Total net yards	300
Pasco	QB	Boller	7	Number of punts	9
Haynes	LH	Phelps	44	Punting average	40
Defilippis	RH	Martin	1	Fumbles lost	0
Wraith	FB	Truman	30	Yards penalized	23

Substitutions—Santa Clara: E. Williams (l), L. Williams (l), Osborn (r), Wiborn (r), ends; Dominick (l), Beatty (l), Cozad (r), House (r), tackles; Duzanica (l), Niehaus (l), Justice (r), Brown (r), guards; Rotticci, Cashman, centers; Napolitano, Toquinto, Richley, quarterbacks; Vogel (l), Dung (l), Vargas (l), Rasmussen (r), Moran (r), Formico (r), halfbacks; Conn, Hakeem, fullbacks. Kentucky: Claiborne (l), Zaranka (l), Netoskie (l), Bruno (r), Frampton (r), McClendon (r), ends; Pope (l), MacKenzie (l), McDermott (r), Vance (r), tackles; Hamilton (l), James (r), Porter (r), Conde (r), guards; Ulinski, Moseley, Schaffnit, Rogers, centers; Parilli, Fucci, Bezuk, quarterbacks; Brooks (l), Clark (l), Webb (l), Jamerson (r), Howe (r), Lawson (r), halfbacks; Leskovar, Genito, fullbacks.

ROSE

On November 19, 1949, at Michigan Stadium in Ann Arbor, Ohio State had marched to a touchdown in the fourth quarter. Now the score stood: Michigan 7, Ohio State 6.

A successful conversion would put the Buckeyes in the Rose Bowl. A miss would send Minnesota to Pasadena. The Gophers had beaten Ohio State 27 to 0 (the Buckeyes' only defeat), but had fallen to Michigan and Purdue. Michigan couldn't go under any circumstances. The Wolverines were prevented by the Big Nine rule prohibiting more than one Rose Bowl appearance in three years.

Jimmy Hague, senior Ohio State end, attempted to placekick the extra point. But it was wide. Would Ohio State stay at home? Maybe not. Michigan was offside. Hague had another chance.

"It was funny but I didn't really feel the pressure until after I had missed that first one," Hague told a close sports writer friend, Jack Clowser of the *Cleveland Press*. "Then it came to me that they'd remember me for the rest of my life as the man who blew the Rose Bowl trip for us, if I didn't make the second try."

Hague's second kick cleaved the posts, giving Ohio State a 7 to 7 tie and the co-championship of the Big Nine with Michigan.

A month and a half after that, Hague was under similar pressure in the closing stage of the Rose Bowl game.

With the score 14 to 14 and three minutes, ten seconds to go, California—playing to win, not to tie—waited until fourth down to punt from its 16.

Center Charlie Harris' snap to quarterback Bob Celeri was low. Before Celeri could bring the ball up, after fumbling it, the Buckeyes rushed toward him from all sides. The desperate Bear ran to his left, closely pursued. Determined to salvage a few yards, he kicked the ball leftfooted from near his own goal line—while on the run—out of bounds on the 13.

"I had a 50-50 chance to handle it but I didn't," Celeri said self-critically.

The stadium lights had been switched on and there was pandemonium in the bowl, filled with 100,963 fans, as Ohio State's offensive platoon streamed onto the field. Halfback Jerry Krall hit for three yards. Fullback Fred Morrison fumbled as he smashed ahead for two but got a lucky bounce. Krall picked up two at right tackle. It was fourth-and-three on the 6.

Coach Wes Fesler made his decision. He sent in Dick Widdoes with the kicking tee. Tom Watson went in to play right end so Hague could drop back for a field-goal attempt. The replacements were somewhat less than warmly received. In a moment they trotted back to the bench saying their teammates on the field wanted to run the ball over.

But Fesler, refusing to have his orders countermanded, returned the pair to the huddle. Referee William Blake stepped off a five-yard penalty against the Buckeyes for delay of the game.

"Three points were enough then," Fesler later explained. "Why should we have risked going for six when we needed only half that many?"

With the ball on the 11, Hague had a better angle, although Fesler didn't draw the penalty deliberately for that reason. Hague kicked it diagonally and true. Time left was one minute, 57 seconds. The score was Ohio State 17, California 14. And that's how it stayed.

The Golden Bears stopped Buckeye drives three times within their own 20 in the first half. They scored their first touchdown in the second quarter. A pass from Celeri to halfback Frank Brunk covered 54 yards to the Ohio State 20. From there it was halfback Jim Monachino twice for seven and two yards, Brunk for four and, finally, Monachino inside left end for the touchdown.

Shortly after the third quarter began, Vic Janowicz, Ohio State back who was to win the Heisman Trophy in 1950, intercepted a Celeri-thrown pass. He ran 46 yards to California's 30.

Ohio State's potent running attack, which totaled 175 yards in the first half as the Buckeyes were held scoreless, wasn't to be checked this time. The combination of Morrison and Krall pounded out most of the yardage. On fourth down from the 1, the 214-pound Morrison crashed into a pileup and simply knocked it back. Now it was 7 to 7.

Directly, Ohio State made another break for itself. Celeri's fourth-down punt was blocked by tackle Bill Trautwein, a 237-pounder. Center Jack Lininger picked up the ball on the 16. He reached the 6 before Celeri brought him down. California fought hard to prevent a touchdown, but Ohio State got it on fourth down when Krall shot through right tackle from the 2.

The Bears counterattacked forthwith. Monachino grabbed a pitchout from Celeri on the fifth play following the kickoff, cut to the outside of the Buckeyes' right flank and ran 44 yards for the tying touchdown. Fullback Pete Schabarum and tackle Jim Turner provided the most needed downfield blocking.

As the fourth quarter began, California moved into Ohio State territory. This drive petered out. But subsequently Janowicz intercepted another pass by Celeri on his 46. Nothing came of this break. So Morrison punted into the end zone and the Bears tried to get under way from their 20. Disaster struck after Schabarum was thrown for a four-yard loss and Celeri fired two long incomplete passes.

Grantland Rice called the contest "one of the bitterest in football history, one of the most exciting of all the bowl games."

"There is one thing you cannot do," California Coach Lynn Waldorf commented. "That is violate the oldest fundamental in the game. Your punting game must be sound. Ours was not."

It was a chilly, overcast day, one of the few times since the Rose Bowl series began that blankets were in evidence.

The bowl was enlarged for this game by the addition of several thousand permanent seats in the end zones.

Tackle Jack Jennings related, "I knocked Celeri down once on a pass and he shook my hand. He said, 'You're going to Hawaii [for an all-star game], aren't you?'

"I said, 'Yeah, you're going too, aren't you?'

"He nodded and said, 'We'll be teammates. So how about taking it a little easier on your teammate?'

"I told him, 'We don't start being teammates until tomorrow.' "

| Ohio State | 0 | 0 | 14 | 3 | 17 |
| California | 0 | 7 | 7 | 0 | 14 |

Ohio State—Touchdowns: Morrison (1, center dive), Krall (2, right tackle). Field goal: Hague (28, placekick). Points after touchdown: Hague 2.

California—Touchdowns: Monachino 2 (7, left tackle; 44, left end). Points after touchdown: Cullom 2.

STATISTICS

Ohio State		California	Ohio State		California
Schnittker	LE	Begovich	19	First downs	12
O'Hanlon	LT	Cullom	221	Net yards rushing	133
Toneff	LG	DeJong	14	Passes attempted	13
Lininger	C	Richter	5	Passes completed	3
Biltz	RG	Franz (c-c)	1	Passes had intercepted	4
Wilson (c)	RT	Turner (c-c)	34	Net yards passing	106
Hague	RE	Pressley	255	Total net yards	239
Savic	QB	Celeri	4	Number of punts	6

Krall	LH	Brunk	28.5	Punting average	22.5
Hamilton	RH	Monachino	1	Fumbles lost	0
Morrison	FB	Schabarum	50	Yards penalized	45

Substitutions—Ohio State: Armstrong (l), Gilbert (l), Watson (r), ends; Jennings (l), Miller (l), Wittman (l), Trautwein (r), Edwards (r), tackles; Mattey (l), Manz (l), Thomas (r), Wittman (r), guards; McCullough, Heid, centers; Widdoes, Wertz, quarterbacks; Swinehart (l), Newell (l), Klevay (r), Sturtz (r), halfbacks; Janowicz, Perini, Gandee, fullbacks. California: Minahen (l), Bartlett (l), Souza (l), LemMon (l), Cummings (r), ends; Muehlberger (l), Nelson (l), Jones (r), Schmalenberger (r), tackles; Klein (l), Harris (l), Solari (l), Dodds (r), Fox (r), guards; Humpert, Stathakis, Harris, centers; Erb, Van Heuit, quarterbacks; Baldwin (l), Montagne (r), halfbacks; Robison, Groger, fullbacks.

GATOR

Missouri, destined for six successive defeats before a bowl victory, returned to Jacksonville in 1950 and suffered considerable embarrassment quite apart from a 20 to 7 lacing by Maryland.

The Tigers' zippy split T offense was well throttled, held to a mere 100 yards on the ground. It was one of the lowest Missouri rushing totals since Coach Don Faurot introduced his personalized style of attack in 1941.

The left side of Maryland's line—end Elmer Wingate, tackle Ray Krouse, and guard Bob Ward—was particularly stout. It was one of the best three-man defensive combinations in college football.

Missouri tried to win with passes in the Gator Bowl. Faurot's men threw 29 but completed only 11. Three were intercepted. Five ball-losing fumbles increased Missouri's misfortunes.

Maryland's touchdowns came easy because of Missouri mistakes. The Tigers' errors, an interception and a pair of muffs, enabled the Terps to score on short drives of only 11, 22, and 15 yards in that order in the first half.

With less than two minutes left, Missouri quarterback Phil Klein topped a 96-yard advance with a five-yard touchdown run.

"It is impossible to beat a good team like Maryland when you don't have possession of the ball," Faurot commented. "The ball beat us. We just didn't have it."

Maryland	7	13	0	0	20
Missouri	0	0	0	7	7

Maryland—Touchdowns: Shemonski 2 (11, right end; 6, right end), Modzelewski (3, right guard). Points after touchdown: Dean 2.

Missouri—Touchdown: Klein (5, right tackle). Point after touchdown: Glorioso.

STATISTICS

Maryland		Missouri		Maryland	Missouri
Wingate	LE	Hulse	11	First downs	13
Krouse	LT	Woodson	226	Net yards rushing	100
Ward	LG	Kadlec	17	Passes attempted	29
Brasher	C	Bob Fuchs	2	Passes completed	11
Troha	RG	Pepper	1	Passes had intercepted	3
Pobiak	RT	Keller	16	Net yards passing	167
Augsburger	RE	Dusenbury	242	Total net yards	267
Tucker	QB	Ghnouly	7	Number of punts	3
Shemonski	LH	Carras	39	Punting average	38
Modzelewski	RH	Stephens	1	Fumbles lost	5
Rowden	FB	Ashley	63	Yards penalized	10

Substitutions—Maryland: Karnash (l), Fox (l), Chiodi (l), Hurd (r), Betz (r), F. Davis (r), ends; O'Connor (l), Maletzky (l), Kensler (r), Gierula (r), Dean (r), tackles; Gayzur (l), McQuade (r), Cianelli (r), guards; Fincke, Keith, centers; Lavine, quarterback; L. Davis (l), Idzik (l), Kuchta (l), Seibert (l), LaRue (r), Scioscia (r), Bolton (r), Condon (r), halfbacks; Early, Roth, fullbacks. Missouri: Ackerman (l), Portman (l), Bounds (r), Armstrong (r), ends; Millican (l), Scholfield (l), Savage (r), Bullock (r), tackles; Marusic (l), Cox (l), Moore (r), guards; Bill Fuchs, Baechle, centers; Klein, Sauer, quarterbacks; Glorioso (l), Braznell (l), Mickens (l), Studer (l), Hailey (r), Henley (r), H. Carter (r), halfbacks; Houston, W. Carter, fullbacks.

— 1951 —

GATOR

Where Bowden Wyatt went, success soon followed—at Wyoming, at Arkansas, and at his alma mater, Tennessee. It was the same in his playing days.

In his book on Tennessee football, published in 1961, sports editor Tom Siler of the *Knoxville News-Sentinel* told of Wyatt's first meeting with Bob Neyland.

"Wyatt was a sophomore in 1936 and Neyland was just back from

a year in Panama," Siler related. "At the time Wyatt was washing
dishes to earn one meal and had an NYA (National Youth Administration) job to pay for other meals and expenses. This was in De-
pression days and times were tough, football and otherwise.

" 'I went to Major Neyland and told him I was hungry,' said
Wyatt. 'If you feed me, I'll make you a good football player. I
meant it.' "

In 1938, Grantland Rice put Wyatt, then Tennessee's captain, on
his All-America team at end.

In his third year as Wyoming's head coach, 1949, single winger
Wyatt's Cowboys won their first Mountain States (Skyline) Conference championship with their first better than .500 record since 1931.
The next season they won the title again with their first perfect campaign of the century.

Wyoming rounded off that 1950 season with a 20 to 7 conquest
of Washington and Lee in the Gator Bowl.

Eddie Talboom, 29-year-old Wyoming tailback and father of three
children, found receivers for ten of his 16 passes. He cracked open
the Generals' defense for 143 yards, scored a touchdown, threw for
one, and set up the third.

Wyoming built up a 20 to 0 lead before Washington and Lee's
split T attack enjoyed any degree of success. Starting from the Cowboys' 49 in the final quarter, the Generals finally penetrated inside
the 20 for the first time and went on to score.

Washington and Lee was handicapped by the absence of fullback
Walt Michaels, maker of 83 points, who underwent an emergency
appendectomy a few days before the game.

MONDAY, JANUARY 1, 1951

Wyoming	0	13	7	0	20
Washington and Lee	0	0	0	7	7

Wyoming—Touchdowns: Campbell (8, pass from Talboom), Talboom (2,
right guard), Melton (16, center). Points after touchdown: Talboom 2.

Washington and Lee—Touchdown: Bocetti (3, left tackle). Point after
touchdown: Brewer.

STATISTICS

Wyoming		Washington and Lee	Wyoming		Washington and Lee
McConnell	LE	Hedge	14	First downs	19
Martin	LT	Delahunty	148	Net yards rushing	270
Sandstrom	LG	Schaub	16	Passes attempted	14
Reeves	C	McCutcheon	10	Passes completed	3

		Washington and Lee	Wyoming		Washington and Lee
Smith	RG	Kay	0	Passes had intercepted	1
Hewgley	RT	Fergusson	143	Net yards passing	31
Parker	RE	Thomas	291	Total net yards	301
Campbell	QB	Bocetti	5	Number of punts	6
Talboom	LH	Stark	39	Punting average	29.5
Gale	RH	Broyles	0	Fumbles lost	4
Melton	FB	Holt	75	Yards penalized	31

Substitutions—Wyoming: Drost (l), Jones (l), Hilpp (r), Layman (r), ends; Schildgen (l), Harp (r), Strauch (r), tackles; Townsend, Taylor, Bowers, centers; Dunn, quarterback; Pederson (l), Geldien (l), Manchak (r), Peters (r), halfbacks. Washington and Lee: Trammell (l), Carpenter (r), Goldsmith (r), White (r), ends; C. Smith (l), Radulovic (l), Thompson (r), R. Smith (r), tackles; Kerneklian (l), George (l), Conard (r), guards; Waters, Brewer, quarterbacks; Abrams (l), Leister (r), halfbacks; Arnold, fullback.

COTTON

In his pregame remarks, General Bob Neyland of Tennessee had told his men, "You may find yourselves behind at the half (they did, 14 to 7). You might be behind by one or two touchdowns. Don't be discouraged. Keep plugging. Keep your poise and pretty soon you'll cut those big men down to your size. Your chance probably will come in the last quarter."

A couple of days after the Cotton Bowl battle of 1951, the plane carrying Tennessee guard Ted Daffer back to Knoxville—he suffered a ruptured kidney and had been left in a Dallas hospital an extra 48 hours—stopped in Nashville.

At the airport, inside the plane, Daffer told a *Nashville Banner* sports writer, "We could sense the coming victory about midway through the third quarter when we noticed the Texas players walking into position. Our team picked up immediately. We began to roll 'em back."

The Volunteers, in excellent condition—this was the most important factor—scored two touchdowns in the last 11 minutes to conquer the weary Longhorns 20 to 14.

"We were never hit as hard as those guys hit us," said Ken Jackson, 240-pound Texas tackle. Against a fearsome line which had yielded an average of 118 yards rushing during the regular season, Tennessee charged for the whopping total of 295.

Tennessee scored first early in the game after tailback Hank Lauricella gained 75 yards of his net of 131 on a dazzling, serpentine breakaway to the 5. On this play Texas end Don Menasco said he

1951—Tennessee tailback Hank Lauricella at start of his long run against Texas.

was blocked four different times. Herky Payne, Lauricella's replacement, passed for a touchdown to end Johnny Gruble four plays later.

Texas earned its second-quarter touchdowns by cracking the Vols' usually armor-plated punt protection and pass defense.

Tackle Jim Lansford blocked Lauricella's punt from the end zone and guard Don Cunningham recovered for Texas on the 8. Fullback Byron Townsend, a punishing runner, scored from the 5 on fourth down.

That tied it, 7 to 7. Quarterback Ben Tompkins maneuvered the Longhorns 67 yards for their second and last touchdown. His climactic play was a fake jump pass, pulling in the Tennessee secondary. Then he passed 34 yards to halfback Gib Dawson, who made the catch in an end-zone corner.

Thirteen minutes of the third quarter had elapsed when Tennessee, remembering what the general had said, started onward from its 17. Fullback Andy Kozar banged across the goal line from the 5 after staging a one-man parade most of the way. But Pat Shires missed the extra point.

A fumble by Dawson recovered by defensive halfback Jimmy Hill enabled the Vols to launch their victory push from the Texas 43.

Lauricella passed for 23 yards to wingback Bert Rechichar. Then Lauricella and Kozar cleaved the Texas forewall for quick, substantial gains before the final plunge by Andy. It was a one-yard burst. Three minutes and 11 seconds were left.

Lauricella came from a well-to-do New Orleans family.

Kozar, from the coal mining town of St. Michael, Pennsylvania, was one of seven children whose father died when Andy was twelve. His two oldest brothers went to work in the mines so he could get an education. Kozar narrowly escaped death from spinal meningitis in 1945. He was told his football playing days were finished but he resumed the next fall. In time Kozar was awarded a Ph.D. degree.

Another among a number of admirable figures in Tennessee's triumph was Captain Jack Stroud, who played despite a fractured jaw. During the week before the game the tackle's wife fed him four times a day, the last meal at midnight. His food was ground into tiny bits to slip between a tooth hole surrounded by a wire brace.

General Neyland wanted this game as much or more than any in his distinguished career. His bowl record up to 1951—one win in four tries—galled him. He was determined to do something about it.

Tennessee	7	0	0	13	20
Texas	0	14	0	0	14

Tennessee—Touchdowns: Gruble (4, pass from Payne), Kozar 2 (5, right guard; 1, center plunge). Points after touchdown: Shires 2.

Texas—Touchdowns: Townsend (5, left end), Dawson (34, pass from Tompkins). Points after touchdown: Tompkins 2.

STATISTICS

Tennessee		Texas	Tennessee		Texas
Gruble	LE	Procter	18	First downs	12
Stroud	LT	Vykukal	295	Net yards rushing	146
Campbell	LG	McFadin	8	Passes attempted	14
Davis	C	Rowan	3	Passes completed	5
Michels	RG	Arnold	2	Passes had intercepted	1
Haslam	RT	Jackson	45	Net yards passing	97
Kaseta	RE	Stolhandske	340	Total net yards	243
Hahn	QB	Tompkins	6	Number of punts	7
Payne	LH	Shands	32.6	Punting average	29
Rechichar	RH	Dawson	1	Fumbles lost	1
Kozar	FB	Townsend	35	Yards penalized	55

Substitutions—Tennessee: Sherrod (l), Atkins (r), ends; Smith (l), Stokes (l), Pearman (r), Donahue (r), tackles; Daffer (l), Bordinger (l), Holohan (r), Lyons (r), guards; Jasper, center; Sizemore, quarterback; Lauricella (l), Sherrill (l), Shires (l), Maiure (l), Hill (r), Morgan (r), halfbacks; Pruett, Polofsky, Ernsberger, fullbacks. Texas: Georges (l), Menasco (l), Williams (r), Adams (r), ends; Wilson (l), Lansford (r), Milburn (r), tackles; Sewell (l), Cunningham (r), guards; Barton, Reeder, centers; Jones, Page, quarterbacks; Ochoa (l), Dillon (r), Raley (r), halfbacks; Davis, Price, Porter, fullbacks.

SUGAR

"When it had to come, we wanted our record broken by a team we respect," Coach Bud Wilkinson of Oklahoma said after the Sooners' 31-game winning streak was shattered in the 1951 Sugar Bowl spectacular. "I can state sincerely we really believe in Kentucky. We lost to a great team, a great coach, a great school and a great state."

In five of their ten games during the 1950 season Oklahoma had battled from behind to win. When Wilkinson's men scored on a 17-yard pass from Claude Arnold to Merrill Green with seven minutes left in the final quarter, a terrible fear arose in the hearts of 13,000 Kentuckians in the roaring crowd of 82,437.

But the Wildcats controlled the ball for twelve of the last thirteen plays. Oklahoma had it for the game-ending play, a long pass thrown in desperation.

That 13 to 7 stunner was Kentucky's most notable football triumph.

Before the game Coach Paul Bryant sent all underclassmen on the team outside the door and addressed himself to the Kentucky seniors. To them he said: "I want you to give your absolute all. Play till you drop on the field."

At halftime he said very little but warned his players about Oklahoma's comeback reputation. He wound up with: "Let's show 'em we can't be had."

Bryant's preparations and his on-the-field directions were classic.

Kentucky confused and contained Oklahoma's virtually unstoppable split T offense with everything from a four- to a nine-man line. The Wildcats' almost impregnable defense was spearheaded by Walt Yowarsky, 208-pound left tackle.

Yowarsky's prime job was to rush Arnold, Oklahoma's sliding quarterback, on the keep-or-lateral play and force early commitment. Mainly because of the thoroughly jolting manner he undertook his assignment, putting heavy physical and mental pressure on Arnold, Oklahoma's timing was badly upset. This led to seven fumbles. Kentucky recovered five.

Against the Sooners, Yowarsky was a defensive end at times. Also he was a tackle flanking the Wildcats' more publicized tackle, Bob Gain, who, with quarterback Babe Parilli, was a consensus All-America choice. On occasion Oklahoma was confronted by a line that included three tackles, one guard, and two ends. Sometimes four big tackles were in there.

Yowarsky's biggest contributions to the victory were his recovery of Arnold's fumble, followed immediately by Kentucky's first touch-

1951—Oklahoma fullback Leon Heath with the ball and Kentucky end Charlie McClendon (87), a very determined fellow, about to pounce on him. McClendon became head coach at Louisiana State in 1962.

down in the first three minutes; his touchdown-saving tackle of speedster halfback Billy Vessels on the Wildcats' seven in the third quarter; his smearing of Arnold for losses totaling 30 yards and his recovery of safetyman Jack Lockett's punt fumble late in the fourth quarter when possession of the ball meant everything. Yowarsky made numerous tackles.

Halfback Wilbur Jamerson, only five feet, nine inches, leaped above Lockett, 5-11, to grasp Parilli's 22-yard pass in the end zone giving Kentucky a touchdown in the early moments. Yowarsky recovered Arnold's fumble on Oklahoma's 22 to set up the opportunity. The Wildcats scored without a minute's delay.

Later in the period end Ben Zaranka dropped a perfect pass from Parilli—or what appeared to be a perfect pass—over the goal line.

"I had nightmares, just dreaming about doing what happened in front of all those folks in New Orleans," Zaranka said. "A child could have caught that ball. But I missed it."

But Parilli attempted to assume the blame, claiming, "It wasn't a good pass. I threw it over the wrong shoulder. Besides, Ben was off balance when it came to him."

In the second quarter Parilli, who completed nine of 12 throws, dropped two well-placed aerial bombs on Oklahoma territory. He placed the ball in Jamerson's hands for a 16-yard gainer and in end Al Bruno's for 48. That put it on the 1. Jamerson cracked the middle for the touchdown.

It seemed incredible that with 7:04 left in the game after Oklahoma scored, there would be time for only thirteen more plays. But Kentucky approached the time allowance on every run, drew three penalties for delay of game, and got a break when Lockett's punt bobble kept the Sooners from trying for a "home run" until the final play.

Bryant was presented with the game ball by his jubilant players. Asked what he would do with it, the Kentucky coach said, "You know that trophy case back in Lexington where they put all those basketballs (national and conference championship trophies won by Adolph Rupp's teams)? Well, this is going right at the top."

Kentucky	7	6	0	0	13
Oklahoma	0	0	0	7	7

Kentucky—Touchdowns: Jamerson 2 (22, pass from Parilli; 1, center smash). Point after touchdown: Gain.

Oklahoma—Touchdown: Green (17, pass from Vessels). Point after touchdown: Weatherall.

STATISTICS

Kentucky		*Oklahoma*	*Kentucky*		*Oklahoma*
Wooddell	LE	Keller	7	First downs	18
Gain	LT	Weatherall	84	Net yards rushing	189
Donaldson	LG	Horkey	12	Passes attempted	8
Wannamaker	C	Moore	9	Passes completed	3
Ignarski	RG	Mayes	0	Passes had intercepted	1
Yowarsky	RT	Cole	105	Net yards passing	38
Martin	RE	Anderson	189	Total net yards	227
Farley	QB	Arnold	8	Number of punts	6
H. Jones	LH	Vessels	41.7	Punting average	33.4
Jamerson	RH	Gray	0	Fumbles lost	5
Webb	FB	McPhail	40	Yards penalized	30

Substitutions—Kentucky: Zaranka (l), Yowarsky (l), Fucci (l), Mackenzie (l), Fuller (l), Bruno (r), McClendon (r), Fry (r), ends; Mackenzie (l), Lukawski (l), Pope (l), Yowarsky (l), Mackenzie (r), Fuller (r), tackles; Wannamaker (l), James (r), guards; Rogers, Moseley, Fuller, Conde, centers; Parilli, Fucci, H. Jones, Griggs, Jamerson, quarterbacks; Clark (l), Farley (l), Zaranka (l), Jamerson (l), Webb (l), Fry (l), Hamilton (l), Webb (r), Martin (r), L. Jones (r), halfbacks; Leskovar, Wooddell, Conde, Clark, Pope, fullbacks. Oklahoma: Lockett (l), Reddell (r), ends; Janes (l), D. Smith (r), tackles; McNabb (l), F. Smith (r), guards; Catlin, center; Lisak, quarterback; Silva (l), Heatly (l), Green (r), Crawford (r), Lisak (r), halfbacks; Heath, Clark, fullbacks.

ORANGE

Never before had there been a 15 to 14 score in a bowl game.

Bowl games had been won by a safety. But never before had one decided the issue so late.

The situation changed in the Orange Bowl when the Smith boys got together for a bit of end zone rough-and-tumble in 1951.

Sterling Smith, stocky Clemson guard, pulled down Frank Smith, Miami's left halfback, behind the latter's goal line in the last six minutes.

The resultant two points enabled Clemson to overcome a 14 to 13 handicap and win the game.

The safety followed an almost unbelievable series of hard-luck plays and damaging penalties, stunning Miami and the record crowd of 65,181 fans.

With time running out the Hurricanes held Clemson at midfield and forced a punt. Harry Mallios snatched the ball and was off on an electrifying 79-yard sprint for an apparent touchdown. But center Pete Mastellone was detected clipping. Instead of a clinching score, Miami had the ball on its 6.

In two plays the Hurricanes appeared to be out of danger on the 22. However, a penalty for illegal use of the hands by tackle Charlie George was inflicted. The end zone was uncomfortably near again. But halfback Jim Dooley came out to the 19.

Miami's abysmal bad fortune now reached a low that Coach Andy Gustafson and his men found almost unbearable. Clipping was called once more, this one against end Ed Lutes. Back the referee marched to the 4.

On the next play Smith met Smith and suddenly Clemson was ahead.

"Nobody touched me," said the Tigers' Sterling Smith. "The guards pulled out and this guy was back there, so I hit him."

Teammates hugged Smith. They pinned him to the end zone turf for a full minute, pounding his back. When he walked to the bench, Coach Frank Howard grabbed his head and gave it a noisy kiss.

"I'd do this to my muddy ole sow if she'd win football games," Howard explained.

| Clemson | 0 | 7 | 6 | 2 | 15 |
| Miami | 0 | 0 | 14 | 0 | 14 |

Clemson—Touchdowns: Cone (1, right guard), G. Smith (21, pass from Hair of 14, run of 7). Points after touchdown: Radcliff. Safety: S. Smith tackled F. Smith in end zone on play from Miami 4.

Miami—Touchdowns: Mallios (5, right end). F. Smith (17, pass from Hackett of 12, run of 5). Points after touchdown: Watson 2.

STATISTICS

Clemson		Miami	Clemson		Miami
Hudson	LE	Lutes	19	First downs	7
Mooneyhan	LT	Allen	144	Net yards rushing	112
Manos	LG	Arcangeletti	18	Passes attempted	15
Brunson	C	Vari	9	Passes completed	5
DiMucci	RG	Diamond	3	Passes had intercepted	4
Gillespie	RT	George	178	Net yards passing	100
G. Smith	RE	Jelley	322	Total net yards	212
Hendley	QB	Schneidenbach	4	Number of punts	5
Calvert	LH	Smith	30	Punting average	40.2
Mathews	RH	Dooley	1	Fumbles lost	0
Cone	FB	Mallios	20	Yards penalized	55

Substitutions—Clemson: Gaskins (l), Calvert (r), Rushton (r), ends; Patton (l), Grigsby (r), tackles; Rogers (l), Crawford (r), Childress (r), S. Smith (r), guards; Wade, center; Wyndham, quarterback; Cook (l), Hair (l), Knoebel (r), halfbacks; Radcliff, fullback. Miami: Martin (l), Chwalik (r), Schultz (r), Czaplinski (r), ends; David (l), Carapella (r), tackles; Lyden (l), Bartolovich (r), Bouyoucas (r), Mariutto (r), guards; Mastellone, center; Hackett, McDonald, quarterbacks; Del Bello (l), Tremont (l), McCloskey (l), Castagno (l), Watson (l), Vacchio (r), Bow (r), Boxx (r), Tedder (r), halfbacks; Stolk, Shiver, Czaplinski, fullbacks.

ROSE

For constant frustration and recurring bad breaks, no school playing in the Rose Bowl could top California. The Golden Bears suffered—that's the word for it—their third straight hard-luck defeat in succession on January 1, 1951, when Michigan beat them 14 to 6.

It was the Big Ten's fifth consecutive victory in the series and the third fourth-quarter collapse in a row by one of Coach Lynn Waldorf's teams, unbeaten in regular season competition in 1948–49–50.

California was in complete command in the first half. Although leading only 6 to 0, the Bears had outgained Michigan 192 yards to 65, crossed the Wolverines' 20 four times, and planted the ball in the end zone twice.

The touchdown that didn't count came on the second play of the game. Pete Schabarum broke off left tackle and apparently scooted 73 yards for six points. A backfield in motion penalty nullified it.

California was checked on the Michigan 17 and the Wolverines were halted on the Bears' 19 in the first quarter. The first break-through occurred when Ray Solari, defensive California guard, intercepted a pass by tailback Chuck Ortmann on Michigan's 46. Solari brought the ball to the 39 and the Bears scored immediately.

Quarterback Jim Marinos, concealing the ball behind exceptional protection, had plenty of time before sending a long pass aloft. Right end Bob Cummings got a step ahead of fullback Don Dufek, playing defensive left half. Cummings caught the ball on the 7 and scored. Linebacker Les Richter, California's extra point man with a record of 24 conversions in 30 tries, missed with a strange ball holder, Brent Ogden. His regular helper, Dick Lee, was injured and unable to play.

With three minutes remaining in the half, California had traveled 70 yards and had a first down on Michigan's 11. On third down from the 3, Jim Monachino slipped on a cutback over right tackle and lost a yard. The path to the goal line was clear. Schabarum was arrested on the 2. The ball went over to the Wolverines for three time-consuming sneaks by quarterback Bill Putich before the half expired.

In the light of this, and what happened in the second half, when Michigan's offense in an astonishing form reversal gained momentum under Ortmann's command, Braven Dyer's game-story lead in the *Los Angeles Times* the next morning read:

"Credit victory to Ortmann.

Charge defeat to Waldorf."

Dyer wrote: "Waldorf pulled a terrible boner when he failed to order a field goal late in the first half. Most of us smarties upstairs nearly fell out of the press coop when Pappy didn't order a three-pointer on fourth down . . . When I picked Cal, I assumed they'd try to win."

Dick Hyland, Dyer's colleague on the *Times,* was equally upset. He objected to the seven-man line, diamond secondary that he said the Bears stayed in throughout the game ("Ortmann passed them silly in the second half, completing 12 of 16").

The friendly, massive coach of the Golden Bears never alibied, never hit back, and that was characteristic of him.

California, which made ten first downs to Michigan's two in the first half, was out-first-downed, 15 to two, in the last half and out-gained, 226 yards to 52. The Maize and Blue's single-wing offense was brilliantly diversified to keep the Bears off balance, at least in the second half. The screen passes to a flank from Ortmann to Dufek were particularly effective.

With ten minutes to play, Michigan began a push from its 20 that California, despite an estimable stand at the goal line, could not repel. Ortmann made good six of eight passes for 64 yards on the way. One of the most important plays was a third-down screen pass from Ortmann to Dufek with seven yards to go from the Michigan 49. It put Michigan on California's 37. Ortmann connected on 15 of 19 throws for 146 yards in the game, setting a record for most completions.

When the Wolverines arrived at the 4 with a first down there, seven minutes remained.

In the huddle, Putich said, "Dufek got us down here and we're going to let him carry it over." The power wedge play with the line tight was called four straight times. On third down, after Dufek had rammed to the 1, Coach Bennie Oosterbaan sent in tackle Tom Johnson with orders to run Dufek twice more. He was unaware that Putich had already decided to do just that. With only the length of the ball to go on fourth down, Dufek dove to the top of a heap of men and scored. End Harry Allis kicked the extra point.

"I kept my head down all the way," Allis said. "I didn't know it was good until Chuck (Ortmann held the ball) yelled, 'Golly, Harry, it's right through the middle.'"

Time left was 5:37.

Michigan's other touchdown was a virtual gift because California gambled to win on fourth down from its 13 rather than punt out of danger and risk not getting the ball again. Marinos' pass was broken up. It was up to Dufek. On his third try he slid to the right, inside the end, and crossed the goal line seven yards away. Dufek gained 113 yards in 23 whacks.

At halftime, it came out that Michigan captain Allen Wahl, 217-pound right tackle, read the riot act.

"Bennie didn't have to talk to us much," said halfback Leo Koceski. "We knew what he wanted done."

"It looked like two different games," Waldorf said. "They knocked the tar out of us in the fourth period."

Rube Samuelsen, sports adviser of the *Pasadena Independent Star-News* and author of the book *The Rose Bowl Game,* published in 1951, paid a warm tribute to Waldorf in *The Sporting News* when the big man resigned as California coach following the 1956 season.

Samuelsen wrote: "He is forever the gentleman—big physically, as everyone knows, and equally big mentally and spiritually.

"Pappy Waldorf can take defeat more gracefully, sans all alibis, better than any man I have ever known. His loyalty to his friends and associates has at times cost him dearly. Even though some person does him dirt—and some have, even cruelly—Waldorf will raise no hand in retaliation, or even defense . . .

"After his final game as coach of the Golden Bears, the football crowd was talking of Pappy's composure under stress . . . his consideration of the feelings of his fellow men . . . his fine sportsmanship . . . his inspirational influence over his players . . . his ability to take it, unwhimperingly and without apologies.

"There isn't a phony bone in his oversized body."

When Fritz Crisler, Michigan's athletic director, reached the dressing room, he hugged Oosterbaan and yelled, "Bennie, I got a much bigger kick out of having you win this one than out of winning mine three years ago."

"That's funny," Oosterbaan replied. "I think I got a bigger kick when you did it in '48."

The unhappy Pacific Coast Conference, meeting soon after the game, deliberated about withdrawing from Rose Bowl participation. However, a month and a half later member schools voted to continue playing there. In the spring another contract between the Big Ten and Pacific Coast Conference was signed, this one to be in force three years.

Under this agreement, and another three-year renewal announced in 1953, both conferences were in accord that no school would be permitted to make two successive appearances in the Rose Bowl. The original stipulation applied only to the Big Ten and limited members to no more than one trip over a three-year stretch. In 1956 the agreement was approved on an indefinite term basis. It was terminated after the game of January 1, 1960.

The academic year of 1950–51 was the first in conference competition for Michigan State. The Western Conference had become, on May 20, 1949, the Big Ten again for the first time since Chicago dropped out following the season of 1939. Michigan State was admitted to membership almost ten years after Chicago gave up football. However, Michigan State's participation in football didn't begin until 1953 because schedules already drawn extended through 1952.

Michigan	0	0	0	14	14
California	0	6	0	0	6

Michigan—Touchdowns: Dufek 2 (1, right guard; 7, right end). Points after touchdown: Allis 2.

California—Touchdown: Cummings (39, pass from Marinos of 32, run of 7).

STATISTICS

Michigan		California	Michigan		California
Perry	LE	Fitzgerald	17	First downs	12
Johnson	LT	Karpe	145	Net yards rushing	175
Kinyon	LG	Laster	21	Passes attempted	8
Kreager	C	Harris	15	Passes completed	4
Wolter	RG	Bagley	2	Passes had intercepted	0
Wahl (c)	RT	Krueger	146	Net yards passing	69
Allis	RE	Cummings	291	Total net yards	244
Putich	QB	Marinos	2	Number of punts	4
Ortmann	LH	Monachino	32.5	Punting average	33.7
Koceski	RH	Schabarum	2	Fumbles lost	2
Dufek	FB	Olszewski	20	Yards penalized	50

Substitutions—Michigan: Clark (l), Pickard (l), Green (r), Popp (r), ends; Zatkoff (l), Ohlenroth (r), Stribe (r), tackles; McWilliams (l), Strozewski (l), Kelsey (r), Timm (r), Jackson (r), guards; Momsen, Padjen, centers; Palmer, Topor, quarterbacks; Osterman (l), Bradford (r), Peterson (r), halfbacks; Straffon, fullback. California: Minahen (l), Ward (l), Bartlett (l), Beal (r), Parker (r), ends; Gulvin (l), Curran (r), tackles; Solari (l), Mering (l), Richter (r), Wardlaw (r), Ely (r), guards; Groger, Cadenasso, centers; Ogden, Van Heuit, quarterbacks; Pappa (l), Robison (l), West (r), LemMon (r), halfbacks; Baham, Richter, fullbacks.

-1952-

ROSE

"The Illini refused to give the Rose Bowl game back to the Indians."

So read the lead to Braven Dyer's story of Illinois' 40 to 7 trouncing of Stanford. The Indians led at halftime 7 to 6, but gave up five second-half touchdowns, four (27 points) in the final quarter.

The incisive football writer Dick Hyland said Stanford lost because its players trained on malted milks.

"The self-indulgent, taste-tickling Stanford belly-pamperers ATE their way out of yesterday's football game," Hyland wrote.

Two days before the 1952 game, Hyland, visiting the Indians at

Arrowhead Springs, where they "trained" (the quotes are his), reported he saw players "loading up with glass after glass of malted milk.

"This Indian team is made up of seniors who never did get in shape in all three varsity years," he continued. "With little more than 11 minutes played in the second half, Stanford was through. It had nothing left except heart and desire. It fell apart and from there on the game was no contest."

Quarterback Gary Kerkorian, one of the "Armenian Armada" that also included Harry Hugasian, Norm Manoogian, and Chuck Essegian, often connected with his receivers scattered in the bewildered Illinois secondary in the first half. He completed five passes, three to end Bill McColl, on an 84-yard march the first time Stanford got the ball. Hugasian bent the line for the last yard and Kerkorian converted.

That overcame a 6 to 0 Illinois lead. The invaders from the Midwest had also started in high gear. They paraded 76 yards in six plays the first time they had possession. Fullback Bill Tate's 41-yard gallop to the 6 was followed by Pete Bachouros' scoring thrust. For the afternoon, the hard-driving Tate pierced Stanford's defense for 150 yards in 20 totes.

In the first quarter Kerkorian completed all of his six passes for 99 yards. After that he added only 67 more yards in the air.

"What won for us, in my estimation, was adjusting our pass defense between halves," summarized Illinois Coach Ray Eliot. "McColl had us pretty much on the spot in the first half. But we checked him at the line. We also hustled our linebackers out to stop the other pass receivers. This is normally a dangerous maneuver but we weren't too much concerned about Stanford's running game."

The Indians netted only 53 yards on the ground. Fullback Bob Mathias, Olympic decathlon champion, was a crippled player, far from his usual form because of injuries sustained during the season.

The touchdown that actually settled the issue was made possible by the Illini defense in the third quarter. Sophomore back Stan Wallace picked off a Kerkorian pass on the Illinois 34 and fled 54 yards to the Stanford 12. That was the turning point. Tate scored on a five-yard romp around right end. He and Bachouros and Johnny Karras riddled the Indian line in the late moments.

Jack Geyer, a *Los Angeles Times* writer, recalled that time was called once when two small dogs entered a Stanford huddle. "That was when the dogs went to Stanford," Geyer observed. "In the second half the situation was reversed."

Chuck Taylor, the Stanford coach, was smiling after the game. "Why not?" he said. "On another day we might play 'em even."

It was the sixth straight triumph for the Big Ten since the intersectional bowl alliance was formed.

One expert, a former college coach living in California, opined, "I do not believe any western team, since the Big Ten started coming out here, has really taken this game seriously or realized that the Big Ten teams go into the Rose Bowl with blood in their eyes and murder —of the football variety—in their hearts."

TUESDAY, JANUARY 1, 1952

Illinois	6	0	7	27	40
Stanford	7	0	0	0	7

Illinois—Touchdowns: Bachouros (6, right tackle), W. Tate 2 (5, right end; 8, right end), Karras (7, left end), D. Stevens (7, right tackle), Ryan (6, pass from Engels). Points after touchdown: Rebecca 4.

Stanford—Touchdown: Hugasian (1, right guard). Point after touchdown: Kerkorian.

STATISTICS

Illinois		*Stanford*	*Illinois*		*Stanford*
Vernasco	LE	Storum	19	First downs	16
Ulrich	LT	Vick	361	Net yards rushing	53
Studley (c)	LG	Manoogian	15	Passes attempted	29
Sabino	C	Garner	7	Passes completed	14
Gnidovic	RG	Bonetti	1	Passes had intercepted	3
Jenkins	RT	Pyle	73	Net yards passing	180
Smith	RE	McColl	434	Total net yards	233
O'Connell	QB	Kerkorian	2	Number of punts	6
Bachouros	LH	Hugasian	50.5	Punting average	30.3
Karras	RH	Cook	0	Fumbles lost	0
W. Tate	FB	Meyers	43	Yards penalized	50

Substitutions—Illinois: Wodziak (l), Nosek (l), Waldbeser (r), L. Stevens (r), Ryan (r), ends; Berschet (l), Baughman (l), Kasap (l), Weddell (r), D. Tate (r), Peterson (r), tackles; Lenzini (l), Valentino (l), Boerio (r), Ernst (r), Murphy (r), Bauer (r), guards; Popa, Cole, Borman, Luhrsen, centers; Engels, Henss, Rebecca, quarterbacks; D. Stevens (l), Neathery (l), Dusenbury (l), Taliaferro (l), Wallace (r), Miller (r), De Moss (r), halfbacks; Brosky, Duke, fullbacks. Stanford: Rye (l), Morley (l), Hoegh (l), Tennefoss (l), Eadie (r), Steinberg (r), ends; Latham (l), Hokanson (l), Calfee (l), Kirkland (r), Broderick (r), tackles; King (l), Griffin (l), Powell (l), Cone (r), Essegian (r), Powell (r), guards; Tobin, Worley, Tanner, centers; Garrett, Horn, quarterbacks; McKay (l), Thompson (l), Laubscher (r), St. Geme (r), halfbacks; Mathias, Crist, Sanders, fullbacks.

GATOR

Revenge-inspired Miami at least partially erased the bitter memory of its 15 to 14 loss to Clemson in the 1951 Orange Bowl with a 14 to 0 Tiger tail-twisting in the Gator Bowl a year later.

Clemson "out-statisticked" the winners. But Miami never failed to erect a stout defense whenever Clemson threatened seriously to score with its potent single-wing offense, more deceptive than many T attacks.

Jim Dooley, tall (six feet, four inches) Miami halfback, blunted Clemson's usually effective passing weapon by intercepting four passes. He was the choice of almost every sports writer present as the game's outstanding player.

Both touchdowns, one in each of the first two quarters, were scored by fullback Harry Mallios.

Clemson made several deep penetrations. Tailback Billy Hair, victim of Dooley's four interceptions, ran 70 yards to Miami's 26 with the opening kickoff. But the Tigers gave up the ball on the 19 and subsequently on the 8, 18, 11 and 4.

The Hurricanes were slowed to a zephyr in the second half. They made up for it with a stubborn defense and the excellent punting of Elmer Tremont.

It was a memorable triumph for Coach Andy Gustafson, who played football at Pittsburgh under two of the masters, Pop Warner and Jock Sutherland.

Miami	7	7	0	0	14
Clemson	0	0	0	0	0

Miami—Touchdowns: Mallios 2 (11, right end; 2, center leap). Points after touchdown: Tremont 2.

STATISTICS

Miami		Clemson	Miami		Clemson
Lutes	LE	Kempson	5	First downs	14
Chickillo	LT	Mooneyhan	119	Net yards rushing	145
Arcangeletti	LG	Manos	2	Passes attempted	20
Vari	C	Bryant	2	Passes completed	6
Mariutto	RG	DiMucci	0	Passes had intercepted	4
George	RT	Byrd	55	Net yards passing	88
McDonald	RE	Smith	174	Total net yards	233
Hackett	QB	Rodgers	9	Number of punts	4
Taro	LH	Hair	44.5	Punting average	30.5
Dooley	RH	George	0	Fumbles lost	1
Mallios	FB	L. Gressette	30	Yards penalized	0

Substitutions—Miami: Martin (l), Nardulli (r), Pagley (r), Chwalik (r), ends;
French (l), Tassotti (l), Behringer (l), Fisher (r), Buccilli (r), tackles; McCloskey
(l), Wilson (l), Lubas (r), Carlstrom (r), Diamond (r), guards; Payne, Shiver,
Castagno, centers; Melear, Harris, Tremont, quarterbacks; Knust (l), Garri-
gus (l), DeBogory (l), Constantino (r), Vacchio (r), halfbacks; Bow, Schneiden-
bach, Stolk, fullbacks. Clemson: Baker (l), Gentry (l), Gaskins (r), ends; Patton (l), N. Gressette (r), Wrightenberry (r), tackles; Barton (l), Crawford (r),
guards; Wade, center; Pate, Quarles, quarterbacks; Cook (l), Knoebel (r), halfbacks; Shirley, fullback.

COTTON

"Babe Parilli is the only guy I ever had who was quick enough to
make three fakes with his hands, then throw; two is above average,"
Coach Paul Bryant once said.

During his three seasons at Kentucky, Parilli completed 331 of
592 passes for 4,351 yards and 50 touchdowns. In one game his tosses
gained 338 yards. In one season, 1950, his throws clicked for 23
touchdowns.

The Kentucky Babe had one of his less spectacular afternoons
against Texas Christian in the 1952 Cotton Bowl game. But his eight
completions, two of which brought touchdowns on five- and 12-yard
shots to halfback Emery Clark, were enough to gig the Horned Frogs
20 to 7.

The Wildcats repulsed four TCU drives at the 4, 24, 5, and 1—
in order—in the first half while scoring twice themselves on advances
of 53 and 57 yards.

"Their spread formation was deceptive and we had a hard time
stopping it between the 10-yard lines," Bryant said. "Our defense on
the goal line saved us. That's what won the game."

Near the close of the third quarter Texas Christian fullback Bobby
Jack Floyd ran 43 yards for a touchdown. The score was 13 to 7
when Keith Flowers added the extra point. TCU was suddenly very
much alive.

Kentucky ended its followers' disquietude only in the last four
minutes. A short punt into a stiff wind by TCU tailback Ray Mc-
Kown put the Cats in an advantageous position on the Frogs' 26.
They quickly cashed in. Halfback Ed Hamilton slammed across
the goal line from the 4.

A telephone call from a high school coach in western Pennsylvania
landed Vito Parilli, son of a glass maker, on the Kentucky campus.
Bryant had sought another player from Parilli's Rochester, Pa., high
school team, overlooking Babe.

Assured Parilli was the better back by his caller, a coach in the
area in which Babe had played, Bryant took a quick look. He im-

1952—A pass by Babe Parilli about to be caught by Kentucky end Steve Meilinger for a gain against Texas Christian.

mediately offered Parilli a Southeastern Conference grant-in-aid contract.

After Babe had been named the conference's Player of the Year in 1950, Lefty Gomez of New York Yankee fame claimed credit for making the award possible.

"I tried my best to sign him to a Yankee contract and failed," Gomez said.

Kentucky	7	6	0	7	20
Texas Christian	0	0	7	0	7

Kentucky—Touchdowns: Clark 2 (5, pass from Parilli; 12, pass from Parilli), Hamilton (4, left guard). Points after touchdown: H. Jones 2.

Texas Christian—Touchdown: Floyd (43, left end). Point after touchdown: Flowers.

STATISTICS

Kentucky		Texas Christian	Kentucky	Texas Christian
Meilinger	LE	George	13 First downs	15
Netoskie	LT	Hughes	213 Net yards rushing	201
Donaldson	LG	Ramsay	20 Passes attempted	17
Griggs	C	McCormack	8 Passes completed	5
Ignarski	RG	Taylor	1 Passes had intercepted	1
Lukawski	RT	M. Harris	85 Net yards passing	99
Proffitt	RE	Vaught	298 Total net yards	300
Parilli	QB	McKown	6 Number of punts	5
L. Jones	LH	Ray	34.3 Punting average	40.8
H. Jones	RH	Medanich	0 Fumbles lost	1
Leskovar	FB	Floyd	40 Yards penalized	32

Substitutions—Kentucky: Fry (l), Carlig (l), Kirk (l), Zampino (l), Farley (r), Claiborne (r), ends; MacKenzie (l), Harper (l), Smith (l), Fuller (r), Baldwin (r), Burrus (r), tackles; Conde (l), Kirn (l), Bailey (l), Correll (r), Weaver (r), Dyer (r), Spicer (r), guards; Moseley, Rudd, centers; Clark, Hunt, quarterbacks; Hamilton (l), Gruner (l), H. Jones (l), Willard (r), Jirschele (r), Hanley (r), Fillion (r), halfbacks; Adkins, Felch, Hennessey, Lawson, fullbacks. Texas Christian: Blair (l), Martin (l), Rogers (r), ends; Conaway (l), Parrett (l), Williams (r), R. Harris (r), tackles; Buck (l), Lambert (l), Zimmerman (r), Teems (r), guards; Pitcock, Moorman, centers; Fowler, Bartosh, Robinson, quarterbacks; Fraley (l), Harville (r), Jones (r), McFarland (r), Morrow (r), halfbacks; Doty, Flowers, Mattern, fullbacks.

SUGAR

For the second successive year a crown was knocked askew in the Sugar Bowl as Tennessee, elected national champion in 1951, came a cropper at Maryland's brawny hands, 28 to 13.

Paul Menton wrote in the *Baltimore Evening Sun*: "If Jim Tatum coaches until he is twice his present age of 37, I doubt if he will bring a team to as magnificent a performance for a big game as he did his unbeaten Terps. Everything he planned and everything he tried, worked. Tennessee was outclassed from start to finish."

"We had been rated well but not on top," Tatum said. "We had something to prove. Our boys were busting with eagerness. They just soaked up coaching. I've got no greater friend in coaching than General Bob Neyland. It was my greatest thrill to beat his team."

Said Neyland: "As for us, we couldn't get any work out of our boys. They had won the national championship and thought just showing up would be enough to win the game. Maryland came out in a blaze of spirit, rushed our unprepared boys off their feet and sewed up the game in the first half."

The Terrapins' line out-toughed the Volunteers' both ways. Tatum's strategy was to direct his split T to the inside. This Maryland did with 215-pound fullback Ed Modzelewski bashing through Tennessee's outcharged front wall for 153 yards in 28 slams. Modzelewski and his halfback cohorts, Ed Fullerton and Bob Shemonski, pierced the Vol barrier and shot into the secondary time and again. The Terps romped on the ground for 289 yards, 208 more than the Vols.

On defense Maryland wouldn't let Tennessee get to the outside and block for tailback Hank Lauricella, their All-American. The Terps' eight-man line, bulwarked by 235-pound tackle Dick Modzelewski, Ed's brother, stifled the Vols most of the game.

Trying to impress Modzelewski with the caliber of an opposing tackle before one of Maryland's games, an assistant coach said, "He's the biggest and strongest and quickest linemen you'll face." Dick didn't widen an eye.

"He's the smartest, too," the coach said.

"Don't worry," Modzelewski replied. "After I hit him a couple of times he'll be as dumb as I am."

With the score 7 to 0 after Fullerton punctured the middle for two yards to cap a half-the-length-of-the-field drive, a turning point came. Lauricella fumbled on the next kickoff on his 13 when hit thunderously by two Terps and Ed Kensler, Maryland guard, recovered. Overcoming a 15-yard penalty from the 1, Maryland scored again on a surprise fourth-down running pass from Fullerton, who took a pitch-out from quarterback Jack Scarbath, to Shemonski. The play covered seven yards.

The unfortunate Lauricella suffered three interceptions and gained only one yard in seven carries.

"I don't feel half as bad over what happened to us as I do over what happened to Hank," Neyland said immediately following the game.

It was 21 to 0 before Tennessee rallied under Herky Payne's direction to move 70 yards. Before that, though, Payne fumbled when gang-tackled on Tennessee's 47. Scarbath's sharp aim and Mighty Mo's plunges covered 46 yards in seven plays. Scarbath sneaked for the touchdown.

The Vols' dim hopes faded completely late in the third quarter. Fullerton erased them by grabbing an errant Lauricella pass and speeding 46 yards to score on a fine bit of open field running.

Tatum presented his players with what he called their "war helmets" as mementos of the victory. He promised to foot the bill himself.

```
Maryland        7   14   7   0    28
Tennessee       0    6   0   7    13
```

Maryland—Touchdowns: Fullerton 2 (2, right guard; 46, intercepted pass by Lauricella), Shemonski (7, pass from Fullerton), Scarbath (1, sneak). Points after touchdown: Decker 4.

Tennessee—Touchdowns: Rechichar (5, pass from Payne), Payne (2, left tackle). Point after touchdown: Rechichar.

STATISTICS

Maryland		*Tennessee*	*Maryland*		*Tennessee*
Lindsay	LE	J. Davis	18	First downs	12
Moss	LT	Stokes	289	Net yards rushing	81
Ward	LG	Campbell	13	Passes attempted	19
Cosgrove	C	R. Davis	7	Passes completed	9
Ladygo	RG	Michels	1	Passes had intercepted	4
Jones	RT	Haslam	62	Net yards passing	75
Weidensaul	RE	Kaseta	351	Total net yards	156
Scarbath	QB	Hahn	8	Number of punts	7
Shemonski	LH	Lauricella	38	Punting average	43
Fullerton	RH	Rechichar	3	Fumbles lost	2
E. Modzelewski	FB	Ernsberger	120	Yards penalized	20

Substitutions—Maryland: Nestor (l), Crytzer (l), Colteryahn (l), Fox (r), Alderton (r), Mahoney (r), ends; R. Modzelewski (l), Fry (l), Christianson (r), Fry (r), Morgan (r), tackles; Hurd (l), Navarro (l), Maletzky (l), Stankus (r), Boeri (r), Kensler (r), Decker (r), guards; Fincke, Keith, Lattimer, Trexler, centers; DeStefano, Faloney, Beightol, quarterbacks; Hanulak (l), Petruzzo (l), David (l), Martine (l), Horning (r), Nolan (r), Felton (r), halfbacks; Cianelli, Scioscia, Martine, fullbacks. Tennessee: Franklin (l), Sekanovich (l), Alexander (r), Kolenik (r), Atkins (r), ends; Herrmann (l), Pearman (l), Fisher (r), Boring (r), Munro (r), tackles; Holohan (l), Powell (l), Bordinger (r), Myers (r), Daffer (r), guards; Barbish, Jasper, centers; Rechichar, quarterback; Payne (l), Blackstock (l), Maiure (l), Crowson (l), Hyde (r), Morgan (r), Wade (r), halfbacks; Kozar, Polofsky, Byrd, fullbacks.

ORANGE

Franklin (Pepper) Rodgers, an uninhibited quarterback, told Bobby Dodd two days before Georgia Tech encountered Baylor in the Orange Bowl, "Coach, maybe I'll kick one that will win the game."

With three minutes remaining and the score tied, Rodgers did precisely that. His toe won it, 17 to 14, in 1952.

The irrepressible Rodgers threw up his arms first as if empowered to signal it was good, although referee F. C. Baccus was still studying the ball's flight and awaiting confirmation on the length from an official in the end zone.

That launched Georgia Tech and Dodd on an unprecedented series of six straight bowl victories in as many seasons.

What accounted for Tech's extraordinary success, apart from fine material and coaching, and perhaps a break or two here and there?

For one thing, no other team had quite as much fun on bowl trips or practiced less.

Dodd's theory is that a bowl invitation is a reward for a good season's work. Also, he thinks a team can become stale by overpracticing in December.

"The boys should be allowed to enjoy themselves as much as possible," Bobby said. "We've sold them on it. We have confidence in that plan. But I'm not saying my idea would work everywhere."

His players were given ten days' Christmas vacation usually, sometimes a day or two longer.

"There's one thing I ask of them while they're at home," Dodd said. "I want them to run on their own. I'm almost a fanatic in my belief football players' legs should be in good shape.

"When we make these trips, we try to give them as much entertainment as possible. We've done that wherever we've gone. Our experience has been that the boys appreciate all this.

"All I ask is that they bear down in their workouts, get plenty of sleep and have a good time—within reason. They've never let me down."

Baylor expended its energy early to take a 14 to 7 halftime lead over the Southeastern Conference co-champions (with Tennessee). The Yellow Jackets' resurgence was attributable in part, Dodd said, to an "Orange Bowl system" of having his men save their strength for a second-half offensive. He played his reserves much of the first 30 minutes.

Tech took charge in the 79 degree temperature in the fourth quarter. Pitch-outs and line stabs off Dodd's "belly T" series, stopped by hard tackles previously, functioned for vital yardage.

The Jackets' tying touchdown drive began on their 41 with ten minutes left. Effective running by Leon Hardeman, Bill Teas, and Darrell Crawford brought Tech to the Baylor 7 where it was fourth down and three yards to go. Crawford nailed end Buck Martin over the middle in the end zone for the touchdown. Rodgers converted for a tie with six minutes, 15 seconds to play.

On the third play after the kickoff, end Pete Ferris intercepted a flat pass by Baylor's talented quarterback, Larry Isbell, on Tech's 36 and ran 55 yards to the Bears' 9. He would have gone all the way but for bumping into a teammate and going down.

Three plays picked up only three yards whereupon Rodgers kicked his field goal with the ball touched down on the 14 by Charlie Brannon. It was made from a difficult angle.

Always quick to glorify his linemen, Dodd said, "Our big, fast defensive team won for us in the second half."

Dodd's teams in the fifties won more games than any other Southeastern Conference school. It wasn't until January 2, 1960, that a Tech team of his lost in a bowl. His men won eight successive bowl games between 1947 and 1956.

Georgia Tech	7	0	0	10	17
Baylor	7	7	0	0	14

Georgia Tech—Touchdowns: Hardeman (3, left end), Martin (7, pass from Crawford). Field goal: Rodgers (24, placekick). Points after touchdown: Rodgers 2.

Baylor—Touchdowns: Parma (1, center plunge), Coody (4, left tackle). Points after touchdown: Brocato 2.

STATISTICS

Georgia Tech		Baylor	Georgia Tech		Baylor
Knox	LE	Williams	9	First downs	17
Snyder	LT	Knowles	107	Net yards rushing	206
Gossage	LG	Bates	14	Passes attempted	18
Brown	C	Sisco	6	Passes completed	8
Beck	RG	Driver	1	Passes had intercepted	3
Lyons	RT	Dowden	84	Net yards passing	93
Martin	RE	Riley	191	Total net yards	299
Crawford	QB	Isbell	7	Number of punts	6
Hardeman	LH	Carpenter	35.3	Punting average	34.3
Hicks	RH	Coody	1	Fumbles lost	0
Maloof	FB	Parma	60	Yards penalized	85

Substitutions—Georgia Tech: Williams (l), Ferris (r), Jones (r), Trainer (r), ends; Thaden (l), Bennett (l), Sherman (l), Wheat (r), Miller (r), tackles; Vereen (l), Shuler (l), Vines (l), Banks (r), Carithers (r), guards; G. Morris, Hunt, Inman, centers; Davis, Rodgers, quarterbacks; Moorhead (l), Patterson (l), Pretz (l), Redford (l), Brannon (r), Grant (r), Teas (r), Ruffin (r), halfbacks; L. Morris, Young, Turner, fullbacks. Baylor: Black (l), Trout (r), Speer (r), Hopkins (r), ends; Welch (l), Casner (r), tackles; Athey (l), Calhoun (r), Hancock (r), Erben (r), S. Davis (r), guards; Galloway, center; J. Reid (l), C. Jones (l), R. Reid (l), G. Jones (r), Davidson (r), Sherman (r), Schleuning (r), halfbacks; Brocato, J. Davis, fullbacks.

– 1953 –

ORANGE

New Year's Day, 1953, was the first on which football fans could see, through the medium of television, bowl games in Pasadena, Dallas, New Orleans, and Miami. Receipts increased greatly with bigger checks for competing schools and their conference brethren.

Alabama crushed Syracuse, champion of the East, 61 to 6, in the Orange Bowl. Many in the crowd of 66,280 left in the third quarter so they could see more of other bowl games on TV at home.

Because the game was lasting so long, an Orange Bowl committeeman reportedly approached the timekeeper and suggested the game, nearly three hours old at the time, might be speeded up because it was about to be cut off the network.

Fifteen records were set in the fiasco. Even the deepest Alabama substitutes among the 46 Crimson Tide players were record-minded. "We didn't want to leave any still standing," explained tackle Van Marcus.

Alabama rushed for 286 yards and passed for 300. Its total offense of 586 yards and the sum of 818 for both teams were among the Orange Bowl records.

It was a close contest for a quarter when Alabama led, 7 to 6. After two periods the score was 20 to 6. And in the second half, "I just couldn't stop them," said Coach Harold (Red) Drew, a native of Maine who came to Alabama as end coach under Frank Thomas and developed Don Hutson, Paul Bryant, and Holt Rast, among others.

Bobby Marlow, who scored the Tide's second touchdown, was one of the finest running backs in Southeastern Conference history. In three years he gained 2,560 yards. That was 693 yards more than the next highest total in the conference in the 1950–59 period made by Billy Cannon of Louisiana State. But Marlow was not picked on the all-decade team in the conference.

Soon after the game the Orange Bowl committee signed contracts with the Big Eight (then Big Seven) and the Atlantic Coast Conference. Their representatives met for the next five years.

THURSDAY, JANUARY 1, 1953

Alabama	7	14	20	20	61
Syracuse	6	0	0	0	6

Alabama—Touchdowns: Luna 2 (27, pass from Hobson; 38, right tackle), Marlow (1, left tackle), Tharp (50, pass from Hobson of 38, run of 12), Lewis 2 (1, center; 30, center), Cummings (22, pass from Starr), Ingram (80, punt return), Hill (60, intercepted pass by Stark). Points after touchdown: Luna 7.

Syracuse—Touchdown: Szombathy (15, pass from Stark of 7, run of 8).

STATISTICS

Alabama		*Syracuse*	*Alabama*		*Syracuse*
Curtis	LE	Ronan	25	First downs	15
Marcus	LT	McClelland	286	Net yards rushing	75
Watford	LG	Rahal	34	Passes attempted	34
Phillips	C	Ringo	22	Passes completed	17
Mims	RG	Beyer	2	Passes had intercepted	5
Smalley	RT	Fleck	300	Net yards passing	157
Ivy	RE	Szombathy	586	Total net yards	232
Hobson	QB	Stark	3	Number of punts	8
Luna	LH	Leberman	30.0	Punting average	35.0
Marlow	RH	Hoffman	2	Fumbles lost	0
Lewis	FB	Wetzel	45	Yards penalized	42

Substitutions—Alabama: Tillman (l), Stewart (l), Lambert (l), Willis (r), Lynch (r), Germanos (r), Cummings (r), ends; Youngleman (l), Mason (l), Shipp (l), Hunt (l), Culpepper (r), Williams (r), tackles; Richardson (l), Eckerly (r), Wilga (r), Davis (r), Emmons (r), guards; DeLaurentis, Snoderly, centers; Wilson, Starr, quarterbacks; Pharo (l), Tharp (l), Oliver (l), Ingram (l), Stone (l), Wilson (r), Conway (r), McBride (r), Hollis (r), Duke (r), halfbacks; Carrigan, Kilroy, Malcolm, Lee, fullbacks. Syracuse: Lessard (l), Karilivacz (l), Yaple (r), Rich (r), Jaso (r), ends; Reimer (l), George (r), Skop (r), Kernaklian (r), tackles; T. Vergara (l), Harshbarger (l), Johnson (l), Skyinskus (r), Perry (r), Cappadona (r), guards; Slick, center; Yancey (l), Dobrowolski (l), Alexander (l), Perkins (r), Hadjis (r), Troilo (r), Brenneman (r), halfbacks; Karilivacz, Althouse, A. Vergara, Voelger, fullbacks.

ROSE

And so, after six long years, and a sequence of beatings by a combined score of 185 to 55, the Pacific Coast Conference finally triumphed over the Big Ten in the Rose Bowl.

Southern California turned back Wisconsin 7 to 0 in 1953 and restored a measure of dignity to the downtrodden Far West.

Few men in sport have attained the variety of distinctions that came to Jesse Hill, coach of the Trojans.

He was a Southern California fullback on the 1930 Rose Bowl winner, a major league outfielder for several years (he hit a home run in his first game), coach of two successive national championship track teams at his alma mater, coach of a conference football champion, and Rose Bowl victor.

In the third quarter tailback Rudy Bukich lofted a 22-yard pass to halfback Al Carmichael in the end zone for the game's only touchdown.

Bukich spent most of his career as an understudy. He got his biggest chance in the Rose Bowl. Jim Sears was forced from the game after only four minutes of action with a broken leg. Rudy came through impressively. He completed 12 of 20 passes for 137 yards.

Alan (The Horse) Ameche, Wisconsin's hard driving fullback who gained 3,345 yards in four seasons of collegiate eligibility, pounded around the left side and ran 54 yards to Southern California's 33 on the first play of the second half.

But, after the Badgers had pressed ahead to the 21, Roy Burks fumbled when tackled vehemently by tackle Bob Van Doren and end Bob Hooks recovered for the Trojans on the 27.

That scare having been withstood, Southern California threw the works at Wisconsin in a follow-up 73-yard offensive ending in the touchdown. En route, Bukich made good five of his six passes for 66 yards against a leaky aerial defense and a line that didn't rush him.

The Trojans' rugged defensive unit had to dig in subsequently to repel the aroused Badgers.

Right after the touchdown, Wisconsin charged 84 yards before being checked on the 2. The Badgers reached the Southern California 15 and 24 as the tension of 101,500 fans mounted in the final quarter. Wisconsin outgained the Trojans' "horse and buggy" single wing, as Hill described it, 211 yards to 48, on the ground. Ameche accounted for 133 yards. But the Trojans were immovable when their goal line was seriously menaced.

One of the main reasons Southern California won was the long distance punting of Bukich and Des Koch. Bukich's only punt traveled 60 yards. Koch got off one for 72 yards and had an average of 50.9 yards on seven kicks.

Luckily for the Far West, Michigan State, voted national champion, had been admitted to the Big Ten in 1949 but wasn't eligible for conference participation in football until 1953.

Arch Ward, *Chicago Tribune* sports editor, wrote prophetically: "Let's give Southern California its due because it may be another

seven years before we'll have an opportunity to congratulate a Pacific
Coast team for victory in the Rose Bowl."
It was.

Southern California	0	0	7	0	7
Wisconsin	0	0	0	0	0

Southern California—Touchdown: Carmichael (22, pass from Bukich). Point
after touchdown: Tsagalakis.

STATISTICS

Southern California		*Wisconsin*	*Southern California*		*Wisconsin*
Miller	LE	Peters	16	First downs	19
Thompson	LT	Prchlik	48	Net yards rushing	211
Willhoite	LG	Steinmetz	27	Passes attempted	26
Welsh (c-c)	C	Simkowski	18	Passes completed	11
Cox	RG	Stensby	2	Passes had intercepted	2
Weeks	RT	Suminski	185	Net yards passing	142
Nickoloff	RE	Andrykowski	233	Total net yards	353
Bozanic	QB	Haluska	8	Number of punts	5
Sears	LH	Hutchinson	52	Punting average	39.2
Carmichael	RH	Witt	0	Fumbles lost	1
Sellers	FB	Ameche	62	Yards penalized	20

Substitutions—Southern California: Hattig (l), Stillwell (l), Hooks (r), Petty
(r), ends; Ane (l), Ashcraft (l), Fouch (l), Van Doren (c-c) (r), Da Re (r), tackles;
Pucci (l), Peviani (r), Pavich (r), guards; Timberlake, center; Goux, Riddle,
quarterbacks; Bukich (l), Welch (l), Dandoy (l), Crow (r), Kirkland (r), Exley
(r), halfbacks; Han, Koch, Tsagalakis, fullbacks. Wisconsin: Wuhrman (l),
Esser (l), Lundin (l), Voss (r), Locklin (r), ends; Hoegh (l), Ursin (l), Berndt (r),
Martin (r), Gulseth (r), tackles; Kennedy (l), Brandt (l), O'Brien (r), Amund-
sen (r), guards; Durkin, Messner, centers; Hable, quarterback; Canny (l), Carl
(l), Shwaiko (l), Gingrass (l), Dornburg (r), Burks (r), halfbacks; Lamphere,
Dixon, fullbacks.

GATOR

Photographic coverage of the 1953 Gator Bowl game was memorable. A touching shot showed a Tulsa player kneeling on the sideline, head in his hands, weeping. It was used in many daily newspapers throughout the country.

Tom Miner, 215-pound Tulsa end, was the player, giving way to
an emotion of the moment.

He had just missed a field goal attempt from the Florida 11 with
two minutes and 55 seconds to play. His team lost, 14 to 13.

Miner was successful on 41 of 45 extra point tries during the season, best mark in the nation. But he had failed after Tulsa's second touchdown, too, which added to his grief.

Except for a penalty against Tulsa following Florida's second touchdown, Miner might not have felt so low. Marvin Matuszak, Tulsa guard and most valuable player for the Golden Hurricane, was charged with illegal use of the arms on the extra point try. Fullback Rick Casares had missed. Given another chance, he made it. Casares had converted after the Gators' first touchdown also.

Tulsa led all major colleges two straight years in total offense with the combined total of 9,948 yards. Coach J. O. (Buddy) Brothers' team scored 328 points in 1952.

But the Golden Hurricane was held in check in the first half, which belonged to Florida, 14 to 0. The Gators scored after two ten-play drives of 78 and 80 yards.

"We loosened our defense in the second half, expecting a lot of passes," Florida Coach Bob Woodruff said. "That's when Tulsa's ground game got rolling."

The halves were like two different games.

Florida capitalized on the biggest break to win in its first bowl appearance.

Florida	7	7	0	0	14
Tulsa	0	0	6	7	13

Florida—Touchdowns: Casares (1, center plunge), Hall (37, pass from Robinson of 13, run of 24). Points after touchdown: Casares 2.

Tulsa—Touchdowns: Roberts (3, right guard), Waugh (4, center plunge). Point after touchdown: Miner.

STATISTICS

Florida		Tulsa	Florida		Tulsa
King	LE	Miner	20	First downs	17
Douglas	LT	Vaughn	233	Net yards rushing	182
Hammock	LG	Hamm	11	Passes attempted	16
Carlton	C	Haas	7	Passes completed	10
May	RG	Matuszak	1	Passes had intercepted	1
Hunter	RT	Reiber	101	Net yards passing	132
O'Brien	RE	W. Roberts	334	Total net yards	319
Dickey	QB	Morris	1	Number of punts	4
Hall	LH	Kercher	38	Punting average	31
Long	RH	Holladay	4	Fumbles lost	1
Casares	FB	Waugh	34	Yards penalized	84

Substitutions—Florida: Horton (l), Balas (l), Manning (l), Kelly (r), Brown (r), Bilyk (r), Sarris (r), Cason (r), ends; LaPradd (l), Medved (l), Kennedy (l), Dahlke (l), Taylor (l), Hatch (r), Chapman (r), Burke (r), tackles; Wright (l), York (l), Chambers (l), D'Agostino (r), Martin (r), Morris (r), Brooks (r), Haygood (r), guards; Jumper, Annis, Dyal, DeLaTorre, Jones, centers; Nichols, Robinson, Wing, Hurse, Lance, quarterbacks; Davis (l), Oosterhoudt (l), Ives (l), Smith (l), Scott (r), Haddock (r), Burgess (r), Burroughs (r), halfbacks; Ware, Quinn, Mueth, Sumner, Stevens, Bass, Schwartzburg, fullbacks. Tulsa: Fabris (l), Pawloski (l), Mantero (l), Cook (r), Austin (r), Kamins (r), ends; Harrawood (l), Prewett (l), Lewon (l), Price (l), St. Clair (r), DePaepe (r), Shrum (r), Brasher (r), tackles; Welch (l), Nolan (l), Kowalski (l), Gilmer (r), Guzzo (r), guards; Hoefling, Malicki, centers; Hudspeth, Finks, Stanton, quarterbacks; Travnick (l), Kelly (l), Hughes (r), J. Roberts (r), Kmet (r), halfbacks; Wells, Walker, fullbacks.

COTTON

Saddened legions of Tennesseans headed home from Dallas on January 2, 1953, still hating to admit what happened to their Volunteers in the Cotton Bowl.

They could have summed it up in a very few words.

To put it plainly, Texas simply booted the stuffing out of Tennessee.

The Vols' single-wing offense was shackled almost as effectively as if each man had been handcuffed. Tennessee backs were thrown in reverse fourteen times for losses of 85 yards. They drove forward 71 yards. The net loss on the ground was 14 yards.

Tennessee's defense, ranked first in the nation statistically in 1952, having allowed 166.7 yards per game, gave up 301. Quick openers with Gib Dawson and Billy Quinn carrying the ball mixed with the power thrusts of fullback Dick Ochoa caved in that defense.

Though the score was not humiliating, the manner in which the Longhorns, coached by Ed Price, earned their 16 to 0 victory was.

Texas played Tennessee-style football in one sense. Their defense forced critical mistakes. Then their offense moved in to capitalize swiftly. That's how Texas got all its points. That's how Tennessee usually gets hers. But not in this game.

The Longhorns' militant defense was headed by burly guard Harley Sewell, 215-pound senior who played 55 minutes. His fierce blocking, tackling, and rushing were something to see.

The first quarter was extraordinary. Tennessee had the ball for exactly two plays.

Dropping back for an end-zone punt the first time the Vols went on offense from their 5, tailback Dave Griffith fumbled the snapback. Charging Texans swarmed over Griffith and downed him for a safety.

Next time Tennessee had the ball, fullback Ray Byrd was separated from it on his 22. Tackle Cliff Polk made the recovery. It was a seven-point break for the Longhorns because Dawson scored seven plays later on a four-yard right end run.

Texas linebacker Jim Rosser smothered tailback Pat Oleksiak's fumble on Tennessee's 26 in the fourth quarter. The Longhorns' offense with unspectacular but consistent gainers bent back the Vols' line. On the seventh jab Quinn cracked tackle for the final inch.

"We just got beat badly," said General Bob Neyland with usual candor. "They kept the pressure on us all the time, never gave us a chance."

Price explained, "We had our linemen slicing and slanting instead of moving straight ahead. It was a gamble but it worked."

Texas line coach J. T. King said, "They like for defensive ends to float wide so they can be blocked out easily. We smashed ours and made their backs cut quickly, in or out."

Ailing with liver trouble, Neyland had turned over his team's bowl preparations to backfield coach Harvey Robinson. He announced on December 30 that Robinson would be in command against Texas but that he (the general) would be instantly available for advice.

Robinson, whom Neyland had previously designated as his eventual successor, became head coach in 1953. The general retired from coaching to devote his energies to the athletic directorship. His remarkable 21-year record included 173 triumphs, 31 defeats, and 12 ties.

Neyland once said, "I have tried to teach my men to accept defeat as a stepping stone to victory, to accept victory without gloating and to accept defeat without bitterness."

The single-wing master died March 28, 1962, in a New Orleans hospital.

Texas	2	7	0	7	16
Tennessee	0	0	0	0	0

Texas—Touchdowns: Dawson (4, right end), Quinn (1, right tackle). Points after touchdown: Dawson 2. Safety: Griffith fumbled center snap on punt formation from Tennessee 5, tackled in end zone by Massey and Price.

STATISTICS

Texas		Tennessee	Texas		Tennessee
Spring	LE	Davis	20	First downs	6
Lansford	LT	Mayock	269	Net yards rushing	−14

Texas		Tennessee	Texas		Tennessee
Sewell	LG	Campbell	8	Passes attempted	6
McDonald	C	Vest	2	Passes completed	3
Branch	RG	Michels	1	Passes had intercepted	0
Genthner	RT	Ussery	32	Net yards passing	46
Stolhandske	RE	Kolenik	301	Total net yards	32
Jones	QB	Hubbard	5	Number of punts	7
Dawson	LH	Griffith	35.4	Punting average	40.0
Quinn	RH	Morgan	3	Fumbles lost	3
Ochoa	FB	Byrd	55	Yards penalized	30

Substitutions—Texas: Kitchens (l), Massey (l), Georges (l), Moon (l), McMurry (r), ends; McGraw (l), Taylor (l), Gawlik (l), Petrovich (r), Polk (r), Miller (r), Kalmus (r), tackles; Johnson (r), Allen (r), guards; Reeder, Barton, Younger, centers; Andrews, quarterback; Parkinson (l), Kelley (l), Raley (l), Anglin (l), Graham (l), Pace (r), Pierson (r), Ingraham (r), Smith (r), Honeycutt (r), halfbacks; Price, Cameron, Matthews, Rosser, Cline, White, Delaney, fullbacks. Tennessee: Sekanovich (l), Franklin (l), Rotroff (r), Gust (r), ends; Fisher (l), McCord (l), Williams (l), Atkins (r), tackles; Holohan (l), McCroskey (l), Adams (r), Myers (r), guards; Moeller, Griesbach, centers; Beutel, Garner, Maiure, quarterbacks; Wade (l), Brengle (l), Godzak (l), Shires (l), Oleksiak (l), Hyde (r), Martin (r), halfbacks; Leachman, Barbish, Schwanger, fullbacks.

SUGAR

Georgia Tech's 24 to 7 victory over Mississippi in the 1953 Sugar Bowl game prompted Bobby Dodd to say of his eminently successful team: "It isn't just the best I ever coached; it's the best I ever saw."

The Yellow Jackets were unbeaten and untied in 12 games.

Both teams were liberally supplied with nationally famous players. One of the Ole Miss Rebels who did not receive wide acclaim, although he led his team in average gain per carry, was Dick Westerman. As a junior, playing against Vanderbilt in 1951, Westerman received a severe head blow. He suffered convulsions and might have died on the field but for emergency treatment by Dr. Brant (Pinky) Lipscomb, Vanderbilt's team physician.

Against speedy, spirited, versatile Ole Miss, Tech didn't get the upper hand until near the end of the first half. The Jackets had to fight off the Rebels twice, on separate drives, within inches of the goal line.

On both occasions, Tech stopped Wilson Dillard, who had scored an early touchdown. Concerning the Jackets' first stand, Ole Miss Coach Johnny Vaught said, "That ball was over but they (the officials) pushed it back two inches. Another score at that time would have meant a different game."

Tech linebacker Larry Morris, who was in a position to see, admitted, "It was mighty close. It could have been called either way."

The Jackets tied the score in the second quarter, the touchdown coming on a one-yard sneak by quarterback Bill Brigman. Then, as the half was ending with Tech on the Ole Miss 6, where a 64-yard drive appeared to be stalled, quarterback Pepper Rodgers booted a field goal with the ball touched down on the 12. It was the second of Rodgers' three field goals in as many bowl games.

Leon Hardeman, a five-foot, six-inch ball-toting wizard with a knack for keeping his feet when hit or bumped, scored for the Jackets in the third quarter. He glided through right tackle from the 6. End Jeff Knox caught a 24-yard touchdown pass thrown by Rodgers in the fourth period.

"Our two goal line stands were the key to the victory," Dodd said. "Our defensive team won the game for us."

What probably saved the game for Tech was an adjustment directed by the coaches in the first half. Instead of rushing slick quarterback Jimmy Lear in a straight-ahead manner, allowing him to emerge from his pocket and pass or run, Jacket ends were instructed to come in from the outside. With the linebackers taking care of the middle, this forced Lear back and deadened the Rebels' most powerful weapon.

Tech's triumph was more than just a football game won. Dodd's considerate way of handling boys seemed to be making a joke of harsh discipline. And the result was a tremendous victory for all wifedom.

It was a resounding slap in the face to all who claim that marriage is a handicap to college football players. There was Tech with twenty-one wives, four of them Christmas brides. Dodd thought the New Orleans trip would make for a nice honeymoon.

Ed Danforth noted, "The Yellow Jackets saw the sights as thoroughly as any visitors, yet without losing sleep or condition."

| Georgia Tech | 0 | 10 | 7 | 7 | 24 |
| Mississippi | 7 | 0 | 0 | 0 | 7 |

Georgia Tech—Touchdowns: Brigman (1, sneak), Hardeman (6, right tackle), Knox (24, pass from Rodgers). Field goal: Rodgers (22, placekick). Points after touchdown: Rodgers 3.

Mississippi—Touchdown: Dillard (1, center plunge). Point after touchdown: Lear.

STATISTICS

Georgia Tech		Mississippi		Georgia Tech	Mississippi
Knox	LE	Slay	16	First downs	15
Lyons	LT	Trauth	194	Net yards running	137
Gossage	LG	Gary	18	Passes attempted	23
Brown	C	Beatty	10	Passes completed	11
Shoemaker	RG	Caldwell	1	Passes had intercepted	3
Miller	RT	Gilbert	101	Net yards passing	150
Martin	RE	Powell	295	Total net yards	287
Brigman	QB	Lear	6	Number of punts	7
Hardeman	LH	Dillard	41.8	Punting average	35.4
Teas	RH	Westerman	2	Fumbles lost	3
Turner	FB	Lofton	42	Yards penalized	60

Substitutions—Georgia Tech: Young (l), Hensley (l), Sennett (l), Willis (l), Trainer (r), Austin (r), Jones (r), Durham (r), Davis (r), ends; Thaden (l), Humphreys (l), Givens (l), Phenix (l), Hall (l), Hunsinger (r), Sherman (r), West (r), Banks (r), Akins (r), Daugherty (r), tackles; Vereen (l), Theodocion (l), Carithers (l), Spears (l), Shuler (r), Frey (r), Banks (r), guards; Johnson, Inman, G. Morris, centers; Teas, Rudolph, Young, Patterson, Rodgers, Davis, Edge, quarterbacks; Rhino (l), Wright (l), J. L. Morris (l), Pretz (l), Moorhead (l), Ruffin (r), Gilliland (r), Patterson (r), Pretz (r), Brannon (r), Hall (r), halfbacks; Ruffin, Wright, Johnson, Hunt, L. Morris, fullbacks. Mississippi: Bridges (l), Mask (l), Yelverton (l), Truett (l), Adams (r), Harris (r), Parker (r), Dickerson (r), ends; Montgomery (l), Weiss (l), Morganti (l), Burleson (r), Linton (r), McKinney (r), tackles; D. Ott (l), May (l), James (l), Brashier (r), Mims (r), Jernigan (r), guards; Hitt, Ingram, Shepherd, centers; Spiers, Reed, Mangum, Patton, quarterbacks; Mangum (l), Childres (l), R. Ott (l), Pasley (l), Patton (l), Matthews (r), Kelly (r), Blair (r), Kinard (r), Muirhead (r), R. Ott (r), Paslay (r), halfbacks; Tuggle, Brenner, Mangum, McCool, Childres, Beatty, fullbacks.

– 1954 –

SUGAR

The 1954 Sugar Bowl match between Georgia Tech and West Virginia was denounced severely by Lloyd Glaudi, *New Orleans Item* sports editor. He referred to it as the "Lemon Bowl," refused to attend, and, instead, stayed at home to watch other bowl games on television. The next day he wrote that he was fortunate not to have gone to the Sugar Bowl game.

However, 76,000 others showed up and saw Georgia Tech complete 20 of 35 passes for 268 yards in a 42 to 19 walkaway. It could have been worse. Dodd was merciful. He issued orders to stay on the ground most of the second half and used his first team only briefly. Tech amassed 233 yards by air in the first two quarters.

Pepper Rodgers had a field day. Against the bulky West Virginia Mountaineers, he made contact on 16 of 26 throws for a total of 195 yards. The Yellow Jackets' first three touchdowns were scored on passes hurled by Rodgers. He pitched to seven receivers in the first half.

West Virginia had set defenses to stop Tech's end sweeps and line blasts off the belly-T offense. The Mountaineers were caught flat-footed by the aerial bombardment.

"Our boys couldn't get their reflexes working fast enough to stop those passes," Coach Art Lewis said shortly after the game, tears welling in his eyes. "We thought we'd get beat, but not by that much."

To West Virginia's credit, it might have been closer. After the Jackets' first touchdown, Tommy Allman whipped through left tackle and sped 60 yards to cross the goal line. The touchdown was nullified by a backfield-in-motion penalty.

There seemed to be a tremor in Dodd's voice as he talked to his victorious squad. He read a telegram to Rodgers that had been delivered to him (Dodd). The wire read: "I am proud of you, daddy." It was signed "Ricky," Pepper's six-month-old son. It was suspected that Ricky's grandfather, Franklin R. Rodgers, Jr., of Atlanta, knew quite a lot about the contents of the message.

Dodd bitterly opposed the new rule, in effect in 1953, which re-established the two-way player and prohibited unlimited substituting. Bobby argued that the two-platoon system had given fans the wide-open game they desired, made it possible for coaches to develop more highly skilled players, and permitted more boys to participate.

But he went right on winning.

FRIDAY, JANUARY 1, 1954

Georgia Tech	14	6	9	13	42
West Virginia	0	6	0	13	19

Georgia Tech—Touchdowns: Hensley (21, pass from Rodgers), Durham (2, pass from Rodgers), Hair (5, pass from Rodgers), Hardeman (26, right tackle), Ruffin (43, left end), Teas (9, left tackle). Field goal: Rodgers (26, placekick). Points after touchdown: Rodgers 2, Turner.

West Virginia—Touchdowns: Williams (5, right end), Marconi (1, center plunge), Allman (1, right guard). Point after touchdown: Allman.

STATISTICS

Georgia Tech		*West Virginia*	*Georgia Tech*		*West Virginia*
Hensley	LE	Papetti	20	First downs	19
E. Gossage	LT	Bosley	170	Net yards rushing	223
O. Vereen	LG	Lamone	35	Passes attempted	18
L. Morris	C	Orders	20	Passes completed	7
Shoemaker	RG	Huff	2	Passes had intercepted	2
Sherman	RT	R. Starkey	268	Net yards passing	78
Davis	RE	Marker	438	Total net yards	301
Rodgers	QB	Jarrett	1	Number of punts	2
Brannon	LH	Stone	36	Punting average	28.5
Teas	RH	Marconi	1	Fumbles lost	4
Turner	FB	Allman	45	Yards penalized	35

Substitutions—Georgia Tech: Durham (l), Trainer (l), Sennett (l), Hair (r), Trainer (r), Jones (r), Juhan (r), ends; Daugherty (l), Christy (l), Powers (l), Miller (l), C. Vereen (r), T. Gossage (r), tackles; Givens (l), Fulcher (l), Brooks (l), Carithers (l), Carlen (l), Brooks (r), Givens (r), Fulcher (r), Willoch (r), Carithers (r), guards; Inman, Summer, J. M. Morris, centers; Mitchell, Brigman, Grant, quarterbacks; Hardeman (l), Volkert (l), Hall (l), Menger (l), Ruffin (l), Rotenberry (l), Ruffin (r), Menger (r), Hall (r), halfbacks; Hunsinger, Mattison, Humphreys, Morrison, fullbacks. West Virginia: Kernic (l), J. Starkey (l), Bunn (l), Hillen (r), Ludwig (r), ends; Sweeney (l), Walsh (r), McCleary (r), tackles; Canton (l), Treadway (l), Federovitch (r), guards; Donaldson, Starr, centers; Wyant, Anderson, McInerney, quarterbacks; Moss (l), Dugan (l), Norman (r), Nicholson (r), Jarrett (r), Forrelli (r), halfbacks; Williams, Wilson, fullbacks.

ORANGE

The tangibles favored Maryland. If you considered only the intangible factors—morale, thoroughness of preparation, hard work, enthusiasm—Oklahoma was the choice. Seldom had a coach asked a team to work so hard for a bowl battle as Bud Wilkinson asked his Sooners.

On the day before the 20th Orange Bowl football game in 1954, an Oklahoma assistant coach commented, "If Maryland was only two touchdowns better at the end of the regular season, we'll beat them. Our boys are ready to overcome that much of a handicap."

Oklahoma scored the only touchdown in the first game bringing representatives of the Big Seven and Atlantic Coast Conferences to the Orange Bowl. Maryland's 7 to 0 defeat marked the third time in four years the national champion fell in a bowl setting.

A 41-yard punt by end Bill Walker, out of bounds on Oklahoma's 1, set up a good chance for Maryland early in the first quarter. Buddy Leake's return boot was for 30 yards—to the 36.

Chet (The Jet) Hanulak, flashy halfback who averaged 9.78 yards per carry, Dick Nolan, and Ralph Felton burst through the Sooners for three first downs. The Terps stood at the 4. The throng of 68,640 fans awaited the first score.

It wasn't to be then. And for Maryland, never.

Hanulak was stopped after a two-yard gain by end Max Boydston. Halfback Larry Grigg nailed Nolan without gain when he tried left end on a reverse. Quarterback Charlie Boxold, taking the place of the renowned Bernie Faloney, who injured his left knee late in the season, sneaked to within a foot of a touchdown. On fourth down Felton might as well have butted the Rock of Gibraltar.

In short order Dick Bielski of the Terps missed a field goal from the 37 and Felton was wide on a try for three points from the 6.

Oklahoma then bent to the task from its 20 and didn't give up the ball again until it had been deposited behind the Maryland goal line by Grigg 11 plays later—and the extra point added by Leake.

Grigg went 25 yards around left end for the touchdown after taking an underhanded flip-out from quarterback Gene Calame. This was the basic split T option run or pitch, executed perfectly as fullback Bob Burris mowed down two Terps.

Grigg, the game's leading gainer with 89 yards, was "one of the best players in the country," Wilkinson said. "We depended on him to make that one play in each series which keeps the first downs piling up. He is the best pass defender I have ever seen."

As the battle wore on, Grigg recovered a Maryland fumble and intercepted a pass, each time at a critical juncture. He wasn't an All-American but Stanley Woodward, the well-respected football authority then with the *Miami Herald,* rated him "the best player we have seen in the past five seasons."

Maryland Coach Jim Tatum sent Faloney onto the field for his first and only series after Hanulak returned a punt 16 yards to Oklahoma's 44 in the third quarter. Bernie handed off to Felton, who ran 15 yards. But the Terps moved no farther against the determined Sooners. It was their only threat since the first period.

Wilkinson greatly appreciated the comment by Bob Addie, *Washington Times-Herald* writer, on his players' conduct during the few downs the crippled Faloney was in the game.

"Not an Oklahoma player laid a hand on Bernie, scotching the insidious rumor that the Sooners were going to 'rack him up,' " Addie reported.

		0	7	0	0	7
Oklahoma		0	7	0	0	7
Maryland		0	0	0	0	0

Oklahoma—Touchdown: Grigg (25, left end). Point after touchdown: Leake.

STATISTICS

Oklahoma		*Maryland*	*Oklahoma*		*Maryland*
Allison	LE	Crytzer	10	First downs	13
D. Brown	LT	Morgan	208	Net yards rushing	176
M. Brown	LG	Bowersox	6	Passes attempted	12
K. Burris	C	Irvine	4	Passes completed	5
Roberts	RG	Palahunik	0	Passes had intercepted	1
Nelson	RT	Jones	22	Net yards passing	36
Boydston	RE	Walker	230	Total net yards	212
Calame	QB	Boxold	7	Number of punts	5
Ging	LH	Hanulak	31.3	Punting average	29
Grigg	RH	Nolan	2	Fumbles lost	1
R. Burris	FB	Felton	45	Yards penalized	15

Substitutions—Oklahoma: Mobra (l), Keller (r), ends; Bowman (l), Hearon (r), tackles; Morris (l), Bolinger (r), guards; Mears, center; Van Pool, quarterback; O'Neal (l), Herndon (l), Leake (r), Green (r), halfbacks; Donaghey, Littlejohn, fullbacks. Maryland: Kramer (l), Dennis (l), Flynn (r), Kilgallen (r), ends; Breunich (l), Brougher (r), tackles; Pellegrini (l), McLuckie (r), Shipley (r), guards; Lattimer, center; Beightol, Faloney, quarterbacks; Waller (l), Burgee (l), Horning (r), Vereb (r), Weiciecowski (r), halfbacks; Bielski, fullback.

ROSE

With five minutes left in the first half of the 1954 Rose Bowl game, UCLA led Michigan State 14 to 0, and seemed to have the situation well in hand.

The Bruins had the ball. Paul Cameron, their poised tailback, prepared to punt while standing on his 15-yard line. Practically everybody in the crowd of 101,000 thought he would "midfield" the ball for the remainder of the half, leaving UCLA with a fairly comfortable lead.

But the snap from center was a bit soft. It was a bit high besides. Left end Ellis Duckett hustled in unchecked. He blocked the kick at almost the instant Cameron's foot thumped the ball. Expertly, Duckett, maintaining his feet, scooped it up on the 6 and ran across the goal line for a sudden, easy touchdown.

The deed staggered UCLA. Simultaneously it picked up the Spartans, who had been stalled until then. It changed the complexion of the game.

1954—Michigan State end Ellis Duckett leaps high to block punt by UCLA's Paul Cameron. Duckett scooped up the ball and scored the touchdown that turned the tide of the game.

"Just what we needed to go on to win," said Michigan State Coach Clarence (Biggie) Munn.

In the second half UCLA couldn't hold back Billy Wells, Evan Slonac, and LeRoy Bolden, swift-striking backs in Michigan State's complex multiple offense directed by Tom Yewcic.

In the five years he had been coaching his unusually deceptive and versatile single-wing system at UCLA, Henry (Red) Sanders had never sustained a blocked punt. Nor had it happened at Vanderbilt, his alma mater, before that.

The Bruins capitalized after recovering fumbles on Michigan State's 37 and 18 to score in each of the first two quarters. Cameron threw a 13-yard pass to halfback Bill Stits in the end zone for the first touchdown. He cracked over from the 2 for the second.

Munn gave his team a brief chalk talk and "a little spirit talk" between halves. Blackboard diagraming outlined wider line splits to give blockers better angles. The splits troubled the Bruins. They reacted very slowly and the Spartans had a lark in the second half. They won, 28 to 20.

Michigan State took the third-quarter kickoff and ripped off 78 yards in 14 plays. The Spartans used split T stuff frequently. Bolden smashed over the goal line from the 1.

The score was tied and the procedure was repeated after Cameron quick-kicked 59 yards. Wells shook loose through right tackle for 27 yards to the 5 for the longest gain on a 73-yard march. Wells, who liked tap dancing, was explosively quick and surprisingly powerful for a five-foot, nine-inch, 175-pounder. Billy bolted over left tackle for the touchdown from the 2.

UCLA had to go only 24 yards for its third touchdown when tackle Jack Ellena recovered Yewcic's fumble on the fourth play of the final quarter. End Rommie Loudd lost four yards trying to circle the right side. On the next play Loudd headed for the goal line and when he got there a touchdown pass from Cameron awaited him.

But where Slonac had made good his first three conversions, Johnny Hermann missed his third try, leaving Michigan State ahead, 21 to 20.

Now UCLA, which had developed the kicking game to a high degree of efficiency, had suffered a morale-shattering blocked punt and failed to make an extra point. More misfortune was on the way.

With less than six minutes left, Cameron toed a low line-drive punt 30 yards. Wells raced up from his safety spot to catch the ball while moving at full speed. He fled 62 yards for the touchdown that laced up the victory.

"Bolden and I got mixed up," Billy revealed. "I was supposed to be on the other side. But it was too late to change. When the kick came straight at me, I thought I had a good chance to go all the way because the field was so spread out."

Munn, who retired as head coach—his teams won 33 of their last 34 games—and became athletic director before another season, said to his players: "I've never been so proud of a game in my life. I want to thank all of you. There are tears in my eyes, but I can't help it. I appreciate it so much. Let's say a prayer."

When Sanders left Vanderbilt, one Los Angeles sports writer professed to be so affronted by the choice of this "unknown" Southerner that he began a column: "Henry R. Sanders, 45, a male Caucasian, is the new UCLA football coach."

Through the 1953 season, his teams lost only two of their last 23 games and those by a total of three points.

"Our system isn't glamorous," Sanders once said. "It's based mainly on the idea of knocking the other fellow down."

With his quick mind and flair for unusual phrasing, Sanders was widely quoted. After his death of a heart attack in 1958, a plaque in his memory was placed at Memorial Coliseum in Los Angeles. Under the plaque were these words of the great coach:

> Blocking is the essence of offense.
> Tackling is the essence of defense.
> And spirit is the quintessence of all.

Michigan State	0	7	14	7	28
UCLA	7	7	0	6	20

Michigan State—Touchdowns: Duckett (blocked Cameron's punt from UCLA 25, recovered on 6 and carried over), Bolden (1, left guard), Wells 2 (2, left tackle; 62, punt return). Points after touchdown: Slonac 4.

UCLA—Touchdowns: Stits (13, pass from Cameron), Cameron (2, left tackle), Loudd (28, pass from Cameron). Points after touchdown: Hermann 2.

STATISTICS

Michigan State		UCLA	Michigan State		UCLA
Duckett	LE	Heydenfeldt	14	First downs	16
Jebb	LT	Ellena	195	Net yards rushing	90
Hallmark	LG	Boghosian	10	Passes attempted	24
Neal	C	Pauly	2	Passes completed	9
Bullough	RG	Feldman	1	Passes had intercepted	2
Fowler	RT	Doud	11	Net yards passing	152
Dohoney	RE	Berliner	206	Total net yards	242
Yewcic	QB	Foster	5	Number of punts	6
Bolden	LH	Cameron	35.4	Punting average	38.6
Wells	RH	Stits	4	Fumbles lost	3
Slonac	FB	Dailey	15	Yards penalized	30

Substitutions—Michigan State: Quinlan (l), Lewis (l), Knight (l), Kauth (r), Diener (r), W. Postula (r), ends; Nystrom (l), Frank (l), Robinson (l), Murphy (r), Dotsch (r), tackles; Hollern (l), Ross (l), guards; Badaczewski, Rody, centers; Morrall, Matsock, quarterbacks; Ellis (l), Zagers (r), halfbacks; Planutis, V. Postula, fullbacks. UCLA: Smith (l), Loudd (l), Long (r), Smith (r), ends; Benjamin (l), Britten (l), Andrews (l), Ray (r), Moreno (r), tackles; Cureton (l), Levy (l), Salsbury (r), guards; Peterson, center; Debay, Okuneff, quarterbacks; Villanueva (l), Brown (l), Davis (l), Stalwick (r), Hermann (r), halfbacks; Davenport, fullback.

GATOR

On the morning of the 1954 Gator Bowl game, Dr. Clifford B. Jones, president emeritus of Texas Tech, was having breakfast with

Bobby Cavazos, high scoring (80 points) halfback of the Red Raiders. As they parted, Dr. Jones wished the player the best of everything against Auburn. He also presented Cavazos with a St. Christopher medal.

"I'd had it 10 years," Dr. Jones said. "I figured that since St. Christopher is the patron saint of travelers, and since Bobby would be traveling a lot that afternoon, it was appropriate."

It certainly was.

Cavazos, son of a foreman on the famous King Ranch in Texas, traveled 141 yards in 13 carries (an average of 10.8). He thrilled the crowd of 28,641 with his open field running. He scored three touchdowns, one on a 59-yard run.

Texas Tech was behind at halftime, 13 to 7. But the Red Raiders turned on 28 points of scoring heat in the last 30 minutes to win, 35 to 13.

Just how keen the Texans were to beat Auburn was shown early. Guard Bobby Hunt suffered a broken leg. He was taken to a hospital. Once there, Hunt insisted on being returned to the stadium to see the rest of the game. Only when convinced his team couldn't lose would he go back to the hospital to have the fracture set.

During the 1953 season, Auburn's so-called X and Y teams, separate two-way units, reaped much publicity. Coach Ralph (Shug) Jordan said there was little to choose between them. In the warmth of victory, Tech Coach DeWitt Weaver remarked, "That X and Y equation didn't work out well today, did it?"

The Red Raiders performed a rare feat in the third quarter. From the Auburn 48, quarterback Jack Kirkpatrick ran to his right and fired straight downfield on the run to left end Paul Erwin at the 30. Erwin sped for an apparent touchdown. But Texas Tech was offside. The penalty moved the ball to its 47.

What appeared to be the identical play was called. Kirkpatrick suddenly halted and shot a diagonal pass. At the Auburn 25, Erwin was waiting by himself. He loped to a touchdown. Kirkpatrick's extra point put Texas Tech in front to stay.

"I knew Texas Tech was good, but I didn't know they were that good," Jordan said. "Cavazos made all the difference."

"Greatest back in the country," Weaver declared.

| Texas Tech | 0 | 7 | 14 | 14 | 35 |
| Auburn | 7 | 6 | 0 | 0 | 13 |

Texas Tech—Touchdowns: Cavazos 3 (5, left tackle; 2, right tackle; 59, right tackle), Erwin (53, pass from Kirkpatrick of 28, run of 25), Spooner (recovered

Lewis' fumble in end zone on play from Auburn 4). Points after touchdown: Kirkpatrick 5.

Auburn—Touchdowns: Duke (1, right guard), Dooley (10, left end). Point after touchdown: Davis.

STATISTICS

Texas Tech		Auburn		Texas Tech	Auburn
Erwin	LE	Crouch	11	First downs	12
Williams	LT	D'Agostino	226	Net yards rushing	195
Gray	LG	Duncan	12	Passes attempted	16
West	C	Baker	6	Passes completed	6
Howard	RG	Atkins	1	Passes had intercepted	2
Walker	RT	Brackett	145	Net yards passing	72
Spooner	RE	Long	371	Total net yards	267
Kirkpatrick	QB	Dooley	6	Number of punts	6
Lewis	LH	James	33.1	Punting average	30.5
Cavazos	RH	Duke	0	Fumbles lost	2
Sides	FB	Hataway	83	Yards penalized	66

Substitutions—Texas Tech: White (l), Bradshaw (l), Kummer (l), Harland (r), Wright (r), Spraggins (r), ends; Wesley (l), Lambert (l), Massey (l), Nelson (r), Kilcullen (r), Thacker (r), W. Bryan (r), tackles; Hurt (l), Fitzhugh (l), Hunt (r), Elliott (r), Cook (r), guards; Martin, Ricketts, McGee, centers; Johnson, Hill, Wilson, quarterbacks; Janes (l), Green (l), Fairley (l), Douglass (r), Thompson (r), W. D. Bryan (r), halfbacks; Spinks, Boyer, Burke, fullbacks. Auburn: Pyburn (l), Hall (r), ends; G. Rogers (l), D. Rogers (l), Neura (r), tackles; Scarbrough (l), Kilpatrick (l), Brame (r), Higgins (r), guards; Locklear, Pugh, centers; Freeman, Davis, Burbank, quarterbacks; Adams (l), Powell (l), Littles (r), Middleton (r), halfbacks; Childress, Minor, fullbacks.

COTTON

A crestfallen player sorrowfully trudged off the field.

"I'm too emotional," he told a reporter. "I kept telling myself, 'I didn't do it. I didn't do it.' But I knew I had.

"I'm just too full of 'Bama. He just ran too close. I know I'll be hearing about this the rest of my life."

What Tommy Lewis, Alabama fullback, had done before 75,504 spectators in the 1954 Cotton Bowl game was the nearest thing to the wrong-way run by Roy Riegels 25 years before.

Rice was leading, 7 to 6, midway in the second quarter. The Owls were in possession on their own 5. Alabama had just muffed a scoring opportunity.

Left halfback Dickie Moegle's signal was called. Taking a handoff from quarterback LeRoy Fenstemaker, he turned right end as his blockers did their job efficiently and headed for the Alabama goal line.

As Moegle approached midfield near the sidelines in front of the Alabama bench, it appeared no player could stop him. No one, that is, except Lewis, who was on the bench, suddenly ran onto the field bareheaded, and threw his body into Moegle's legs. Moegle was felled on Alabama's 41. Referee Cliff Shaw awarded a touchdown to Rice. Moegle was credited with a 95-yard run.

1954—Alabama's Tommy Lewis (42) leaves the bench and is about to tackle Dickie Moegle of Rice.

"I think he'd probably have made the touchdown anyway," said Alabama Coach Red Drew.

Moegle told John Bibb of the *Nashville Tennessean*, "As I was running down the sideline, I caught a glimpse of a player getting off the bench. I thought he was just picking up something. I turned back to watch the players chasing me and he got me from the side.

"He sort of body-blocked me and I was dazed for a little. I believe I would have scored. The Alabama players apologized. They slapped me on the back practically every time they tackled me after that."

Although Drew said the Lewis incident had no demoralizing effect

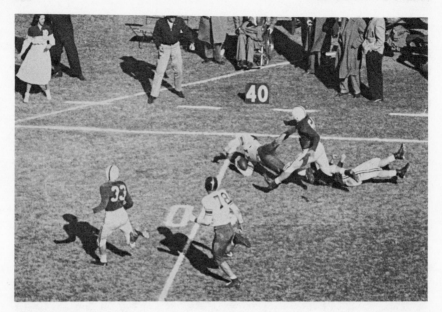

1954—Lewis, on the ground, fells Moegle on Alabama's 41. The referee allowed a touchdown and Moegle was credited with a 95-yard run.

on his team, the Southeastern Conference champions were never the same again. A letdown was evident. Rice went on to smash Alabama, 28 to 6.

It was Lewis who plunged the final foot for a touchdown on a 47-yard advance in the first quarter.

Rice went ahead on Moegle's 79-yard scamper followed by Fenstemaker's extra point. Dick scurried 34 yards for another touchdown in the third period. He gained 265 yards of his team's whopping 379 rushing. He carried the ball only 11 times, averaging 24.1 yards. After this game Moegle held four Cotton Bowl records and three all-time major bowl records.

At the half Lewis went directly to the Rice dressing room to ask if apologies would be accepted.

"My heart went out to him," Rice Coach Jess Neely said. "I told him, 'Don't let it bother you.' "

The *Dallas Morning News,* in an editorial written by managing editor Felix R. McKnight, a former sports writer, asked Texans to "drop Tommy Lewis a line . . . and let him know he hasn't lost his last friend . . . (he) committed a forgivable error that will live with him forever . . . he's quite a fighter—and we like them that way in Texas."

Tommy couldn't sleep on the night after the game. "I sat on the edge of the bed all night," he said. "My wife tried to comfort me, but she couldn't."

Rice	0	14	7	7	28
Alabama	6	0	0	0	6

Rice—Touchdowns: Moegle 3 (79, right tackle; 95, right end; 34, right end), Grantham (7, right tackle). Points after touchdown: Fenstemaker 3, Burk 1.
Alabama—Touchdown: Lewis (1, center plunge).

STATISTICS

Rice		Alabama	Rice		Alabama
Hart	LE	Cummings	14	First downs	11
Chapman	LT	Mason	379	Net yards rushing	188
Hudson	LG	Lee	10	Passes attempted	16
Rucka	C	Carrigan	4	Passes completed	7
Paul	RG	Eckerly	2	Passes had intercepted	0
Schuebel	RT	Youngleman	59	Net yards passing	67
Bridges	RE	Willis	438	Total net yards	255
Fenstemaker	QB	Starr	8	Number of punts	7
Moegle	LH	Luna	25.1	Punting average	42.7
Kellogg	RH	Tharp	0	Fumbles lost	4
K. Johnson	FB	Lewis	89	Yards penalized	65

Substitutions—Rice: Holland (l), Ward (l), Crawford (r), Worthan (r), Costa (r), ends; Golemon (l), Cox (r), Riviere (r), tackles; Treadway (l), Lee (r), Rayburn (r), Harpold (r), guards; Lundstedt, Wilson, centers; Grantham, Nisbet, Proctor, quarterbacks; Nesrsta (l), Rogers (l), Laviage (r), Burk (r), C. Johnson (r), Stone (r), halfbacks; Taylor, Garbrecht, Whittaker, fullbacks. Alabama: Tillman (l), Lynch (r), ends; Shipp (l), Culpepper (r), Smalley (r), tackles; Wilga (l), Moorer (r), guards; DeLaurentis, center; Ingram (l), McBride (l), Oliver (r), Hollis (r), halfbacks; Stone, fullback.

– 1955 –

COTTON

Bobby Dodd's sparkling postseason record, which started with a 41 to 19 victory over St. Mary's in the 1947 Oil Bowl game, remained unsullied when Georgia Tech overcame a 6 to 0 halftime deficiency and bludgeoned the Arkansas Razorbacks, 14 to 6, in the 1955 Cotton Bowl encounter.

That made it six straight—on the road to eight—bowl triumphs for the former Tennessee All-American.

At a meeting of the Atlanta Quarterback Club a few years ago, General Bob Neyland expressed his feeling toward Dodd and Bowden Wyatt, the Arkansas coach who was also an All-American under him.

"People are always asking me how he (Dodd) was as a football player at Tennessee," Neyland said in his speech. "He's built up a reputation of being lazy, lackadaisical, a fellow who didn't like to practice. They also say he looked as cool as a cucumber.

"The only laziness he ever showed was in not liking to run laps. Dodd actually was the first player on the field and the last one off.

"He had the greatest competitive spirit of any player I ever saw. His senior season against Alabama, Dodd dropped a pass that could have won the game. It turned out to be the only losing game he played in at Tennessee. He cried all the way home. That shows you how much he wanted to win."

Wyatt, said the general, "was a savage, driving, resourceful scrapper —the hard-bitten type."

"To be so different as players, they are remarkably alike as coaches. They have the knack of getting every bit of effort and cooperation out of their assistants and players, better than any coaches I've ever seen."

Wyatt, in his second year at Arkansas, produced the university's finest and most surprisingly successful team in nearly three decades. Arkansas won eight games and the Southwest Conference championship. Dodd's team was runnerup in the Southeastern Conference.

At halftime in the Cotton Bowl, the Yellow Jackets told Dodd they thought they could move Arkansas linemen so an inside ground attack would click. Tech's first-half passing and wide stuff hadn't met with much success.

"We found out we couldn't run wide against Arkansas and we couldn't pass on them too well," said quarterback Wade Mitchell. "So in the second half we began wedging up the middle and trapping and that worked pretty well."

With sledge hammering George Humphreys and impish little, 148-pound Jimmy Thompson romping through the Arkansas line, Tech whirled to touchdowns on drives of 58 and 44 yards. Speedy Paul Rotenberry hot-footed around right end for three yards to get the first one. Mitchell punched over from a yard away for the second.

"It was the complete switch in strategy that won for the Jackets," wrote Furman Bisher in the *Atlanta Constitution*.

SATURDAY, JANUARY 1, 1955

Georgia Tech	0	0	7	7	14
Arkansas	0	6	0	0	6

Georgia Tech—Touchdowns: Rotenberry (3, right end), Mitchell (1, right guard). Points after touchdown: Mitchell 2.
Arkansas—Touchdown: Walker (1, right guard).

STATISTICS

Georgia Tech		Arkansas			Arkansas
Durham	LE	Souter	19	First downs	10
Vereen	LT	Bradford	285	Net yards rushing	141
Brooks	LG	Roberts	15	Passes attempted	10
L. Morris	C	Ford	4	Passes completed	7
Fulcher	RG	Brooks	0	Passes had intercepted	1
Anderson	RT	Roth	31	Net yards passing	86
Hair	RE	McFadden	316	Total net yards	227
Mitchell	QB	Carpenter	4	Number of punts	4
Rotenberry	LH	Walker	30	Punting average	30.5
Menger	RH	Thomason	0	Fumbles lost	0
Humphreys	FB	Moore	30	Yards penalized	30

Substitutions—Georgia Tech: Ellis (l), Sennett (l), Huff (l), Webster (r), Jones (r), ends; Christy (l), Daugherty (l), Phenix (r), Thrash (r), tackles; Ecker (l), Willoch (l), Miller (r), Roberts (r), Gossage (r), guards; J. M. Morris, Carlen, Summer, centers; Brigman, Shamburger, Vann, Grant, quarterbacks; Volkert (l), J. L. Morris (l), Thompson (r), Gookin (r), halfbacks; Hunsinger, Mattison, Owen, fullbacks. Arkansas: Burns (l), Matthews (l), Lyons (r), ends; Smith (l), Fuller (r), tackles; Martin (l), Hardwick (l), Gilliam (r), guards; Steelman, center; Proctor, Kolb, quarterbacks; Benson (l), Underwood (r), halfbacks; Berry, fullback.

SUGAR

Three direct hits torpedoed Mississippi as Navy, in its first bowl appearance in 31 years, scuttled the Southeastern Conference's championship team.

Coach Eddie Erdelatz's "team called desire," minus two regulars, fastest halfback Bob Craig (tonsillitis) and tackle Jim Royer (hip injury), and playing against a squad that was heavier, deeper, more experienced, and speedier, stunned the Rebels, 21 to 0, in the 1955 Sugar Bowl game.

The Middies, in a victory that was priceless from a prestige and publicity standpoint, outcharged, outhit, out-tackled, outsmarted, outhustled, and outclassed Ole Miss. The lighter Navy line ripped up the big—and on this day, sluggish—Mississippi line that statistically ranked first in the nation on defense.

Rebel halfback Allen Muirhead analyzed accurately. "We broke down on defensing their split T option," he said. "Offensively, our line didn't do any blocking. We underrated 'em."

Ole Miss didn't cross its opponents' 40 until the fourth quarter was well under way. A scoring chance was wasted due to a fumble.

"Confidentially," paragraphed Pete Baird in the *New Orleans Times-Picayune,* "Ole Miss sunk."

The Rebs, winning the coin toss, chose the goal with the wind at their backs, although it wasn't an important factor. Ole Miss hoped to force a punt, then open up near midfield on offense.

The strategy failed utterly. Receiving the kickoff, Navy rammed the ball down the field 70 yards in 18 plays for a touchdown, even gambling on fourth down with a foot to go at its 39.

Quarterback George Welsh, halfback Johnny Weaver, and squatty, smashing fullback Joe Gattuso broke through the Ole Miss primary defense repeatedly on trap plays. A 15-yard penalty didn't bother the Middies. Weaver flashed 24 yards on a pitch-out to the 3 on the next play. Gattuso crashed into the end zone.

Navy did a repeat in the third quarter, taking the kickoff and punching over a touchdown forthwith. Two defenders, Eagle Day and Billy Kinard, blanketed Weaver when he went up in the end zone for a 15-yard pass thrown by Welsh on the tenth play of the drive. But Weaver came down with the football, a spectacular catch.

A moment or so later Day punted 72 yards over Welsh's head to put Navy on its 7. The Middies simply couldn't be contained. They rushed 93 yards with Gattuso slashing the tackles punishingly. He plowed the last yard.

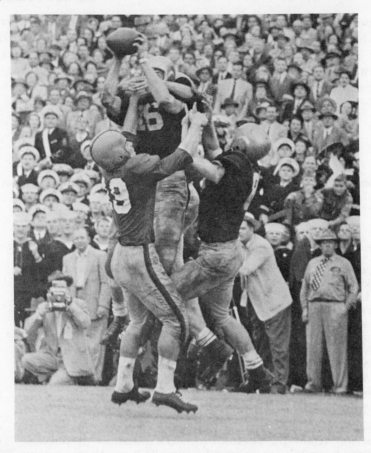

1955—Timing his jump just right, Navy's John Weaver catches a touchdown pass from George Welsh. That's Eagle Day (19) of Ole Miss in front and behind (arms around Weaver's neck) is Billy Kinard. Ron Beagle, Navy's All-America end, is on the right.

Gattuso gained 111 yards and Weaver, 106, as the Annapolis crew accumulated 295 on the ground and 147 in the air—to a meager 78 rushing and 43 passing for Ole Miss.

The Navy line played exceptionally well.

Deft little Welsh kept the gigantic Rebels befuddled with his slick running, passing, and handling of the option keep or lateral play. "He was a genius at calling the right plays," Erdelatz said.

"They sure lived up to that 'team called desire' stuff, corny as it sounds," Day said.

The man behind the scene, most responsible for Navy's appearance in the bowl, was E. E. (Rip) Miller, the Academy's assistant director of athletics. Miller was a civilian who came to Annapolis in 1926, a year after he played for Notre Dame in the Rose Bowl. Miller did invaluable spade work in selling the Navy Department on the idea of the Midshipmen going to a bowl.

Navy	7	0	14	0	21
Mississippi	0	0	0	0	0

Navy—Touchdowns: Gattuso 2 (3, right tackle; 1, right tackle), Weaver (15, pass from Welsh). Points after touchdown: Weaver 3.

STATISTICS

Navy		Mississippi	Navy		Mississippi
Beagle	LE	Harris	20	First downs	5
Hopkins	LT	Weiss	295	Net yards rushing	78
Benzi	LG	Alliston	28	Passes attempted	18
Whitmire	C	Dubuisson	12	Passes completed	5
Aronis	RG	Brashier	4	Passes had intercepted	0
McCool	RT	Boggan	147	Net yards passing	43
Smith	RE	Dickerson	442	Total net yards	121
Welsh	QB	Day	4	Number of punts	9
Weaver	LH	J. Patton	33.7	Punting average	36.1
Garrow	RH	Kinard	0	Fumbles lost	1
Gattuso	FB	Cothren	15	Yards penalized	50

Substitutions—Navy: Freeman (l), Byrom (l), Owen (r), Barker (r), ends; House (l), Webster (r), Vaselenko (r), tackles; Bendrick (l), Mohn (l), Textor (r), Dander (r), Wittner (r), guards; Dutnell, Davis, Hower, centers; Echard, Korzep, quarterbacks; Hepworth (l), Burchett (l), Malynn (l), Gober (r), Monahan (r), halfbacks; Guest, Monto, fullbacks. Mississippi: Fisher (l), Drewry (r), Harbin (r), ends; Yelverton (l), Walters (l), Goehe (r), Powers (r), tackles; James (l), Williams (l), Shepherd (r), McKay (r), guards; McKinney, Stone, centers; H. Patton, Blalack, Jenkins, quarterbacks; Blair (l), Thomas (l), Crawford (l), Muirhead (r), Barber (r), halfbacks; McCool, Baker, fullbacks.

ORANGE

The hard and fast provisions of the Orange Bowl's pact with the Atlantic Coast Conference and the Big Seven resulted in a mismatch in 1955.

As had been feared by most knowledgeable football people, Duke's superior Blue Devils whaled Nebraska's four times beaten Cornhuskers, 34 to 7. The Big Seven's agreement stipulated no consecutive return appearances for its members. This prevented Oklahoma's perfect-record Sooners, champions for the ninth straight year of the Big Seven and 55 to 7 lambasters of runnerup Nebraska, from giving Duke all it might desire in the way of a rugged contest.

Nebraska Coach Bill Glassford was a veteran of Pittsburgh's 1937 Rose Bowl victors and, therefore, well schooled in the value of psychological warfare. He saw to it that his men fully appreciated the scope of disparaging comments written about them.

His Cornhuskers, although outpersonneled, made things uncomfortably, even embarrassingly close for the Atlantic Coast Conference champions until well into the third quarter.

Duke led at the half, 14 to 0. Nebraska had earned only two first downs. In the third period Glassford's willing battlers gained title to a 35-yard piece of ground in eight slices with Don Comstock, Ron Clark, and Bob Smith whacking the Blue Devil line. Comstock banged into the end zone for the touchdown.

Nebraska was in hot contention now, it seemed. But it was only an appearance. For now Duke buckled down with consummate dedication.

Captain Jerry Barger, whose punt bouncing crazily backward 20 yards for a net loss of two provided the Cornhuskers with their big chance, shot a pass from the Nebraska 17 to end Sonny Sorrell on the 5. Sorrell twisted out of Clark's grasp and scored. It capped a 65-yard shove immediately following the Cornhuskers' kickoff.

That broke open the game in Duke's favor. There were two more touchdowns within the next ten minutes.

Two sports writers from Lincoln charged the Cornhuskers with indifference toward training and breaking training rules. But Bill Murray, the generous winning coach, said, "It may not have looked like it in the stands, but it was a good tough game—much tougher than the statistics showed."

Despite lack of intense fan interest in the game, 68,750 saw it, a new record. The Orange Bowl Committee formally announced a three-year renewal of its contract with the Big Seven and Atlantic Coast Conferences.

Duke	0	14	6	14	34
Nebraska	0	0	7	0	7

Duke—Touchdowns: Pascal (7, right end), Kocourek (2, pass from Barger), Sorrell (17, pass from Barger of 12, run of 5), McKeithan (2, left tackle), Eberdt (3, left tackle). Points after touchdown: Nelson 4.

Nebraska—Touchdown: Comstock (3, left tackle). Point after touchdown: Smith.

STATISTICS

Duke		Nebraska	Duke		Nebraska
Sorrell	LE	Loehr	23	First downs	6
Campbell	LT	Holloran	288	Net yards rushing	84
Birchfield	LG	Bryant	13	Passes attempted	9
Palmer	C	Oberlin	7	Passes completed	1
Torrance	RG	Wagner	0	Passes had intercepted	2
Knotts	RT	Glantz	82	Net yards passing	26
Moon	RE	McWilliams	370	Total net yards	110
Barger	QB	Brown	5	Number of punts	7
Pascal	LH	Comstock	23.6	Punting average	28.9
Bass	RH	Greenlaw	1	Fumbles lost	0
Aldridge	FB	Smith	30	Yards penalized	20

Substitutions—Duke: Benson (l), Sebastian (l), Kocourek (r), Black (r), Stallings (r), ends; Deloatch (l), Hord (l), Cox (r), Konicek (r), tackles; Nelson (l), Fesperman (l), Klinger (r), guards; Falls, Snowberger, Murray, centers; Jurgensen, Murray, quarterbacks; McKeithan (l), Post (l), Beasley (l), Kredich (l), Blaney (r), Conner (r), halfbacks; Eberdt, Lutz, fullbacks. Nebraska: Butherus (l), Westervelt (l), Hewitt (r), Harris (r), Giles (r), ends; Peterson (l), Neal (l), Evans (r), Fleming (r), tackles; Murphy (l), Taylor (l), Kripal (r), guards; Torczon, Berguin, centers; Erway, Fischer, quarterbacks; Clark (l), Johnson (l), Korinek (r), halfbacks; Edwards, fullback.

ROSE

For the third time in the history of the Tournament of Roses parade, rain fell in Pasadena in 1955. For the first time since 1934, spectators at the Rose Bowl game got wet.

A crowd of 89,191 watched Ohio State defeat Southern California, 20 to 7, in a driving rain. Playing conditions were never worse. The spectators were treated to the usual halftime show with marching bands.

"They turned it into a quagmire," beefed Ohio State's forthright coach, Woody Hayes, when the game was over. "Eighty million people saw those bands on television marching in the parade, so why did they have to march on that muddy field at the time? They shouldn't have been permitted on the field. They don't have any business ruining it when the game is the big thing. The bands are great and I am for them. But football comes first. If you don't think so, put the bands in the Rose Bowl without the football teams and see how many people you draw."

In the course of his remarks to the press, Hayes said, "There are four, and possibly five, Big Ten teams I'd rate ahead of the Trojans." He also chided the writers for not ranking his team higher in pre-season forecasts.

Ohio State was voted national champion in the Associated Press poll. UCLA topped the United Press ratings. "I definitely think we are still the best college ball club in the country," Hayes declared. "I don't think UCLA could have lived up to that schedule of ours."

Countering hard, Dick Hyland of the *Los Angeles Times* observed: "The UCLA Bruins could take them both (Ohio State and Southern California) on the same afternoon. If the Buckeyes are the best collegiate team in the country . . . then the United States Marine Corps is a bunch of sissies."

Unbeaten, untied UCLA was ineligible for the 1955 Rose Bowl game, having played in it the year before. The Bruins routed Southern Cal, 34 to 0, in the season of 1954.

Southern California Coach Jesse Hill was complimenting the conquerors at his press conference when someone relayed Hayes' statement that four Big Ten teams could beat his Trojans.

"Just say for me I'd like to play Ohio State again on a fast field," Hill snapped.

Mud-coated players weren't identifiable a minute after going into action. Southern California fumbled the slippery ball seven times and lost it thrice. The Buckeyes scored after two of the recoveries in the second quarter.

Also in the second period Aramis Dandoy of the Trojans galloped through the mire and murk (the stadium lights had been turned on at 1 P.M.) 86 yards for a touchdown on a punt return. Oliver Kuechle of the *Milwaukee Journal* called it, "The finest play of the game, the finest in all Rose Bowl history. Taking the kick on his own 14, and with a flock of Buckeyes apparently down on him, he wiggled this way and that, tore away from several men who apparently had him, and then just beyond midfield ran away from the last Buckeye with an outside chance to catch him." Dandoy suffered a recurrence of his chronic leg muscle injury and missed the second half.

However, the game's brightest light was Dave Leggett, Ohio State's quarterback. He flawlessly handled the wet ball on quick opener handoffs and pitch-outs. He threw six completed passes, one of 21 yards to Bob Watkins for a touchdown and another that offset a penalty and led to his team's third touchdown in the fourth quarter. Leggett scored the Buckeyes' first touchdown. In addition he recovered a Trojan fumble and time after time made substantial yardage on the split T keeper.

Late in the third quarter Southern Cal stopped Ohio State on its 4. Jon Arnett, the Trojans' breakaway runner with unusually good balance developed as a high school gymnast, cut through right tackle and sped 70 yards before he was downed by Howard (Hopalong) Cassady, the Buckeyes' All-America halfback.

"I thought he had it made but his fake against Cassady didn't work," Hill said.

Ohio State dug in and took possession on its 23. From there the Buckeyes moved to their clinching touchdown. Jerry Harkrader slithered around left end for the last nine yards.

Ohio State dominated the game with its ball-control type of attack. The Buckeyes got off 80 scrimmage plays to the Trojans' 36, netted 305 yards rushing, and made 22 first downs.

But Southern California had the most effective ball carrier in the elusive Arnett, whose nine sprints totaled 123 yards (13.7 average). Cassady acquired 92 yards in 21 tries. He played admirably on defense.

"We intended to do a lot of throwing but the rain hurt us," said Hill. "We depend more on speed than power, so we were handcuffed both ways."

Leggett's replacement was a junior named Bill Booth. He was the son of a bowl-playing father. His dad, Dr. A. A. Booth, a dentist in Sharon, Pa., was a fullback for Pittsburgh against Stanford in 1928.

In the 1949–50 games, Charles F. (Boots) Erb III, son of the famous California quarterback in the early 1920's, had played against Northwestern and Ohio State.

Ohio State	0	14	0	6	20
Southern California	0	7	0	0	7

Ohio State—Touchdowns: Leggett (3, left guard), Watkins (21, pass from Leggett of 12, run of 9), Harkrader (9, left end). Points after touchdown: Weed, Watkins.

Southern California—Touchdown: Dandoy (86, punt return). Point after touchdown: Tsagalakis.

STATISTICS

Ohio State		Southern California	Ohio State		Southern California
Dugger	LE	Clarke	22	First downs	6
Hilinski	LT	Da Re	305	Net yards rushing	177
D. Williams	LG	Galli	11	Passes attempted	8
Thornton	C	Goux	6	Passes completed	3
Reichenbach	RG	Ferrante	1	Passes had intercepted	0
Machinsky	RT	Fouch	65	Net yards passing	29
Brubaker	RE	Greenwood	370	Total net yards	206
Leggett	QB	Contratto	4	Number of punts	5
Cassady	LH	Dandoy	38.3	Punting average	46.6
Watkins	RH	Crow	0	Fumbles lost	3
Bobo	FB	Duvall	40	Yards penalized	60

*Substitutions—*Ohio State: Michael (l), Spears (l), Ellwood (l), Ludwig (r), Kriss (r), Collmar (r), ends; Swartz (l), Stoeckel (l), Krisher (r), Guy (r), Cummings (r), tackles; Parker (l), Jobko (l), Howley (l), Weaver (r), Blazeff (r), Ramser (r), guards; Vargo, Bond, Dillman, centers; Booth, Weed, quarterbacks; Howell (l), Archer (l), Roseboro (r), Young (r), Harkrader (r), Thompson (r), halfbacks; Gibbs, Vicic, L. Williams, fullbacks. Southern California: Leimbach (l), McFarland (l), Perpich (l), Bordier (r), Griffith (r), Hilario (r), ends; Belotti (l), Fletcher (l), Westphal (l), Pavich (r), Adams (r), Smith (r), tackles; Miller (l), Isaacson (l), Torena (l), Spector (r), Enright (r), Willott (r), guards; Sampson, Eldredge, centers; Hall, Kissinger, quarterbacks; Arnett (l), Clayton (l), Pierce (l), Calabria (r), Merk (r), halfbacks; Brown, Tisdale, Kurlak, Tsagalakis, fullbacks.

GATOR

A unique distinction was attained by Auburn on December 31, 1954.

Auburn became the first school ever to play in a major bowl twice in the same year.

Actually, of course, these were two distinct teams and two separate seasons, 1953 and 1954.

The Gator Bowl was now of age. The Association wisely switched its presentation from New Year's Day. Starting in 1955, it was held on the Saturday before (or the Saturday after) to avoid television competition with the four other big bowl games.

Disgusted with its collapse against Texas Tech on the previous January 1, Auburn ripped "innocent" Baylor, 33 to 13. After a 7 to 7 first-quarter deadlock, the Tigers unsheathed their claws. Fullback Joe Childress and halfbacks Fob James and Dave Middleton tore off huge strips of yardage.

Childress slammed out 134 yards on 20 handoffs. He scored twice. James had 71 yards on six carries for an 11.8 average. Middleton added 60 yards. James' touchdown run of 44 yards was the longest sprint.

Auburn's total of 423 yards rushing was an all-time bowl rushing record until broken in 1959 when Iowa amassed 429 in Pasadena.

This was the second of three straight trips to the Gator Bowl for Auburn and Jordan, who restored his alma mater's football prestige soon after he became head coach in 1951. In 1957 Auburn won the national championship but was ineligible for bowl game consideration because of a probation sentence imposed by the National Collegiate Athletic Association for a recruiting violation.

There was a feeling in the Southeastern Conference that Auburn, which won its last six games after losing three of its first four, might have been the strongest team at the finish, although Mississippi won the championship.

Jack Gallagher wrote in the *Houston Post*: "Auburn was a wondrous football team. The Tigers played perfect football, never had to punt for the first 50 minutes and scored five of the first six times they had their hands on the ball."

FRIDAY, DECEMBER 31, 1954

Auburn	7	14	12	0	33
Baylor	7	0	6	0	13

Auburn—Touchdowns: Childress 2 (7, center; 5, center), James (44, left tackle), Long (4, pass from Freeman), Freeman (5, left end). Points after touchdown: Childress 3.

Baylor—Touchdowns: Saage (1, left guard), Dupre (38, center). Point after touchdown: C. Smith.

STATISTICS

Auburn		Baylor	Auburn		Baylor
Pyburn	LE	C. Smith	25	First downs	16
D'Agostino	LT	J. Smith	423	Net yards rushing	105
Scarbrough	LG	Dierking	7	Passes attempted	18
Locklear	C	Glass	3	Passes completed	10
Atkins	RG	Rutherford	0	Passes had intercepted	1
Brackett	RT	Parsley	53	Net yards passing	134
Long	RE	Gremminger	476	Total net yards	239
Freeman	QB	Hooper	2	Number of punts	3
James	LH	Shofner	41	Punting average	42
Middleton	RH	Dupre	2	Fumbles lost	1
Childress	FB	A. Jones	52	Yards penalized	25

Substitutions—Auburn: Elliott (l), Sansom (l), Whatley (l), Hall (r), Coleman (r), ends; Rogers (l), Warren (l), Clark (l), Neura (r), Terry (r), tackles; Maxime (l), Higgins (l), Danjean (r), Brame (r), Steber (r), guards; Reeves, Strain, centers; Tubbs, Peerson, Burbank, quarterbacks; Adams (l), Powell (l), Shell (r), Cunningham (r), halfbacks; Minor, Walsh, fullbacks. Baylor: De-Grazier (l), Stinson (l), P. Smith (l), Meyer (l), McNair (r), Amyet (r), ends; Ritchie (l), Robinson (r), tackles; Culvahouse (l), Froebel (l), Pearce (r), Barnett (r), guards; Harris, center; R. Jones, quarterback; Guess (l), Berry (l), Holley (r), halfbacks; Saage, fullback.

– 1956 –

GATOR

Don Orr's wonderfully competent and plucky performance in Vanderbilt's 25 to 13 Gator Bowl triumph over Auburn was superior to that of any of the other quarterbacks in the major bowls that topped off the 1955 season.

The Commodore quarterback sustained a severely dislocated right elbow five weeks before against Tennessee. Dr. Brant Lipscomb, Vanderbilt's team physician, didn't think it would be possible for him to recover in time to play in the Gator Bowl. Orr insisted all along he would be in the game.

"Don never let himself think anything but that he'd play," Dr. Lipscomb said. "We helped him all we could. But it was he who did it with his determination. Normally, this type of injury disables a person seven to 10 weeks."

Orr's passing, running, bold but smart play-calling, and inspirational qualities give him all-time Gator Bowl team eminence. With poise, finesse, and intelligence he steered the Commodores in their first bowl game and brought them through in front.

Auburn's coach, Ralph Jordan, remarked at the postgame banquet, "I'm so glad, Don, you didn't dislocate both elbows."

As he received the most valuable player award, Orr responded, "No one individual can win this. Determination and desire on the part of all 39 Vanderbilt players won that game—that and the spirit and confidence and knowledge instilled in us by our great coaching staff."

That staff was headed by Art Guepe, former Marquette star who scored the first touchdown in the Cotton Bowl on a 60-yard punt return. Later, he played for the Iowa Seahawks and learned the split T offense as taught by Don Faurot.

Guepe coached successfully at Virginia and came to Vanderbilt in 1953, the year after his Cavaliers submerged the Commodores, 27 to 0. There was no immediate improvement. In his third season he restored its football prestige and was elected Coach of the Year in the Southeastern Conference.

His offense, which Elmore (Scoop) Hudgins, Vanderbilt's athletic publicity director, ingeniously called the "Kaleidoscopic T," was varied and extremely difficult to scout, as the title suggested. In the Gator Bowl, his T featured a diversified spread formation with a man in motion.

Orr might not have lasted a minute, if hit at a certain angle on his right arm. But he was on the field 57 minutes.

As the teams warmed up before the opening kickoff, Tennessee Coach Bowden Wyatt, who was in the press box, commented, "Vanderbilt looks on fire to me."

A 15-yard holding penalty probably deprived the Commodores of a quick early touchdown. Orr, on fourth down with five to go from Auburn's 30, shot a 25-yard pass to halfback Charlie Horton, who was tackled on the 5. The infraction forced a punt.

However, shortly thereafter Orr engineered a 39-yard touchdown surge. He threw a seven-yard pass to end Joe Stephenson for the score.

Auburn came back strong and tied the score. But under Orr's direction, Vanderbilt swiftly recaptured the lead. Four plays were needed to travel 76 yards. Fullback Phil King hammered center for four. Orr ran 44, passed to Joe Scales for 24, and scored from the 4 on a fake pitchout to King.

In the third quarter Stephenson, after recovering Howell Tubbs' fumble on Vanderbilt's 49 (one of five by Auburn), maneuvered into the clear and caught a pass from Orr for an apparent touchdown. But holding was detected again.

Orr scored his second touchdown from the 1 to crown a 51-yard drive. A short 12-yard punt by Bill Burbank plus an unnecessary roughness penalty gave Vanderbilt the ball on Auburn's 26 and made the fourth touchdown, this one by Horton, easy.

Alex Orr of Miami was as proud as a father possibly could be. And he didn't mind admitting it.

He related, "When Don left home to go to Jacksonville last week, he told us, 'I'm going there to play my best game.' So I knew he would do it. He has a habit of doing what he says.

"Don overcame his share of misfortunes—polio, a facial injury in high school that was pretty bad, concussion and double vision at Vanderbilt, and finally, this dislocated elbow. But he's always battled back. Yes, a man is lucky to have a son like that."

At a late January banquet for the team given by the Nashville

1955—Vanderbilt quarterback Don Orr, holding trophy, with his most valuable player award, which he received from Dick Stratton of the Gator Bowl executive committee.

Quarterback Club, Vanderbilt vice-chancellor Madison Sarratt said something many have wanted to say and tried to say after a notable accomplishment but couldn't put in just these fitting words: "The blood, sweat and tears of Vanderbilt men through the years helped to bring this about. Back of these boys as far as you can see into the distance are those who have worked to make Vanderbilt good and strong."

SATURDAY, DECEMBER 31, 1955

Vanderbilt	7	6	6	6	25
Auburn	0	7	0	6	13

Vanderbilt—Touchdowns: Stephenson (7, pass from Orr), Orr 2 (4, left tackle; 1, right guard), Horton (1, right tackle). Point after touchdown: Jalufka.

Auburn—Touchdowns: James (38, pass from Tubbs of 13, run of 25), Phillips (7, pass from Tubbs). Point after touchdown: Tubbs.

STATISTICS

Vanderbilt		Auburn	Vanderbilt		Auburn
Harkins	LE	Elliott	15	First downs	15
Woodroof	LT	D'Agostino	177	Net yards rushing	159
Hayes	LG	Danjean	8	Passes attempted	13
Cunningham	C	Scarbrough	5	Passes completed	8
Frank	RG	Maxime	1	Passes had intercepted	0
Demmas	RT	Brackett	94	Net yards passing	142
Stephenson	RE	Phillips	271	Total net yards	301
Orr	QB	Tubbs	4	Number of punts	3
Horton	LH	James	32	Punting average	29
Scales	RH	Hoppe	1	Fumbles lost	5
King	FB	Childress	54	Yards penalized	59

Substitutions—Vanderbilt: Jalufka (l), Laws (l), Brown (l), Taylor (r), Tyler (r), ends; Swan (l), Toups (l), Wodka (r), Linville (r), Ward (r), tackles; Lamberson (l), Parker (l), Davie (l), Tatum (r), Williamson (r), Donaldson (r), guards; Heywood, Richardson, Allen, centers; Holmes, Sturm, quarterbacks; Hudson (l), Tkac (l), Morgan (r), Jabaley (r), halfbacks; Hunt, Pepoy, Ahrens, fullbacks. Auburn: Sansom (l), end; Preston (l), Terry (r), tackles; Weekley (l), Steber (l), Baker (r), guards; Reeves, center; Burbank, Cook, quarterbacks; Adams (l), Shell (r), Grider (r), halfbacks; Walsh, fullback.

COTTON

The Cotton Bowl game of 1956 may have been decided on the opening kickoff by Mississippi. Chuck Curtis, Texas Christian's All-Southwest Conference quarterback, suffered two fractured ribs and an injured right shoulder when tackled ruggedly.

His removal left the Horned Frogs like a rudderless ship. Yet even without him the Southwest Conference champions led the Southeastern Conference kings 13 to 0 in the second period. The Rebels scored the tying touchdown and added the scales-tipping extra point with less than five minutes remaining in the game.

The climactic play of the second Ole Miss touchdown drive of 66 yards was a 25-yard skedaddle by quarterback Eagle Day to the 5. From there, Billy Lott, speedy sophomore halfback who entered the game two plays before, whirred around right end and reached the end zone. Fullback Paige Cothren's trusty toe proved the difference.

As the ball cleared the crossbar and the referee's arms flew up, the scoreboard read: Ole Miss 14, TCU 13.

Curtis admitted Coach Abe Martin told him not to run back a kickoff if he got the ball. Martin reasoned Ole Miss probably would try to direct the kick to Curtis.

"I was supposed to lateral to Jim [Swink] but I just didn't," Curtis explained. "Somebody hit me from behind when I was going down and that was it."

Martin said Curtis' injury caused him to make a radical change in battle plans.

"We figured to pass quite a lot," Martin said, unhappily, immediately after the game. "We couldn't do it with Dick Finney. He did a heck of a job. But he can't pass like Curtis and he hadn't run a down with the No. 1 backfield.

"Finney isn't used to Swink either. I thought Jim was tremendous. But Curtis has worked with him all year and he knows how to get the most out of him. There are other things Curtis can do that we counted on and had to throw out.

"They just ignored our passing in the second half and massed to stop the running."

Swink, TCU's junior All-America halfback who netted 1,283 yards rushing in 1955 and scored 125 points, gave a valiant all-around performance. He scored both of his team's touchdowns, the first on a short plunge and the second on a 39-yard dash. He gained 107 yards in 19 carries and was a standout on defense.

However, player-of-the-game honors went to Day. The slender, part-Cherokee Rebel fired completed passes that covered 137 yards completing ten of 21 throws, punted for a 42.7 average and called a smart game in addition to producing the knockout punch with his late fourth-quarter run.

Might-have-beens haunted the dreams of the Horned Frogs for a long time. Fullback Harold Pollard kicked the extra point after Swink's second touchdown. TCU was penalized for an illegal formation. Pollard missed his next try.

On Day's important scamper, two Frogs, tackle Norman Hamilton and guard Vernon Uecker, said they should have grabbed him.

With this victory Ole Miss and Coach Johnny Vaught began a remarkably successful run in the bowls.

MONDAY, JANUARY 2, 1956

Mississippi	0	7	0	7	14
Texas Christian	7	6	0	0	13

Mississippi—Touchdowns: Cothren (3, left tackle), Lott (5, right end). Points after touchdown: Cothren 2.

Texas Christian—Touchdowns: Swink 2 (1, left guard; 39, right tackle). Point after touchdown: Pollard.

STATISTICS

| | | *Texas* | | | | *Texas* |
Mississippi		*Christian*		*Mississippi*		*Christian*
Fisher	LE	Engram	12	First downs		11
Weiss	LT	Hamilton	92	Net yards rushing		233
Alliston	LG	J. Williams	21	Passes attempted		5
Dubuisson	C	Pitts	10	Passes completed		2
Duck	RG	Uecker	0	Passes had intercepted		2
Goehe	RT	Cooper	137	Net yards passing		20
Drewry	RE	O. Williams	229	Total net yards		253
Day	QB	Curtis	6	Number of punts		5
Blair	LH	Swink	42.7	Punting average		29
Kinard	RH	Taylor	1	Fumbles lost		1
Cothren	FB	Hallbeck	80	Yards penalized		80

Substitutions—Mississippi: Harbin (l), D. Williams (r), ends; Yelverton (l), Hickerson (r), tackles; J. Williams (l), McKay (r), guards; Stone, center; Blalack, quarterback; Crawford (l), Reed (l), Bowman (l), Lott (r), halfbacks; Baker, fullback. Texas Christian: Nikkel (l), Bull (r), ends; Laswell (l), Groom (r), tackles; Alexander (l), Yung (l), McCullough (r), guards; Ozee, center; Finney, quarterback; Shofner (l), Wineburg (r), Miller (r), halfbacks; Pollard, fullback.

SUGAR

In Pittsburgh's dressing room after the Panthers' 7 to 0 loss to Georgia Tech in the 1956 Sugar Bowl game, Bob Grier, first Negro ever to play in it, sobbingly told newsmen the decisive penalty against him "should have been called the other way. He pushed me from behind. That's why I fell forward."

On the ninth play of the game, Wade Mitchell, Tech's brainy quarterback, had, from Pittsburgh's 32, tossed a high pass toward the end zone aimed for end Don Ellis.

Back judge Frank Lowry ruled that defensive halfback Grier pushed Ellis. The Panthers were penalized for pass interference and the ball was placed on the 1. Mitchell sneaked through the middle for the game's only touchdown.

Pitt Coach John Michelosen, whose team outgained the Yellow Jackets 311 yards to 142, out-first-downed them 19 to 10, and put the ball in play 70 times to 46, said "It could have been called either way."

Bobby Dodd commented, "I couldn't see the play at all. Ellis told me Grier pushed him and I guess that was the way it was."

Ellis said Grier "must've stumbled against me. Otherwise, I think I could've caught the ball."

"I was in front of him," Grier insisted. "How could I have pushed

1956—This action resulted in a pass interference penalty setting up the only touchdown as Georgia Tech beat Pittsburgh 7 to 0. Tech end Don Ellis reaches for a pass throw by Wade Mitchell. Bobby Grier, on the ground, was charged with pushing.

him? They were good sportsmen, perhaps the best I've played against all season. They played hard, but clean. It was a good game. But believe me, I didn't push that man."

Bill Keefe of the *New Orleans Times-Picayune* wrote: "I followed the ball in flight with my binoculars and was just in time to see Grier seemingly push himself off Ellis and fall."

Describing the controversial play, Al Abrams of the *Pittsburgh Post Dispatch* reported, "Grier pushed the intended receiver."

Tech didn't complete a pass. The Jackets scored on an early double break, first of which came when Pitt quarterback Pete Neft fumbled and Tech guard Allen Ecker recovered on the Panthers' 32.

Seconds before the half ended, Pitt quarterback Corny Salvaterra failed to dent the line on a fourth-down jab from the Jackets' 1. The Panthers had rolled 79 yards in 20 plays.

Protecting the last few feet of its own territory with zealous ferocity had been a Tech characteristic for years.

When the final gun sounded, the Panthers were on Tech's 5, second down and four yards to go, having moved from their 28. Left-handed third-string quarterback Darrell Lewis had picked up his team at midfield and had handed off to fullback Ralph Jelic for six yards on the last play.

"I thought we had 30 seconds left," Lewis said. "I thought we could get off another play easily."

The field clock stopped working in the first quarter.

Salvaterra said he was under the impression time was running out on Pittsburgh when he was stopped on a hurried call in the last minute of the second quarter. As it happened, Tech got the ball for one long count play.

After the game, Dodd said, "I expected them to dominate things like they did. Once we were on top, I didn't care how long they kept the ball, just so long as they didn't score."

Georgia Tech	7	0	0	0	7
Pittsburgh	0	0	0	0	0

Georgia Tech—Touchdown: Mitchell (1, sneak). Point after touchdown: Mitchell.

STATISTICS

Georgia Tech		Pittsburgh	Georgia Tech		Pittsburgh
Rose	LE	Walton	10	First downs	19
Vereen	LT	Pollock	142	Net yards rushing	217
Brooks	LG	Scorsone	3	Passes attempted	18
Morris	C	Cenci	0	Passes completed	8
Ecker	RG	Schmitt	1	Passes had intercepted	1
Thrash	RT	Canil	0	Net yards passing	94
Ellis	RE	Paluck	142	Total net yards	311
Mitchell	QB	Neft	6	Number of punts	4
Rotenberry	LH	Bowen	33.8	Punting average	38.7
Volkert	RH	DiPasquale	0	Fumbles lost	2
Mattison	FB	Grier	15	Yards penalized	72

Substitutions—Georgia Tech: Nabors (l), Huff (l), Bagwell (r), ends; Christy (l), Gossage (l), Anderson (r), Askew (r), tackles; Fulcher (l), Baum (l), Miller (r), Glazier (r), guards; Stephenson, center; Vann, quarterback; Noe (l), Flowers (l), Menger (l), Thompson (r), halfbacks; Owen, Gookin, fullbacks. Pittsburgh: Glatz (l), Kiesel (l), Rosborough (r), ends; McCusker (l), Linn (l), Linn (r), McCusker (r), Kissel (r), tackles; Hunter (l), Bolkovac (r), guards; Bose, Brueckman, centers; Salvaterra, Lewis, quarterbacks; Cost (l), Cimarolli (r), Passodelis (r), halfbacks; Jenkins, Jelic, fullbacks.

ORANGE

The double-quick huddle was not new.

The Oklahoma Sooners jumped to their feet when a play was over, held a split-second conference, sprinted to position, and were off and running. What made it seem novel was that most modern teams operate with much more deliberation.

Bob Pellegrini, Maryland's All-America center, had just downed a Sooner back and was taking his time arising when Mike Sandusky, giant Terp tackle, holloed, "Get up, Bob. Here they come again!"

Despite Maryland's plight at the time, not to mention the fact he was hot, tired, and hardly able to catch his breath, Pellegrini had to grin.

"Two things result from shortening the huddle time," Coach Bud Wilkinson explained. "First, we're able to move before the defense can become set. Second, there's no real time for reflection by the quarterback. On the other hand, there's none for the defensive signal-caller either, and this helps us.

"One of the basic things about our offense is that we use so few plays. This speeds up the quarterback's choice, of course."

Late in the second quarter of the 1956 Orange Bowl game Maryland halfback Ed Vereb, racing wide to his right as if to pass or sweep that side of the line, suddenly reversed his field and ran 15 yards for a touchdown around the left terminal.

"Even at halftime when Maryland led, 6–0, I felt sure Oklahoma would win," said a press box observer, James T. (Slick) Welsh of Nashville, who in 1954 was named America's No. 1 sports fan because of his avid lifetime interest. "I timed Bud's boys in one sequence and believe it or not, they got off three running plays in 40 seconds."

Oklahoma quarterback Jimmy Harris disclosed that at the half, Wilkinson "told us we had been stopping ourselves by our own mistakes. He told us to come out fast and drive and never let up. He said we would beat Maryland if we would just stick to our bread-and-butter inside plays. He wound up saying, 'If you're men, you'll snap out of it and play the way you know how.' After the game, Coach Wilkinson said we played the greatest second half of any team he ever had or had seen."

The Sooners hadn't made a scoring threat in the first half. Touch-downs followed the first two times they got possession of the ball in the third quarter. Fleet Tommy McDonald blew around right end on a pitch-out from the 4 for the first touchdown to cap a seven-play drive of 46 yards. McDonald, always dazzling to the opposition on punt returns, had brought back one 33 yards by way of a hint of things to come.

All those gainers and all those on a 17-play thrust of 51 yards that resulted in a touchdown by quarterback Jay O'Neal of Wilkinson's second unit, on a one-yard sneak, were sustained at high speed.

Near the end, Carl Dodd picked off a pass by Lynn Beightol and

1956—Oklahoma's Carl Dodd sprints past Maryland Coach Jim Tatum and goes 82 yards to score on an intercepted pass.

ran 82 yards to put the icing on his team's victory cake, 20 to 6. On that run, Wilkinson said, "I found out I was in pretty fair shape because I stayed with him about 60 yards on the sideline."

Maryland's split T offense was impotent in the second half. The better-conditioned Sooners, using the rapid-fire huddle against the beefy Terps, exhibited unusual split T speed and power in a lean, tough, mobile line as well as the backfield.

Maryland Coach Jim Tatum, who died of a violent virus infection just before the start of the 1959 season at North Carolina, said: "I've never seen a team with better equipment than Oklahoma. Every boy they had was a threat."

This was Oklahoma's thirtieth straight triumph. The streak ended in November of 1957 after 47 consecutive victories. The Sooners scored in 123 successive games before being beaten by Notre Dame 7 to 0.

Pete Elliott, an assistant coach for five years at Oklahoma, once said Wilkinson's success couldn't be accounted for by "any one thing but rather it is due to a combination of reasons.

"It's just that everything he plans or is responsible for is done to the highest degree of imagination, intelligence and effort.

"He's a master at instilling in a boy the desire and determination to win. I don't mean to win at all costs. I mean he makes a boy see that the only way to play is to play hard, to give it his maximum effort all the way.

"Bud is completely in command of himself always and this rubs off on his players and shows in their confident, poised play. Then, too, he has the keenness of mind and knowledge of football to give a boy the best possible teaching."

Oklahoma	0	0	14	6	20
Maryland	0	6	0	0	6

Oklahoma—Touchdowns: McDonald (4, right end), O'Neal (1, sneak), Dodd (82, intercepted pass by Beightol). Points after touchdown: Pricer 2.
Maryland—Touchdown: Vereb (15, left end).

STATISTICS

Oklahoma		*Maryland*	*Oklahoma*		*Maryland*
Mobra	LE	Walker	16	First downs	9
Woodworth	LT	Heuring	202	Net yards rushing	187
Bolinger	LG	Tullai	10	Passes attempted	10
Tubbs	C	Pellegrini	4	Passes completed	3
C. Morris	RG	Davis	1	Passes had intercepted	3

Oklahoma		Maryland	Oklahoma		Maryland
Gray	RT	Sandusky	53	Net yards passing	46
Bell	RE	Vereb	255	Total net yards	233
Harris	QB	Dennis	8	Number of punts	7
McDonald	LH	Tamburello	34.5	Punting average	40.4
Burris	RH	J. Healy	1	Fumbles lost	2
Pricer	FB	Hamilton	35	Yards penalized	61

Substitutions—Oklahoma: Stiller (l), Long (l), Timberlake (r), Ballard (r), ends; Greenlee (l), Searcy (l), Loughridge (l), Emerson (r), Ladd (r), tackles; Oujesky (l), Jennings (l), Krisher (r), Broyles (r), guards; Northcutt, Darnell, centers; O'Neal, Sturm, quarterbacks; Thomas (l), Sherrod (l), Dodd (r), Derrick (r), halfbacks; D. Morris, Brown, fullbacks. Maryland: Parsons (l), Waters (l), Cooke (r), Flynn (r), ends; Wharton (l), D. Healy (r), tackles; Dyson (l), Kolarac (l), Tonetti (l), DeCicco (r), guards; Alderton, Weber, centers; Beightol, quarterback; Nusz (l), McVicker (l), Dare (r), Burgee (r), halfbacks; Perlo, Skarda, Laughery, fullbacks.

ROSE

"Nervous? I didn't have time to get nervous."

"The boot felt good but I was afraid to look. I wasn't sure I made it until the official near me raised his arms and then Buck Nystrom (team captain) barreled into me and hugged me down on the grass."

In the bedlam of the Michigan State dressing room, Dave Kaiser was describing his 41-yard field goal with seven seconds left that gave the Spartans a 17 to 14 victory over UCLA on Monday, January 2, 1956.

Kaiser's long placekick ended, to all intents and purposes, the Rose Bowl game with the most frantic finish of all. The three-pointer climaxed a succession of events which confused 100,809 spectators in Pasadena and millions more watching on television.

The strange doings began just after Gerry Planutis of Michigan State missed a field goal following UCLA's tying touchdown. And with one minute, 34 seconds left, UCLA took possession of the ball on the 20, apparently sure of a tie.

Then the funny business started with head linesman Carlisle Dollings of the Big Ten catching Jim Myers, assistant UCLA coach, signaling from the sidelines for a pass while the Bruins were huddling. Fifteen yards were walked off against UCLA for unsportsmanlike conduct (coaching from the sidelines).

Coach Red Sanders explained, "I didn't see it, but they tell me one of our assistant coaches was yelling to Ronnie Knox to pass. If so, the officials were right."

On the next play, tailback Knox was trapped in the end zone. He threw a desperation pass. One official signaled intentional grounding of the ball. Referee Ross Dean repeated it. At the same time two other officials verbally called a penalty for UCLA having an ineligible receiver downfield. Intentional grounding of the ball would have given Michigan State a safety since the pass was thrown from the end zone. The ineligible receiver violation calls for a 15-yard penalty. That was the penalty that was assessed.

So now the ball was on the 1.

Knox chose to punt out of danger. It was short and high and as it came down on the 34, Bruin All-America guard Hardiman Cureton bumped into receiver Clarence Peaks. Peaks meant to make a fair catch but was brushed before he touched the ball. The resultant 15-yard penalty put the Spartans in possession on their 19. There was less than a minute to play.

Halfback Dennis Mendyk was stopped and fumbled, Planutis recovering. But a holding penalty against Michigan State moved the ball to the 30. Halfback Don Zysk fumbled, too, but gained a yard. Quarterback Earl Morrall threw a pass to Zysk on the 19.

At that point, Coach Duffy Daughterty purposely sent in Peaks to draw a five-yard delay of game penalty. This enabled Michigan State to stop the clock and get the kicking tee on the field.

Kaiser kicked the field goal from the 31. However, it wasn't until 25 minutes after the game ended that reporters realized he was the hero, not Planutis, who missed two earlier attempts. The public address announcer told the crowd Planutis was the kicker. The official play-by-play credited Planutis. Even Clarence Munn, Michigan State athletic director, yelled to reporters from his vantage point just below the press box that it was Planutis.

"We were going to gamble on passing at the end (Myers' signal was unnecessary) but those penalties killed us," Sanders commented.

Wilfrid Smith of the *Chicago Tribune* indicated the unsportsmanlike conduct penalty would never have been called but for the fact that the head linesman worked the entire game from the east sideline where the UCLA bench is located. Television cameras were placed on the west side.

Smith wrote: "Thus, by agreement, the down marker and ten-yard chain were operated during all of the game on the east sideline. Except for agreement to give the television audience the best view of all measurements, the head linesman and his assistants would have officiated on the west sideline for one half of the game.

"Dollings called the 15-yard penalty after he had been the target for criticism by the Bruins on several occasions . . . Dollings was given 60 minutes exposure to one team—and he made the 'call' many other officials would have avoided when faced by a 14–14 tie with less than two minutes to play."

UCLA wingback Jim Decker intercepted Morrall's first-play pass, flipped from the 12, and the Bruins scored first inside of four minutes. Advancing from the 16, tailback Sam Brown and fullback Bob Davenport were unstoppable. Davenport crashed into the end zone from the 2.

Morrall began to hit his targets in the second quarter. He threw a 13-yard touchdown pass to Peaks as the final play on an 80-yard drive. Most damaging to the Bruins on this march was a 30-yard run by sophomore halfback Walt Kowalczyk. Sanders referred to the strapping, speedy native of Massachusetts as the "sprinting blacksmith." Kowalczyk led all ball carriers with 88 yards in 13 trips.

In the first minute of the final hectic quarter a 67-yard pass play electrified the throng and boosted Michigan State into the lead 14 to 7. Morrall handed off to Peaks, who faded deep and flung a pass to end John (Big Thunder) Lewis. The Spartan wingman ran away from Brown after catching the ball on UCLA's 37. Brown was knocked out when he dived at Lewis' feet.

The Bruins battled back to earn a tie with the clock showing six minutes, seven seconds to play. Knox and Decker teamed up on a 47-yard pass. That put the ball on the Spartans' 7. Knox hit the line for five, then one. Fullback Doug Peters plunged over a pile for the touchdown.

Michigan State took the kickoff and charged from its 17 to the UCLA 22 where Planutis' field-goal attempt fell short, leading to the most extraordinary chain of circumstances ever helping to determine the result of a bowl game.

Daugherty, nonsecretive, revealingly conversational, was a decided contrast to most of the other Big Ten coaches who had barred the California press from practices. Daugherty welcomed Pacific Coast sports writers with open arms.

He worked four years following his graduation from high school to earn enough money to enter Syracuse. He was named Munn's line coach at Syracuse in 1946. The next year Daugherty went to Michigan State with Munn. When Biggie became athletic director in 1954, Duffy was promoted to head coach and continued to teach the multiple offense.

One day Daugherty received a letter addressed: "Duffy the Dope." When asked, "Didn't that make you mad?" he answered, "I didn't mind getting the card. It was pretty funny. The thing that bothered me was that the East Lansing post office knew exactly where to deliver it."

Michigan State   0   7   0   10   17
UCLA   7   0   0   7   14

Michigan State—Touchdowns: Peaks (13, pass from Morrall of 12, run of 1), Lewis (67, pass from Peaks of 30, run of 37). Field goal: Kaiser (41, place-kick). Points after touchdown: Planutis 2.
UCLA—Touchdowns: Davenport (2, left guard), Peters (1, dive). Points after touchdown: Decker 2.

STATISTICS

Michigan State		UCLA		Michigan State		UCLA
Lewis	LE	Hermann	18	First downs		13
Masters	LT	White	251	Net yards rushing		136
Currie	LG	Cureton	18	Passes attempted		10
Badaczewski	C	Palmer	6	Passes completed		2
Nystrom (c)	RG	Moreno	2	Passes had intercepted		1
Haidys	RT	J. Brown	130	Net yards passing		61
Kaiser	RE	Loudd	381	Total net yards		197
Morrall	QB	Ballard	2	Number of punts		7
Peaks	LH	S. Brown	40	Punting average		39.6
Kowalczyk	RH	Decker	1	Fumbles lost		0
Planutis	FB	Davenport	98	Yards penalized		60

Substitutions—Michigan State: Kolodziej (l), Jones (l), Jewett (l), Hinesly (r), ends; Rutledge (l), Burke (r), tackles; Matsos (l), Hollern (r), guards; Matsko, center; Wilson, quarterback; Mendyk (l), Wulff (r), Zysk (r), Gaddini (r), halfbacks; Lowe, fullback. UCLA: J. Smith (l), O'Garro (l), Adams (r), H. Smith (r), ends; Shinnick (l), Hampton (l), Penner (r), tackles; Birren (l), Harris (r), guards; Matheny, center; Bergdahl, quarterback; Bradley (l), Knox (l), Hollaway (r), halfbacks; Peters, fullback.

– 1957 –

ROSE

The night before Oregon State and Iowa met at Iowa City, October 6, 1956, John Eggers, sports publicity director for the Beavers, was the house guest of the Eric Wilsons. During the course of a pleasant evening, Eggers remarked to his host, drum beater for Iowa's athletic teams, "I wouldn't be surprised if our teams played each other again in the Rose Bowl."

Just that summer the Wilsons, vacationing in California, had visited the Pasadena stadium. As they sat there in the sunshine surrounded by 100,000 empty seats, Wilson said to his wife, "Do you suppose we'll live long enough to see an Iowa team play here?"

Under robust, sensible, solid, straightforward, approachable Forest Evashevski, Iowa came a long way to play there. The Hawkeyes, employing a winged T attack that Evashevski molded to fit his players' capabilities, won eight games and lost only to Michigan, 17 to 14, on a touchdown scored with 66 seconds remaining.

Iowa won its first undisputed Big Ten championship since 1921. At the end of the season, Evy said, "We're not a really good club. We've been getting more mileage out of six points this year than any team I've ever seen. No, we aren't great but we try to be."

One of the memorable sports pictures of the year, 1956, was made November 17. It showed three of Evashevski's four sons rushing into his outstretched arms a moment after Iowa had beaten Ohio State, 6 to 0. That clinched at least a tie for the Big Ten title. The family picture was used later to illustrate an Iowa Development Commission advertisement in the official Rose Bowl program.

The striking photograph was taken as Evashevski's right arm embraced his 14-year-old boy, Forest, Jr., a freshman quarterback at Iowa City High School. The young man later matriculated at Michigan, his father's alma mater. One Friday night, after seeing a high school game, typical dad Evashevski came home and told his wife, Ruth, "I just don't think that coach is playing Frosty enough."

Mrs. Evashevski is the daughter of Prentiss Brown, wealthy former United States senator from Michigan. A few years ago Evashevski was pondering renewal of his contract at a reported salary of $15,000 annually. He received a wire from his father-in-law advising, "Better take it. I'm not as rich as you think."

Oregon State was built from a downtrodden lot into Pacific Coast Conference champion by single-wing disciple Tommy Prothro. This was the year UCLA, Southern California, and Washington weren't permitted to play in the Rose Bowl. They were under ban charged with excessive aid to athletes. It was a three-year suspension for UCLA, two years for Washington and Southern California. When the 1960 Rose Bowl game was played, Southern California was under National Collegiate Athletic Association probation again.

Prothro came from UCLA to Oregon State in 1955, bringing with him the concepts of Wallace Wade, under whom he played at Duke in 1939–40–41, and Red Sanders, under whom he coached at Vanderbilt and UCLA.

His Beavers were doomed to quick calamity in the 1957 Rose Bowl game and eventual defeat, 35 to 19 in their second meeting with Iowa after losing the first, 14 to 13.

Wingback Earnel Durden and tailback Joe Francis ran impressively on the first two plays. Fullback Tom Berry fumbled, though, when Iowa's All-America tackle, Alex Karras, "undressed" him. End Frank Gilliam recovered for the Hawkeyes on their 40. Four plays after that quarterback Kenny Ploen, the Big Ten's most valuable player, slanted inside Oregon State's left end and ran 49 yards for a touchdown. It was a brilliant combination of personal exploit and team cooperation.

Iowa's second touchdown was virtually a duplicate. Again the Beavers handed over the ball involuntarily when center Don Suchy's rock-and-sock jolting caused Francis to cough it up for halfback Mike Hagler to recover on Iowa's 34. The Hawkeyes went 66 yards to score in four plays. Biggest chunk of yardage was a burst of 37 by halfback Don Dobrino to the Oregon State 9. From there little Hagler whizzed to his left and scored.

With a little less than four minutes left in the first quarter, Ploen sustained an injured right knee. He was carried off the field in pain, apparently through for the day.

Each team scored in the second quarter. Ploen returned to the lineup, his knee heavily taped, when the Beavers kicked off to start the second half. With the ball on Iowa's 34, a double reverse executed with speed and precision brought the crowd of 97,126 to its feet.

Here's how the play unfolded: Ploen fed the ball to Dobrino coming right. Hagler took it from Dobrino who shoved it forward. The right halfback darted in at left guard and cut back sharply. Sprinting diagonally, he outran pursuers in what amounted to a footrace to the goal line.

In the opening seconds of the fourth period Ploen's seventh successive completion since the game began was an on-the-run touchdown pass to end Jim Gibbons on a fourth-and-two situation from the 16.

At the finish Governor Elmo Smith of Oregon congratulated Governor Leo Hoegh of Iowa. Hoegh had given Smith nine points in a friendly bet of a 15-pound Iowa ham against a 45-pound Oregon salmon.

Harry Stapler of the *Detroit News* revealed that the tragic death of Calvin Jones was a factor in the victory. Jones, Iowa's All-America guard in 1954 and 1955, was aboard a Canadian airliner that disappeared in the mountains of British Columbia early in December.

Stapler wrote that the Iowa coaches did not direct the players' decision. They got the notion themselves shortly following the tragedy. A week after they reached California, Evashevski, then somewhat discouraged by mediocre workouts, told them, "You don't deserve to dedicate a game to Cal the way you're going out here. Forget it."

Three days before the game, however, the players held one of their regular morale meetings. No coaches attended these sessions. The squad voted unanimously to play the game for Jones. The ball was to be given to his mother in Steubenville, Ohio.

Cynics, Stapler acknowledged, "won't be able to take this but it happened: before the game, someone told Frank Gilliam, who had come with Jones to Iowa from Steubenville, 'Remember, Frank, Cal will be playing beside you today.' "

The game hadn't quite ended when the goal posts at the south end were knocked down by jubilant Iowans. An estimated 15,000, including 2,500 students, crossed the country to see the classic.

"I can't wait to get back home and roll in that rich Iowa dirt," Evashevski remarked. He could hardly turn anywhere in public without bumping into a representative of the *Des Moines Register,* which blanketed the event with four sports writers, two news reporters, and a photographer. They contributed heavily to the record press file of 115,000 words from the Rose Bowl on the day of the game.

Evy's wife beamed as she prepared to board a plane to the Midwest, January 3. "It's a great relief to be returning like this," she said. "You feel as though you let the Big Ten down if you don't win out here."

TUESDAY, JANUARY 1, 1957

Iowa	14	7	7	7	35
Oregon State	0	6	6	7	19

Iowa—Touchdowns: Ploen (49, right end), Hagler 2 (9, left tackle; 66, left guard), Happel (5, left end), Gibbons (16, pass from Ploen). Point after touchdown: Prescott 5.

Oregon State—Touchdowns: Berry (3, left guard), Beamer (1, center plunge), Hammack (35, pass from Francis of 33, run of 2). Point after touchdown: Beamer (plunge).

STATISTICS

Iowa		Oregon State	Iowa		Oregon State
Gibbons	LE	Thiel	16	First downs	16
A. Karras	LT	Witte	301	Net yards rushing	166
Bloomquist	LG	Sniffen	15	Passes attempted	14
Suchy (c-c)	C	Corrick (c-c)	11	Passes completed	10
Commings	RG	Brackins	1	Passes had intercepted	0
Klein	RT	Jesmer	107	Net yards passing	130
Gilliam	RE	DeGrant	408	Total net yards	296
Ploen	QB	Laird (c-c)	2	Number of punts	3
Dobrino	LH	Francis	36	Punting average	35
Hagler	RH	Durden	3	Fumbles lost	3
Nocera	FB	Berry	50	Yards penalized	60

Substitutions—Iowa: Ahlgren (l), Haussman (l), Jenkinson (l), Prescott (r), Hatch (r), ends; Burroughs (l), Kress (l), Scott (l), Deasy (c-c) (r), Rigney (r), tackles; Theer (l), Grouwinkel (l), Drake (r), P. Karras (r), guards; Pierce, Lewis, centers; Duncan, Veit, Coppotelli, quarterbacks; Gravel (l), Kloewer (l), Knotts (l), Happel (r), Furlong (r), halfbacks; Harris, Walker, Janda, Stifter, fullbacks. Oregon State: Fournier (l), Negri (r), Clarke (r), ends; Zwahlen (l), Bates (r), Rogers (r), tackles; McKittrick (l), Ellison (r), guards; Randall, Anagnos, centers; Searle, Lukehart, quarterbacks; Lowe (l), Arana (l), Hammack (r), Marsh (r), Owings (r), halfbacks; Beamer, Milum, fullbacks.

GATOR

Bobby Dodd, that master of bowl preparation, did it again at Jacksonville.

"Whatever the touch may be, he has it," the *Atlanta Journal's* Ed Danforth wrote at the Gator Bowl scene. "It is not accidental that eight of his teams have played their brilliant best in bowl games."

As in the past the swift moving Yellow Jackets followed the do-it-the-easy-way plan. They kept their bowl record under Dodd clean with a 21 to 14 victory over Pittsburgh.

Although Pittsburgh worked a week later than Tech getting ready for a late season game with Miami, the Panthers took only a four-day Christmas vacation before returning to the scrimmage grind. The Jackets were given an 11-day vacation. In actual practice time they spent only a week on the gridiron.

The Tech team of 1956 was tough, sharp, eager, and won its sixth bowl game in as many seasons.

Seven players participated in their fourth straight bowl contest. One of them was quarterback Wade Mitchell, a straight A textile engineering student who was ranked highest scholastically in his school. He received the most valuable player trophy.

Among other feats Mitchell completed both passes he threw en route to Tech's third touchdown. His play judgment was beyond criticism. He was involved in one unusual situation. He felt he would have broken up a long throw by Corny Salvaterra, which went for a touchdown, if he hadn't fallen over back judge Sam Bartholomew while covering receiver Dick Bowen.

"I'm sure it wasn't intentional, but the official blocked me out," Mitchell said. Bowen made a diving, rolling catch of the 42-yard pass.

That was 16 seconds before the first half ended. The extra point was scored on a fake kick and pass by Salvaterra to All-America end Joe Walton, son of Frank (Tiger) Walton, Pitt tackle in the early thirties. Joe's father died of cancer two days after he enrolled.

The Jackets had already scored twice. On one of the plays during the first touchdown drive, fullback Ken Owen was shaken up by a gang tackle. The team trainer went out on the field and asked, "What's the matter, Ken?"

"It's my neck," Owen answered. "It's broken. But being as this is my last game, I'll just stick it out."

Owen kept his teammates relaxed and laughing with his natural wit. He scored the first touchdown from the 2. The second was

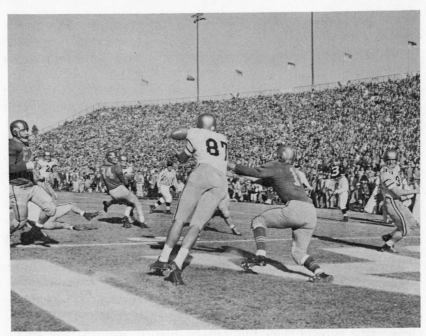

1956—Georgia Tech end Jerry Nabors (87) catches a running pass by George Volkert (24) for a touchdown against Pittsburgh.

notched on a six-yard running pass from George Volkert to end Jerry Nabors, and the third on a five-yard end run by Paul Rotenberry.

Pitt fell behind by two touchdowns twice and got the next one but not the important one. It was the second straight bowl game in which the massive, powerful Panthers decisively outgained and out-first-downed the Jackets but couldn't score as many points. It happened 361 days before in New Orleans.

In the course of his talk at the postgame banquet Pitt Coach John Michelosen turned to the table where his players sat and said, "Rub shoulders with these Tech seniors. I want you to become a band of opportunists, too."

SATURDAY, DECEMBER 29, 1956

Georgia Tech	7	7	7	0	21
Pittsburgh	0	7	7	0	14

Georgia Tech—Touchdowns: Owen (2, left tackle), Nabors (6, pass from Volkert), Rotenberry (5, right end). Points after touchdown: Mitchell 3.

Pittsburgh—Touchdowns: Bowen (42, pass from Salvaterra), Salvaterra (2, right guard). Points after touchdown: Walton (pass from Salvaterra), Bagamery (placekick).

STATISTICS

Georgia Tech		Pittsburgh		Georgia Tech	Pittsburgh
Nabors	LE	Walton	10	First downs	16
Vereen	LT	Pollock	162	Net yards rushing	246
Johnson	LG	Scorsone	3	Passes attempted	11
Stephenson	C	Brueckman	3	Passes completed	3
Ecker	RG	Wisniewski	0	Passes had intercepted	2
Anderson	RT	Canil	45	Net yards passing	67
Ellis	RE	Rosborough	207	Total net yards	313
Mitchell	QB	Salvaterra	5	Number of punts	3
Rotenberry	LH	Bowen	41	Punting average	36
Thompson	RH	Theodore	1	Fumbles lost	2
Owen	FB	Jelic	13	Yards penalized	0

Substitutions—Georgia Tech: Rose (l), Gibbs (r), Smith (r), ends; Christy (l), Henry (l), Thrash (r), tackles; Miller (l), Askew (r), guards; Wiley, center; Vann, quarterback; Flowers (l), Volkert (r), Menger (r), halfbacks; Mattison, Gookin, fullbacks. Pittsburgh: Scherer (l), Brown (r), ends; Kissel (l), Mc-Cusker (r), tackles; Michaels (l), Carr (r), guards; Salwocki, center; Lewis, quarterback; Haley (l), Passodelis (l), Bagamery (r), DiPasquale (r), halfbacks; Jenkins, fullback.

COTTON

The stars shone brilliantly, as advertised, but an unknown second team end named Chico Mendoza determined the final score as Texas Christian bested Syracuse 28 to 27, in the Cotton Bowl tingler of 1957.

Mendoza didn't score a point. He charged into the backfield and blocked mighty Jim Brown's try for the extra point after Syracuse's third touchdown.

"I had a straight shot in there," said Mendoza. Brown's toe was just inches away from the ball when the tall end leaped sideways. The ball hit his left arm.

It was a great day for TCU, stung with five straight bowl losses.

Harold Pollard, who had missed the extra point in the 14 to 13 defeat by Ole Miss in 1956, kicked four vital conversions.

Quarterback Chuck Curtis, carried off the field with broken ribs after the opening kickoff the year before, completed 12 of 15 passes for 174 yards. He pitched for a pair of touchdowns, ran for one himself, and set up the fourth, scored by Jim Swink, with a 30-yard pass to the All-America halfback.

It was undoubtedly TCU's most needed triumph in its annals.

Actually, the Frogs wouldn't have had the opportunity except that Texas A&M, champion of the Southwest Conference and 7 to 6 victor over TCU, was under bowl probation imposed by the National Collegiate Athletic Association.

Syracuse also had some redeeming to do. Coach Floyd (Ben) Schwartzwalder's 1952 team had been routed, 61 to 6, by Alabama in the Orange Bowl.

"Does this atone for that Miami defeat?" an interviewer asked.

"No," Schwartzwalder answered. "When you've lost a game, you've lost it. You're out to win a game, not to atone for another."

All four of TCU's touchdowns followed Syracuse mistakes—a pass interception and three fumbles. The scoring drives of 70, 35, 60, and 69 yards were evenly divided among the quarters.

The Orangemen got their final touchdown on a 27-yard pass play from Chuck Zimmerman to Jim Ridlon with 1:16 left. But rather than try an onside kick in an effort to gain possession of the ball, Syracuse kicked off deep, apparently hoping for the miracle of a fumble. TCU ran three plays and the game ended.

The muscular Brown, who had scored 106 points and amassed 986 yards in Syracuse's eight-game season, put on the most awesome demonstration of carrying a football forward by sheer power a Cotton Bowl crowd ever saw. Brown often lugged several Frogs on his back as he whanged ahead for 132 yards in 26 blasts. He scored 21 points.

"Any man who wouldn't call Brown a great player would have to be ignorant or blind," said TCU Coach Abe Martin.

"We hope to come back some day and do a little better," Schwartzwalder said as he departed for home.

Three years later he did.

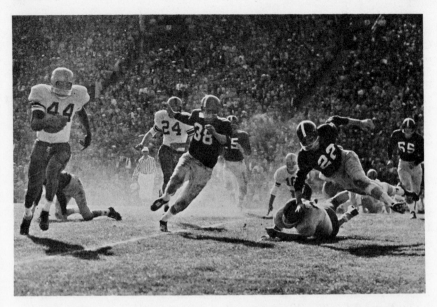

1957—Syracuse's Jim Brown heads around Texas Christian's left side.

| Texas Christian | 7 | 7 | 7 | 7 | 28 |
| Syracuse | 0 | 14 | 0 | 13 | 27 |

Texas Christian—Touchdowns: Nikkel (6, pass from Curtis), Shofner (8, pass from Curtis), Curtis (7, left end), Swink (3, right tackle). Points after touchdown: Pollard 4.

Syracuse—Touchdowns: Brown 3 (2, right guard; 4, right end; 1, right tackle), Ridlon (27, pass from Zimmerman of 26, run of 1). Points after touchdown: Brown 3.

STATISTICS

Texas Christian		*Syracuse*	*Texas Christian*		*Syracuse*
Nikkel	LE	Baccile	15	First downs	16
Hamilton	LT	Strid	133	Net yards rushing	235
Groom	LG	Farmer	16	Passes attempted	7
J. Williams	C	W. Brown	13	Passes completed	3
Uecker	RG	Bailey	0	Passes had intercepted	1
Cooper	RT	Cashman	202	Net yards passing	63
H. Williams	RE	Lasse	335	Total net yards	298
Curtis	QB	Zimmerman	4	Number of punts	2
Swink	LH	J. Brown	37.5	Punting average	46.5
Wineburg	RH	Ridlon	2	Fumbles lost	3
Dike	FB	Coffin	40	Yards penalized	5

Substitutions—Texas Christian: Sanford (l), Mendoza (l), Pollard (r), ends; K. Miller (l), Robb (r), tackles; Holland (l), Mitchell (r), Salley (r), Few (r), Carter (r), guards; Walker, Ozee, centers; Finney, quarterback; Vacek (l), Shofner (r), V. Miller (r), halfbacks; Hallbeck, fullback. Syracuse: Althouse (l), Stephens (l), Aloise (r), ends; Hershey (l), Benecick (r), tackles; Warholak (l), Bill (r), guards; Krivak, center; Kuczala, Fogarty, quarterbacks; Ackley (l), Jackson (r), Danigelis (r), halfbacks; Cann, Zaso, fullbacks.

SUGAR

"It Was The Vols By 7 . . .
The Sun Was Shining"

The headline in the *Knoxville News-Sentinel,* January 1, 1957, whether intentionally subtle or not, carried just a hint that by late afternoon, when the game would be over and the paper would be read, the picture might have changed.

It had. Again, as on six other New Year's Day evenings in Knoxville, home of the University of Tennessee, dinners were cheerless. The Volunteers, favored by seven points, had lost to Baylor in the Sugar Bowl 13 to 7. They became the fourth perfect-record Tennessee team with a bowl smudge.

The result was no surprise to Baylor Coach Sam Boyd and his men. Boyd felt his twice-beaten team could and should zoom to its zenith of performance.

Tennessee's 1956 schedule, in Bowden Wyatt's second season as his alma mater's coach, was the toughest in school history. There were games with five bowl teams of the previous year. The Vols flattened all opposition to win the Southeastern Conference title.

Athletic director Bob Neyland pronounced 162-pound Johnny Majors the finest all-around tailback in Tennessee history. He seemed to have a built-in sense of timing.

Tennessee's first three foes scored 47 points and the firmness of its defense was questioned. Captain John Gordy bristled at this. Said the 215-pound tackle: "Other teams can run all over our defense —on the blackboard. And maybe between the 20-yard lines. But we are men, not 'x's'."

Most formidable figure in the big Baylor line, which averaged 211 pounds per man—to Tennessee's 196—was guard Bill Glass, whose 230 pounds were spread on a six-foot, five-inch frame. His chosen field was child welfare religious work. He was booked for dinner or church meeting speaking engagements for a solid month after returning from the Sugar Bowl to Waco.

Halfback Del Shofner in Baylor's multiple T offense was timed in 9.8 seconds in the 100-yard dash and 20.6 in the 220. In a game against Nebraska, Shofner demonstrated such propulsion the Bears frequently were penalized for having a back in motion (moving forward before the center snap). Boyd insisted his speed boy was only shooting forth at the precise instant the ball was passed back. At halftime he complained to an official.

"He wasn't in motion," Sam maintained.

"No, it wasn't for that," the official replied. "Those penalties were against the rest of the team for delaying the game."

Majors prevented a Baylor touchdown on the opening kickoff with a last-man tackle of Bobby Peters, who ran 51 yards to the Tennessee 44. A subsequent drive reached the 4 where Baylor was penalized five yards for unaccountably not getting off its next play in the prescribed 25 seconds. This forced a field goal attempt by Donnel Berry that was wide.

In the second quarter Baylor moved 80 yards and this time didn't stop until the ball was planted in the end zone on a 12-yard pass play from quarterback Bobby Jones to end Jerry Marcontell. Longest gainer was a 54-yard sprint by Shofner.

Four Vols gang-tackled Peters on the Baylor 14 as the second half got under way in contrast to the first. A Bear punt was compulsory and Tennessee had 39 yards to traverse after a 15-yard penalty for piling on when Majors returned the kick. It took ten plays to score with Johnny carrying on eight. He went over from the 1. Sammy Burklow's placement was true—Berry's hadn't been—and the Vols led 7 to 6.

The Vols held on the ensuing kickoff. They were in another favorable position as they lined up at the Bears' 42 on offense. Three plays later, when Majors was swarmed over for a six-yard loss, the crowd was horrified. Baylor fullback Larry Hickman suddenly ran a few steps and kicked Bruce Burnham, Tennessee's left guard, in the face as he was getting off the ground. Burnham, unconscious, went into convulsions and lay trembling on his back.

The player was carried from the field on a stretcher and rushed to Touro Infirmary in New Orleans. Two hours later Burnham revived. He recovered quickly from the concussion.

Referee Fred Koster said Burnham had drawn a personal foul for continuing aggressive action against Baylor guard Charley Horton by moving his elbows and legs after he'd blown his whistle. Burnham would not have been ejected. Hickman was.

The most important kick of the game, by Shofner, occurred in the fourth quarter. Booted from the Tennessee 48, it appeared to be headed for the end zone until Majors elected to catch the spiral on the 7. Johnny struggled back to the 15. There he fumbled when tackled.

To Baylor fullback Reuben Saage, who pounced on the ball, "it was the happiest moment of my life. I knew we would score from there."

Saage was right. On the sixth play Buddy Humphrey, one of four Baylor quarterbacks, negotiated the final yard as linemen wedged a gap in the middle he could leap through.

One of the first things Boyd did when the game ended was to seek and receive permission to speak to the Tennessee squad.

"All of us at Baylor are terribly sorry this happened," he said, referring to the kicking of Burnham. "We hope you can forgive us." Boyd was in no mood to rejoice. "This is the first ball game I ever won that I can't be happy about," he told the press.

Glass joined other Baylor representatives in apologizing, saying "Hickman is a fine boy, a religious boy and a fine player, but I guess he just lost his head."

At the awards dinner that night, Hickman accepted his wrist watch, then asked permission to speak. "I want to apologize to the University of Tennessee and to Bruce Burnham and to my own school for what happened today," he said. "I'm as sorry as a person can be. I sincerely hope the boy will be all right and that you will find it in your hearts to forgive me."

Pete Baird, front page paragrapher of the *New Orleans Times Picayune,* said he knew a broker who had resolved not to work so hard, explaining, "There are other things in life besides money . . . stocks, bonds, travelers' checks."

For quite a while it would have been difficult to convince the despondent Vols and their followers there are other things besides victory in football.

But the pain eased as the hours passed.

Next morning, as he opened his motel room door, end Buddy Cruze called to his roommate, "See, I told you the sun would come out."

Baylor	0	6	0	7	13
Tennessee	0	0	7	0	7

Baylor—Touchdowns: Marcontell (12, pass from Jones of 7, run of 5), Humphrey (1, center plunge). Point after touchdown: Berry.

Tennessee—Touchdown: Majors (1, left tackle). Point after touchdown: Burklow.

STATISTICS

Baylor		Tennessee	Baylor		Tennessee
DeGrazier	LE	Cruze	13	First downs	10
Oliver	LT	Rader	275	Net yards rushing	146
Glass	LG	Burnham	11	Passes attempted	10
Harrington	C	Howe	3	Passes completed	1
Horton	RG	Johnson	0	Passes had intercepted	4
Lunceford	RT	Gordy	24	Net yards passing	16
Marcontell	RE	Roger Urbano	299	Total net yards	162
Jones	QB	Adkins	8	Number of punts	5
Shofner	LH	Majors	32.6	Punting average	41.6
Peters	RH	Anderson	0	Fumbles lost	1
Dupre	FB	Bronson	60	Yards penalized	55

*Substitutions—*Baylor: Miller (l), Anderson (r), ends; Bradshaw (l), Kelley (l), Dickson (r), Britton (r), tackles; Pearce (l), Letbetter (r), Bennett (r), guards; Cowart, center; Traylor, Humphrey, Overton, quarterbacks; Fisher (l), Berry (r), Beall (r), Clark (r), halfbacks; Hickman, Saage, Baker, Pavliska, fullbacks. Tennessee: Darty (l), Cantrell (r), ends; Smelcher (l), Kolinsky (r), tackles; Bob Urbano (l), Herzbrun (r), guards; Lanter, center; Gleaves, quarterback; Gordon (l), Carter (l), Sandlin (r), halfbacks; Smith, Burklow, fullbacks.

ORANGE

Within a second-quarter segment of five minutes and six seconds, Colorado scored a bunch of three touchdowns. An intercepted pass and blocked punt paved the way for two of them. At halftime in the 1957 Orange Bowl game, the Buffaloes seemed securely ahead, 20 to 0.

The Clemson Tigers shuffled to their dressing room before 73,280 pairs of eyes, whipped and crestfallen. There they found an irate coach awaiting them with fire in his eyes.

"I told 'em if they didn't get in there and play, I was gonna resign," Frank Howard said. "I meant it, too. I said I didn't want to be associated with boys who played like that. They simply refused to block and their tackling was sloppy."

His message got through to his men. It so inspired them that with 11 minutes, 12 seconds left in the fourth quarter, they had taken a 21 to 20 lead over the Colorado team, which was runner-up to Oklahoma's national champions in the Big Seven.

But then, quarterback Charlie Bussey tried an onside kick that fooled no one. After its second touchdown, Clemson had recovered an onside kickoff against the surprised boys from Boulder, although tackle Dick Marazza, the kicker, said, "I just missed the ball. We didn't plan it that way."

Bussey was pressing his luck this time. He kicked the ball squarely into the arms of John Wooten, 228-pound Colorado guard. In eight quick strikes, with rangy halfback Eddie Dove and 217-pound full-back John (The Beast) Bayuk as the driving forces, Colorado advanced 53 yards to score and win, 27 to 21.

"I wanted to get the ball again because I thought we had them on the run," Bussey said. "But it wasn't a very smart call."

"At least we had enough pride to fight back," said Clemson half-back Joel Wells, top rusher with 125 yards in 18 carries. He made two touchdowns, the second on a 58-yard run. Wells gained four yards more than Bayuk, who also scored twice.

"Fifty million folks (television watchers) would have remembered us by that comeback," Howard said. "But then we go get ourselves beat."

After the game Howard was asked if he still had any thoughts of quitting. He pondered for a moment, shifted the tobacco from one side of his mouth to the other, and replied, "Son, a man's gotta make a living."

Colorado	0	20	0	7	27
Clemson	0	0	14	7	21

Colorado—Touchdowns: Bayuk 2 (2, center smash; 1, right tackle), Dowler (6, left end), Cook (26, right end). Points after touchdown: Indorf 2, Cook.

Clemson—Touchdowns: Wells 2 (3, left tackle; 58, right tackle), Spooner (1, left guard). Points after touchdown: Bussey 3.

STATISTICS

Colorado		Clemson	Colorado		Clemson
Leahy	LE	Rivers	16	First downs	14
Stapp	LT	Marazza	279	Net yards rushing	217
Wooten	LG	Greene	4	Passes attempted	8
Uhlir	C	Bunton	2	Passes completed	3
Jones	RG	Grdijan	0	Passes had intercepted	2
Schlagel	RT	Hudson	27	Net yards passing	25
Merz	RE	Smith	306	Total net yards	242
Dowler	QB	Bussey	5	Number of punts	7
Stransky	LH	Wells	36.6	Punting average	37.9
Dove	RH	Coleman	3	Fumbles lost	0
Bayuk	FB	Hayes	55	Yards penalized	40

Substitutions—Colorado: Clarke (l), Nady (l), Lotz (r), ends; Salerno (l), Giek (l), Himelwright (r), Call (r), tackles; Golder (l), Vest (l), Joslin (l), Mondt (r), guards; Brown, Pruit, centers; Herbst, Morley, Hyson, quarterbacks; Cook (l), Worden (r), Indorf (r), Briddle (r), halfbacks; Warner, Clark, fullbacks. Clemson: Masneri (l), Few (l), Breedlove (r), Jordan (r), ends; McCanless (l), Sease (r), tackles; Kaltenbach (l), DeSimone (r), Bruorton (r), guards; Thomas, center; Turbeville, quarterback; Lawrence (l), Horne (r), halfbacks; Spooner, Dukes, fullbacks.

– 1958 –

ORANGE

The two-line, eight-column streamer on the *Miami Herald's* first sports page on January 2, 1958, told the story succinctly.

'GIFT-WRAPPED' TDS MADE WILKINSON BLUSH
—BUT HIS WAR CRY WAS 'GET ANOTHER ONE'

"Get another one," Bud Wilkinson shouted as his Oklahoma Sooners piled up touchdown after touchdown (four of them) in the wild fourth quarter.

When he met Duke Coach Bill Murray in the center of the Orange Bowl afterward, he said, with some embarrassment, "I never had so many touchdowns given to me."

As Oklahoma line coach Gomer Jones explained it: "We put our defensive men in gaps and shot them through. This is a pretty chancy sort of thing. You either throw them for a loss or they get by you.

"They got by us on their three long touchdown drives. But it took a lot of steam out of them.

"Meanwhile, we forced them into other errors with the penetrating defense. We got every score the easy way—after two fumbles, a blocked punt, poor snap from center, two pass interceptions and a good punt return. We never had to grind them out."

A look at the statistics gave no indication that the score was 48 to 21. Duke led in first downs, rushing, and total yardage, had a better pass completion percentage, and intercepted more passes. Also, Oklahoma was penalized 150 yards, a record. Duke ran 69 plays to 44 for the Sooners.

Yet there was no doubt that Oklahoma was the superior team. In the last analysis, breaks, stamina, speed, depth, alertness, never letting up, plus a few surprise plays won for the Sooners.

Center Bob Harrison offered this viewpoint:

"We hit so hard in the first half [when Oklahoma led 14 to 7] they can't stay with us in the second half. We wear 'em out. When

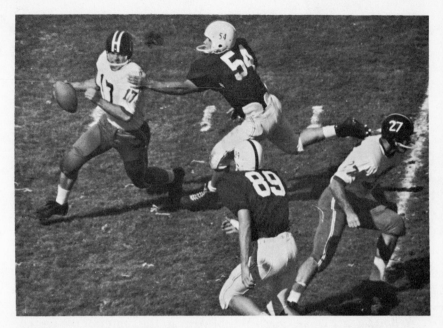

1958—Bob Harrison (54), Oklahoma's All-America center, rushes in to throw Duke quarterback Bob Brodhead for a 14-yard loss.

they're so tired they start to coast, then bang! That's when we explode. We just consider the second half ours."

Oklahoma was being outplayed in the first quarter until quarterback David Baker intercepted a pass thrown by third-string Duke quarterback George Harris from the Sooners' 17. Baker whisked away 94 yards for the first touchdown.

Practically everyone agreed that the play that broke open the game was a third-down (with goal to go) shovel pass from quarterback Carl Dodd to Jackie Sandefer. It was good for 13 yards to the Duke 4 early in the fourth quarter. Sandefer immediately wheeled for a touchdown, making it 27 to 14.

Murray blamed himself for one of the touchdowns. It was supposed to be a pass off a fake quick-kick. There was confusion, a fumble. Oklahoma recovered the ball and scored.

"We should never have put in a play like that at the half," Murray said. "You can't expect a team to execute it with no practice."

After each of their team's touchdowns, Oklahoma cheer leaders set off a small but loud explosive. As the dazed Blue Devils dejectedly made their way to the dressing room, the yell leaders fired the cannon once more in tribute to the one-sided victory. One battered lineman stopped short and glanced back at the scoreboard. "Don't tell me they scored again," he said.

The Atlantic Coast Conference's contract with the Orange Bowl terminated with this game. Under a new pact, the Big Eight was to furnish the host Orange Bowl team for the next three years.

WEDNESDAY, JANUARY 1, 1958

Oklahoma	7	7	7	27	48
Duke	0	7	7	7	21

Oklahoma—Touchdowns: Baker 3 (94, intercepted pass by G. Harris; 29, pass from Hobby of 7, run of 22; 9, pass from Hobby), Thomas (13, double reverse, left end), Dodd (1, left guard), Sandefer (4, right end), Carpenter (73, Watts intercepted pass by Brodhead, run of 28, lateral to Carpenter, run of 45). Points after touchdown: Dodd 4, Boyd, McDaniel.

Duke—Touchdowns: McElhaney 2 (1, center plunge; 4, center), Dutrow (8, left end). Points after touchdown: Carlton 3.

STATISTICS

Oklahoma		*Duke*	*Oklahoma*		*Duke*
Stiller	LE	Hurm	11	First downs	16
Searcy	LT	Topping	165	Net yards rushing	231
Northcutt	LG	Hord	18	Passes attempted	13
Harrison	C	Byrd	9	Passes completed	8
Krisher	RG	McGee	3	Passes had intercepted	2
D. Jennings	RT	Recinella	114	Net yards passing	97
Rector	RE	Thompson	279	Total net yards	328
Baker	QB	Brodhead	7	Number of punts	10
Sandefer	LH	Carlton	34.7	Punting average	28.1
Thomas	RH	Dutrow	1	Fumbles lost	2
Morris	FB	McElhaney	150	Yards penalized	25

Substitutions—Oklahoma: Coyle (l), Jackson (l), S. Jennings (r), Durham (r), Levonitis (r), ends; Thompson (l), Wells (l), Lewis (l), Lawrence (r), Shilling (r), Morford (r), tackles; Oujesky (l), Bowman (l), Gwinn (l), Corbitt (r), Moore (r), Bradley (r), guards; Davis, Johnson, Payne, centers; Dodd, Watts, Sherrod, quarterbacks; Boyd (l), Holt (l), Gautt (l), Hobby (r), Pellow (r), Carpenter (r), halfbacks; Rolle, McDaniel, Sears, fullbacks. Duke: Lattimore (l), Bartal (l), Atherholt (r), Padgett (r), Spada (r), ends; Denne (l), Swofford (l), Gardner (r), Royal (r), tackles; Kersey (l), Keyser (l), Guy (r), guards; Hoch, Culp, centers; Millner, G. Harris, quarterbacks; Rushton (l), Bell (l), Fetsko (r), Lee (r), halfbacks; Dupler, Cottingham, J. Harris, Eberdt, fullbacks.

ROSE

So they carried Coach Len Casanova of Oregon off the field.

Did his Ducks, 19-point underdogs in what was supposed to be the most unequal match in Rose Bowl history, upset Ohio State's national champions (United Press poll)?

No. But those scorned Oregonians gave those terrific Buckeyes a giant-sized scare. They did themselves proud. They thought Casanova was a remarkable coach and a fine fellow.

So they carried him off the field, even though reserve Ohio State halfback Don Sutherin had come off the bench in the first minute of the fourth quarter to kick a game-winning 34-yard field goal.

1958—Don Sutherin of Ohio State kicks the field goal that downed Oregon 10 to 7.

Oregon was nosed out by Oregon State, 10 to 7, on the November 23rd before the same-score defeat by Ohio State. Oregon State, which finished in a tie with Oregon for the Pacific Coast Conference title, could not return to the Rose Bowl again because of the once-in-two-years rule.

Oregon was one of four teams in the conference eligible to play in the Rose Bowl in the season of 1957. The others were California, Stanford, and Washington State. Under National Collegiate Athletic Association probation for infractions of the athletic code were UCLA, Washington, and Southern California.

Thirty-eight years before, a team from Eugene, Oregon, had come to Pasadena and lost to Harvard, 7 to 6. In that game, an Oregon field-goal try that would have won the game just missed. Some of the Oregon players never were convinced it wasn't good.

Just a few minutes before Sutherin delivered his game-clincher, Oregon fullback Jack Morris had a chance for a field goal from almost the exact spot—the 24-yard line—and almost the same angle.

"Morris' kick was so close I thought sure it went between the goal posts," Ohio State Coach Woody Hayes said. "It's lucky the officials were calling it instead of me."

But Oregon quarterback Jack Crabtree, who was voted the outstanding player, said it missed by five or six feet. "Right from the start I was afraid it wouldn't go through," said Crabtree, who held the ball for Morris. "I held my breath and hoped, but it had a little too much angle."

However, what may have hurt Oregon most was end Ron Stover's fumble on Ohio State's 24 in the fourth period. The Ducks had driven desperately from their 20 after the score went to 10 to 7. Stover caught a pass from Crabtree, thrown from the Buckeyes' 47. He was tackled from behind and as he fell the ball squirted from his hands like a cake of wet soap. Stover caught ten passes for 144 yards.

"I lost it all right," Stover said. "I was shifting the ball to stiff-arm a guy and got hit from the other side." Halfback Joe Cannivino recovered for Ohio State and the Buckeyes controlled the ball most of the remaining 11 minutes.

A rout, as predicted, seemed imminent when Ohio State's physically superior forces traveled 79 yards in 13 plays, concentrating the attack mostly inside the ends, to score following the opening kickoff. Quarterback Frank Kremblas sneaked the last yard.

Before the first quarter ended, inspired Oregon began a drive from its 20 with an imaginative offense. Crabtree's pitch-outs and keepers baffled the Buckeyes. Near the completion of the march, Crabtree connected with halfback Charlie Tourville for 11 yards from the Ohio State 21. Then he picked up five more himself at right tackle and on the next play flipped a running lateral pass to halfback Jim Shanley, who toured left end untouched for the matching touchdown.

While the Ducks rolled down the field several times afterward, and outgained Ohio State 351 yards to 304, they couldn't sustain any more pushes.

Morris' unsuccessful field-goal attempt in the third quarter was like a signal for a determined offensive by the aroused Big Ten boys. Hard working fullback Bob White hacked out most of the yardage. He gained 49 of the 63 yards advanced by the Buckeyes to set up Sutherin's field goal.

Joe St. Amant of International News Service may have gotten off the best game lead. He wrote:

"That dry gulch, the Arroyo Seco, where the celebrated Rose Bowl is located, was heartbreak hollow for Oregon's spunky football team today."

Hayes, whose Ohio State teams won three out of four Big Ten championships in the 1954–57 period, admitted the breaks were "the only real edge in the game and we got them all." But he added, "We won, and the better team always wins."

Casanova said, "For my money, ours is the best team in the country. It out-gutted everybody, and it came from nowhere this season to play a game like this.

"Nobody can be humiliated like our boys were and take it. They were derided but they showed them.

"All I said beforehand was that I wanted to be proud of them when the game was over. And I couldn't be prouder."

On an airplane taking Casanova to a coaches convention one winter, a pert stewardess was asking the passengers for their name and destination. When Casanova gave her his, she said, "My, what a nice name. Tell me, does a name like that do you any good?"

He laughed and answered, "It may have 20 years ago. But now it may as well be Smith."

Ohio State	7	0	0	3	10
Oregon	0	7	0	0	7

Ohio State—Touchdown: Kremblas (1, sneak). Point after touchdown: Kremblas. Field goal: Sutherin (34, placekick).

Oregon—Touchdown: Shanley (5, left end). Point after touchdown: Morris.

STATISTICS

Ohio State		Oregon		Ohio State	Oregon
Houston	LE	Wheeler	19	First downs	21
Schafrath	LT	Kershner	245	Net yards rushing	160
Jobko	LG	Mondale (c-c)	6	Passes attempted	21
Fronk	C	Peterson	2	Passes completed	14
Thomas	RG	Grottkau	0	Passes had intercepted	2
Marshall	RT	Linden	59	Net yards passing	191
Bowermaster	RE	Stover	304	Total net yards	351
Kremblas	QB	Crabtree	2	Number of punts	0
LeBeau	LH	Tourville	19	Punting average	0
Cannavino	RH	Shanley (c-c)	0	Fumbles lost	2
White	FB	Morris (c-c)	15	Yards penalized	25

Substitutions—Ohio State: Morgan (r), Brown (C-C) (r), ends; Crawford (l), Arnold (r), tackles; Baldacci (l), Spychalski (r), guards; White, James, centers; Okulovich, quarterback; Clark (l), Sutherin (l), Trivisonno (r), Sutherin (r), halfbacks; Cisco (C-C), fullback. Oregon: Kimbrough (l), Brenn (l), Altenhofen (r), Robinson (r), ends; Aschbacher (l), Willener (l), Keele (r), White (r), Frost (r), tackles; Schaffeld (l), Heard (l), Newsom (l), Reeve (r), Todd (r), guards; Fish, Powell, centers; Fraser, Grover, quarterbacks; West (l), Phelps (l), Read (r), Laudenslager (r), halfbacks; Osborne, Holland, fullbacks.

GATOR

The situation was this:

Texas A&M and Tennessee were tied, 0 to 0, with five minutes, 30 seconds to play. It was fourth down on the Texas A&M 1, the ball in the Volunteers' possession.

Tennessee Coach Bowden Wyatt called Sammy Burklow, a fourth-string fullback, to his side and said, "Son, go in there and kick it. It's just like a point after touchdown."

Burklow calmly did what he was told. Tennessee won 3 to 0, and after so many sorrowful bowl excursions, Vol supporters were positively ecstatic.

The victory, achieved before a record crowd of 41,160 in the enlarged Gator Bowl, was only Tennessee's fourth in eleven bowl games.

There was an unpublicized hero this day that ushered in the bowls ending the 1957 season. He was quarterback (blocking back in the single-wing offense) Stockton Adkins. When he mowed down two Texas Aggies on Burklow's kick, he made possible the field goal.

Roddy Osborne, the Aggies' quarterback, threw a fresh slant on what had appeared to be merely a routine mass blocking effort against a fast charging line.

"I lined up at the extreme right," Osborne said. "I was racing in there and I thought I was a cinch to bat it down. But that Tennessee back, No. 20 (Adkins), took care of the man just inside me. And then at the last second he stuck out his leg and knocked me off my feet. You have to give him plenty of credit, maybe as much as the kicker."

The question arose, of course, as to why Tennessee hadn't gone for the touchdown. Several reasons were brought to light.

In the first place, tailback Bobby Gordon had figured in every play, running or passing, in a drive that had covered 50 yards. Bobby had been knocked cold in a head-on collision with the Aggies' powerful All-America back, John Crow, three plays earlier. He had bounced back remarkably to carry the ball from the 7 to the 1 in three slams into the line. But he was a tired boy.

Hurdling, diving fullback Tommy Bronson was not in the game at the time. To have inserted him would have telegraphed the plunge on fourth down.

Twice before in the second half Tennessee had wasted scoring chances because of fumbles. Appreciating the rugged quality of the Aggies' defense, Wyatt didn't care to stake his chances on another march down the field, if a running attempt from the 1 failed to produce a touchdown. Also, Burklow had made good 15 of 17 extra point attempts, two being blocked, from almost this same distance.

These things, plus the almost certain knowledge that the first score would hold up, dictated Wyatt's judgment.

"It was the only decision," said Texas A&M Coach Paul Bryant. "Frankly, I was glad. Osborne had won two games for us, charging in there to block placekicks. I thought he could save us this time."

Texas A&M never threatened the Tennessee goal line, never moved inside the Vols' 35. The Aggies had the ball for only 18 plays in the second half.

Gordon, who ran 32 times, executed a marvelous 82-yard punt return for a seeming touchdown in the first quarter. It was nullified by clipping against wingback Bill Anderson.

Bill Rives, *Dallas Morning News* sports editor, called Crow "Superman with shoulder pads." But if that were so, the Heisman Trophy winner found plenty of his own kind wearing the orange jerseys of Tennessee in the Gator Bowl.

SATURDAY, DECEMBER 28, 1957

Tennessee	0	0	0	3	3
Texas A&M	0	0	0	0	0

Tennessee—Field goal: Burklow (17, placekick).

STATISTICS

Tennessee		Texas A&M	Tennessee		Texas A&M
Darty	LE	Marks	14	First downs	8
Smelcher	LT	Krueger	135	Net yards rushing	142
Herzbrun	LG	Goehring	6	Passes attempted	8
Stottlemyer	C	Gilbert	4	Passes completed	3
Johnson	RG	Brown	0	Passes had intercepted	0
Kolinsky	RT	Beck	56	Net yards passing	27
Potts	RE	Tracey	191	Total net yards	169
Adkins	QB	Osborne	8	Number of punts	7
Gordon	LH	Crow	36	Punting average	38
Anderson	RH	Conrad	2	Fumbles lost	1
Bronson	FB	Gay	30	Yards penalized	35

Substitutions—Tennessee: Overholt (l), Armstrong (r), ends; Shafer (l), Schaffer (r), tackles; Urbano (l), Lukowski (r), guards; Moss, center; Bennett, Emory, quarterbacks; Carter (l), Grubb (r), halfbacks; Smith, Burklow, fullbacks. Texas A&M: Pearson (l), Smith (r), ends; Simmons (l), (r), tackle; Stanley (l), Howard (l), Munson (r), Payne (r), guards; Oliver, center; Milstead, quarterback; Sanders (l), Taylor (r), halfbacks; LeBouef, Newcomb, fullbacks.

COTTON

Through the season Navy Coach Eddie Erdelatz maintained Tom Forrestal of Cleveland, whose father once captained the national championship curling team in Ireland, was America's best quarterback.

The Midshipmen's 20 to 7 mastery of Rice in the 1958 Cotton Bowl conflict, in which Forrestal outshone King Hill, the Owls' All-America quarterback, may have proved Erdelatz was right.

Forrestal completed 13 of his 24 passes for 153 yards, shoveled pitch-outs accurately and imaginatively, and led his team to a triumph that caused Erdelatz to say, "This was my greatest team at Annapolis."

Navy's second unit swept 33 yards to the first touchdown late in the first quarter after Rice quarterback Frank Ryan fumbled and Middie halfback Roland Brandquist recovered. Quarterback Joe Tranchini slammed through right guard for the last yard.

Forrestal skippered the first team on a 66-yard touchdown cruise in the second quarter. Halfback Harry Hurst took a pitch-out and darted 13 yards around left end to score.

End John Ruth seized a fumble by fullback Ray Chilton on the fourth play of the second half and it was anchors away for 20 yards. Only two plays were required. Fullback Ray Wellborn, once a member of the Rice freshman team, made a yard. Then halfback Ned Oldham raced for a touchdown around right end.

Also in the third quarter Rice scored after a Forrestal pass bounced out of end Pete Jokanovich's hands and was intercepted by halfback Bobby Williams. He ran seven yards to Navy's 36. Four plays later (four straight pass completions by Ryan, who had 13 of 22 for 151 yards for the day) the Owls acquired a slightly consoling touchdown. Halfback Ken Williams made it on an eight-yard flip.

Navy's big, fierce charging line had a lot to do with inducing five ball-losing fumbles by Rice backs.

Guard Tony Stremic, whose father played baseball for Carnegie Tech, sustained a badly sprained ankle in pregame practice. The injury was so severe that three days earlier Erdelatz said Stremic couldn't possibly play. He was voted the outstanding lineman in press box balloting.

Navy	6	7	7	0	20
Rice	0	0	7	0	7

Navy—Touchdowns: Tranchini (1, right guard), Hurst (13, left end), Oldham (19, right end). Points after touchdown: Oldham 2.

Rice—Touchdown: K. Williams (8, pass from Ryan of 7, run of 1). Point after touchdown: Hill.

STATISTICS

Navy		Rice	Navy		Rice
Jokanovich	LE	Dial	21	First downs	14
Anthony	LT	Whitmire	222	Net yards rushing	137
Stremic	LG	Gorges	27	Passes attempted	27
Moncilovich	C	Gillis	13	Passes completed	14
Fritzinger	RG	McCraw	1	Passes had intercepted	1
Reifsnyder	RT	White	153	Net yards passing	164
Ruth	RE	Jones	375	Total net yards	301
Forrestal	QB	Hill	3	Number of punts	5
Oldham	LH	Dueitt	36.6	Punting average	42
Hurst	RH	K. Williams	3	Fumbles lost	5
Wellborn	FB	Kelley	65	Yards penalized	53

Substitutions—Navy: Kanuch (l), Hyde (l), McKee (r), Shirreffs (r), ends; Meisel (l), Helweg (l), Boyer (r), Valentine (r), tackles; Caldwell (l), Harris (l), Chomicz (r), Boyle (r), guards; Witzmann, Bannan, centers; Tranchini, Flood, quarterbacks; Brence (l), Zembrzuski (l), Brandquist (r), Correll (r), halfbacks; Swanson, Ehlers, fullbacks. Rice: Veltman (l), Miller (r), ends; Cauley (l), Smith (r), Phillips (r), tackles; Gusler (l), Peebles (r), guards; Graves, Kramer, centers; Ryan, quarterback; R. Williams (l), Speer (l), Bailey (r), Searcy (r), halfbacks; Chilton, Hoelscher, fullbacks.

SUGAR

Ole Miss did it up BROWN.

In the *New Orleans Item,* Tom Fox revealed:

"Fourteen years ago a Memphis doctor told Raymond Lloyd Brown he would never walk again but you saw him."

Amid the hurrah of her boy's finest hour, Mrs. C. J. Mason, Ray's mother, remembered, "Ray had osteomyelitis; that's a disease of the bone."

Raymond Brown's performance was almost legendary in character as Mississippi trounced Texas, 39 to 7, in the Sugar Bowl game of 1958.

He ran for two touchdowns. He galloped for 92 yards from punt formation to score with less than two minutes left and gained 157 yards in all from scrimmage. One of his passes produced a touchdown.

On defense Brown stopped George Blanch on a kickoff return when only he remained between the Texas halfback and the Ole Miss goal line. Another time Brown tackled Blanch when he might have gone all the way. He intercepted three passes. One led to an Ole Miss touchdown.

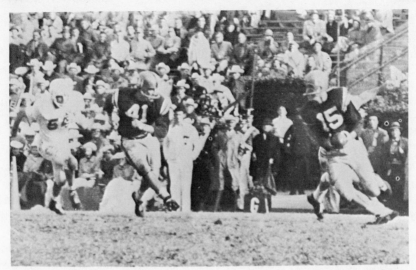

1958—Start of the Sugar Bowl record touchdown run of 92 yards. Mississippi quarterback Ray Brown, in his own end zone, takes off against Texas.

Before his impromptu Sugar Bowl record run from scrimmage, Ray said, "I started to ask for another kicker. I was so weary. I told the fellows in the huddle I might not kick it 20 yards.

"I was going to punt but the snap from center was a bit high and I saw a lineman from their right side bearing in on me. I knew that if he blocked the kick, it probably would give them a touchdown. So I decided to run and lit out to my left. I almost fell just past the line of scrimmage but kept going."

Brown started running from three yards behind his own goal line. Rebel guard Jackie Simpson, downfield expecting to cover a punt, picked him up. Simpson said he kept shouting for a lateral pass because "Ray looked like he was gonna collapse."

Charlie Flowers, conversational sophomore Ole Miss fullback, said, "This victory makes up for those two awful showings Mississippi teams made previously here in the Sugar Bowl."

Brown agreed.

"I think our performance goes back to that defeat by Navy three years ago," he said. "After we got the invitation this time, all we heard was Navy, Navy, Navy and how Ole Miss usually failed in the big games. We made up our minds to be the Mississippi team that rubbed out this Sugar Bowl jinx."

Three weeks after the game, Warren Averitte, a former Alabama lineman, told Wirt Gammon of the *Chattanooga Times* about an experience he had at Greenville, Miss., High School.

"When I was coach there a few years ago, I had a boy who could get so few things right on the football field that I suggested he give up that sport," Averitte related. "I put it to him in a nice way. I said, 'It's just that football isn't for you, so put your extra work into one of your studies and go all out for that instead.' It was his first year out for high school football and I thought I was doing the right thing in stopping him before he got started.

"Can you guess who that boy was?

"Raymond Brown of Ole Miss."

Said Brown: "Ambition is the thing. If a fellow doesn't have ambition, he's not going to make it.

"When they told me I wouldn't walk again, I had enough ambition to say I would walk. And I had an ambition to play high school football and then college football.

"I had an ambition to whip Texas, too. One of our coaches told us about this trophy [Warren V. Miller Memorial Trophy to the game's outstanding player]. He said an Ole Miss boy had never won it. I thought about it the night before the game and I had an ambition to win it [he did].

"I've got another ambition—to play pro football."

That same year he was a member of the world champion professional Baltimore Colts.

| Mississippi | 6 | 13 | 7 | 13 | 39 |
| Texas | 0 | 0 | 0 | 7 | 7 |

Mississippi—Touchdowns: Brown 2 (1, right guard; 92, punt formation, left end), Williams (3, pass from Brown), Lovelace (8, left end), Franklin (3, left tackle), Taylor (12, pass from W. Brewer). Points after touchdown: Khayat 3.

Texas—Touchdown: Alvis (2, center smash). Point after touchdown: Lackey.

STATISTICS

Mississippi		Texas	Mississippi		Texas
Templeton	LE	Doke	15	First downs	13
West	LT	Seaholm	304	Net yards rushing	192
Simpson	LG	Wilson	16	Passes attempted	11
Crain	C	Del Homme	7	Passes completed	2
W. Hickerson	RG	R. Lee	0	Passes had intercepted	4
R. Hickerson	RT	Kennon	71	Net yards passing	17
Williams	RE	M. Lee	375	Total net yards	209
Brown	QB	Fondren	7	Number of punts	5
Reed	LH	Blanch	34.7	Punting average	38.2
Lovelace	RH	Alvis	2	Fumbles lost	4
Hurst	FB	Dowdle	95	Yards penalized	50

Substitutions—Mississippi: Grantham (l), Burke (l), Barkley (l), Cavin (l), J. Brewer (r), Jenkins (r), ends; Smith (l), Khayat (l), Owens (l), Sanders (r), Winston (r), tackles; Cooper (l), Terrell (l), Churchwell (r), Kempinska (r), guards; Kirk, Pruett, Terry, centers; Franklin, W. Brewer, quarterbacks; Hall (l), Champion (l), Rittman (l), Woodruff (r), Lott (r), Taylor (r), halfbacks; Flowers, Partridge, Cavin, fullbacks. Texas: Stephens (l), Halm (l), Bryant (r), Schulte (r), ends; Wes Wyman (l), Stolhandske (l), Will Wyman (r), Williams (r), tackles; Anderson (l), Muennink (l), Schultz (l), Shillingburg (r), Padgett (r), Wells (r), guards; Parkhurst, Harwerth, Wetzel, centers; Lackey, Clements, Moffatt, quarterbacks; Smith (l), Grubbs (l), Ramirez (r), Castleberry (r), halfbacks; Allen, Welch, Bednarski, fullbacks.

– 1959 –

SUGAR

By mid-December of 1958, the most notable of the many honors and awards attained by Louisiana State could be distinguished. They were:

1. First LSU team to win the national collegiate football championship.

2. Only major college team to come through the season with a perfect record.

3. Team of the year over such as the New York Yankees and Baltimore Colts, both world's champions.

4. Left halfback Billy Cannon, with a series of remarkable all-around performances, picked on every All-America eleven.

5. Paul Dietzel, handsome, able, charming, elected "Coach of the Year" in the biggest landslide vote of his fellow coaches in the award's history.

Imaginative and resourceful, Dietzel ingeniously solved his problem of small, inexperienced linemen. He did it by developing three platoons that were known as the White Team (on which Cannon played and that was used on both offense and defense), the Go Team (chiefly used on offense), and the colorfully titled Chinese Bandits (whose forte was defense).

The Bandits captured the nation's fancy. Years before, Dietzel, a

fan of the comic strip *Terry and the Pirates,* came across this statement by one of the characters: "Chinese bandits are the most vicious
people in the world."

Dietzel hit on the idea of glamorizing his defensive platoon by
something borrowed. The response of the players, and the public,
surpassed his expectations. His men took special pride in being
chosen for this unit. A Memphis radio announcer wrote a song in
their honor. The LSU school band played it whenever the Bandits
trotted on the field. They felt tougher, more ruthless and courageous
than ever.

Honors galore were bestowed on Cannon. He was sometimes referred to as "either the fastest shotputter or the strongest sprinter in
track annals." He had run the 100-yard dash in 9.5 seconds and had
heaved the shot more than 53 feet.

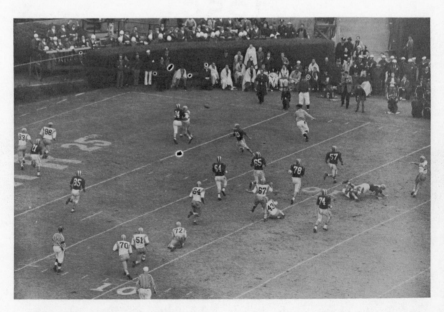

1959—LSU All-America Billy Cannon passes to end Mickey Mangham for
the touchdown that beat Clemson.

Billy's impressive 211-pound physique was strengthened by a
weightlifting program that he took under the supervision of Alvin
Roy, United States weightlifting trainer in the 1952 Olympic Games
and proprietor of a health emporium in Baton Rouge.

This was one of the fastest teams ever assembled in the South.
Dietzel said: "Everything today is based on speed. We tell our boys

we don't care what mistakes they make as long as they make them full speed."

As the Southeastern Conference champions (picked in advance of the season to finish ninth) turned to their Sugar Bowl date with Clemson, General Troy Middleton, president of the university, cautioned them at a banquet: "Remember, the season isn't over yet. All I'm going to ask from you is one more victory."

Clemson, in winning the Atlantic Coast Conference title, had lost to South Carolina, 26 to 6, and had also been beaten by Georgia Tech of the Southeastern Conference. Its choice by the New Orleans Mid-Winter Sports Association to meet LSU was sharply criticized. Clemson was a two-touchdown underdog, a psychological factor that Coach Frank Howard made the most of. "They keep telling us we're not worth a darn," he said. "I don't know, maybe we're not. But you keep telling a feller that long enough and it begins to get under his hide."

Against Howard's highly keyed up Tigers, LSU passed up three scoring opportunities in the first half but capitalized on a wild center snap in the third quarter to win 7 to 0.

LSU tackle Duane Leopard recovered the errant pass into the backfield by Clemson center Paul Snyder. Clemson intended to punt from its 20. The mistake gave the ball to LSU only 11 yards from a touchdown.

"A little wet grass got between my hand and the ball," Snyder explained. "It slipped when I threw it and it got away." The snap bounced off the leg of fullback Doug Cline, who was blocking for the punter, Bill Mathis.

LSU advanced the ball two yards on the next two plays. Dietzel sent in the next one. Quarterback Durel Matherne handed off to Cannon, who moved from left to right on a run or pass option. Billy slowed up after he'd gone a few yards laterally and cast a strike into the arms of right end Mickey Mangham in the end zone.

"I didn't throw it . . . The Lord did," Cannon said. "I looked for Johnny Robinson but they had him covered. Then I spied Mickey and let go. I wasn't sure it would get to him until he grabbed it. It went off with a prayer."

Clemson struck back after that, reaching the LSU 24 where George Usry dropped a fourth-down screen pass. That ended a 59-yard march.

"If that boy had been able to hold onto that little screen pass, I was shore going for those two points and beat them if we'd have scored," said Howard.

The LSU attack was handicapped in the second half by the absence of quarterback Warren Rabb, who suffered a broken hand in the second quarter.

Cannon netted 51 yards in 13 carries, completed his only pass, punted three times for an average of 34.7 yards, and was brilliant on defense.

And what of the Bandits?

"God bless them," Dietzel said. "I don't think I've ever seen them play more courageously—and against a team which dwarfed them."

THURSDAY, JANUARY 1, 1959

Louisiana State	0	0	7	0	7
Clemson	0	0	0	0	0

Louisiana State—Touchdown: Mangham (9, pass from Cannon). Point after touchdown: Cannon.

STATISTICS

Louisiana State	Clemson	Louisiana State	Clemson
Hendrix	LE Masneri	9 First downs	12
LeBlanc	LT Padgett	114 Net yards rushing	168
Kahlden	LG Payne	11 Passes attempted	4
Fugler	C Thomas	4 Passes completed	2
McCreedy	RG Lynn	0 Passes had intercepted	0
Strange	RT Cordileone	68 Net yards passing	23
Mangham	RE Anderson	182 Total net yards	191
Rabb	QB White	6 Number of punts	6
Cannon	LH Usry	41.4 Punting average	29.6
Robinson	RH Horne	2 Fumbles lost	2
Brodnax	FB Hayes	35 Yards penalized	20

Substitutions—Louisiana State: Bourgeois (l), McClain (l), Kinchen (r), Norwood (r), ends; Branch (l), McCarty (l), Leopard (r), Frayer (r), tackles; Fournet (l), Dampier (l), Lott (r), Stupka (r), guards; Langan, center; Matherne, Roberts, quarterbacks; Purvis (l), Daye (r), Bourque (r), halfbacks; Davis, Schexnaildre, fullbacks. Clemson: DeBardelaben (l), Cox (r), ends; McCanless (l), Smith (r), H. Olson (r), tackles; Crout (l), Wagner (l), Gobble (r), Pilot (r), D. Olson (r), guards; Snyder, center; Shingler, Eberhart, Daigneault, quarterbacks; Mathis (l), Morgan (r), halfbacks; Cline, Dukes, fullbacks.

ORANGE

Syracuse's day in a bowl was coming, but it was not to be in Miami on January 1, 1959. However, the Orangemen deserved kudos for the most unexpected comeback on the bowl front.

Syracuse was humiliated 61 to 6, by Alabama six years before. It may have been with some misgivings that the Orange Bowl Commit-

1959—Oklahoma's Steve Jennings stretches Art Baker's jersey and slows up the Syracuse fullback for teammates to grab.

tee invited Syracuse to meet strong Oklahoma. The stipulation that the Big Eight champion could not return to Miami in successive years was waived. The Sooners were asked to come back because the committee wanted to be certain of a powerful team from that conference for its 25th anniversary game.

When Oklahoma scored on its second play, a 42-yard run around left end by fullback Prentice Gautt, committee members blanched somewhat. It was a fake handoff that drew in the Syracuse ends. It was followed by a pitch-out from Bob Cornell to Gautt, a new play.

Before the first quarter ended, Oklahoma's All-America center, Bob Harrison, recovered a fumble by Tom Stephens, halfback for the Orange, on the Sooners' 19, halting a long march. Cornell made two yards. Then Brewster Hobby tossed a short, running, flat pass to end Ross Coyle near the sideline. Coyle, dodging tacklers cleverly, filtered through the secondary, and reached the goal line 73 yards away. The play covered 79 yards.

Halfback Jakie Sandefer passed to Hobby for the two-point conversion, made possible under the revised rule in effect for the first time in the 1958 season.

Oklahoma led now 14 to 0. Many in the crowd of 75,281 imagined it would be another rout. Such thoughts proved to be groundless. Syracuse never stopped trying. The Orangemen battled valiantly to gain the admiration of and provide an interesting show for the spectators. The Easterners didn't lose their zip this time in the 78 degree heat. But they lost the game 21 to 6.

Coach Ben Schwartzwalder's team won the meaningless statistical contest, including control of the ball. The Orange got off 80 plays to 52 for the Sooners.

Syracuse scored when halfback Mike Weber burst through a hole at right tackle and beat a 15-yard path to the goal line in the fourth quarter. It was Weber's first carry, capping a drive of 69 yards.

Before that, though, Hobby had grabbed a punt and scooted 40 yards for the touchdown that put Oklahoma on top 21 to 0.

"I couldn't convince my kids Oklahoma was fast," Schwartzwalder said. "They believe it now. We didn't play good football. We were tense and made too many errors."

Oklahoma Coach Bud Wilkinson was magnanimous as usual.

"If we played Syracuse tomorrow, they might beat us," he said.

Assistant coach Dick Beyer of Syracuse, in an interview with Bill Roberts of the *Nashville Banner* a few days after the game, said, "This team worked harder than any I've seen in the 10 years I've been at Syracuse. At the end of the game we were in better shape than they were. Of course, Oklahoma was superior in overall team speed, especially in the backfield. Our inability to contain their fast backs on certain plays probably cost us the game."

It wasn't a popular victory with some of the box seat holders on the Oklahoma side.

New dugout benches had been built on each side of the field in front of the box seats. Syracuse players occupied their dugout. But the Sooners quickly abandoned theirs. They lined up behind Wilkinson on the sideline and ignored the shouts and pleas of fans, police, and bowl officials that they were blocking the view.

"I feel very badly about it and I'm sorry," Wilkinson said. "But you can't be in a dugout as a spectator one minute and be playing the next. Besides, it's an Oklahoma tradition."

Oklahoma	14	0	7	0	21
Syracuse	0	0	0	6	6

Oklahoma—Touchdowns: Gautt (42, left end), Coyle (79, pass from Hobby of 6, run of 73), Hobby (40, punt return). Points after touchdown: Hobby (pass from Sandefer), Boyd.
Syracuse—Touchdown: Weber (15, right tackle).

STATISTICS

Oklahoma		*Syracuse*	*Oklahoma*		*Syracuse*
Coyle	LE	D. Baker	12	First downs	18
Lewis	LT	Yates	152	Net yards rushing	239
Thompson	LG	Davis	4	Passes attempted	25
Harrison	C	Applehof	3	Passes completed	10
Davis	RG	Benecick	0	Passes had intercepted	2
Lawrence	RT	Luciano	93	Net yards passing	72
Rector	RE	Mautino	245	Total net yards	311
Cornell	QB	Zimmerman	8	Number of punts	8
Sandefer	LH	Stephens	37	Punting average	31.2
Hobby	RH	Schwedes	1	Fumbles lost	2
Gautt	FB	Keiffer	35	Yards penalized	20

Substitutions—Oklahoma: McDaniel (l), Tillery (r), ends; Jennings (l), Durham (r), tackles; Payne (l), Moore (l), Corbitt (r), guards; Johnson, center; Boyd, quarterback; J. Carpenter (l), R. Carpenter (r), halfbacks; Rolle, fullback. Syracuse: Gilburg (l), Bartlett (l), Skonieczki (r), ends; Hershey (l), Gill (l), Gerlick (r), tackles; Youmans (l), Lamey (l), Tarbox (r), guards; Nichols, Bemiller, centers; Fogarty, quarterback; Weber (l), Reimer (r), halfbacks; Jackson, A. Baker, Anderson, fullbacks.

ROSE

Swift Iowa backs raced to records galore as the Hawkeyes crushed California 38 to 12, in the 1959 Rose Bowl game. It wasn't expected to be close and it wasn't.

Exciting, fleet Bob Jeter, who flew 81 yards for a touchdown in the third quarter to make the score 32 to 6, set a record for the longest run from scrimmage.

That was the only time the 182-pound junior halfback from Weirton, W. Va., scored. But he flashed for a total of 194 yards in nine carries (another record) and a glittering 21.6 average (also a record).

Iowa's rushing total of 429 yards was a record, as was the net of 516. Twenty-four first downs tied yet another as the Big Ten made it 12 victories, five of them one sided, in the 13 games since the Rose Bowl alliance with the Pacific Coast Conference was formed.

Jeter was superbly supported on offense by 173-pound sophomore

1959—Electrifying Bob Jeter of Iowa on one of his dashes against California.

halfback Willie Fleming of Detroit.   He ran only nine times, too, but
achieved a 9.4 average and scored two touchdowns on sprints of 37
and seven yards.   Between them, the starting halfbacks scudded 279
yards.

All-America quarterback Randy Duncan, renowned for his passing
prowess, didn't use this weapon often.   It wasn't necessary.

The halftime score was 20 to 0.   At the outset of the third quarter
California exhibited a slick double-spread offense.   The Golden
Bears, with quarterback Joe Kapp working the option successfully,
amazed the crowd of 98,297 by sweeping 74 yards in 11 plays for a
touchdown.   California fans hoped that somehow their team could
score some more while checking faster, more powerful Iowa.

It was not to be.   Iowa adjusted its defense.   California returned
to its tight, orthodox offense.   And the Bears did not score again until the game's last minute when a number of Hawkeye fourth-stringers
were on the field.

"I am probably the lousiest-feeling winning coach in Rose Bowl
history," said Iowa's Forest Evashevski.   "I don't even know the final

score." Evy was in bed with flu and a temperature of 101 degrees the
day before the game.

Evashevski's accomplishments, and those of his teams, in a three-
year stretch included the winning of two Big Ten championships and
two Rose Bowl games by a combined score of 73 to 31.

Pete Elliott, California coach who as a Michigan halfback had participated in the 49 to 0 rout of Southern California 11 years before,
bravely came up with a cheerful viewpoint. "At least we got a good
scouting report," he said. California and Iowa met in the opening
game for the Hawkeyes in 1959. Iowa won, 42 to 12.

The nine-member Pacific Coast Conference disbanded on July 1,
1959. The beginning of the end dated back to December 13, 1957,
when California, which served a year's probationary period, UCLA,
and Southern California announced they would withdraw from the
conference. This was a consequence of the bitterness engendered by
heavy penalties imposed on the California schools and Washington
for illegal assistance to athletes.

However, under the terms of the contract, the Rose Bowl series
between the Big Ten and a Pacific Coast school was assured through
the 1960 game.

Iowa	7	13	12	6	38
California	0	0	6	6	12

Iowa—Touchdowns: Fleming 2 (37, left tackle; 7, left tackle), Duncan (1,
right guard), Langston (7, pass from Duncan), Horn (4, center), Jeter (81, right
tackle). Points after touchdown: Prescott 2.

California—Touchdowns: Hart 2 (1, right guard; 17, pass from Kapp).

STATISTICS

Iowa		California			Iowa		California
Langston	LE	Lundgren	24		First downs		20
Burroughs	LT	Newell	429		Net yards rushing		214
Grouwinkel	LG	Domoto	14		Passes attempted		20
Lapham	C	Jones	9		Passes completed		9
Drake	RG	Piestrup	0		Passes had intercepted		2
Lewis	RT	Sally	87		Net yards passing		130
Norton	RE	T. Bates	516		Total net yards		344
Duncan	QB	Kapp (c-c)	3		Number of punts		5
Jeter	LH	Olguin	40.7		Punting average		37
Fleming	RH	Hart (c-c)	1		Fumbles lost		2
Nocera (c)	FB	Patton	55		Yards penalized		35

Substitutions—Iowa: Miller (l), Merz (l), Prescott (r), Spaan (r), Clauson (r),
ends; Lee (l), Scott (l), Sawin (r), Hain (r), tackles; Novack (l), Ringer (l),
Mielke (l), Clark (l), Shipanik (r), Manders (r), Dunn (r), Sonnenberg (r),
guards; Humphreys, Turner, Leshyn, centers; Ogiego, Treadway, Moore, quarterbacks; Furlong (l), Gravel (l), McMeekins (l), Jauch (r), Mauren (r), Gajda

(r), halfbacks; Horn, Brown, Long, Mosley, fullbacks. California: Holston (l), George (l), Fraser (l), Huber (r), Cooper (r), ends; Streshly (l), Dinkler (l), Michael (r), Thomas (r), tackles; Green (l), Gonzales (l), Lasher (r), Snow (r), Johnson (r), Byrd (r), guards; Segale, Doretti, centers; Parque, quarterback; Garvin (r), Crow (r), S. Bates (l), halfbacks; Arnold, Yerman, Perrin, fullbacks.

GATOR

At the Gator Bowl banquet on the night of the late December game of 1958, Florida's captain Don Fleming, speaking to several hundred guests, said, "It's like Coach Woodruff told us before the game; the best team doesn't always win."

When his turn came on the rostrum, Bob Woodruff, blushing somewhat, corrected the statement. "What I said was that the team which made the fewest mistakes would win," he declared.

Briefly, that was the story. Mississippi won, 7 to 3.

Florida had four scoring opportunities inside the Mississippi 15. Fumbles ruined two advances.

Earlier, the Gators scored on a field goal of 27 yards by halfback Billy Booker. Ole Miss took the opening kickoff and rammed 70 yards in 11 plays with fullback James (Hoss) Anderson going for the touchdown on a one-yard plunge.

Little Jimmy Dunn legged it 56 yards with the ensuing Ole Miss kickoff. Immediately, Dunn raced around right end for 14. The next three plays netted only five yards. That's when Booker kicked his field goal.

The Rebels were in a hole most of the fourth quarter. On the first play of the period, Bobby Greene quick-kicked 76 yards. The ball glanced off the leg of Ole Miss center Milt Crain, who was trying to block. End Dave Hudson recovered for Florida on the 11.

A subsequent fourth-down try by Dunn from the 2 resulted in a three-yard loss when guard Dick Price nailed the Gators' 142-pound quarterback.

Woodruff praised Dunn as "pound for pound and ounce for ounce, the finest football player I've seen in 20 years in the Southeastern Conference."

SATURDAY, DECEMBER 27, 1958

Mississippi	7	0	0	0	7
Florida	3	0	0	0	3

Mississippi—Touchdown: Anderson (1, right guard). Point after touchdown: Khayat.
Florida—Field goal: Booker (27, placekick).

STATISTICS

Mississippi		Florida		Mississippi	Florida
Grantham	LE	Fleming	9	First downs	13
Smith	LT	Schutz	157	Net yards rushing	157
Cooper	LG	Cox	7	Passes attempted	11
Crain	C	Hergert	2	Passes completed	5
Terrell	RG	Johns	0	Passes had intercepted	1
Churchwell	RT	Heckman	27	Net yards passing	58
Jenkins	RE	Hudson	184	Total net yards	215
Franklin	QB	Dunn	10	Number of punts	7
Woodruff	LH	Lucey	34.4	Punting average	44.1
Lovelace	RH	Deal	2	Fumbles lost	3
Flowers	FB	Milby	10	Yards penalized	25

Substitutions—Mississippi: Templeton (l), Daniels (r), ends; Sanders (l), Robertson (l), Owens (r), Benton (r), tackles; Price (l), Kempinska (r), Roberson (r), guards; Kirk, Alford, centers; Brewer, Gibbs, quarterbacks; Hall (l), Champion (l), Blair (l), Crespino (r), Taylor (r), halfbacks; Anderson, Partridge, Robinson, fullbacks. Florida: Patchen (l), McGriff (l), Edgington (r), Arfaras (r), ends; Brantley (l), Slack (l), Royal (r), Davidson (r), tackles; Giannamore (l), Miranda (r), guards; Graves, Hood, centers; Ellenburg, quarterback; Booker (l), Dilts (l), Partin (l), Green (l), Newbern (r), Page (r), halfbacks; MacBeth, Giles, fullbacks.

COTTON

Five field-goal attempts were unavailing as the 1959 Cotton Bowl struggle between the Air Force Academy and Texas Christian ended in a 0 to 0 stalemate.

Air Force halfback George Pupich missed tries from the 12, 24, and 35-yard lines. TCU fullback Jack Spikes failed to put the ball through the posts from the 29 and 35. A tricky wind bothered the kickers.

Early in the third quarter the Air Force reached the TCU 2 on a jump pass from Rich Mayo to end Tom Jozwiak. That advance was nullified by a penalty for illegal procedure.

Longest sustained drive was for 86 yards by the Horned Frogs at the outset of the fourth period. It went for naught when quarterback Hunter Enis fumbled on the 8 and Dave Phillips, Falcon tackle who was the outstanding lineman, recovered.

Coach Ben Martin told his Air Force team, "I'm proud of every one of you. You were a better team out there but the ball just didn't bounce right."

"I'm not satisfied," TCU Coach Abe Martin said. "The last thing I ever expected was a scoreless tie."

The Air Force graduated its first class in June of 1959.

Air Force	0 0 0 0 0
Texas Christian	0 0 0 0 0

STATISTICS

Air Force		Texas Christian	Air Force		Texas Christian
Rodgers	LE	Gilmore	13	First downs	9
Phillips	LT	Floyd	140	Net yards rushing	190
Bronson	LG	Headrick	23	Passes attempted	11
Gulledge	C	Walker	12	Passes completed	3
Zaleski	RG	Armstrong	2	Passes had intercepted	0
Strom	RT	Robb	91	Net yards passing	37
Jozwiak	RE	Meyer	231	Total net yards	227
Mayo	QB	Enis	7	Number of punts	9
Lane	LH	Lasater	38.1	Punting average	38.8
Quinlan	RH	Harris	3	Fumbles lost	3
Galios	FB	Spikes	15	Yards penalized	61

Substitutions—Air Force: Brickey (l), McCain (l), Hardage (r), Wagner (r), ends; Wideman (l), Cwach (r), tackles; Cubero (l), Johnson (r), guards; Mitchell, center; Kuenzel, Rosane, quarterbacks; Pupich (l), Rawlins (r), halfbacks; Thomson, fullback. Texas Christian: Ham (l), Linne (l), Peebles (r), Rowland (r), ends; Roach (l), Lilly (r), Pitts (r), tackles; Rambo (l), McSpedden (r), guards; Martin, Cumpton, centers; Dawson, George, quarterbacks; Moreland (l), Vacek (l), Gault (r), Terrell (r), halfbacks; Priddy, fullback.

– 1960 –

Hail Houston and Philly

COTTON

A 15-yard penalty on the second play of hostilities had set back the national champions to their own 17-yard line.

The crowd of 75,504 at the 1960 Cotton Bowl game, most of them roaring Texans hoping for the "fanatical effort" Darrell Royal, coach of the Longhorns, said it would take to beat Syracuse, believed they sniffed an enormous upset in the making.

They couldn't have been more wrong.

On second down, right halfback Ger Schwedes turned, ran laterally to his left, and took a pitch-out from quarterback Dave Sarette. He took a few more steps, whirled, and flung a pass to left halfback Ernie Davis. That fast sophomore, who had lined up as the left flanker, caught the ball at midfield as he sped between two Texas defenders. He was gone in a flash.

The 87-yard touchdown play, longest passing gain in bowl history, stunned the partisan throng that only a moment before had envisioned the beginning of something wonderful for Texas, co-champion of the Southwest Conference. Only one minute and 23 seconds had elapsed.

It set the tempo for an intensely exciting battle, replete with gridiron deeds—and some, it must be recorded, not so noble.

There was a near free-for-all just before the end of the first half. At the time, Syracuse, ultimate 23 to 14 victor, led 15 to 0. The Orangemen had scored again in the second quarter on a jab of less than two feet by Davis, capping an 80-yard offensive.

Dick Easterly passed from the Texas 41 to Ken Ericson. The end

Ernie Davis, Syracuse halfback who played brilliantly in the Cotton Bowl and Liberty Bowl games.

made the catch at the 12 and was hit by Longhorn halfback Jack Collins just short of the goal line. He fumbled. The ball bounced through and out of the end zone for a touchback.

As the play unfolded, a shoving, swinging flare-up erupted near the line of scrimmage. John Brown, Negro Syracuse tackle, took a swing at Texas tackle Larry Stephens. Both benches were emptied. Both coaches, Ben Schwartzwalder of Syracuse and Royal, ran onto the field. A near gang fight was narrowly averted.

Each side charged the other with making remarks of a racial nature, uncomplimentary on the one hand to Syracuse's Negro players and on the other to Rene Ramirez, Texas halfback of Latin-American descent. Accusations of dirty play were hurled. The game was marked by displays of temper and considerable arguing.

Schwartzwalder came on the field in the first quarter to ask for an interpretation of a defensive holding penalty. The Syracuse party strenuously objected to rulings of umpire Julius Truelson, a Southwest Conference official.

"Early in the game the umpire told us we couldn't hit 'em like this," said Coach of the Year Schwartzwalder, lashing out with his right arm. "We've been doing it all year in every section of the country. Now how can you play football under those conditions?"

Truelson said, "The basic interpretation of blocking in the East and down here in the Southwest was the foundation for Syracuse's

1960—A short gain and end of the line for Bobby Franklin of Ole Miss.

disagreement with my calls. Every foul I called was there in great big bold letters."

The Longhorns, trailing 15 to 0 at the start of the second half, outgained the nation's No. 1 team, 198 yards to 88, and outscored it, 14 to 8, in the final 30 minutes.

The third quarter had barely begun when Bobby Lackey fired a 39-yard pass to Collins, who ran 30 more to score. Syracuse countered before the period ended. Davis, named the game's outstanding player, intercepted a pass thrown by Collins and returned six yards to the Texas 24. Employing blockers expertly and reversing his field, Davis then raced to the 3 to set up a touchdown by German-born Schwedes, who ripped off left tackle for the last three yards.

The noisy multitude booed the officials often. One of the times was in the fourth quarter when Texas recovered its own onside kick on the Syracuse 47 but had to take a five-yard penalty for being offside. Syracuse got the second kick.

Texas had just scored on a thrust by Lackey from the 1. Putting the ball there, fullback Clair Branch exploded up the middle for 36 yards, assisted by end Monte Lee's timely block.

Chick Meehan, former Syracuse player and coach, called his old school's 1959 team "the best I've seen in collegiate circles in my lifetime."

The Orangemen averaged scoring 39 points per game with their unbalanced T formation "ride" attack. They moved the ball an average of 451 yards per game. The forwards, agile, quick, heavy, and hard hitting, were known as the Sizable Seven. They held ten regular season foes to an average of 96 yards.

Bob Rule wrote in the *Houston Press*: "Syracuse was clearly superior to the Longhorns in everything but heart."

Texas played with the fervor Royal hoped for.

Syracuse proved its claim to the national title. It also vindicated eastern football and three previous bowl defeats, including that terrible 61 to 6 smearing in Miami.

FRIDAY, JANUARY 1, 1960

Syracuse	7	8	8	0	23
Texas	0	0	6	8	14

Syracuse—Touchdowns: E. Davis 2 (87, pass from Schwedes of 37, run of 50; 1, right guard), Schwedes (3, left tackle). Points after touchdown: E. Davis (pass from Sarette; pass from Sarette), Yates.

Texas—Touchdowns: Collins (69, pass from Lackey of 39, run of 30), Lackey (1, right guard). Points after touchdown: Schulte (pass from Lackey).

STATISTICS

Syracuse		Texas		Syracuse	Texas
Skonieczki	LE	Schulte	12	First downs	10
Yates	LT	Talbert	133	Net yards rushing	145
R. Davis	LG	Doke	12	Passes attempted	15
Bemiller	C	Muennink	9	Passes completed	4
Tarbox	RG	Dreymala	1	Passes had intercepted	1
Youmans	RT	Jones	181	Net yards passing	99
Mautino	RE	Lee	314	Total net yards	244
Sarette	QB	Lackey	6	Number of punts	5
E. Davis	LH	Collins	33	Punting average	42
Schwedes	RH	Gurwitz	3	Fumbles lost	1
Baker	FB	Branch	67	Yards penalized	61

Substitutions—Syracuse: Ericson (l), Lemieux (l), Gilburg (r), Bartlett (r), ends; Gerlick (l), Cholakis (l), Brown (r), tackles; Feidler (l), Grabosky (r), Godfrey (r), guards; Stem, Appelhof, centers; Easterly, quarterback; Weber (l), Hart (l), Bowers (l), Brokaw (l), Reimer (r), halfbacks; Nichols, fullback. Texas: Cooper (l), Gott (l), Halm (r), Moses (r), ends; Stephens (l), Padgett (r), Brockermeyer (r), tackles; Harwerth (l), Kristynik (r), guards; Laughlin, Jackson, centers; Cotten, Saxton, Newman, quarterbacks; Shirley (l), Russell (l), Ramirez (r), halfbacks; Dowdle, Blanch, fullbacks.

SUGAR

"In all honesty," Coach Paul Dietzel had said, "I must choose my own team—Louisiana State—tops in the South."

So did everyone else in 1959. Thirty-one lettermen returned from the national champions' three units of the year before.

But surprising Georgia won the Southeastern Conference championship. Tennessee played almost superhuman football to defeat LSU 14 to 13. It was the Tigers' only defeat. Georgia was unbeaten in the conference.

In the Sugar Bowl, LSU met a Mississippi team in a cold fury.

The Rebels' national title hopes had been dashed by the Bayou Bengals on Halloween Night when Billy Cannon returned a punt 89 yards to beat them, 7 to 3.

They avenged themselves in the Sugar Bowl on a murky day on a muddy field, 21 to 0. It was Ole Miss' fourth bowl victory in five years.

"The score was closer than the game indicated," noted Peter Finney in the *New Orleans Times-States.*

He continued: "I doubt if any game was ever won more clearly in the line—both offensively and defensively. I don't think there's any question but that a combination of the Ole Miss line and LSU backfield would have beaten the Ole Miss backfield and LSU line."

In three starring years Cannon gained 1,867 yards rushing, scored 24 touchdowns, and led his team in punt and kickoff returns, pass receiving, pass interceptions, and punting average.

Ole Miss' smothering defense held the Heisman Trophy winner to eight yards in six carries in the 1960 New Orleans game. The Rebels threw LSU backs for losses totaling minus 15 yards. Never before had a team been so thoroughly shackled in the Sugar Bowl.

Assistant Ole Miss coach Junie Hovious said, "We have never been so aggressive. What I mean is we never went after folks like we did today. It was murder."

Thirty-eight seconds before the end of the first half, with the ball on LSU's 43 in Mississippi's possession, Coach Johnny Vaught ordered a favorite long pass play.

Ends Johnny Brewer and Larry Grantham headed downfield, taking LSU's deep defenders with them. Left halfback Cowboy Woodruff delayed a moment, then hurried after Grantham. Turning slightly to the center of the field, Woodruff reached out and caught quarterback Jake Gibbs' perfectly timed pass on the 12. His touchdown gave Ole Miss a 7 to 0 halftime lead.

The Rebels wore down the staunch LSU defense in the second half. Speed, power, and the roll-out or sprint-out pass combined to put constant pressure on their foes.

Senior quarterback Bobby Franklin, voted the game's outstanding player, passed for two touchdowns. Grantham scored on an 18-yard play in the third quarter and halfback George Blair took a nine-yard touchdown throw in the fourth period, climaxing drives of 64 and 75 yards, respectively. Franklin completed 10 of 15 passes for 148 yards.

LSU didn't cross midfield to invade Rebel territory until the middle of the last quarter and then the stay was short.

Why did LSU players agree to a Sugar Bowl rematch after having already conquered Ole Miss?

A number of them did not approve in the beginning. Cannon's talk to the squad after the first ballot showed a majority, but not an overwhelming one, was credited with changing attitudes.

Billy said he would go along with the wishes of the majority. But he said he wouldn't be interested in half-hearted approval or playing with a team not prepared for hard football.

The public was eager from the start.

"We must have had 50 orders for every ticket we had to sell," said Ace Higgins, LSU's athletic publicity director.

Claude (Monk) Simons, Tulane star who set the Sugar Bowl record for longest kickoff return in 1935. He was president of the New Orleans Mid-Winter Sports Association, which sponsors the Sugar Bowl game, 25 years later.

A crowd of 83,000 saw the game. Each school received $165,000 but was permitted to keep just over $100,000. The remainder went to the Southeastern Conference office and other schools in the league.

The seven major bowls climaxing the 1959 season paid nearly $2,-500,000 to the competing schools and conferences.

Mississippi	0	7	7	7	21
Louisiana State	0	0	0	0	0

Mississippi—Touchdowns: Woodruff (43, pass from Gibbs of 31, run of 12), Grantham (18, pass from Franklin of 14, run of 4), Blair (9, pass from Franklin of 8, run of 1). Points after touchdown: Khayat 3.

STATISTICS

Mississippi		Louisiana State		Mississippi	Louisiana State
Grantham	LE	McClain	19	First downs	6
Kempinska	LT	LeBlanc	140	Net yards rushing	−15
Price	LG	Fournet	27	Passes attempted	25
Kirk	C	Fugler	15	Passes completed	9
Terrell	RG	McCreedy	2	Passes had intercepted	1
Khayat	RT	Strange	223	Net yards passing	89
J. Brewer	RE	Mangham	363	Total net yards	74
W. Brewer	QB	Rabb	6	Number of punts	12
Blair	LH	Cannon	37.5	Punting average	34.1
Partridge	RH	Robinson	2	Fumbles lost	0
Anderson	FB	Daye	65	Yards penalized	30

Substitutions—Mississippi: Smith (l), Bell (l), Goodwin (l), Daniels (r), Regan (r), ends; J. Robertson (l), Basham (l), Owens (r), Benton (r), Brown (r), tackles; Alford (l), Mitchell (l), Lamar (l), Khayat (r), Roberson (r), guards; Lentjes, Green, Jones, centers; Franklin, Gibbs, Elmore, quarterbacks; Woodruff (l), Hall (l), Champion (l), Khayat (l), Crespino (r), Robinson (r), halfbacks; Flowers, Adams, R. Robertson, fullbacks. Louisiana State: Bourgeois (l), Bond (l), Kinchen (r), Norwood (r), ends; Branch (l), McCarty (l), Leopard (r), Frayer (r), tackles; Winston (l), Stupka (l), Booth (l), Lott (r), Guillot (r), Booth (r), guards; Langan, Greenwood, centers; Jenkins, Matherne, quarterbacks; Purvis (l), Bourque (r), Neck (r), halfbacks; Schexnaildre, Gros, fullbacks.

ORANGE

"The 1959 Georgia team has given me my greatest thrills in a lifetime of football."

The finest tribute to the players Wally Butts coached in his twenty-first year at Georgia came from the "Little Round Man" himself.

Harold M. Walker, Georgia football's poet laureate, composed the following lines in praise of the unheralded Bulldogs, picked for ninth place in the Southeastern Conference in advance of the season:

> This was the team that came storming back
> When all was dark along the track
> With nothing left to reach the goal
> But a champion's heart and a champion's soul
> So here's to the champions of Wallace Butts
> The football team that won on guts.

Georgia unexpectedly won the championship, Butts' fourth, clinching the title with a 14 to 13 victory over Auburn when Francis Tarkenton passed to Bill Herron for a touchdown with 30 seconds left.

Tarkenton, son of a Methodist minister, was a marksman throwing a football and a smart field general.

"In 30 years in sports I've never met a better boy or better leader of men," said Butts. "I thank him for making me a better coach."

To protect and escort Tarkenton: breakaway runner Fred Brown, nephew of Alabama's Johnny Mack Brown; Bobby Walden, No. 1 punter in the nation in 1958 who was an excellent all-purpose back in '59, and fullback Bill Godfrey, the Bulldogs' leading ground gainer, a keenly aggressive line had been fashioned by J. B. (Ears) Whitworth. This warm-hearted man died of a heart attack a few months after Georgia's 14 to 0 triumph over Missouri in the 1960 Orange Bowl game.

1960—Bill McKenny (24) of Georgia scores as high-leaping Fred Brossart of Missouri descends on him.

Missouri, coached by boyish-looking Dan Devine, was runnerup to Oklahoma in the Big Eight. The Sooners couldn't return because of the no-repeat rule.

Georgia scored in the first quarter when Tarkenton and halfback Bill McKenny collaborated on a 29-yard pass play. The Bulldogs notched their second touchdown in the third quarter. Tarkenton threw 33 yards to end Aaron Box.

Devine said his team was "the slowest I was ever associated with but our pursuit on defense just about made up for it except on those two passes. If our rush on Tarkenton had worked on those two plays, they might not have scored. We almost had him on the first one. We didn't quite get to him the last time."

Butts once said, "Hard work and confidence make a good pass receiver. If a player thinks he can catch the ball, he can. It's vital that a receiver relax as he tries to take in the ball. We work on relaxation drills regularly.

"Our passers know exactly where their receivers will be. Knowing this, they watch the defensive man. We figure every defensive man can't be right. When somebody makes a mistake, our passer hits the man who is open."

Georgia safetyman Charley Britt picked off a pair of Missouri passes to thwart the Tigers. He also tackled Norm Beal after he returned a punt 44 yards to Georgia's 48, preventing the swift halfback from going for a touchdown.

Butts said it was Georgia's "worst game," but his players remarked about how vigorously they were hit.

"You have to get a pretty good lick to have a big dent knocked in your helmet," Britt said, "and I had to go to the sidelines to get a new one."

Georgia	7	0	7	0	14
Missouri	0	0	0	0	0

Georgia—Touchdowns: McKenny (29, pass from Tarkenton of 23, run of 6), Box (33, pass from Tarkenton of 32, run of 1). Points after touchdown: Pennington 2.

STATISTICS

Georgia		Missouri	Georgia		Missouri
Vickers	LE	Sloan	14	First downs	17
Lancaster	LT	Wegener	88	Net yards rushing	80
Dye	LG	Henley	21	Passes attempted	24
Thompson	C	Swaney	9	Passes completed	14

Georgia		Missouri		Georgia	Missouri
Roland	RG	Garvis	2	Passes had intercepted	3
Leebern	RT	Magac	128	Net yards passing	180
Kelley	RE	LaRose	216	Total net yards	260
Britt	QB	Snowden	7	Number of punts	6
Walden	LH	West	46.9	Punting average	38.7
Towns	RH	D. Smith	0	Fumbles lost	0
Godfrey	FB	Miles	44	Yards penalized	72

Substitutions—Georgia: Herron (l), Box (r), ends; Case (l), Lawrence (r), tackles; Ramsey (l), Davis (r), guards; Ashe, center; Tarkenton, quarterback; Pennington (l), Brown (l), Paris (l), McKenny (r), Guisler (r), halfbacks; Soberdash, Taylor, Lewis, fullbacks. Missouri: Carpenter (l), Pidcock (r), G. Smith (r), T. Smith (r), ends; Blaine (l), Brinkman (r), Rittman (r), tackles; Moyer (l), Vanderlinde (l), Calhoun (r), guards; McCartney, center; Haas, quarterback; Beal (l), Snyder (l), Brossart (r), halfbacks; Toman, McCoy, fullbacks.

ROSE

Until the 1960 Rose Bowl game, last year of the contract binding Big Ten and Pacific Coast Conference teams to play in Pasadena, the Midwest had outscored the long suffering Far West, 333 to 141, and had won 12 of the 13 encounters.

The pact officially ended as it began—in a runaway. But this time it was the Big Ten champion, Wisconsin, that was manhandled 44 to 8 by Washington.

Washington was co-leader of the new Athletic Association of Western Universities (Big Five), which replaced the defunct Pacific Coast Conference in 1959. Other members were California, Southern California, UCLA, and Stanford.

Under the contract the Pacific Coast Conference was obligated to furnish a team through the 1960 game. The school was picked from eligibles in the dissolved conference by the nine athletic directors. The AAWU signed a new contract with the Tournament of Roses Association to provide the western team, starting in 1961.

It was Washington's first appearance against the Big Ten's best, although the Huskies had played in the Rose Bowl four times previously without winning. It was also the first bowl game for young (thirty-two) Jim Owens as a head coach. No stranger to bowls, however, he played in the Gator Bowl, two Sugar Bowl games, and the Senior Bowl while at Oklahoma.

Washington's 9–1 season and its emergence as the strongest team on the Pacific slope was a rewarding climax to three years of painstaking, sometimes discouraging rebuilding that the former Sooner All-America end and his staff undertook. Its chances were not well thought of. From a 1–6 record in the conference in 1958, Washington improved to 3–1 in the Big Five, losing to Southern California. The Trojans, also 3–1 in the Big Five, were under National Collegiate Athletic Association probation and were, therefore, ineligible to play in the Rose Bowl. UCLA, 3–1 too, was whipped by Washington.

Owens came to Washington in 1957 after Darrell Royal, also an Oklahoma alumnus, accepted an offer from Texas. Royal stayed in Seattle only a year. Many Washington alumni were somewhat disenchanted with the selection of Owens, an assistant under Paul Bryant at Texas A&M.

Following the 1958 season (3–7), athletic director George Briggs got the jump on dissatisfied Huskie fans by signing Owens to a new two-year contract.

On the eve of the Rose Bowl game with Wisconsin, former Washington All-America tackle Paul Schwegler, who was president of his school's alumni group in southern California, said:

"Don't overlook the fine coaching job Jim Owens has done. Here's a team without any big stars, without even any first-string seniors. But Owens has done an excellent welding job. These Huskies are well balanced, full of desire, trying all the time. I think they can do it."

They did and after the pounding Wisconsin took, stars aplenty were acclaimed. The disaster that befell Coach Milt Bruhn's Badgers was almost unbelievable.

Washington shocked the crowd of 100,809–and Wisconsin–by taking a 17 to 0 lead at the end of the first quarter. In the first 15 minutes Wisconsin failed to make a first down and was in possession of the ball for only nine plays.

The Huskies' line, although outweighed ten pounds per man, consistently outcharged and outblocked Wisconsin's. Sharp tackling helped to induce four ball-losing fumbles.

Superlative was the word for quarterback Bob Schloredt's passing, running, and audacious field generalship. Once he ran on fourth down from the Washington 16 and made it. This was late in the game. Washington went on to score its last touchdown. The drive covered 93 yards and Schloredt went over.

Schloredt completed four of his seven passes for 102 yards and carried 21 times for 81 yards, in addition to scoring on a three-yard run. He became a fine player despite almost complete blindness in his left eye as a result of a boyhood firecracker accident.

"It isn't really a handicap," Schloredt insisted. "I can make the good eye do the work of two by moving my head back and forth. That way I can see almost as well as a quarterback with perfect eyesight."

Owens said, "His depth perception is limited. Yet he can put a ball into the arms of a weaving receiver 50 yards away."

Dazzling were the exploits of halfback George Fleming. He returned three punts for 122 yards and also brought back three kick-offs for 80 yards. Fleming carried one punt 53 yards over the Badgers' goal line as the first quarter expired and raced 55 yards with another to set the stage for a touchdown in the second period.

In addition, Fleming kicked a 36-yard field goal against the wind and caught a pass from Schloredt for a 65-yard gain that made possible the final touchdown.

Brilliant, but typical of the Huskies' efforts, was end Lee Folkins' finger-tip, diving, end zone clutch of Schloredt's 23-yard pass that put

1960—Typical of Washington's extra effort against Wisconsin was this diving catch of Bob Schloredt's touchdown pass made by end Lee Folkins.

Washington ahead, 24 to 8, at halftime. At that time the Huskies had scored more points than any Pacific Coast team since the beginning of the pact. When the game was over, they had scored more than any Far West Rose Bowl team in 30 years.

"We knew they were aggressive," said Bruhn. "But we weren't prepared for all that speed."

The tall, handsome Owens said, "I'm on top of the world."

In his third year as head coach he had abandoned split T "plunge and punt" tactics that had not produced results pleasing to Washington followers and delighted them with a "swing T" attack featuring flankers, wingbacks, unbalanced lines, and deceptive pass patterns.

The Huskies' performance was a revelation.

His players were beside themselves with joy in their locker room after their Rose Bowl triumph. Don McKeta, a halfback who scored the first touchdown, did an unusual thing. He leaped on a training table and shouted: "We've been reading that our line was too light and was gonna get pushed around. Well, every back on this team should take our linemen out and buy them a dinner—they're the best."

Washington	17	7	7	13	44
Wisconsin	0	8	0	0	8

Washington—Touchdowns: McKeta (6, right end), Fleming (53, punt return), Folkins (23, pass from Schloredt), Jackson (2, right tackle), Schloredt (3, left tackle), Millich (1, pass from Hivner). Points after touchdown: Fleming 5. Field goal: Fleming (36, placekick).

Wisconsin—Touchdown: Wiesner (4, left tackle). Points after touchdown: Schoonover (pass from Hackbart).

STATISTICS

Washington		Wisconsin	Washington		Wisconsin
Folkins	LE	Schoonover	16	First downs	13
Gegner	LT	Lanphear	215	Net yards rushing	123
Allen	LG	Perkins	13	Passes attempted	32
McKasson	C	Nelson	7	Passes completed	14
Kinnune	RG	Stalcup (c-c)	0	Passes had intercepted	0
B. Bullard	RT	Heineke	137	Net yards passing	153
Meyers	RE	Derleth	352	Total net yards	276
Schloredt	QB	Hackbart	6	Number of punts	6
Fleming	LH	Hobbs	36	Punting average	36
McKeta	RH	Zeman (c-c)	0	Fumbles lost	4
Jackson	FB	Hart	85	Yards penalized	18

Substitutions—Washington: Claridge (l), Peasley (l), Quessenberry (r), Chapple (r), ends; White (l), Cordes (l), Echols (r), Davidson (r), Enslow (r), tackles; Walters (l), Clanton (l), Skaggs (r), Crawford (r), guards; Pitt, F. Bullard, Dunn, Nelson, centers; Hivner, Everett, quarterbacks; Millich (l), Gayton (l), Wooten (r), halfbacks; Jones, Hurworth, Wheatley, fullbacks. Wisconsin: Holmes (l), Rogers (r), ends; Holzwarth (l), Huxhold (l), Jenkins (r), Moore (r), Zouvas (r), tackles; Schade (l), Kulcinski (r), guards; Gotta, center; Bakken, quarterback; Clark (l), Kunesh (r), halfbacks; Wiesner, Neumann, fullbacks.

GATOR

The teacher vs. pupil angle was too appetizing not to be swallowed by the Gator Bowl Association that paired Georgia Tech and Arkansas.

Frank Broyles, 35-year-old Arkansas coach, spent 10 years at Georgia Tech, the last six as an assistant to Bobby Dodd.

In 1959, his second season at Arkansas, the Razorbacks earned a share of the Southwest Conference title and won eight of their ten games. Tech was less successful, losing four.

But the Dodd-Broyles match was so appealing that the Gator Bowl was sold out in mid-December. A crowd of 45,104 attended.

Dodd and Broyles had more combined bowl experience than any two coaches ever matched.

It was Bobby's thirteenth bowl battle, four as backfield coach under W. A. Alexander at Tech and nine as head coach. The Yellow Jackets had been beaten only twice, both times when Dodd was serving as an assistant.

Broyles played in three bowl games as quarterback of Tech teams that lost once. He was an assistant coach to Bob Woodruff at Baylor when that team defeated Wake Forest in the Dixie Bowl game of 1949. He was Dodd's backfield coach in the six straight years the Jackets won bowl games, beginning in 1952.

"Coach Dodd has had the greatest effect on my life of any person I've ever known," Broyles once said.

Before the game at Jacksonville, he said, "They've got tradition working for them. Their players will be telling one another, 'Let's don't be the first bowl team to lose under Coach Dodd.' They'll go into the game determined to win somehow."

Which was probably true.

Nevertheless, Dodd's string of bowl successes was snipped 14 to 7.

"It was so simple," wrote Orville Henry, sharply analyzing the game in the *Arkansas Gazette*. "Arkansas won with two basics:

"1. By far the better halfbacks, Jim Mooty and Lance Alworth, perhaps the finest pair ever in harness at Arkansas.

"2. Quick-hitting, scrambling little linemen who came prepared to play all day, getting tougher all the time, while the bulky Yellow Jackets, as one of the Porkers put it, 'just plain wore out.'"

Before the game Mooty was talking to trainer Bill Ferrell as he was being taped.

"Ground Hog," said Mooty, using the nickname the players applied to their trainer, "this has got to be my best day. I want it to be in the worst way."

With the score tied at 7 to 7 in the second half, Mooty started a 78-yard push with a 24-yard run and hustled 19 yards to finish it.

There had been considerable doubt in July whether Mooty would play again because of a head injury. A late-August medical examination gave him clear sailing. He missed two complete games because of a knee injury but led his team in rushing with 519 yards (5.6 average) and became an All-American.

At Jacksonville, Mooty was superb.

Tech received the kickoff and used up 22 plays and 11 minutes, 41 seconds before a 75-yard drive fizzled with an unsuccessful field goal try by Cal James at the Arkansas 8.

Arkansas had the ball for three unproductive plays before being forced to punt. On Tech's second down, quarterback Marvin Tibbetts faked a handoff to his fullback, rolled out through left tackle, cut back to take advantage of blocks, and sped 51 yards to score. En route, Tibbetts ran through Mooty's arms. Tibbetts suffered a back injury on the second-half kickoff, eliminating him from the remainder of the game.

In the second quarter Arkansas pieced together 62 yards in 19 plays for its first touchdown. Fullback Joe Paul Alberty, only bachelor in the starting backfield, came through three times to get the first down on one-yard-to-go situations. The 175-pounder plunged the final yard for the touchdown and the half ended 7 to 7.

Mooty and his sophomore sidekick, Alworth, running swiftly and shiftily, broke wide for important gains in the third quarter as the Razorbacks, normally a wing T team, swept down the field from their 22.

The key play, Broyles thought, was an eight-yard run by Alworth to the Tech 39 on third down with seven to go. Both ends lined up on the left side with Mooty in a slot between the inboard wingman and the left tackle. Alworth had three backs and two ends in front of him.

Finally, with Alworth cutting down Tech's left end, Mooty bolted inside that block and with more aid plus his own drive made it to the goal line 19 yards away.

At a day in Mooty's honor held in El Dorado, Ark., his home town, Broyles said, "We found out, grading our films, that every time Mooty's number was called—and some of our plays even carried his name—there was more effort by our linemen blocking at the hole and

1960—Jim Mooty of Arkansas utilizes blocks, leg power, speed to score against Georgia Tech.

better downfield interference. They believed in Jim Mooty. They knew if they gave him a chance, he'd make the most of it."

Dodd was philosophical about the defeat.

"If streaks must end, it is better that they end in the family and I would rather lose to Frank than anyone else," he said.

Broyles was stuck under the dressing room shower by his players.

"The speed of our two halfbacks (Mooty was voted the outstanding player on the winning team) was the difference," he said, emerging. "Except for their speed the game was as even as it possibly could be. Of course, I'm sorry Coach Dodd's fine record had to be broken. But you don't expect me to be sorry we won, do you?"

SATURDAY, JANUARY 2, 1960

Arkansas	0	7	7	0	14
Georgia Tech	7	0	0	0	7

Arkansas—Touchdowns: Alberty (1, left tackle), Mooty (19, right tackle). Points after touchdown: Akers 2.

Georgia Tech—Touchdown: Tibbetts (51, left tackle). Point after touchdown: Faucette.

STATISTICS

Arkansas		Georgia Tech	Arkansas		Georgia Tech
Butler	LE	Burch	15	First downs	13
Epp	LT	Shaw	218	Net yards rushing	172
Luplow	LG	Ericksen	6	Passes attempted	18
Harris	C	Baughan	2	Passes completed	7
Gardner	RG	Reed	1	Passes had intercepted	1
Hollander	RT	Deese	21	Net yards passing	64
Letsinger	RE	Rudolph	239	Total net yards	236
McKinney	QB	Tibbetts	4	Number of punts	4
Mooty	LH	Faucette	36	Punting average	40
Alworth	RH	Williamson	1	Fumbles lost	0
Alberty	FB	Anderson	56	Yards penalized	15

Substitutions—Arkansas: Gaston (l), Tranum (r), ends; Henderson (l), Childress (r), tackles; Garrett (l), Green (l), Fields (r), guards; Switzer, center; Monroe, quarterback; Williams (l), Akers (l), Kyser (r), Horton (r), halfbacks; Cox, fullback. Georgia Tech: Powell (l), Carter (l), Beasley (l), Murphy (r), ends; Foret (l), Nutting (r), tackles; McKinney (l), Moss (l), Pilgrim (r), Nicholl (r), guards; McGaughey, center; Braselton, quarterback; Graning (l), Nix (r), Thompson (r), James (r), halfbacks; Smith, fullback.

BLUEBONNET BOWL

On January 1, 1958, Elvin M. Smith, a Houston pipeline executive who once played football at Southern Methodist, was in New Orleans watching his son, Elvin, Jr., a Texas halfback, against Ole Miss.

"I came home and thought what a fine thing this Sugar Bowl game was for New Orleans," he said. "I was determined that Houston should and could put on as fine a bowl game as any city in the nation."

Eight days after the Texas-Mississippi game, Smith suggested to the athletic committee of his city's Chamber of Commerce that such a possibility be investigated.

On the committee appointed with Smith to make the study were Eddie Dyer, former Rice player and one-time manager of the St. Louis Cardinals, and Lou Hassell. Several enthusiastic responses later the nonprofit Greater Houston Bowl Association was formed with Smith as its first president. There were 84 directors. The number was subsequently increased. Rice University granted the use of its stadium. And the game was officially certified by the National Collegiate Athletic Association on August 29, 1959.

Thus the Bluebonnet Bowl (the bluebonnet is the state flower of Texas) came into being. A crowd of 55,000 attended the game between Clemson, champion of the Atlantic Coast Conference, and Texas Christian, co-champion (with Texas and Arkansas) of the Southwest Conference. No other bowl drew that many in its first year. Each school received $84,000 to be split according to the dictates of its conference.

Rice Stadium in Houston, home of the Bluebonnet Bowl, seats 70,000.

Forestalling protests often voiced by vacationers in some bowl cities, Bluebonnet Bowl officials obtained written pledges of Houston motels, hotels, and restaurants that there would be no advance in regular prices during game week. The hotels assured visitors they would not be required to pay for reservations for a longer period of time than they desired to stay.

"They made the normal amount of mistakes expected in a new venture, and still the Bluebonnet Bowl has been widely acclaimed an outstanding success," wrote Bob Rule, sports editor of the *Houston Press,* two days after Clemson's 23 to 7 victory over Texas Christian in the first game.

"A tremendous start has been made. There can be no reasonable doubt it can quickly take its place alongside the big ones."

As the fourth quarter began, TCU led 7 to 3. Within a period of seven minutes, six seconds, Clemson manufactured 20 points.

With 10:22 left, Coach Frank Howard's Tigers had the ball on their 32, third down and 18 to go. Right end Gary Barnes went down, cut left, and took a long, perfectly timed "home run" pass from quarterback Harvey White on the TCU 30. Barnes galloped unhindered for a touchdown.

Then Howard sent in "Shingler's Raiders." They had struck for eight of Clemson's 14 longest plays during the season. They never started but they played almost as much as the first unit.

Alternate quarterback Lowndes Shingler and his band had gotten the field goal that gave Clemson a brief 3 to 0 lead in the second quarter. Now, two plays after the White to Barnes pass, they took the ball away from the Horned Frogs when Lon Armstrong intercepted Don George's throw. He returned it 17 yards to the TCU 27. On fourth down, with six yards to go, Shingler shot a pass to Tommy King, who made a wrong-shoulder catch in the end zone.

The "Raiders" paraded 63 yards in seven plays through a disorganized defense to score again. Fullback Ron Scrudato hammered out the last yard.

It was essentially a battle of two "bull elephant" lines until Shingler and White riddled the TCU secondary in the closing minutes.

During that 1959 season Howard's son, Jimmy, a halfback, was a highly praised high school senior. Someone asked Howard, while he was in Houston, why he wanted the boy to play his college football at Clemson.

"So he'll have the advantage of brilliant coaching," Howard answered characteristically.

SATURDAY, DECEMBER 19, 1959

Clemson	0	3	0	20	23
Texas Christian	0	7	0	0	7

Clemson—Touchdowns: Barnes (68, pass from White of 38, run of 30),

T. King (23, pass from Shingler), Scrudato (1, right tackle). Points after touchdown: Armstrong 2. Field goal: Armstrong (22, placekick).

Texas Christian—Touchdown: Moreland (19, pass from Reding). Point after touchdown: Dodson.

STATISTICS

Clemson		Texas Christian	Clemson		Texas Christian
Anderson	LE	Gilmore	16	First downs	12
Cordileone	LT	Floyd	203	Net yards rushing	89
Crout	LG	Rambo	13	Passes attempted	17
Snyder	C	Martin	6	Passes completed	7
Lynn	RG	Armstrong	1	Passes had intercepted	4
H. Olson	RT	Lilly	103	Net yards passing	70
Barnes	RE	Peebles	306	Total net yards	159
White	QB	Sledge	3	Number of punts	5
Mathis	LH	Lasater	37	Punting average	32
Usry	RH	Harris	2	Fumbles lost	0
Cline	FB	Spikes	23	Yards penalized	35

Substitutions—Clemson: Bost (l), DeBardelaben (l), T. King (r), Crolley (r), ends; J. King (l), Smith (l), Osborne (r), Keller (r), tackles; West (l), Killen (l), D. Olson (r), Gue (r), Armstrong (r), guards; Andreo, Veronee, centers; Shingler, quarterback; Pavilack (l), Daigneault (r), Coleman (r), halfbacks; Scrudato, fullback. Texas Christian: Ham (l), Linne (l), Meyer (r), Glasscock (r), Iles (r), ends; Crenwelge (l), Prince (l), Roach (r), Plummer (r), tackles; Moffett (l), Lucas (l), McSpedden (r), Pinion (r), guards; Cumpton, Biehunko, centers; George, Dawson, Gonzales, quarterbacks; Moreland (l), Rowland (l), Reding (r), Terrell (r), halfbacks; Priddy, Pierce, Dodson, fullbacks.

LIBERTY BOWL

Three weeks before, 100,000 football fans watched Navy thrash Army, 43 to 12, in Philadelphia Stadium.

Now, on December 19, 1959, in the nationally televised Liberty Bowl premiere, Penn State's 7 to 0 victory over Alabama was viewed by a shivering, blanketed assemblage of 36,211 spectators.

But they contributed enough to the gate receipts to insure that the bold promoters, Ambrose F. (Bud) Dudley and George J. Kerrigan, wouldn't lose their laundry. Each school received $98,000. No other bowl paid out so much in its first year.

"It was a wonderful start, better than the first effort of such bowls as the Sugar and Orange," said Dudley, who sought to prove, among other things, that a bowl game could succeed in the cold latitude of eastern Pennsylvania, even near Christmas.

The Liberty Bowl Association headed by Dudley petitioned the National Collegiate Athletic Association for approval of the game in March 1957. Twenty-two months later the bowl was certified.

Philadelphia Stadium, where the Liberty Bowl game is played, has a capacity of 100,000.

Canvassing began for 500 charter members who were asked to contribute $100 each to launch the project. In the program (which sold for one dollar) the Association expressed gratitude that almost 700 individuals and organizations furnished support.

Incidentally, this may have been the only football program ever printed that carried the names in a band, Penn State's, complete with each musician's uniform number, instrument, age, weight, height, class, and home town.

In a letter to Dudley, printed in the program, Philadelphia mayor Richardson Dilworth wrote, "A game of this magnitude will undoubtedly generate a considerable amount of business in our city."

Penn State, coached by Charles (Rip) Engle, was picked to represent the East. The Nittany Lions won eight and lost two. They were beaten by Syracuse's national champions, but only by 20 to 18, and dropped their final game to Pittsburgh 22 to 7.

In the Syracuse game, 18-year-old sophomore halfback Roger Kochman ran 100 yards to score on a kickoff return. However, the team's ace was Richie Lucas, a multiply talented quarterback.

Alabama under Paul Bryant lost its opener to Georgia's Southeastern Conference champions but never another, although tied twice. After yielding twenty-nine times in four years, the Crimson

Tide had rebounded to a 5–4–1 season in 1958 as Bryant returned to his alma mater to coach.

Thus, he repeated performances at Maryland, Kentucky, and Texas A&M where he rebuilt football programs and converted also-rans into winners. In 1959, Alabama, despite a dull offense that produced only 12 touchdowns, won seven games.

The Crimson Tide reached Penn State's 28 early in the first quarter. It never got that close to scoring again.

The play that beat Alabama was put in by Engle two days before the game. It was a fake field goal, quickly sprung and well executed, as the clock ran out ending the first half.

A 20-mile-an-hour wind held up punts against it all afternoon and caused an almost straight-up kick by Tommy White. It netted Alabama only three yards. This provided Penn State with its fourth scoring opportunity of the first half. Previously, the Nittany Lions failed on penetrations to the 1, 5, and 8.

With the ball on Alabama's 18, second down and six yards to go, Penn State speedily went into field-goal formation without huddling. Quarterback Galen Hall knelt on the 25. Guard Sam Stellatella

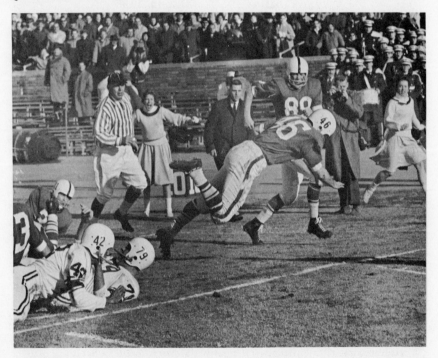

1959—Penn State's Roger Kochman crosses the Alabama goal line after taking a short pass from Galen Hall on a fake field-goal attempt.

stood on the left side of him, head down, apparently intent on kicking.

Hall took a high snap, rose, and rolled to his right. He threw back diagonally a few yards. Kochman, well screened near the sideline, took the pass on the 20 and bolted for the goal line, charging behind a convoy of teammates. He was tripped near the end zone but tumbled in.

"We had never scouted Alabama," Engle explained. "We had studied game movies, though. From them we learned that Alabama's right side rushed much harder than the left. So we sent in the fake field goal-screen pass left which would be to their right side. You see, the right side rushed so hard, it was drawn in."

Lucas was forced from the scene early in the second quarter because of a hip injury after playing a brilliant first period.

"We were fortunate not to be beaten by four or five touchdowns," said Bryant. "We just got a good sound thrashing."

"We get a little tired of people belittling Eastern football," said Engle. "Nobody's too decadent around here that I know of."

SATURDAY, DECEMBER 19, 1959

Penn State	0	7	0	0	7
Alabama	0	0	0	0	0

Penn State—Touchdown: Kochman (18, screen pass from Hall). Point after touchdown: Stellatella.

STATISTICS

Penn State		*Alabama*	*Penn State*		*Alabama*
Bozick	LE	Rice	18	First downs	8
Stynchula	LT	Phillips	278	Net yards rushing	104
Kohlhaas	LG	Hannah	10	Passes attempted	8
Huffman	C	Blevins	2	Passes completed	2
Popp	RG	Cochran	0	Passes had intercepted	0
Janerette	RT	Neighbors	41	Net yards passing	27
Mitinger	RE	Brooker	319	Total net yards	131
Lucas	QB	Trammell	6	Number of punts	8
Hoak	LH	Richardson	29	Punting average	34.4
Pae	RH	Morrison	4	Fumbles lost	4
Botula	FB	Wesley	45	Yards penalized	45

Substitutions—Penn State: Oppermann (l), Neff (r), ends; Barber (l), Mulraney (r), tackles; Stellatella (l), Korbini (r), guards; Wilson, center; Hall, quarterback; Kochman (l), Kerr (r), halfbacks; Sobczak, fullback. Alabama: Patton (l), Moore (r), Spruiell (r), ends; Boylston (l), Allen (r), tackles; Sims (l), Holsomback (l), Rutledge (r), guards; Moseley, center; Skelton, quarterback; Fuller (l), Rich (l), Dyess (r), Johnson (r), halfbacks; White, O'Steen, Stickney, fullbacks.

– 1961 –

GATOR

Almost three months earlier, when Florida met Georgia Tech, the Gators scored a touchdown with 32 seconds to play. That left Tech leading, 17 to 16.

What would Florida do? Go for the almost certain extra point placekick and a tie? Gamble for victory with a pass or run for the two-point conversion?

Well, Ray Graves started his new job at Florida not 12 months before with the promise the Gators would play wide open, take-a-chance football. With his approval, 138-pound sophomore quarterback Larry Libertore, who with fellow sophomore quarterback, Bobby Dodd, Jr., helped to bring about the defeat of Bobby Dodd, Sr.'s Yellow Jackets, passed into the end zone. Fullback Jon MacBeth caught it and Florida won, 18 to 17.

In the Gator Bowl game played on the last day of 1960, the shoe was on another foot. It didn't fit.

Baylor halfback Ronnie Bull smashed three yards for a touchdown after quarterback Ronnie Stanley had teamed up with halfback Ronnie Goodwin on a 44-yard pass to put the Bears in scoring position.

It was Florida 13, Baylor 12 now with one minute left.

Would the Bears, who achieved an 8–2 record with equal devotion to passing and running—using the pass as a trusted weapon on which half of their offensive practice time was spent—be satisfied with kicking for a possible tie?

They didn't give it a thought. Bobby Ply dropped back and threw a pass, perhaps a bit high, aimed at Goodwin, who was running toward the right sideline. Goodwin reached for the ball, juggled it, and couldn't hold on.

"It was a good pass," said the skilled receiver who caught seven throws, a record, for 129 yards. "I should have had it."

And so Florida gained its ninth victory under Graves, Dodd's right-hand man at Georgia Tech for many years. Under Graves' command, the Gators enjoyed their finest, most exciting season in 31 years.

Just four points, a 10 to 7 loss to Auburn, kept Florida from tying for the Southeastern Conference championship. They were supposed to finish ninth or lower.

Few sensed their strength. But as Edwin Pope of the *Miami Herald* wrote, "When you get right down to it, one group alone called the turn on this Florida team. That was the Florida team itself.

"Before the season started, someone suggested to Libertore the Gators would be lucky to break even. 'Break even!' he cried. 'Who we gonna lose to?' "

In the Gator Bowl game Florida's aggressive line harassed Baylor's two passing aces, Ply and Stanley, held the Bears to a meager 40 yards rushing, stopped them four straight times when they had driven to a first down on the 4, and created the opportunities that won the game.

Bull fumbled a pitch-out in the second quarter. Guard Chet Collins recovered on Baylor's 20. This led to a touchdown by fullback Don Goodman, who plunged over from the 3.

With two minutes remaining in the half, Baylor halted a long Florida advance on the 3 by blocking Billy Cash's attempted field goal. The Bears, refusing to play conservatively despite their position on the field and the little time left, went into the air. On third down Collins burst through Stanley's protective pocket and jolted him so hard that he dropped the ball.

Tackles Ronnie Slack and Gerald Stephens and guard Larry Travis grasped for it. Travis was incorrectly credited with the touchdown. He said he didn't score it, that Slack did, and the pictures seemed to prove he was right.

"I had the ball between my legs," Travis said. "Slack got it in his hands. But I never scored any points before and I'm glad to have a part in this one anyway."

Florida sat on that 13 to 0 lead in the third quarter.

On the first play in the fourth period Ply passed 11 yards to Goodwin for Baylor's first touchdown. The Bears had moved 61 yards. Larry Corley failed to make good the placekick conversion attempt.

Then, with almost three-fourths of the field's length to travel and less than three minutes to do it in, Baylor got 63 yards on two quick passes, both to Goodwin, the first by Ply and the second by Stanley. Bull did the rest. But ultimately, the dramatic missed conversion by air closed the book on the happiest season Florida ever had.

The seven major bowls drew approximately 460,000 fans. Gross receipts amounted to upward of $3,000,000. Of that total, television and radio network companies paid more than $1,000,000.

The Rose Bowl led with the biggest crowd—97,314; gate receipts —$975,000, and television receipts—approximately $500,000.

SATURDAY, DECEMBER 31, 1960

Florida	0	13	0	0	13
Baylor	0	0	0	12	12

Florida—Touchdowns: Goodman (3, left tackle), Slack (recovered fumble by Stanley from Baylor 2). Point after touchdown: Cash.

Baylor—Touchdowns: Goodwin (11, pass from Ply), Bull (3, right tackle).

STATISTICS

Florida		Baylor	Florida		Baylor
Patchen	LE	Davis	11	First downs	15
Slack	LT	McLeod	176	Net yards rushing	40
Norris	LG	Frazier	8	Passes attempted	27
Hood	C	Hicks	5	Passes completed	13
Miranda	RG	Adkins	0	Passes had intercepted	0
Beaver	RT	West	57	Net yards passing	211
Smith	RE	Moore	233	Total net yards	251
Libertore	QB	Ply	7	Number of punts	5
Infante	LH	Goodwin	37	Punting average	33
Deal	RH	Bull	1	Fumbles lost	3
MacBeth	FB	Evans	70	Yards penalized	5

Substitutions—Florida: Kelley (l), Cash (l), Holland (r), Gregory (r), ends; Odom (l), Dean (l), Seals (r), Stephens (r), tackles; Collins (l), Gill (l), Travis (r), guards; Wehking, Culpepper, centers; Dodd, White, Ringgold, quarterbacks; Starling (l), Skelly (l), Partin (l), Hoover (r), Page (r), halfbacks; Goodman, Ewell, fullbacks. Baylor: Harlan (l), Plumb (l), Lane (r), ends; Frongillo (l), Nicklas (r), tackles; Manasco (l), Burk (r), guards; Hays, center; Stanley, Corley, White, quarterbacks; Minter (l), Tate (r), Gowen (r), halfbacks; Starr, Whorton, Adams, fullbacks.

COTTON

During the 1958 football season, when things weren't going well for Duke, students of a fraternity house on the Durham campus hanged the coach, Bill Murray, in effigy. This prompted an attractive Duke coed to write an open letter to Murray. She wrote, in part:

I was so busy with my school work someone had to tell me. Well, that's us students for you. Full of pranks and awfully demanding without knowing the situation or the problems.

Since I'm such a rabid fan, I know some of my classmates expected me to defend you and the boys. I just go my way—for I don't think you need my defense . . .

You're a coach and nobody forced you to become one. You're in coaching because you love football and the youngsters who play it and all that goes with the game. Winning and losing are part of it . . .

I've been a Duke backer for a long time—and one of yours in particular.
Your record here is pretty impressive . . . You've got a strong neck and a good
sense of humor . . .

I'll be pulling for you and the boys the rest of the way. So will a lot of
other Duke fans.

> With love and understanding,
> Carolyn Kirby Murray
> (Duke class of '59)

The student was a young grandmother, completing work for her
degree almost 30 years after she dropped from school to marry the
campus football hero who later became his alma mater's football
coach.

Late in the afternoon of January 2, 1961, Murray and his Duke
Blue Devils were sitting on top of the world. They had just struck
down favored Arkansas, 7 to 6, in the Cotton Bowl. Their selection
to oppose the Southwest Conference champions had been roundly
criticized after late season losses to North Carolina and UCLA.

Murray regarded the victory as a "rewarding vindication."

So stunned was Arkansas Coach Frank Broyles that after the game
he asked football writers what the score was.

"The extra point is the most important play in football," he commented.

Late in the third quarter Lance Alworth, exceptionally talented,
exceedingly fast Arkansas halfback, had kicked 38 yards out of bounds
on the Duke 1. It was a remarkable effort. The center snap was
high. Alworth had to skedaddle to his right and punt on the run.

He followed up that with a sparkling feat of another kind. He
caught Randy Clark's return punt and scurried 49 yards for a touchdown. He left Clark, the last defender, standing flatfooted with his
darting fake.

End Dave Unser blocked Mickey Cissell's extra point attempt because, as he put it, "I had to." Unser said, "I felt that I was the one
who let Alworth make his touchdown run. My job defending on
punt returns is to protect the right side. I cut him inside all right,
but I had a chance to make the tackle and didn't."

Duke had been held to 26 yards rushing and 38 in the air in the
first half. When the Blue Devils got the ball 73 yards from the
Arkansas goal line with 10:13 left in the fourth quarter, prospects
of reaching it looked bleak to their rooters in the crowd of 74,000.
Duke hadn't crossed midfield under its own steam.

Orville Henry explained what happened then quite clearly in the
Arkansas Gazette—"a patient, short-play surge, one tough play after
another, to get the winning points."

"I just knew we were going to score," said Duke tackle Dwight

Bumgarner. "I felt it in my heart. The extra point they missed after their touchdown spurred us on."

During the lengthy march quarterback Don Altman twice threw completed fourth-down passes for the necessary yardage to keep it alive. Finally, from the 9, Altman spiraled a touchdown pass to end Tee Moorman, who made eight catches that day and 46 during the season.

"I was supposed to go down and in, but our other ends told me their halfback was going with the first fake," said Moorman. "So I went down, faked in and cut outside. Their halfback (Alworth) went in and I was open. It seemed like it took a year for the ball to get to me."

The play was called a 31-rollback. Altman pitched back to right halfback Jack Wilson, who headed in at left tackle. Wilson gave the ball to Altman, who rolled to his right, looking.

"Wright (Dean Wright, the left halfback) should have been wide open," Altman said. "We never had thrown that pass to the right, always had gone left, and I was scared to death when I saw he was covered. Then I saw old Tee all by himself in the right corner."

Alworth admitted, "Moorman was my man and I didn't cover him. I was trying to watch the play and keep him in the corner of my eye, too."

Altman completed eight of nine passes on the drive (13 of 17 in all). Moorman caught six of them. One of his grabs went for a three-yard loss. However, it was the most important catch he made, except for the touchdown.

Alworth was in the clear and had his hands on the ball as he ran past Moorman, who wound up with it in his possession. Alworth appeared headed for a 67-yard touchdown trip for an instant.

"I should have had it," Lance said. "If I had, I think we would have won."

Two minutes, 45 seconds remained when Moorman scored and guard Art Browning converted.

Even then, there was still a chance for Arkansas. But Alworth fumbled on the kickoff runback to his 40 and Duke controlled the ball until the end. At the finish the Blue Devils were on the Arkansas 1.

MONDAY, JANUARY 2, 1961

Duke	0	0	0	7	7
Arkansas	0	0	6	0	6

Duke—Touchdown: Moorman (9, pass from Altman). Point after touchdown: Browning.
Arkansas—Touchdown: Alworth (49, punt return).

STATISTICS

Duke		Arkansas	Duke		Arkansas
Moorman	LE	Butler	10	First downs	12
Bumgarner	LT	Epp	96	Net yards rushing	148
Browning	LG	Garrett	17	Passes attempted	13
Allie	C	Harris	13	Passes completed	5
Berry	RG	Fields	1	Passes had intercepted	2
Bosson	RT	Henderson	93	Net yards passing	71
Spada	RE	Collier	189	Total net yards	219
Altman	QB	McKinney	8	Number of punts	6
Wright	LH	Alworth	37	Punting average	30.1
Wilson	RH	J. Williams	2	Fumbles lost	1
McGee	FB	Cox	15	Yards penalized	40

*Substitutions—*Duke: Widener (l), Chesnutt (l), Unser (r), ends; Gregory (l), Kotchin (r), tackles; Markas (l), Havens (r), guards; Bengel, Williams, centers; Clark, Rappold, quarterbacks; Garda (l), Leggett (r), halfbacks; Tinnell, Burch, fullbacks. Arkansas: Langston (l), Gaston (l), Letsinger (r), Evans (r), ends; Mazzanti (l), Childress (r), tackles; Trail (l), Brabham (r), guards; Gramlich, Lineberger, centers; Moore, quarterback; Horton (l), Worthington (l), D. Williams (r), halfbacks; Alberty, Moody, Cissell, fullbacks.

SUGAR

Charley Thornton, who covered Mississippi's 14 to 6 win over Rice in the 1961 Sugar Bowl game, neatly analyzed it like this in the *Arkansas Gazette*:

"Everybody said that Jake Gibbs would be the difference and he was. Statistically, Gibbs didn't have a great day. He was like Babe Ruth striking out three times, but on his fourth trip putting the ball out of the park with a game-winning homer."

The All-America quarterback of the undefeated Rebels gained only 15 yards running. But two of his carries were good for touchdown yardage on sweeps of eight and three yards. He completed only five of his 15 passes for 43 yards, although several misses were no fault of his. But two hits were good for vital yardage on the scoring drives.

Ole Miss' first touchdown came so easy it caused many in the crowd of 82,851 packing the double-decked steel stadium to wonder if they were to see a mismatch. Actually, the outcome wasn't certain until the final gun.

But Rice had only just kicked off to start the game when the Rebels bounded 65 yards in seven well-selected plays. Big gains were fullback James (Hoss) Anderson's 13-yard up-the-middle slash, wingback Bobby Crespino's 21-yard reverse run, Gibbs' seven-yard pass to halfback George Blair to the 8, and, from there, Jake's roll-out to the left to score after faking a throw.

Center Allen Green kicked the extra point. It was 7 to 0 and only three minutes, 20 seconds had elapsed.

"If we hadn't let them get that first one so easy, it might have been a different story," said Rice Coach Jess Neely. "We started playing football after that."

Indeed, the lightly regarded Owls outplayed Ole Miss from that point until the fourth quarter. However, their only advantage was statistical. They gained the most yardage, 281 to 186. They made the most marches, four to two. Four pass interceptions, two of them stemming touchdown-bound drives, were fatal.

On Rice's fifth penetration of Rebel soil, a touchdown resulted. Previously, the Owls had been at the 31, at the 10 (where Green intercepted a pass by quarterback Randy Kerbow), the 18 (where Johnny Robinson picked off a pass by Butch Blume), and the 13. Following a nine-yard loss from the latter spot, Max Webb missed a field-goal try from the 29.

At last Rice was rewarded. Capping a 76-yard, 18-play offensive, Blume, a stubby runner with incalculable determination, carried a couple of Rebels on his back as he charged into the end zone on a two-yard dash. It was a single wing-type play. He took a pitch-out and skirted right end behind a wall of interference. This was late in the third quarter.

Again, Webb's toework was inaccurate.

"I hurried it," he said. "The boys told me the missed kick didn't beat us, but if I had made it, it would have given us a lift and put more pressure on them."

Johnny Vaught, the Ole Miss coach, said, "Our boys proved themselves champions by the manner in which they came back to score after Rice almost tied it up."

Gibbs said he "almost fouled up that second score. I came out too fast (running right from the three) and slipped. My knee almost hit the ground at the six but when I straightened up and saw all my blockers in front of me I knew I was going in."

That rounded out a 57-yard expedition by the Rebels, who revived perceptibly when their lead became insecure.

In the last 16 seconds, Green attempted to kick a field goal from the 36. It was short. Conceivably, Rice could have blocked it, scored a touchdown, and added a two-point conversion to tie Ole Miss.

While Rice quarterback Billy Cox's 11 pass completions in 20 tosses bettered Gibbs' figures, it was no surprise that the senior from

Ole Miss, heart of his team and greatest athlete in his school's history, was named the outstanding player in the Sugar Bowl game.

To Bob Rule of the *Press* in Houston, home of Rice University, "It was the most soul-satisfying defeat I've ever witnessed."

It was also a treasury-enriching appearance for both schools. Each received record checks of $165,029, much of which was shared with other schools in their conferences.

Officials of the Sugar Bowl announced that they distributed $5,-247,501.20 to competing schools from the gates of their first 27 games. In addition they retired $1,003,631 of the $1,298,431 spent on three Tulane Stadium enlargement and improvement projects. Other contributions were made to the United States Olympic Fund.

Mississippi	7	0	0	7	14
Rice	0	0	6	0	6

Mississippi—Touchdowns: Gibbs 2 (8, left end; 3, right end). Points after touchdown: Green 2.
Rice—Touchdown: Blume (2, right end).

STATISTICS

Mississippi		Rice	Mississippi		Rice
Daniels	LE	Burrell	13	First downs	19
Brown	LT	Karam	143	Net yards rushing	103
Price	LG	Simmons	15	Passes attempted	28
Green	C	B. King	5	Passes completed	14
Bolin	RG	Lively	0	Passes had intercepted	4
Benton	RT	Johnston	43	Net yards passing	178
Brewer	RE	Raesz	186	Total net yards	281
Gibbs	QB	Cox	5	Number of punts	3
Blair	LH	Wayt	40.4	Punting average	34
Crespino	RH	Webb	1	Fumbles lost	0
Anderson	FB	Jackson	10	Yards penalized	30

Substitutions—Mississippi: Smith (l), Ball (l), Dabbs (r), Sullivan (r), ends; J. Robertson (l), Ferrill (l), Dunaway (r), tackles; Alford (l), Lamar (l), Jones (r), Dickson (r), guards; Ross, Maxwell, centers; Elmore, Griffing, quarterbacks; Doty (l), Taylor (l), Robinson (r), Guy (r), Halbert (r), Holloway (r), halfbacks; Adams, R. Robertson, fullbacks. Rice: Stellman (l), Brast (l), ends; Cornett (l), Alborn (r), tackles; R. King (l), Anthony (l), Ligon (r), guards; Stroud, center; Hartman, Kerbow, quarterbacks; Candler (l), Blume (l), Poage (r), halfbacks; Caddell, Smith, fullbacks.

ORANGE

When Greg Mather took off on a 98-yard run with an intercepted lateral pass to give Navy a 6 to 0 lead in the first quarter, a little boy in the stadium began to cry softly. He was Danny Devine, Jr., six-year-old son of the Missouri coach.

Within a few moments, however, his emotions changed. So did those of all the 72,212 spectators at the 1961 Orange Bowl game, including John F. Kennedy, then President-elect of the United States.

Pounding down the field and across the Navy goal line, after intercepting a pass, was Missouri halfback Norm Beal. His father, Arthur Beal of Normandy, Mo., was in the crowd to see the 90-yard run. Was it a thrill? "If you had a son who had done it, you'd know how I felt," said Mr. Beal.

It was a fantastic pace that could not last, of course. But when Beal scored and Bill Tobin kicked the extra point, Missouri led and the trend of the game was set. The Tigers' superiority was established and maintained to the finish.

Missouri, beaten twice previously in the Orange Bowl and without a victory in six earlier bowl games, ended that losing streak in convincing fashion despite the score, which was 21 to 14.

"I enjoyed the game very much," Mr. Kennedy said. "Both teams were good."

But Missouri's line and its ends in particular were better. And its blocking was top-hole, where Navy's was virtually non-existent.

Missouri, with an overpowering T attack predicated on massed single-wing blocking, had steam-rolled 80 and 64 yards for touchdowns in the second and fourth quarters, respectively, to forge a 21 to 6 advantage.

It was a game dominated by a mauling Tiger forewall on defense. Its dedicated blocking tore down Navy resistance and opened the gates for Mel West (108 yards in 21 carries), Donnie Smith, Ed Mehrer, and Norris Stevenson. On their sweeps, cutbacks, and slants, Missouri backs gobbled up 296 yards.

Navy was held to minus eight yards rushing. All-America halfback Joe Bellino, gainer of 834 yards in the season, was all but handcuffed. Lacking blocking and finding no holes, he wound up with four yards net in eight rather discouraging tries.

Yet suddenly, on another pulse-quickening play, the Midshipmen roused Mr. Kennedy and everybody else. With an almost unbelievable burst of speed, after faking two defenders out of his path, Bellino caught a 27-yard touchdown pass from quarterback Hal Spooner. It was a super effort. Bellino grabbed it with a leap while looking straight up and over his right shoulder.

"It was the greatest catch I've ever seen," said Coach Dan Devine.

Mr. Kennedy jumped to his feet and slammed a friend on the back. "That Bellino is good!" he shouted. "A beautiful pass! Beautiful!"

1961—Navy's Joe Bellino makes a sensational end-zone catch for a touch-down against Missouri.

Almost ten minutes were left but charging Tiger linemen, prominent among whom were ends Danny LaRose and Tom Carpenter and tackle Ed Blaine, rushed Spooner so hard he had no chance to engineer an eleventh hour offensive in the air.

Spooner completed 13 of his 21 passes for 176 yards. But he suffered four interceptions. Missouri's charging linemen pressured the Middie quarterback, hurried him, and several times mowed him down behind the line. The interceptions cost Navy 114 yards.

"Missouri was just too strong up front," said Navy's 32-year-old coach, Wayne Hardin. "Their linemen kept breaking through and stopped us dead."

"I was sure we could halt Bellino," Devine said. "In fact, I was never surer of anything in my life. He's a great player but we were a great team."

Missouri's only defeat on the way to the Orange Bowl was by Kansas, 23 to 7. But Kansas, after winning the Big Eight championship, was required by conference faculty representatives at a December meeting to forfeit the title to Missouri, as well as late season victories over both the Tigers and Colorado, for violating league recruiting rules. Earlier in the fall of 1960, Kansas was placed on probation by the National Collegiate Athletic Association on charges of breaking recruiting regulations. Oklahoma, winner of the championship for 12 straight years up to 1960 and sharer of honors for two years before 1948, was also under N.C.A.A. probation in 1960 and ineligible for a bowl.

The Big Eight had agreed at its spring meeting to let Missouri return to the Orange Bowl for a second successive appearance if it finished first or second and if invited in the event of a runnerup berth in its conference.

The Orange Bowl's contract with the Big Eight expired with the playing of this game. It was renewed in the spring of 1961.

| Missouri | 7 | 7 | 0 | 7 | 21 |
| Navy | 6 | 0 | 0 | 8 | 14 |

Missouri—Touchdowns: Beal (90, intercepted pass by Spooner), Smith (4, right guard), Taylor (1, sneak). Points after touchdown: Tobin 3.

Navy—Touchdowns: Mather (98, intercepted lateral pass by D. Smith), Bellino (27, pass from Spooner). Points after touchdown: Luper (pass from Spooner).

STATISTICS

Missouri		Navy	Missouri		Navy
Carpenter	LE	Dattilo	19	First downs	9
Blaine	LT	Driscoll	296	Net yards rushing	—8
Henley	LG	Hoy	6	Passes attempted	23
Langan	C	Visted	1	Passes completed	13
Garvis	RG	Hewitt	0	Passes had intercepted	4
Calhoun	RT	Erchul	5	Net yards passing	176
LaRose	RE	Luper	301	Total net yards	168
Taylor	QB	Spooner	4	Number of punts	7
West	LH	Bellino	30.5	Punting average	35.4
D. Smith	RH	Prichard	3	Fumbles lost	0
Mehrer	FB	Matalavage	15	Yards penalized	4

Substitutions—Missouri: G. Smith (l), Hitchler (r), ends; Wallach (l), Moyer (r), tackles; T. Smith (l), Hertz (r), guards; McCartney, center; Snyder, quar-

terback; Beal (l), Brossart (r), Stevenson (r), halfbacks; Russell, Tobin, fullbacks. Navy: Kellner (l), McQuade (l), Mather (r), ends; Graham (l), Testa
(l), Fitzgerald (r), Huffman (r), tackles; Falconer (l), Von Sydow (r), guards;
Lucci, Pierce, centers; Dietz, quarterback; Hardison (l), Kisiel (l), Zenyuh (r),
Meyer (r), halfbacks; McKeown, fullback.

ROSE

The University of Washington card section was tricked by ingenious California Institute of Technology pranksters into spelling out
"CALTECH" during halftime of the 1961 Rose Bowl game. Washington students, all unsuspecting, also spelled their football team's
nickname, Huskies, backward and came up with a picture of the Caltech beaver instead of their own canine mascot.

But the Washington football team fell into no such preconceived
trap.

Because Minnesota was voted national champion and because, as
the *New York Herald Tribune's* Red Smith expressed it, "Rose Bowl
ground rules forbid West Coast teams to abuse the Big Ten representative except Wisconsin," the Gophers were favored by a touchdown.

They were toppled 17 to 7, in the first of three games under a new
contract signed by the Athletic Association of Western Universities
(Big Five) with the Tournament of Roses that had an open-end clause
providing for the extension of the pact.

In the spring of 1960 the Big Ten decided against continuing Rose
Bowl competition on a conference contract basis but still permitted
an individual member school to accept an invitation to play the Big
Five champion.

Executive director Tom Hamilton of the Big Five said, "Our
policy will be to invite the No. 1 team in the nation to play us in the
Rose Bowl. Minnesota is not here as a representative of the Big Ten
but as the national champion."

Minnesota's invitation was accepted, somewhat grudgingly, by its
faculty senate, which had consistently opposed bowl games and voted
against renegotiation of the contract.

"I think, after taking part in the Rose Bowl game, the Minnesota
people will find it to be a wholesome event," said Tug Wilson, who
retired as Big Ten commissioner in 1961 and was succeeded by William R. Reed.

Sure enough, five months after the trip, the faculty representatives
who govern athletics at Minnesota voted, 70 to 42, for renewal of
the Big Ten's Rose Bowl contract. This about-face broke the deadlock and gave pro Rose Bowl schools in the Big Ten a six to four

majority. It appeared to clear the way for the writing of a new permanent pact with the Big Five. However, executive director Hamilton said later the Big Five did not plan to initiate action leading toward a new contract.

Minnesota's Murray Warmath was elected national Coach of the Year. The year before, when the Gophers won two games and were tenth-place finishers in their conference, Warmath had been hung in effigy on the campus. The year before that, after a season with only one victory, the Minnesota lettermen's "M" club openly campaigned for his ouster. Attempts were made to buy his contract.

"The whole difference between 1960 and 1959 was that we were a senior-junior team and didn't make the mistakes that killed us," Warmath, a native of Tennessee, explained. "We scored every time we got the ball inside the opposition's 20. Last year we had no such punch."

In the Rose Bowl the success story ended sadly for Minnesota. The Big Ten co-champion (with Iowa) lost the game in the first half.

"They kept us on the defensive throughout the first half and we didn't recover until it was too late," Warmath said.

Said assistant coach Bob Bossons, "We got hit too fast, too quick and too early. We let them get too good a start."

"Our early troubles were caused by our failure to field two punts that rolled dead near the goal line and our inability to contain a couple of Washington's wide pitchouts and passes," added Warmath.

Washington, showing the same speed and striking power that overwhelmed Wisconsin in the 1960 game, and the same players, too, was in front 17 to 0 when the Gophers first trudged to their dressing room. In the first half Minnesota made only two first downs, only 61 yards net, and didn't cross midfield on its own power.

The Gophers' pride and courage enabled them to dominate and "win" the second half and come out on top statistically before 97,314 fans.

"We took our tip from the movies of the Minnesota-Nebraska game and first moved inside to bring their defense together," said Washington quarterback Bob Schloredt. "Then we moved outside. That allowed us to make those sweeping end runs."

The diversified attack engineered by Schloredt "bewitched, bothered and bewildered" the Gophers, reported Yale Coach Jordan Olivar, writing in the *Los Angeles Times*.

"In rapid succession, the resourceful Washington offense employed the double slot formation, wing T, double wing, lonesome end, man in motion, and balanced and unbalanced lines. Seldom did the Gopher defenders guess right during that devastating first half."

Washington led off early with a 44-yard field goal, longest in bowl history, by halfback George Fleming. A double touchdown parade in the second quarter on successive 62- and 68-yard marches made catching up by Minnesota all but impossible against the tiring but relentless team from the Northwest.

Schloredt, playing his first game since he sustained a broken collar bone against UCLA in mid-October, was named the outstanding performer in the Rose Bowl for the second straight year. He guided both scoring drives, flipping a fourth-down pass to Brent Wooten for the first touchdown from the 4 and notching the second himself from the 1 after a 31-yard run on a routine keeper play. Schloredt was brilliant passing, running, and punting.

The Huskies' outweighed line—due largely to the presence of Minnesota's All-America guard Tom Brown, 243, and tackle Frank Brixius, 250—had gouged the Gophers' forewall and paved the way for Schloredt, fullback Ray Jackson, and halfbacks Charlie Mitchell, Don McKeta, and Fleming in the first half.

Now Minnesota counterattacked fiercely. Washington halted an early third-quarter advance on its 35. But Husky quarterback Bob Hivner fumbled and Gopher end Bob Deegan recovered on the 32.

Quarterback Sandy Stephens on a roll-out to the right went nine yards. Dave Mulholland picked up five. Next, Stephens headed left on another roll-out and as a defender closed in Sandy tossed the ball to halfback Bill Munsey, who scored.

Washington was held to a single first down, against 12 for Minnesota, and surrendered 192 yards in the second half. However, center Roy McKasson, guard Chuck Allen, tackles Kurt Gegner and Barry Bullard, end Stan Chapple, and other teammates in the primary defense fought off the heftier Gophers except for a lone lapse. A sign over the counter of the Washington locker room in Seattle reads: "We issue everything here but guts." It was never more convincingly put into practical application than in the Rose Bowl.

Actually, Minnesota's chances of winning didn't become hopeless until the final minutes. With just less than half of the period to play, the Gophers reached the Washington 6 by driving 70 yards with Stephens, Roger Hagberg, Judge Dickson, and Munsey in attacking roles.

On third down, McKeta, lining up at left end, broke through and spilled Stephens for a 13-yard loss. Minnesota went into field-goal formation. It was a fake, though, for which the Huskies were prepared. McKeta intercepted Stephens' pass on the 1 to end the Gophers' hopes once and for all.

Owens seemed to think his team should be ranked first in the nation after defeating Minnesota.

"We beat the best and that's all that counts," he said.

Washington	3	14	0	0	17
Minnesota	0	0	7	0	7

Washington—Touchdowns: Wooten (4, pass from Schloredt of 1, run of 3), Schloredt (1, left tackle sneak). Points after touchdown: Fleming 2. Field goal: Fleming (44, placekick).

Minnesota—Touchdown: Munsey (18, left end). Point after touchdown: Rogers.

STATISTICS

Washington		Minnesota	Washington		Minnesota
Claridge	LE	R. Larson	11	First downs	14
Gegner	LT	Bell	177	Net yards rushing	202
Allen	LG	Mulvena	5	Passes attempted	18
McKasson	C	G. Larson (c)	2	Passes completed	5
Kinnune	RG	Brown	0	Passes had intercepted	3
Enslow	RT	Brixius	16	Net yards passing	51
Chapple	RE	Deegan	193	Total net yards	253
Hivner	QB	Stephens	8	Number of punts	6
Fleming	LH	Dickson	41.3	Punting average	43.3
McKeta	RH	Munsey	2	Fumbles lost	0
Jackson	FB	Hagberg	50	Yards penalized	35

Substitutions—Washington: Folkins (l), Meyers (r), Davidson (r), ends; Mansfield (l), B. Bullard (l), tackles; Hurworth (l), Skaggs (r), Scheyer (r), T. Bullard (r), Locknane (r), guards; Nelson, center; Schloredt, Jorgensen, quarterbacks; Mitchell (l), Wooten (r), halfbacks. Minnesota: Prawdzik (l), Hall (r), ends; Frisbee (l), Miller (r), Wheeler (r), tackles; Hook (l), Tellor (l), Odegard (r), Perkovich (r), guards; Annis, center; Johnson, Salem, quarterbacks; Mulholland (l), Kauth (r), King (r), halfbacks; Enga, Rogers, fullbacks.

LIBERTY

"Bad Day For Ducks" read the headline.

"Liberty Bowl Snarled By Snow" said another.

And this: "Bowl In Frigid Climate Strains Fans' Credulity."

Penn State's Nittany Lions ("Arctic Champs") overpowered Oregon's Ducks, 41 to 12, in refrigerated Philadelphia Stadium ("Winter Wonderland").

Six days before the Liberty Bowl game, one of the heaviest snowfalls of the 20th century covered eastern Pennsylvania. The 14-inch blanket ruined advance ticket sales. Presenting a reasonably exciting lure, president Bud Dudley of the Liberty Bowl Association hoped for 40,000 or 50,000 customers. But that was before the snowstorm.

Tons of snow were shoveled off the field tarpaulin during the week of the game. Drifts covered the less attractive seats. A courageous group of 16,624 customers sat stiffly in cleared rows nearest the 50-yard line.

Although spectators shivered in biting 30-degree cold, semitropical temperature warmed the players' benches. A string of infrared lamps overhead produced sideline temperature twice that of what it was on the field.

"Sure, we took a cold bath on this one," said George Kerrigan, vice president of the Association. "You might say we were subdued by the weather. But we'll be back next year and don't you forget it."

After watching Penn State's impressive victory, many Eastern writers wondered if this were not the best team in their section. Coach Rip Engle said, "I believe we could take on any team in the country."

This was the second time within a period of a few months that a scrappy individual named Hoak had a major role in a signal triumph by a Pennsylvania team.

It was Don Hoak, fiery third baseman of the 1960 world champion Pittsburgh Pirates in baseball. In football, it was Dick Hoak, Penn State quarterback.

As quarterback of the "Reddies," the Lions' alternate or second eleven (but never called that), Hoak led Penn State in total offense. Twelve of Penn State's last 17 touchdowns in the season were scored by the "Reddies." Dick declined an invitation to direct the first team in favor of sticking it out with the "Reddies."

Against outclassed Oregon, Hoak was superb. He conducted the split T, wing T attack during the making of five of the six touchdowns. He ran for a pair himself on roll-outs of six and 11 yards. He threw a 28-yard pass that Dick Pae caught and carried five yards for a touchdown. Hoak fired only five times, hitting three receivers for gains of 67 yards.

Speedy Oregon traveled 88 yards to score the second time it had possession of the ball, using a double flanker with slots. Swift halfback Dave Grayson started it with a 27-yard scamper. Quarterback Dave Grosz finished it by moving 14 yards to the 1 on the option, then finding an opening at right tackle to score.

Physically superior Penn State, employing two units of virtually equal ability, wore down the Webfoots in the second quarter with three touchdowns. Oregon reduced the spread of points in the third quarter, cutting the score to 21 to 12 when Grayson sped ten yards for a touchdown on a cutback. But the Lions pushed over three quick touchdowns in the fourth period, all within a four-minute segment. Hoak set up two by intercepting passes.

Oregon Coach Len Casanova was greatly distressed by his team's mistakes. "We made more in this game than we did the rest of the season," he said. "We let them get off the hook when we were in the running."

Interviewing Engle, a teeth-chattering reporter asked, "Wwwould you lllikke mayybe the Rrose or Ooorangge Bowlll next year?"

"Maybe they'll have an Equator Bowl," Engle replied. "That would suit me."

SATURDAY, DECEMBER 17, 1960

Penn State	0	21	0	20	41
Oregon	6	0	6	0	12

Penn State—Touchdowns: Hoak 2 (6, left tackle; 11, left end), Jonas (1, right guard), Gursky (2, right tackle), Caye (1, center plunge), Pae (33, pass from Hoak of 28, run of 5). Points after touchdown: Oppermann 4, Jonas.
Oregon—Touchdowns: Grosz (1, right tackle), Grayson (10, right tackle).

STATISTICS

Penn State		Oregon	Penn State		Oregon
Oppermann	LE	Bauge	25	First downs	17
Barber	LT	Snidow	301	Net yards rushing	187
Blasenstein	LG	Rose	14	Passes attempted	16
Huffman	C	Clesceri	8	Passes completed	10
Popp	RG	Urell	0	Passes had intercepted	2
Smith	RT	Barnett	119	Net yards passing	173
Mitinger	RE	Burnett	420	Total net yards	360
Hall	QB	Grosz	4	Number of punts	4
Jonas	LH	Grayson	25	Punting average	34
Kerr	RH	Jones	1	Fumbles lost	2
Sobczak	FB	Snyder	40	Yards penalized	12

Substitutions—Penn State: Robinson (l), Davis (l), Truitt (r), Schwab (r), ends; Sieminski (l), Tietjens (l), Farkas (r), Gilmour (r), tackles; Berfield (l), Wilson (l), Butterfield (l), Hart (r), Waresak (r), Maiello (r), guards; Saul, Galardi, Raisig, centers; Hoak, Lang, quarterbacks; Gursky (l), Caye (l), Pae (r), Kline (r), Wayne (r), halfbacks; Hayes, Torris, Schaeffer, fullbacks. Oregon: Tarr (l), Peterson (r), Willener (r), Herron (r), ends; Mattson (l), Prozinski (l), Anderson (r), Stensland (r), tackles; Weigel (l), Thomas (l), Ording (r), Delbiaggio (r), guards; Swain, Dixon, centers; Arbuckle, Fraser, quarterbacks; Brown (l), McKinney (l), Bruce (r), Gaechter (r), halfbacks; Cargill, Josephson, Owens, fullbacks.

BLUEBONNET

A unique field-goal standoff, something new in big league bowl action, left 68,000 fans neither happy nor hurt as Texas and Alabama fought to a 3 to 3 tie in the 1960 Bluebonnet Bowl defensive struggle.

It was a strange contest from this standpoint, too: if the Longhorns of Texas had won, they would have done so on a play that began after time had officially expired.

End Tommy Brooker kicked a 30-yard field goal to put Alabama in the lead in the third quarter when a drive stalled on the Texas 13.

Dan Petty, a third-team tackle, booted the equalizer. He kicked it from the 10. The play started on Alabama's 3. There were three minutes, 44 seconds remaining.

With 28 seconds to go, Texas took possession of the ball on its 48. An Alabama pass, thrown on fourth down, was complete. But it failed to make the required yardage. No doubt existed about what Texas would do.

The Crimson Tide secondary defense broke up Johnny Genung's first long fling. Alabama's Leon Fuller and Texas end Bob Moses both jumped for Genung's second lengthy throw. The big clock's second hand stopped at zero. Part of the crowd flocked onto the field thinking the game had ended. But a handkerchief had been dropped. Interference was called against Fuller. Since a game cannot end on a penalty, Texas was awarded another play.

The ball was placed on Alabama's 18. It would be a field-goal try, of course. Thumped from the 25 by Petty, who in the third quarter had missed from the same spot, it was wide to the left.

Another penalty break had helped to sustain the 71-yard offensive that culminated in Petty's successful kick. Fullback Ray Poage's hard running brought the Longhorns storming into Tide territory. After they reached the 34, a personal foul penalty called against fullback Mike Fracchia for grabbing a Texan's face mask, moved them 15 yards closer. However, they needed six yards on fourth down from the 15.

What to do? Quarterback Mike Cotten knelt. Alabama wasn't deceived. Cotten wasn't Petty's regular ball holder. It had to be a fake field-goal attempt. Cotten rose and passed to halfback Jack Collins who ran to the 7.

"We knew about that play," said Alabama Coach Paul Bryant. "We had two men sitting out there waiting for it. That Collins did a terrific job of getting the yardage."

This was the third penetration of Tideland in the second half by a Texas team that didn't threaten to score once in the first 30 minutes.

Alabama did, though. Late in the first quarter Bobby Skelton tossed a look-in pass to end Bill Rice, who took it on the Texas 40 and ran to the 7 before David Russell overhauled him. It was a 49-yard gain.

On third down from the 3, Skelton cut in at left tackle. Millions watching on television thought he had carried the ball across the goal line before being halted. So did many at the game.

"I was in there," Skelton said. "I had chalk all over my jersey when I got up."

A moment later, fullback Billy Richardson was stopped within an inch or two of scoring.

"Naturally, we all were hoping that last kick by Petty would go through," said Texas Coach Darrell Royal. "But it would have been a shame to win it that way. I think the score was indicative of the comparative strength of the two teams."

At the awards dinner, taskmaster Bryant looked at his players, grinned, and said, sincerely, "I want to thank you tonight for putting up with me all this season. I know I've been rough at times, but I hope you won't hold it against me."

SATURDAY, DECEMBER 17, 1960

Alabama	0	0	3	0	3
Texas	0	0	0	3	3

Alabama—Field goal: Brooker (30, placekick).
Texas—Field goal: Petty (20, placekick).

STATISTICS

Alabama		*Texas*	*Alabama*		*Texas*
Battle	LE	Moses	4	First downs	11
Pell	LT	Moffett	65	Net yards rushing	124
Rutledge	LG	Lee	14	Passes attempted	17
Jordan	C	Laughlin	8	Passes completed	7
Neighbors	RG	Kubin	0	Passes had intercepted	1
Boylston	RT	Jones	155	Net yards passing	108
Ronsonet	RE	Cooper	220	Total net yards	232
Skelton	QB	Cotten	7	Number of punts	3
Fuller	LH	Russell	40.4	Punting average	39.8
B. Wilson	RH	Saxton	1	Fumbles lost	0
Fracchia	FB	Poage	49	Yards penalized	20

Substitutions—Alabama: Rice (l), Spruiell (l), Brooker (r), O'Dell (r), Box (r), ends; Moore (l), Moore (r), Sisia (r), tackles; Sharpe (l), Holsomback (r), J. Wilson (r), guards; O'Linger, Moseley, centers; Trammell, Stapp, quarterbacks; Piper (l), Abruzzese (l), White (r), halfbacks; Richardson, Stapp, Clark, Holt, Wesley, fullbacks. Texas: Lucas (l), York (l), Fults (r), ends; Talbert (l), Petty (l),

Padgett (r), Mann (r), tackles; Treadwell (l), Seals (l), Anderson (r), guards; Kristynik, center; Genung, quarterback; Collins (l), Cook (l), Nunis (l), Gurwitz (r), Morris (r), halfbacks; Culpepper, fullback.

– 1962 –

ROSE

It was, as executive sports editor Bill Boni of the *St. Paul Dispatch and Pioneer Press* wrote in the 48th Tournament of Roses football program: "A Minnesota team about which most people said before the season started that it wasn't going anywhere. Not even in its own Big Ten."

But, Boni hurried to add, "Minnesota football players didn't buy that story."

The Gophers upset the advance dope. They won seven games. They earned ranking as the sixth best team in the land. Then they returned to the Rose Bowl in 1962 an unprecedented—for a Big Ten school—second straight year with a special job to do. They did it overpoweringly, jarring UCLA's Big Five champions, 21 to 3.

Minnesota, whipped by Washington 17 to 7 the year before, never would have had the chance to atone except for an unusual turn of events.

Ohio State Coach Woody Hayes and his Big Ten champions wanted to play in Pasadena. They were prevented by the university's policy-setting faculty council that voted to reject a tentative Rose Bowl invitation. The decision was vigorously protested but to no avail by thousands of demonstrating students. No less than three effigies of John Fullen, secretary of the alumni association and a long-time outspoken opponent of bowl games, were hung.

A few days afterward Minnesota's faculty senate did just the opposite. It voted to accept a bid for its Big Ten runnerup team if tendered by the Big Five. Twenty-four hours later the invitation was received.

It was the second successive year Minnesota was picked from the nation at large. There was a touch of irony in this. The Big Ten had refused to allow a team to go to the Rose Bowl on consecutive New Year's Days during the length of its contract with the old Pacific Coast Conference between 1947–60, inclusive.

At its winter meeting in December of 1961 the Big Ten initiated action leading to another Rose Bowl agreement. Previous overtures had been made by the West Coast. Minnesota's two straight appearances were permitted under a Big Ten loophole giving a member school the right to accept a Rose Bowl invitation.

As one of the terms in the new pact, the Big Ten again insisted that none of its teams could play in the Rose Bowl two years in a row. The Big Five champion was the annual host. The renewed contract was to run indefinitely with a two-year notice required by either party for cancellation.

On his return to California soil, Minnesota Coach Murray Warmath told the reception committee, "We are happy to be back and we hope the scoreboard will be a little different from a year ago."

It was a lot different.

This was a tense and eager team. It was bent on redemption. It did not underestimate its foe. It was actually stronger than Minnesota's national champions of 1960. It had more mobility, a quicker line starring All-America Bobby Bell and a swifter, more versatile backfield.

Minnesota's winged T attack hinged on All-America quarterback Sandy Stephens, an astute play caller. Shadows were beginning to purple the San Gabriel slopes overlooking the fully peopled bowl when Stephens was elected the Rose Bowl game's most valuable player. He shredded UCLA's defenses with a skillful blend of powerful, speedy, and shifty running, accurate passing, and play selection that unbalanced his adversary.

Stephens scored the first and last Minnesota touchdowns in the romp. UCLA's classy all-around tailback Bobby Smith kicked a 28-yard field goal in the early minutes. Quickly surmounting that handicap, the Gophers, spearheaded by Stephens, bludgeoned the Bruins as they outrushed them, 222 yards to 55. Sandy threw only 11 passes. Seven were completed, including six in succession.

Although Minnesota was not long in establishing superiority, its first touchdown was a virtual gift.

UCLA fullback Almose Thompson fumbled on his 6. Stephens capitalized almost immediately, punching over from the 1.

In the second quarter halfback Bill Munsey wound up a 75-yard advance, taking 16 plays, with a three-yard scoring cutback. The Bruins were unable to contain critical third-down plays and the outcome was not really in much doubt.

Stephens cracked left tackle on a two-yard touchdown slant as a 19-play, 83-yard drive on the ground came to a successful climax against the drooping coast boys in the fourth period.

While the Gopher offense got kudos, its defense was not overlooked in the reviews. The ends in particular, and John Campbell especially, smothered UCLA's passing game and with their smashing tactics took the power sweep from the Bruins, too.

UCLA went into battle with some scores to settle, having never won in previous bowl engagements. But it was soon evident to the 98,214 fans and the television audience of possibly 86,000,000 that this would have to be postponed to another time.

Gross receipts came to $1,018,000. Of this $500,000 was paid by the National Broadcasting System for television rights. The Tournament of Roses Association received one-third of the first $100,000, twenty-five per cent of the next $50,000 and 15 per cent of the remaining receipts under the contract. The Big Ten and Big Five divided the remainder. After expenses the Big Ten split its share into twelve parts with the participating team getting two shares (about $60,000) and the Big Ten office one share. Officials received $250 plus expenses.

"Bill, I'm sorry it had to be you," said Warmath to UCLA Coach Bill Barnes, who, like himself, had been schooled under General Bob Neyland at Tennessee.

"For Murray Warmath a long wait was over and a galling memory was gone," wrote Bert McGrane in the *Des Moines Register*.

MONDAY, JANUARY 1, 1962

Minnesota	7	7	0	7	21
UCLA	3	0	0	0	3

Minnesota—Touchdowns: Stephens 2 (1, left guard; 2, left tackle), Munsey (3, left guard). Points after touchdown: Loechler 3.
UCLA—Field goal: B. Smith (28, placekick).

STATISTICS

Minnesota		UCLA	Minnesota		UCLA
Hall	LE	Vena	21	First downs	8
Eller	LT	Andersen	222	Net yards rushing	55
Hook	LG	Macari	11	Passes attempted	8
Frisbee	C	Hull	7	Passes completed	5
Tellor	RG	Paton	0	Passes had intercepted	0
Bell	RT	Shirk	75	Net yards passing	52
Deegan	RE	Gutman	297	Total net yards	107
Stephens	QB	Stevens	3	Number of punts	5
Mulholland	LH	B. Smith	40	Punting average	37
Munsey	RH	Alexander	2	Fumbles lost	2
Dickson	FB	Thompson	70	Yards penalized	5

Substitutions—Minnesota: Park (l), Prawdzik (l), Rognlie (l), Campbell (r), Rude (r), Lothner (r), ends; Wheeler (l), Tyskiewicz (l), Maus (l), Loechler (r), Sunde (r), Schwantz (r), tackles; Mulvena (l), McNeil (l), Hartse (l), Perkovich (r), Mudd (r), guards; Enga, center; Teigen, Pelletier, Blaska, quarterbacks; King (l), Fischer (l), Cashman (l), Cairns (r), Smith (r), halfbacks; Jones, Benson, fullbacks. UCLA: Profit (l), Geverink (l), Hicks (r), Gibbs (r), ends; Fiorentino (l), S. Bauwens (l), Jones (l), Oram (r), Weeden (r), tackles; J. Bauwens (l), Allen (l), Stout (r), Dathe (r), guards; Von Sonn, Truesdell, centers; Walker, LoCurto, quarterbacks; Singleton (l), Haffner (l), Jensen (l), R. Smith (r), DiPoalo (r), Rosenkrans (r), halfbacks; Dimkich, Zeno, Rojas, fullbacks.

GATOR

Even Bobby Dodd, whose play-hard, practice-lightly bowl plan as contrasted to the hard-play, energetic-scrimmage policy of his bowl opponents was hugely successful in the forties and fifties, admitted Georgia Tech's preparations to meet Penn State were "slightly ridiculous."

Prior to mustering at the Gator Bowl site 48 hours before the game, the Yellow Jackets had worked out, as a team, only five hours on five days since their last regular season contest 26 days previously. Then they had been excused for Christmas vacation.

A strong, big, poised, stable, and versatile Penn State outfit laughed at a 9 to 0 Tech lead, fought back, and beat the bowl-frequenters from Atlanta, 30 to 15.

The Jackets didn't give out. But at least one writer suggested that possibly Bobby overdid his do-it-yourself training theme this time.

The decisive play followed an extraordinary effort by Penn State end Dave Robinson, first Negro to play in the Gator Bowl. In the third quarter, with the Nittany Lions in front 14 to 9, Robinson crashed into the Tech backfield, leaped over a blocker, grabbed quarterback Stan Gann, and forced him to fumble. Robinson seized the ball himself on the Jackets' 35.

Galen Hall had already thrown two touchdowns passes of 13 and 32 yards to Al Gursky and Roger Kochman, respectively, in the first half. Now, on the very next play, he launched another. It was caught by halfback Hal Powell on the 14. There was no Tech man within a whoop and a holler. Powell jumped in his joy and literally gambolled into the end zone.

"If the touchdown didn't kill Tech's hopes, Powell's infectious spirit probably did," wrote Tommy Devine in the *Miami News*.

On the important play Penn State huddled quickly and took advantage of the Jackets' slowness in coming out of their defensive assembly. Hall, who completed eight passes in succession in the second and third periods, made an adroit fake as Powell pretended to be

After several enlargements, the Gator Bowl in Jacksonville now will accommodate 50,000 fans.

engaged in a blocking assignment but suddenly darted away and got far behind the Tech secondary defense.

The final quarter was young when elusive, give-and-go Jacket halfback Joe Auer restored his team to contention. He recovered a wild pitch-out by quarterback Billy Lothridge far behind the scrimmage line and ran 25 yards in the opposite direction of his blockers for a touchdown (14 yards, officially).

That made it 20 to 15.

Early in the game, after Tech had picked up two points on a safety when Hall was charged with intentionally grounding a pass thrown from behind his goal line, Auer sprinted 68 yards to score.

Gambling desperately after Auer's second touchdown, Dodd ordered a fourth-down screen pass with six yards to go from Tech's own 12. Lothridge threw it and it failed. Penn State profited by three points. Don Jonas kicked a field goal from the 23.

A late-game pass interception by Jim Schwab of a flip by Gann gave the Nittany Lions a chance to run up the score. When fullback Buddy Torris bent back the Tech line from a yard away, the Jackets had surrendered more points than in any game since 1950.

Winning Coach Rip Engle prized this message, received from Oklahoma Coach Bud Wilkinson: "Penn State's offense in the game —and I watched every minute—was the greatest I've ever seen."

SATURDAY, DECEMBER 30, 1961

Penn State	0	14	6	10	30
Georgia Tech	2	7	0	6	15

Penn State—Touchdowns: Gursky (13, pass from Hall), Kochman (32, pass from Hall), Powell (35, pass from Hall of 21, run of 14), Torris (1, right guard). Points after touchdown: Jonas 3. Field goal: Jonas (23, placekick).

Georgia Tech—Touchdowns: Auer 2 (68, right guard; 14, left end). Point after touchdown: Lothridge. Safety: Hall (passing from Penn State 9, intentionally grounded pass).

STATISTICS

Penn State		Georgia Tech	Penn State		Georgia Tech
Schwab	LE	Davis	13	First downs	19
Sieminski	LT	Griffin	137	Net yards rushing	212
Blasenstein	LG	Ericksen	22	Passes attempted	24
Huffman	C	McGaughey	12	Passes completed	12
Wilson	RG	Watson	0	Passes had intercepted	2
Smith	RT	Stallings	175	Net yards passing	201
Mitinger	RE	Solomon	312	Total net yards	413
Hall	QB	Gann	8	Number of punts	5
Kochman	LH	Auer	41	Punting average	27.6
Jonas	RH	Williamson	1	Fumbles lost	3
Sabol	FB	McNames	63	Yards penalized	14

Substitutions—Penn State: Robinson (l), Davis (l), Anderson (r), Baker (r), ends; Tietjens (l), Farkas (r), Monaghan (r), tackles; Galardi (l), Ricevuto (l), Rosdahl (r), Schleiden (r), Raisig (r), guards; Saul, Williams, Bendik, centers; Liske, Caum, quarterbacks; Gursky (l), Kline (l), Sincek (l), Powell (r), Wydman (r), Popp (r), Weber (r), halfbacks; Torris, Hayes, fullbacks. Georgia Tech: Sexton (l), Chapman (l), Martin (r), ends; Swanson (l), Nicholl (r), tackles; Matlock (l), Biddle (l), Guthrie (r), guards; Caldwell, Chancey, centers; Lothridge, Toner, quarterbacks; Winingder (l), Sircy (r), halfbacks; Mendheim, Nail, fullbacks.

COTTON

Darrell Royal of Texas said, "It might be the biggest thing that ever happened to me, winning from a team like Ole Miss."

His Longhorns pulled it off in the 1962 Cotton Bowl game, 12 to 7. They did it with something new, something stolen, and something basic.

Unfamiliar to the Mississippians was an option pitch-out to the fullback, Ray Poage, in motion toward a widely split end. It helped cover the 34 yards Texas had to travel for its first touchdown in the first quarter after halfback Tommy Ford's diving interception of a pass thrown by quarterback Glynn Griffing. The Rebels were caught off guard by the fullback in motion stuff.

Just before the end of the first half, with Texas on top 12 to 0, Mississippi arrived at the Longhorns' 7.

Passing on first down, Griffing spotted an open receiver in the end zone. But guard Johnny Treadwell, leaping high, tipped the ball. The effort enabled halfback Jerry Cook to intercept it, one of the most crucial plays of the duel that provided the crowd of 75,504 with oodles of thrills.

Cook seized two more passes. Linebacker Pat Culpepper grabbed another.

Ole Miss, the nation's total offense leader (418.7 yards per game average), relied utterly on the aerial weapon, once behind, but wasn't able to use that route to conquer a team that rushed eight determined men on the passer.

Ends Bob Moses and Tommy Lucas, along with Culpepper, seemed to be looking down the throats of Griffing and Doug Elmore, who threw for the Rebels, most of the afternoon.

Hurried tosses resulted in fatal interceptions—five of them in 37 attempts. That was only three more than Ole Miss suffered in 202 passes during the entire regular season. In a sense, Ole Miss died by its own hand.

As for the basic ingredients, the Longhorns simply blocked more destructively when it counted most and tackled more vehemently when it meant most.

They put forth what wingback Jack Collins called "the best team effort since I've been at Texas." Collins' pretty run after catching a roll-out pass cast by quarterback Mike Cotten gave Texas a 12 to 0 lead in the second quarter. The play spanned 24 yards.

Texas spent most of the second half fighting off one aerial attack after another. Only one was successful. The Rebs drove 86 yards in the third quarter. They scored on a 20-yard pass from Griffing to end Reed Davis, who made an excellent jumping catch between two Longhorns.

In the final minutes Ole Miss traveled from its 45 to the Texas 23, needing two yards for a first down—on fourth down—and a chance to press on for what would be the winning touchdown. Charging energetically, Moses confronted Griffing, off balance anyway after slipping, on a pass or run option play and brought him down for a yard loss.

That settled the issue.

It was a match of teams noted for their speed. Texas got there "fustest with the mostest" (points) as well as "fustest with the fastest" in All-America halfback James Saxton, Collins, and companions. Saxton wasn't allowed to travel far, but a one-yard burst was one of the game's most important plays since it scored a touchdown. His 74-yard quick-kick helped greatly in holding Ole Miss at bay.

1962—Jimmy Saxton follows blockers and jabs Mississippi line for a Texas touchdown.

The Longhorns' extra-alert defense limited the Rebels to total yardage amounting to 100 yards less than they had been accustomed to make. However, the Ole Miss offense, as well as its defense, was handicapped by the absence of All-Southeastern Conference fullback Billy Ray Adams, who sustained severe injuries in an early December automobile accident. The Rebs were all but forced to turn to their air game when Adams' replacement, Buck Randall, left early due to an injury.

"They had a tough pass rush, and they had the quickest secondary I ever played against," said Griffing, who was certainly in an excellent position to know.

Texas	6	6	0	0	12
Mississippi	0	0	7	0	7

Texas—Touchdowns: Saxton (1, right guard), Collins (24, pass from Cotten of 9, run of 15).

Mississippi—Touchdown: Davis (20, pass from Griffing). Point after touchdown: Sullivan.

STATISTICS

Texas		Mississippi	Texas		Mississippi
Moses	LE	Smith	12	First downs	17
Padgett	LT	Brown	123	Net yards rushing	127
Kubin	LG	Jones	13	Passes attempted	37
Kristynik	C	Ross	6	Passes completed	15
Treadwell	RG	Bolin	3	Passes had intercepted	5
D. Talbert	RT	Dunaway	60	Net yards passing	192
Lucas	RE	Dabbs	183	Total net yards	319
Cotten	QB	Elmore	5	Number of punts	4
Saxton	LH	Doty	40	Punting average	32.5
Collins	RH	Guy	1	Fumbles lost	1
Poage	FB	Randall	35	Yards penalized	30

Substitutions—Texas: York (l), C. Talbert (l), Gott (r), Sands (r), ends; Appleton (l), Phillips (l), Ferguson (r), tackles; Brucks (l), Bass (l), D. McWilliams (r), Gamblin (r), guards; P. McWilliams, center; Carlisle, quarterback; Cook (l), Ford (l), Russell (r), Moritz (r), halfbacks; Culpepper, fullback. Mississippi: Davis (l), Tempfer (l), Sullivan (r), ends; McKay (l), Hall (l), Roberts (r), tackles; Mitchell (l), Dickson (r), guards; Lentjes, Dill, centers; Griffing, Dunn, quarterbacks; Morris (l), Holloway (r), halfbacks; Roberts, Halbert, fullbacks.

SUGAR

A play that failed but if it had clicked might have besmirched national champion Alabama's perfect season record with an unsightly blot will be remembered longest by the 82,910 fans who saw plucky Arkansas fall, 10 to 3, in the 28th Sugar Bowl battle.

Two minutes remained and the Razorbacks were trying to penetrate the Crimson Tide's deep defense by long range aerial bombardment.

A long, well timed pass was arched by quarterback George McKinney from midfield. Forty-eight yards away swift halfback Lance Alworth had gotten a bit of a jump on two defenders and was running full tilt. The pass floated down over his shoulder. He reached and touched the ball and seemed almost to have it in his fingertips. But he couldn't hold on.

Right there Coach of the Year Paul Bryant of Alabama suffered what must have been the fifth of nine heart attacks he said he had during the conflict.

Two plays later McKinney shot another 50-yard pass. Bryant caught his breath again but his halfback, Butch Wilson, intercepted this one. Wilson's momentum carried him out of bounds approximately six inches from the Alabama goal line.

Bama had the ball now and would certainly win if it didn't have to give up possession. Arkansas' five allotted timeouts in the second half had been taken. Long counts by the Tide's cool quarterback, Pat Trammell, could be expected. But what if there was a fumble? Bryant shuddered.

For three straight plays Trammell held on tightly as he butted into a wall, going nowhere but not retreating. Bryant's anguish ended before a punt was required as the game ended.

Alabama's big asset, said assistant coach Sam Bailey, who was assigned to compile the scouting report on Arkansas, was that Bryant "gets more out of boys than anyone I know."

Bryant was never quite so proud of any of his seniors as those on his 1961 team that carried the fight to the enemy and then some. They came to him three years before, he said, and told him they would someday win the national championship.

"Regardless of who was coaching them, they still would have been a great team," Bryant said.

Those seniors formed the backbone of a defense that yielded only 22 points and didn't allow Alabama's goal line to be crossed in the last seven games.

"I said early in the season that they were the nicest, even the sissiest bunch I'd ever had," remarked Bryant, referring to the squad as a whole. "I think they read it, because later on they got unfriendly."

Speed and extraordinary quickness, control of the line of scrimmage, hit and keep hitting—those were Alabama characteristics.

Arkansas, which tied Texas for the Southwest Conference title (although losing to the Longhorns, 33 to 7), was that kind of team but not quite as agile or as strong or as poised as Alabama.

Nervousness, which the Razorbacks admitted, was evident at the start.

On the fifth play of a drive that began on Alabama's 21, fullback Mike Fracchia, a high stepper with terrific drive, burst through two tacklers' arms and sped 43 yards to the Arkansas 12 before Billy Joe Moody overtook and spilled him.

Trammell carried the ball on the next play, rolling wide to the

1962—Alabama quarterback Pat Trammell dives over Arkansas goal line.

left and through tackle. As teammates obliterated all opposition, Trammell ran unhindered into the end zone.

Placekick specialist Tim Davis toed a 32-yard field goal in the second quarter. A fumble by Fracchia, a missed field-goal try by Davis, and a holding penalty after a successful third-quarter effort by the Tide kicking expert thwarted other penetrations.

The Razorbacks, pitted against a hotly pursuing, ultra-aggressive line, weren't entirely cooped up on their own side of the 50, although they had difficulty breaking out on their own initiative.

The first time they did—Bama already had its ten points and less than three minutes of the first half were left—right halfback Paul Dudley escaped around left end and down the sideline 38 yards to the 10. Left defensive end Tommy Brooker caught him from behind to prevent a touchdown.

Quarterback Billy Moore gained two. But when Dudley was called on to repeat the play that succeeded a moment before, linebacker Lee Roy Jordan rode him to earth for a four-yard loss. After an incomplete pass, Mickey Cissell missed a field-goal attempt.

Field-goal opportunities arose twice for Arkansas in the third quarter following fumbles in Alabama territory by Billy Richardson and Trammell. One by Jim Grizzle failed when Richardson absolved himself by rushing in and blocking the kick. Cissell made good on his from the 13.

McKinney pierced the Tide secondary late in the game on a 31-yard pass to Alworth. But Lance fumbled as he was tackled and Richardson recovered on the Alabama 43. An interference penalty called against Wilson on Bama's 40 furnished Arkansas and Mc-Kinney with their last chance in the air.

Statistics showed Alabama's leader in tackles to be, unsurprisingly, All-America tackle Billy Neighbors with eight clasps. On one series he brought down Alworth three straight times.

"We looked like the nation's No. 1 team for a few minutes of the first quarter," Bryant said. "After that we were lucky not to be the second best team on the field."

At the Sugar Bowl party given for both teams on the night of the game, Governor Orval Faubus of Arkansas told Frank Broyles, coach of the Razorbacks, "Win or lose, we still love you."

When it was his turn to speak, Bryant grinned at Broyles and cracked, "Frank, don't believe that stuff about them loving you, win or lose. It just ain't so."

Alabama	7	3	0	0	10
Arkansas	0	0	3	0	3

Alabama—Touchdown: Trammell (12, left tackle). Point after touchdown: Davis. Field goal: Davis (32, placekick).
Arkansas—Field goal: Cissell (23, placekick).

STATISTICS

Alabama		Arkansas	Alabama		Arkansas
Battle	LE	John	12	First downs	7
Pell	LT	Mazzanti	234	Net yards rushing	113
J. Wilson	LG	Trail	10	Passes attempted	12
Jordan	C	Brabham	4	Passes completed	2
Sharpe	RG	Garrett	0	Passes had intercepted	3
Neighbors	RT	Childress	20	Net yards passing	55
Brooker	RE	Collier	254	Total net yards	168
Trammell	QB	McKinney	6	Number of punts	7
Richardson	LH	Alworth	23	Punting average	33.8
B. Wilson	RH	Dudley	3	Fumbles lost	1
Fracchia	FB	Moody	53	Yards penalized	34

Substitutions—Alabama: Williamson (l), Wilkins (r), Layton (r), ends; Rice (l), Crenshaw (l), Wright (r), Bible (r), tackles; Pettee (l), Allen (l), Rutledge (r), Lewis (r), guards; O'Linger, center; Culwell, Holt, Sanford, quarterbacks; Martin (l), Abruzzese (l), Clark (l), Oliver (r), Nelson (r), halfbacks; Wall, Davis, fullbacks. Arkansas: Grizzle (l), Evans (r), ends; Bryant (l), Adams (r), tackles; Howard (l), Polk (r), guards; Lineberger, center; B. Moore, quarterback; Williams (l), T. Moore (l), Horton (r), halfbacks; Branch, Cissell, fullbacks.

ORANGE

"This was the best football team I have ever been associated with," said Louisiana State Coach Paul Dietzel.

After his Tigers did everything but rope, tie, and brand the Buffaloes of Colorado in the Orange Bowl game, played in a light rain. Dietzel added that he didn't know of a better team in the country. Some were inclined to agree.

Dietzel's 1961 team was also the last he coached at LSU. It was a published fact, before the Orange Bowl game, that West Point authorities had received permission to talk to him and that he would become Army's new coach, once the formality of being released from his contract with LSU was attended to.

LSU was sought by the Sugar Bowl people but let them know before ending the season with nine straight victories (after an opening loss to Rice) that only an invitation to play out of the state would be entertained. The jaunt to a bowl site only 90 miles away from the campus and to a city familiar to and often visited by most of the players offered little attraction.

Belaboring Colorado, LSU demonstrated greater drive, more speed, better depth, and won overwhelmingly, 25 to 7. The score didn't show it. Yet it was an easy triumph.

Colorado could neither probe nor outflank the LSU line. The Buffaloes were able to gain only 24 yards net on the ground. Their ends were whipped time and again. Colorado could not stop the sprint-out pass or the circling runs.

Dietzel's three interchangeable units—the White team (two-way players), Go team (essentially offensive), and Chinese Bandits (primarily defensive)—gave the Southeastern Conference team an edge in experienced personnel.

In view of all this, it was passing strange that Colorado led by the odd score of 7 to 5 in the early minutes of the second quarter. At that time the Buffaloes had not made a first down and hadn't gained a yard. The scoreboard presented an almost ludicrous sight.

LSU drove 54 yards to the Colorado 14 immediately after receiving the opening kickoff. When the Tigers were seemingly stalled there, Dietzel decided on a field goal. Halfback Wendell Harris delivered it from the 20.

Within two more minutes the score became 5 to 0. Attempting to punt from the Colorado 12, Chuck McBride juggled the snap long enough for linebacker Gary Kinchen to loom large in front of him and block the kick with his upraised left arm. Kinchen slapped the ball out of the end zone for a safety.

On the fifth play of the second period, quarterback Jimmy Field tried to reach Harris on a pass. Fullback Loren Schweninger intercepted it and lighted out on a 59-yard touchdown scamper.

That gave Colorado an insecure and brief lead that vanished before the Buffaloes could put their hands on the ball again. An eight-play, 82-yard march was capped by fullback Charles Cranford's scoring smash from the 1. That made it 11 to 7.

It took LSU six plays to travel 43 yards for a third-quarter touch-

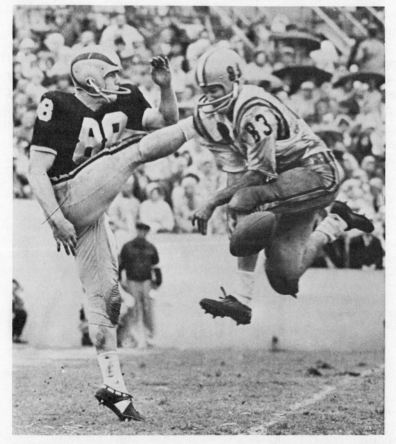

1962—Gene Sykes, Louisiana State end, blocks an attempted punt by Colorado's Chuck McBride. Sykes immediately covered the ball for a touchdown.

down notched by Field on a nine-yard slant through left tackle. The advance began after a McBride punt was partially blocked and went only 18 yards.

Just before the period ended, end Gene Sykes blocked still another McBride punt, this one from the 9.

"They just didn't line up very well to protect that punter," Sykes said. "I didn't feel anybody even nudge me. The ball thumped off my chest and I fell down. I looked around and there was the ball spinning around a few feet away. All I had to do was to reach out and scoop it in."

Thus was the Tigers' third touchdown scored.

Colorado Coach Sonny Grandelius was convinced by halftime his only chance was in the air. Of the Buffaloes' 39 passes, an Orange Bowl record, 30 were flung in the last two quarters and all but three of the total by quarterback Gale Weidner. Only 12 were complete, none for long yardage.

The Big Eight team, playing in Miami in that conference's first appearance under a renewed pact with the Orange Bowl, was able to make only one real scoring threat under its own steam. Colorado penetrated to the LSU 11 in the final period before surrendering the ball. The cause then was already quite hopeless.

"I don't want to sound corny but it's only a game," said Grandelius. "I've been beaten before."

Louisiana State	5	6	14	0	25
Colorado	0	7	0	0	7

Louisiana State—Touchdowns: Cranford (1, right guard), Field (9, left tackle), Sykes (blocked punt by McBride from Colorado 9, fell on ball in end zone). Points after touchdown: Harris 2. Field goal: Harris (30, placekick). Safety (Kinchen blocked McBride's punt from Colorado 12, ball rolled through end zone).

Colorado—Touchdown: Schweninger (59, intercepted pass by Field). Point after touchdown: Hillebrand.

STATISTICS

Louisiana State		Colorado	Louisiana State		Colorado
Sykes	LE	Blair	19	First downs	7
Estes	LT	Denvir	206	Net yards rushing	24
Winston	LG	Heck	18	Passes attempted	39
Gaubatz	C	Klinker	8	Passes completed	12
M. Guillot	RG	Romig	3	Passes had intercepted	0
Booth	RT	Perkins	109	Net yards passing	105

Louisiana State		Colorado		Louisiana State		Colorado
Gates	RE	Hillebrand	315	Total net yards	129
Field	QB	Weidner	4	Number of punts	8
Stovall	LH	Woods	33.8	Punting average	22.1
Harris	RH	Mavity	1	Fumbles lost	1
Gros	FB	Schweninger	65	Yards penalized	35

Substitutions—Louisiana State: Flurry (l), Neumann (l), Morgan (r), Truax (r), Young (r), Rice (r), ends; Richards (l), Pere (l), R. Guillot (r), Miller (r), tackles; Hargett (l), Gary (l), Hucklebridge (l), Odom (r), Habert (r), guards; Kinchen, center; Robinson, Amedee, quarterbacks; Neck (l), Campbell (l), Wilkins (r), Soefker (r), Mercer (r), halfbacks; Hamic, Cranford, fullbacks. Colorado: Hold (l), McBride (l), Bell (l), Meadows (r), ends; Grimm (l), Bearss (l), Frank (r), tackles; Vardell (l), Houk (l), McCullough (r), Young (r), guards; Christensen, Harper, centers; Montera, quarterback; Harris (l), Crabb (l), Graham (l), Johnson (r), Somerville (r), Coleman (r), halfbacks; Raisis, fullback.

BLUEBONNET

John Hadl, who could play either quarterback (his position in 1961) or halfback with equal facility, nimbly maneuvered Kansas to a 33 to 7 thrashing of Rice in the Bluebonnet Bowl.

The first half was touch-and-go. With less than three minutes to play in the second quarter, Rice was ahead, 7 to 6.

Hadl gave ground on fourth down and six yards to go from the Kansas 40, intending to punt. But he fumbled the wet ball in the rain that fell throughout the game. Then he grabbed it and sped away, twisting and bulling 41 yards before he was felled on the Rice 19.

Fullback Ken Coleman exploded through the middle for 18 yards, running over three Owls. On the next play he plunged for the touchdown that gave the Jayhawkers a 12 to 7 advantage. Coleman scored twice and piledrove 107 yards.

When Hadl got away from his 40, almost everybody thought he had been faking a punt. But Coach Jack Mitchell said, "That would have been a stupid play. John was being rushed hard by the Rice end (Gene Raesz). He saw daylight at the last second and he was off. It was the turning point of the game."

George Bernhardt, Kansas line coach, said, "I told our linemen at halftime that if they would give the passer a better rush, we'd win." Randy Kerbow had completed eight of 12 passes for 129 yards in the first half. One of five yards to Johnny Burrell put Rice in the lead in the first quarter.

The fired-up Jayhawkers had things all their own way in the last half. They ran 45 plays to the Owls' 15, amassed 14 first downs to

1961—Winding up a double reverse, halfback Roger McFarland of Kansas scores against Rice.

two, outrushed the Southwest Conference team, 184 yards to minus one, and outscored it 21 to 0.

Unexpected by Rice, Kansas aimed its attack with power slants off tackle while the defense was primed to halt Hadl's dangerous pass-run options. Coleman and his backfield cronies tore Rice's bigger but less mobile line to tatters.

The Owls found a double reverse particularly difficult to fathom. Halfback Rodger McFarland scored twice on it with neatly executed runs of 12 and 9 yards. Halfback Curtis McClinton made the other touchdown on a four-yard scoot.

In the consensus All-America backfield for 1961 were Sandy Stephens of Minnesota, Ernie Davis of Syracuse, James Saxton of Texas, and Bob Ferguson of Ohio State.

But Hadl was the most talented all-around back in the nation in all probability.

SATURDAY, DECEMBER 16, 1961

Kansas	6	6	13	8	33
Rice	7	0	0	0	7

Kansas—Touchdowns: Coleman 2 (1, center plunge; 1, right guard), McFar-

land 2 (9, right tackle; 12, right tackle), McClinton (4, left tackle). Points
after touchdown: Barnes, Boydston (pass from Hadl).

Rice—Touchdown: Burrell (5, pass from Kerbow). Point after touchdown:
Blume.

STATISTICS

Kansas		*Rice*	*Kansas*		*Rice*
Allen	LE	Burrell	21	First downs	11
Lousch	LT	Karam	293	Net yards rushing	58
Basham	LG	Woods	10	Passes attempted	20
Staab	C	Cole	7	Passes completed	11
Mills	RG	Simmons	2	Passes had intercepted	0
Kirshman	RT	Johnston	64	Net yards passing	163
Boydston	RE	Raesz	357	Total net yards	221
Hadl	QB	Kerbow	3	Number of punts	6
McFarland	LH	Blume	37	Punting average	31
McClinton	RH	Candler	0	Fumbles lost	3
Coleman	FB	Jackson	15	Yards penalized	0

Substitutions—Kansas: Graham (l), Green (l), Roberts (r), Deer (r), ends;
Fisher (l), Walker (l), Eiseman (r), Davis (r), tackles; Collins (l), Barnes (l),
Tiger (r), Clothier (r), guards; Converse, Quatrochi, centers; Keating, quarterback; Leiker (l), Wilson (l), Doughty (r), Marshall (r), halfbacks; Jarrett, Baughman, Michaels, fullbacks. Rice: Sylvester (l), Schultz (l), Kelley (r), Rees (r),
ends; Mims (l), Cornett (l), Alborn (r), Moore (r), tackles; Anthony (l), Hubbard (l), Nichols (r), Fritsch (r), guards; Malin, center; Cox, quarterback; Wayt
(l), Poage (r), Brown (r), halfbacks; Bowen, Caddell, fullbacks.

LIBERTY

It was all Miami in the first half, 14 to 0.

In the second half of the Liberty Bowl game, it was all Syracuse,
15 to 0.

On a numbingly cold, 22-degree afternoon in Philadelphia, before
a sparse turnout of 15,712, the lads from Syracuse won, 15 to 14, on
a successful pass good for two extra points.

Victorious Coach Ben Schwartzwalder, self-described as "the
world's worst deliverer of pre-game pep talks," could thank, chiefly,
four senior veterans of his 1959 national championship squad.

They were All-America halfback Ernie Davis, whose three-year
totals of 2,386 yards rushing and 220 points broke the celebrated Jim
Brown's school records; halfback Dick Easterly, quarterback Dave
Sarette, and end Ken Ericson.

But it took them 30 minutes to get going.

"Just to show you what an inspiration I am to my boys," said
Schwartzwalder, "take a look at our record. Why, we were behind
at the start of seven of our 10 games."

A 12-yard gallop off left tackle by halfback Jim Vollenweider and a 60-yard punt return by halfback Nick Spinelli propelled Miami into a surprising two-touchdown lead.

Davis, limited to 38 yards in ten carries in the first half and hurting from an accidental kick in the back, was a changed man when he returned to the field for the third quarter. And so were his teammates. Exhibiting the grace and force that earned for him the Heisman Trophy, Ernie swept and smashed 102 yards in the last two periods. He who had fumbled away Syracuse's only first half scoring opportunity piloted both of his team's touchdown drives.

Sarette, who connected with receivers on 13 of his 26 passes, shot one of 15 yards to Easterly during a 42-yard offensive in the third quarter. Davis ripped off the last seven yards on six- and one-yard thrusts.

After Ernie's first touchdown, Syracuse gambled in an attempt to get the bonus conversion. Sarette, aiming for Easterly in the end zone, threw low. But the halfback dived and caught the ball, narrowing the score to 14 to 8.

A 51-yard march following a recovery of a Miami fumble put Syracuse on top for keeps in the fourth quarter. Again, the biggest gainer was another Sarette to Easterly flip that covered 13 yards. But Davis was the kingpin of the attack, netting 25 yards on four tries.

From the 7, where Davis was stopped on his last blast, Sarette floated a payoff pass into Easterly's hands, tying the score. Ericson sent a placekick over the crossbar and Miami was whipped.

Miami Coach Andy Gustafson paid Davis the supreme compliment. He said, "He is the best back by far I've seen in college ranks since Doc Blanchard and Glenn Davis played for Army. It doesn't look like he is moving very fast. But quite often his teammates whom he couldn't push out of his way had more to do with stopping him than our tacklers did."

Ernie, called on twenty times in the second half, said, "I felt I could have carried the ball twice as often as I did." The great back died of acute monocytic leukemia on May 18, 1963.

SATURDAY, DECEMBER 16, 1961

Syracuse	0	0	8	7	15
Miami	6	8	0	0	14

Syracuse—Touchdowns: Davis (1, center plunge), Easterly (7, pass from Sarette). Points after touchdown: Easterly (pass from Sarette), Ericson.

Miami—Touchdowns: Vollenweider (12, left tackle), Spinelli (60, punt return). Points after touchdown: Miller (pass from Mira).

STATISTICS

Syracuse		Miami		Syracuse		Miami
Sweeney	LE	Miller	21	First downs		11
Feidler	LT	Maluty	221	Net yards rushing		109
Spillett	LG	Reynolds	27	Passes attempted		21
Stem	C	Lillimagi	13	Passes completed		7
Francovitch	RG	Eggert	0	Passes had intercepted		0
Brown	RT	Watts	148	Net yards passing		94
Mackey	RE	L. Wilson	369	Total net yards		203
Sarette	QB	Mira	7	Number of punts		0
Davis	LH	Vollenweider	31.4	Punting average		30.3
Easterly	RH	Bahen	2	Fumbles lost		1
Fallon	FB	Fernandez	35	Yards penalized		29

Substitutions—Syracuse: Ericson (l), Howard (l), Mingo (r), ends; Paglio (l), Archer (r), Hnat (r), tackles; Seager (l), Meggyesy (r), Mazurek (r), guards; Stancin, Huettner, centers; Snider, quarterback; King (l), Giardi (r), Humphreys (r), halfbacks; Schoonover, fullback. Miami: Reinhart (l), Simon (l), Foster (l), Rizzo (r), R. Wilson (r), ends; Conners (l), Smerdel (r), tackles; Diamond (l), Strieter (l), O'Mahony (r), guards; Losego, center; Timmons, quarterback; Ryder (l), Bennett (l), Spinelli (r), halfbacks; Parsons, Bruno, fullbacks.

– 1963 –

ORANGE

In the Alabama dressing room after the Crimson Tide's 17 to 0 Orange Bowl victory over Oklahoma, a photographer asked Coach Paul Bryant how to spell the name of a player whose picture he had just taken.

"That's Namath, son—N-A-M-A-T-H," Bryant said. "But don't worry about it. You'll learn how to spell it in the next couple of years."

If the cameraman were unfamiliar with the name, the crowd of 73,380 attending the 1963 Orange Bowl game and millions more watching on television were not.

Long before that game, Bryant said the precocious young man

from Pennsylvania was ahead of Babe Parilli (whom he coached at Kentucky) as a sophomore. He rated Namath "potentially the finest quarterback I've ever coached."

Namath piloted his team 61 yards in ten plays for a touchdown in the first quarter. From the Oklahoma 25, he faked a handoff and a short pass, whirled, and sailed a long pass into end Dick Williamson's hands in the end zone.

A sleight of hand pitch-out to halfback Cotton Clark resulted in a 15-yard scoring sprint in the second period. It was the third play after Billy Piper returned a punt by Joe Don Looney to the Sooners' 34. First, Namath threw a pass to Williamson, good for 20 yards. Clark's touchdown was his sixteenth of the year.

Next, and finally, Namath conducted a Tide surge from Oklahoma's 33 to the 2. There, it was fourth down. Tim Davis, Bama's placekicking specialist, toed a 19-yard field goal. This third-quarter opportunity arose when Looney, the nation's leading punter with an average of 43.4 yards, was hurried by guard Frankie McClendon's rush and got off a kick of only seven yards.

Fumbles ruined Oklahoma's chances of making it a closer contest. Fullback Jim Grisham, a hard-running sophomore, was the offender twice within a seven-minute part of the first period. Flaming work by the smaller but faster Alabama line, spearheaded by All-America center Lee Roy Jordan, suppressed the Sooners' offense and caused Grisham's fumbles on the Alabama 6 and 8.

Grisham, the game's top ground gainer with 107 yards on 28 carries, was picked by only one All-America team selector, Lacy Lockert, a retired professor living in Nashville and one of football's keenest scholars and most exhaustive historians.

Striving for at least a consoling touchdown in the last few minutes, Oklahoma struggled first to the Alabama 16, then to the 10. But the Tide's more agile, quicker-striking defenders denied the Sooners further passage. With the checking of the last drive in the final minutes, President Kennedy, a spectator sitting on the Oklahoma side, left the scene.

Sooner backs were hounded relentlessly by swift-pursuing Bamans who on offense blocked to the end of every play. There were Charley Pell, Jimmy Wilson, Jimmy Sharpe, Bill Battle, Butch Wilson, Ed Versprille, Dan Kearley, and McClendon—all bristling with desire. But the greatest of all, in another superb performance, tackling and blocking, was Jordan.

He was as fine a linebacker as ever played in the South. Perhaps nobody else in college football in 1962 had his almost instinctive ability to seek out the ball carrier so quickly and bring him down so abruptly. It is doubtful if Bryant ever praised a player quite as much.

Jordan once expressed his philosophy this way: "I would be dishonest with myself and short-changing myself and the team if I didn't put everything I had into it. I always thought you had to put 100 per cent into anything to make it worthwhile."

Fifteen seniors finished the best three years (29–2–2) Alabama ever knew in football. Only a matter of a few inches, the distance by which Jack Hurlbut failed to make a two-pointer after the only touchdown against Georgia Tech (Tech won, 7 to 6), apparently separated the Tide from two straight national championships.

Said Bryant: "Walking around the dressing room shaking hands with them after their last game, it was all I could do to keep from completely choking up. You just love them, that's all."

Alabama and Oklahoma struck the second richest pay lode in the game's history. In 1958, when the Columbia Broadcasting System paid $275,000 for television and radio rights, Duke and Oklahoma each collected $224,308.50. The American Broadcasting Company gave $205,000 for those rights in 1963. Rival teams each got $190,-000, some of which, of course, was shared with schools in the Big Eight and Southeastern Conference.

Five Southeastern Conference teams played in bowl games. Collectively, they netted four victories and an estimated $475,000.

TUESDAY, JANUARY 1, 1963

Alabama	7	7	3	0	17
Oklahoma	0	0	0	0	0

Alabama—Touchdowns: Williamson (25, pass from Namath), Clark (15, left end). Points after touchdown: Davis 2. Field goal: Davis (19, placekick).

STATISTICS

Alabama		Oklahoma	Alabama		Oklahoma
Williamson	LE	Flynn	15	First downs	10
Henry	LT	Ward	174	Net yards rushing	154
J. Wilson	LG	Burton	17	Passes attempted	8
Jordan	C	Garrett	9	Passes completed	4
Sharpe	RG	Cross	1	Passes had intercepted	0
Pell	RT	Metcalf	86	Net yards passing	106
Battle	RE	McCurdy	260	Total net yards	260
Namath	QB	Deere	8	Number of punts	10
Clark	LH	Lea	40.5	Punting average	34
B. Wilson	RH	Sandersfeld	1	Fumbles lost	2
Versprille	FB	Grisham	5	Yards penalized	12

Substitutions—Alabama: C. Stephens (l), Dill (l), Hopper (r), ends; O'Dell (l), Boler (l), Allen (r), Kearley (r), Wright (r), Fowler (r), tackles; Freeman (l), Pettee (l), Cook (l), Mitchell (l), Simmons (l), Wieseman (r), Lewis (r), McClendon (r), guards; G. Stephens, McCollough, centers; Hurlbut, Culwell, Moore, quarterbacks; Nelson (l), Piper (l), Davis (l), Andrews (l), Martin (r), Elmore (r), Harris (r), halfbacks; Rankin, Ogden, fullbacks. Oklahoma: Porterfield (l), Bumgardner (r), ends; Neely (l), Hill (l), Cook (r), Stokes (r), tackles; McQuarters (l), Vermillion (r), guards; Lee, center; Mayhue, quarterback; Looney (l), Boll (r), halfbacks; Voiles, fullback.

ROSE

Wisconsin was hopelessly beaten, overwhelmed, in danger of being humiliated.

Southern California, national champion for the first time in 31 years, led by a whopping score, 42 to 14, in the Rose Bowl and there were 12 minutes left—plenty of time to break Michigan's record of 49 points made in 1902 and duplicated in 1948.

Or so it seemed.

Yet at the finish the Trojans, so splendid a few minutes before, were almost paralyzed and bewildered, holding on for dear life to a shrunken lead, praying the clock would run out before the Badgers could get the ball again.

What happened, fantastically, was this as Wisconsin fiercely counterattacked:

1. Speedy halfback Lou Holland tore around right end for 13 yards and a touchdown with 11:41 to play. Score: 42 to 21.

2. Quarterback Ron VanderKelen threw a four-yard pass to Gary Kroner for a touchdown with 8:32 to go. Score: 42 to 28.

3. Pete Lubisich sailed the center snap so far over Ernie Jones' head that the Trojan punter had to down it in the end zone for a safety with 2:40 left. Score: 42 to 30.

4. VanderKelen, completing his 33rd and last of 48 passes for the amazing total of 401 yards, arched one of 19 yards to All-America end Pat Richter for a touchdown (his 11th catch) with 1:19 remaining. Score: 42 to 37.

Wisconsin's attempted recovery of an onside kick failed and Southern California controlled the ball for three downs on which 10 yards were lost. The final gun sounded after Jones' punt, nearly blocked, was returned for scanty yardage. Trojan fans unloosed a great shout of triumph. Many envisioned a 44 to 42 score if Wisconsin could have gotten the ball once more in good field position.

"What I wouldn't give for just one minute more," said Milt Bruhn, coach of the Big Ten champions.

It was Southern California's tenth victory in thirteen Rose Bowl appearances in the most sensational game ever played in that classic.

All sorts of records were set.

Pete Beathard, quarterback for the Trojans and co-winner of the outstanding player award, with VanderKelen, fired four touchdown passes, two more than the Badgers' ace. A total of 69 passes was thrown and 44 completed for 672 yards. There were 47 first downs (32 by Wisconsin) and 79 points.

The drawn out game lasted three hours, five minutes. It was pitch-dark outside the bowl when the crowd of 98,698 left. The fourth quarter was played under dim, inadequate lighting. It took 43 minutes to play the first quarter after the kickoff had been delayed.

"The game was over-officiated from start to finish by a whistle-happy striped-shirt quintet," wrote Paul Zimmerman in the *Los Angeles Times*. "Only the remarkable play of the two teams kept them from spoiling the contest."

What happened up to the moment of Wisconsin's valiant come-back was this:

First Quarter

1. On a tackle-eligible play, Ron Butcher received a 13-yard touch-down pass from Beathard with 5:37 gone. Score: 7 to 0.

2. Wisconsin stormed back, mainly on VanderKelen's passing. Fullback Ralph Kurek's one-yard plunge climaxed an 82-yard drive at 13:06. Score: 7 to 7.

Second Quarter

1. Damon Bame, a demon of a linebacker, set up a touchdown by intercepting a VanderKelen pass and returning 25 yards to the Badgers' 30. Fullback Ben Wilson smashed over from the 1 with 5.05 played. Score: 14 to 7.

2. What Bruhn called an "awfully fast whistle" deprived Wisconsin of the ball when end Ron Carlson hit the Trojans' No. 2 quarterback, Bill Nelsen. Badger guard Ronnie Parr covered the ball on S.C.'s 22. Instead, it was ruled dead on the 30 before the fumble. Heartened, the Trojans quickly scored.

Nelsen passed far into Wisconsin territory and fleet halfback Willie Brown made a marvelous catch 45 yards away. Halfback Ron Heller, declared out of the game only two days before—he sustained a severely sprained knee December 27—started wide, cut in, and sped 25 yards at 9:49. Score: 21 to 7.

With four seconds left in the second period, Holland, diving and rolling, caught a 28-yard pass from VanderKelen for an apparent touchdown. But clipping was called against Parr.

The instant the half ended, Bruhn, irate, charged after the officials.

"I asked them about a quick whistle on the fumble and about the penalty when they called back the touchdown pass," he said. Obviously, he felt the officials were all wrong.

THIRD QUARTER

1. On the first play from scrimmage, All-America end Hal Bedsole fastened onto a short toss from Beathard. He right-angled across the field to his own right to pick up an escort. Brown and Ken Del Conte leveled menacing Badgers. Their aid, plus his own pretty footwork, freed him for a 57-yard run. Bedsole crossed the goal line with 50 seconds showing. Score: 28 to 7.

2. Now Wisconsin wheeled 67 yards with VanderKelen himself breezing the last 17 and 5:15 elapsed. Score: 28 to 14.

3. Southern Cal pulled three touchdowns ahead again at 9:20. Bedsole, outspokenly anxious to equal or excel Richter's performance, faced Beathard deep in the end zone and leaped to catch a 23-yard pass thrown at least eight feet off the ground. Score: 35 to 14.

FOURTH QUARTER

1. As the third period closed, Tom Lupo was tackled on Wisconsin's 13. He had run 29 yards with an intercepted VanderKelen pass. Immediately, Beathard shot a pass to end Fred Hill on the goal line. Score: 42 to 14.

It began then—the wildest rally the old bowl ever knew.

The Badgers couldn't prevent their third straight Pasadena defeat, or the Big Ten's third in the last four Rose Bowl games. But there was nothing to be ashamed of this time.

Deserved praise went to the brilliant VanderKelen, who played only 90 seconds of varsity competition prior to his senior season, and to Beathard and Bedsole and Richter. Southern California's John McKay, 1962 Coach of the Year, agreed and then talked about an overlooked fellow.

He said, "All that Willie Brown did for us was to catch three passes for 108 yards, return four kickoffs for 124 yards, intercept a crucial pass (just before the safety) that kept Wisconsin from winning, make one of the greatest catches in Rose Bowl history and tackle Gary Kroner when he missed a big first down (in the second period) by inches."

Most of the Trojans could hardly muster a smile in their dressing room. One who could was the genial Wilson. He said, "You just can't feel sad when you got 42 points and they only got 37, now can you?"

McKay felt the same way.

"Fifty years from now it'll still be in the records that we won the game, 42–37," he said. "And they will have forgotten how we almost blew a 42–14 lead."

Southern California	7	14	14	7	42
Wisconsin	7	0	7	23	37

Southern California—Touchdowns: Bedsole 2 (57, pass from Beathard of 5, run of 52; 23, pass from Beathard), Butcher (13, pass from Beathard of 9, run of 4), Wilson (1, left tackle), Heller (25, right end), F. Hill (13, pass from Beathard). Points after touchdown: Lupo 6.

Wisconsin—Touchdowns: Kurek (1, left tackle), VanderKelen (17, right end), Holland (13, right end), Kroner (4, pass from VanderKelen), Richter (19, pass from VanderKelen of 16, run of 3). Points after touchdown: Kroner 5. Safety: Lubisich's center snap to E. Jones from Southern California 25 went over punter's head who downed it in the end zone.

STATISTICS

Southern California		Wisconsin		Southern California	Wisconsin
Bedsole	LE	Leafblad	15	First downs	32
Kirner	LT	Pillath	114	Net yards rushing	67
Fisk	LG	Gross	20	Passes attempted	49
Sagouspe	C	Bowman	10	Passes completed	34
Lubisich	RG	Underwood	0	Passes had intercepted	3
Marinovich	RT	Wojdula	253	Net yards passing	419
Pye	RE	Richter	367	Total net yards	486
Beathard	QB	Norvell	5	Number of punts	4
Brown	LH	Holland	40.4	Punting average	40.3
Del Conte	RH	Kroner	1	Fumbles lost	0
Byrd	FB	Kurek	93	Yards penalized	77

Substitutions—Southern California: Hoover (l), E. Jones (l), Thurlow (l), Brownwood (r), F. Hill (r), Potter (r), Austin (r), ends; Byrd (l), Butcher (l), Eaton (r), R. Jones (r), Gonta (r), tackles; Johnson (l), Svihus (l), Ratliff (l), Smedley (r), Gonta (r), guards; Schmidt, Sanchez, centers; Lupo, Nelsen, quarterbacks; Clark (l), G. Hill (l), Heller (r), Hunt (r), halfbacks; Bame, Wilson, McMahon, E. Jones, Pye, fullbacks. Wisconsin: Carlson (l), Ezerins (l), Howard (r), ends; Bernet (l), Jacobazzi (r), tackles; Paar (l), Monk (l), Schenk (r), guards; Heckl, Bruhn, centers; VanderKelen, Frain, Reichardt, quarterbacks; Nettles (l), Silvestri (l), W. Smith (r), R. Smith (r), halfbacks; Purnell, Norvell, fullbacks.

GATOR

Cocky described to a T the Florida quarterback Tom Shannon. Several days before the 1962 Gator Bowl game, this supremely confident sophomore remarked to Florida's defensive coach, Gene Ellenson, "If Penn State is real lucky, they might make a game out of it for a half."

Shannon did his part well enough to win the award to the most valuable player on the winning team. Against Penn State, he threw a seven-yard touchdown pass to Larry Dupree and another of 19 yards to Hagood Clarke among his seven completions in nine attempts.

Shannon, explained Ellenson, "believes in himself and the team. That's good."

Inflamed by scoffs, even among their own followers, that they were unworthy to appear on the same field with the powerful Eastern champion, the Gators soundly thumped the favorite, though the score was only 17 to 7.

Penn State, ragged and lacking the quickness of their "we'll show 'em"-minded opponents, did stay close for a half, trailing then, 10 to 7. But this day the Nittany Lions were no match for unwanted, but undaunted Florida, which attacked furiously in an unrelenting crusade to prove its merit after four regular season defeats.

During the season Penn State piled up more yardage than any other team in the school's history but was held to 139 yards running and passing by the Gators.

Jacksonville writers gave credit to a new "monster" defense installed by Ellenson. He was promoted from offensive line coach to head the defense after Jack Green left the staff to become Vanderbilt's head coach in early December. It was basically a nine-man front with the secondary drawn up closer.

Just before the half ended, Penn State pulled itself together offensively for the first and only time and brought off a 76-yard advance. It wound up with quarterback Pete Liske legging the final yard around right end.

Before that Bob Lyle had kicked a towering 43-yard field goal into a brisk wind and Dupree had caught Shannon's high, soft toss deep in the end zone.

When the teams returned to the field for the third quarter, many thought Penn State would forge in front in a demonstration of predicted superiority. Nothing doing. The aroused Gators kept the ball most of the time (41 minutes in all), scored another touchdown, and never let the Nittany Lions launch a sustained offense.

Penn State coach Rip Engle thought the turning point was a fumbled interception chance on Florida's 35 by Don Caum of the Lions in the third period but conceded, "We were outplayed all day in everything. Florida came up with the key plays. We did not."

Three Penn State fumbles and two passes thrown with erring aim were gratefully accepted by the Gators. Fumbles by Roger Kochman and Caum set up their first half point-making. An interception of Liske's pass led to the second touchdown, although Florida then had to travel 49 yards.

Dave Robinson, Penn State's giant end, played superbly in defeat and was honored with a trophy as the losers' outstanding man.

This was the only bowl game ever officiated by six men on the field. There were two back judges.

At the awards banquet after the game, Penn State President Eric A. Walker pointed out the difference, to him, between winning and losing in the Gator Bowl.

"Last year, when we won, I sat next to Miss America," he said. "Today, we are the losers and I am sitting next to my wife."

SATURDAY, DECEMBER 29, 1962

Florida	3	7	0	7	17
Penn State	0	7	0	0	7

Florida—Touchdowns: Dupree (7, pass from Shannon), Clarke (19, pass from Shannon). Points after touchdown: Hall 2. Field goal: Lyle (43, placekick).

Penn State—Touchdown: Liske (1, right end). Point after touchdown: Coates.

STATISTICS

Florida		*Penn State*	*Florida*		*Penn State*
Brown	LE	Anderson	14	First downs	8
Odom	LT	Sieminski	162	Net yards rushing	89
Travis	LG	Blasenstein	13	Passes attempted	21
Pettee	C	Galardi	8	Passes completed	5
Katz	RG	Rosdahl	1	Passes had intercepted	2
Lasky	RT	Monaghan	86	Net yards passing	50
Holland	RE	Robinson	248	Total net yards	139
Shannon	QB	Liske	6	Number of punts	6
Dupree	LH	Kochman	23.7	Punting average	40.8
Newcomer	RH	Gursky	1	Fumbles lost	3
O'Donnell	FB	Hayes	42	Yards penalized	10

Substitutions—Florida: Gregory (l), Starling (l), Starling (r), Dean (r), ends; Murphy (l), Pearson (l), Lyle (l), Peters (r), Dent (r), tackles; Entzminger (l), Thompson (l), Hosack (l), Richbourg (r), Jones (r), MacLean (r), guards; Morgan, Culpepper, centers; Libertore, Batten, Dodd, Hall, quarterbacks; Clarke (l), Stoner (l), Mack (r), halfbacks; Kelley, fullback. Penn State: Yost (l), Stepanausky (l), Walter (l), Bowes (r), Pickup (r), ends; Buchan (l), Tietjens (l), Farkas (r), Deibert (r), tackles; Sabol (l), Waresak (l), Ressler (r), Hart (r), guards; Baker, Williams, Raisig, centers; Caum, Coates, quarterbacks; Hershey (l), Weber (l), Powell (r), Klingensmith (r), Sincek (r), halfbacks; Torris, Stuckrath, fullbacks.

COTTON

It was a rather hot spot Coach Charlie McClendon occupied as successor to Paul Dietzel at Louisiana State in 1962.

In Dietzel's last year at LSU before he moved to West Point, the Tigers won ten consecutive games and a share of the Southeastern Conference championship. Twenty-six of the men he lettered returned to play under McClendon.

The former Kentucky end filled that warm seat remarkably well. LSU won nine (counting its bowl triumph), lost one, and tied one.

"I'm very stingy," McClendon, who directed LSU's defense under Dietzel, told John Foster of the *New Orleans Times-Picayune* after becoming head coach. "I'm selfish—I want the ball. There are about 150 offensive plays in a game. If you hold the ball 75 or 85 of these plays, chances are you're going to win, providing—and this is all-important—your defense is equal to your opponent's."

The 1963 Cotton Bowl game was a case in point.

Counting punts, there were 146 plays. LSU was in possession of the ball for 88 plays and Texas for 58. Texas was outgained, rushing and passing, 258 yards to 172. LSU recovered two fumbles (one leading to a touchdown and the other stopping a Texas drive) and intercepted three passes.

Little wonder LSU won, 13 to 0.

Surprising, though, was the merited recognition of stubby Lynn Amedee, quarterback of LSU's No. 2 or "Go" team, as the game's outstanding back. In the voting he outdistanced the Bengals' All-America halfback Jerry Stovall.

Amedee kicked 23- and 37-yard field goals. He completed nine of his 13 passes for 94 yards. He kicked off at the start of the third quarter and seconds later recovered Texas tailback Jerry Cook's fumble.

LSU capitalized almost immediately. On the fifth play "White" (No. 1) team quarterback Jimmy Field, intending to pass but finding receivers blanketed, took off to his left and escaped for a 22-yard touchdown run.

The Tigers actually wrapped up the game within a space of just over two minutes. Amedee's first field goal was booted with eight seconds left in the first half. The victors had hammered out 75 yards. On the advance Amedee passed for 33 yards and ran for ten.

The only Texas scoring threat of any consequence petered out when a field goal effort failed after a 61-yard march to LSU's 25. The Tigers took the ball and carried it into position for Amedee's first three-pointer.

With ten minutes to go LSU linebacker Buddy Hamic jerked the ball away from Cook, ending the Longhorns' last penetration on the Tigers' 31. The steal set in motion a drive to the Texas 21. Amedee climaxed it with a Cotton Bowl record-breaking field goal.

Amedee's wife, Judy, celebrated her 20th birthday on the day of the game. At the party at which he received his trophy, the quarterback cracked, "It will have to serve as a birthday present for Judy since it's the only thing I can afford."

Louisiana State	0	3	7	3	13
Texas	0	0	0	0	0

Louisiana State—Touchdown: Field (22, left end). Point after touchdown: Amedee. Field goals: Amedee 2 (23, placekick; 37, placekick).

STATISTICS

Louisiana State		Texas	Louisiana State		Texas
Sykes	LE	Lucas	17	First downs	9
Estes	LT	Appleton	126	Net yards rushing	80
Guillot	LG	Kubin	21	Passes attempted	22
Gaubatz	C	P. McWilliams	13	Passes completed	8
Hucklebridge	RG	Treadwell	0	Passes had intercepted	3
Miller	RT	Ferguson	132	Net yards passing	92
Gates	RE	Sands	258	Total net yards	172
Field	QB	Carlisle	9	Number of punts	8
Stovall	LH	Ford	41.8	Punting average	46.8
LeBlanc	RH	Dixon	0	Fumbles lost	2
Ward	FB	Culpepper	15	Yards penalized	44

Substitutions—Louisiana State: Neumann (l), Flurry (l), Truax (r), Morgan (r), ends; Pere (l), Simmons (l), Langley (r), Cox (r), Trosclair (r), tackles; Young (l), Prudhomme (l), Habert (r), Turner (r), guards; Kinchen, Rodrigue, centers; Amedee, Robinson, quarterbacks; Campbell (l), Graves (l), Mercer (r), Soefker (r), Wilkins (r), halfbacks; Cranford, Hamic, fullbacks. Texas: House (l), Crosby (l), Fults (r), Talbert (r), ends; Besselman (l), Faulkner (l), Lacy (r), Roberts (r), tackles; Brucks (l), Bass (l), Gamblin (r), Underwood (r), guards; D. McWilliams, center; Genung, Wade, quarterbacks; Cook (l), Green (l), Koy (r), King (r), Hudson (r), halfbacks; Poage, Doerr, fullbacks.

SUGAR

"The difference," said Arkansas Coach Frank Broyles as he relaxed on a rubbing table, "was Glynn Griffing. Without a doubt, he is the greatest college passer in America."

With Griffing directing the performance, Ole Miss beat Arkansas 17 to 13 before a crowd of 82,900 in the Sugar Bowl.

Broyles continued: "In fact, he's the best college passer I've ever seen. The big third down plays when he would get away from us broke our backs.

"His receivers came up with some fantastic catches. This boy Louis Guy looked like a juggler in a side show act. I thought he was equipped with radar. Any pass within five yards of him he caught."

Griffing completed 14 of his 23 passes for 242 yards, 17 more than Davey O'Brien's old Sugar Bowl record. Guy, who ran 103 yards with an intercepted pass against Tennessee, caught five of Griffing's throws for 107 yards. But it was by no means a two-man show.

Left cornerback Buck Randall was a particularly sharp and timely tackler. Among others perhaps devoted beyond the call of duty were 261-pound tackle Jim Dunaway, guards Tommy Lucas and Don Dickson, tackle Whaley Hall, and tailback Chuck Morris.

"Griffing was the difference all right," said Ole Miss Coach Johnny Vaught. Then, diplomatically, "but this was a tremendous team effort."

He wouldn't say his undefeated, untied 1962 squad was better than some of his others. "That's just like choosing between children," Vaught said. "You love them all."

The score was a contradiction of the statistical evidence. Ole Miss led in first downs, 22 to seven, and in net yardage, 429 to 170.

The victory narrowed the interval between Vaught's winning percentage and Bud Wilkinson's of Oklahoma. Wilkinson's winning percentage of .827, based on a record of 137–27–4, was highest among active coaches. Vaught's record was now 130–31–7 (.795). Each had been a head coach for 16 years.

Vaught's Southeastern Conference championship in 1962 was his fifth. It was his sixth trip to the Sugar Bowl and fourth straight win in New Orleans. Ole Miss had now gone to bowl games six successive years and ten in all under Vaught.

With Ole Miss ahead, 17 to 10, Arkansas had the ball on the Rebels' 5, fourth down and goal to go. Tom McKnelly was ordered to attempt a field goal, which he made.

"It was still the third quarter and we figured we could make them punt and then go for the winning touchdown," Broyles explained. "We were having trouble moving the ball anyway."

Vaught agreed with this decision when questioned after the game.

But the Razorbacks never got beyond their own 25 in the remaining 17 minutes and they could not force a punt. They spent most of the time fending off their opponents, who reached the Arkansas 3, 24, 8, and 10 on successive fourth-period drives but scored no more.

All of that time the Porkers' ace, quarterback Billy Moore, was on the sideline. His right knee, hurt in the final game of the season, was reinjured on the play just before McKnelly's second field goal and he had to leave.

In the second quarter, first Billy Carl Irwin of Ole Miss and then McKnelly kicked 30-yard field goals. McKnelly's followed a 68-yard pass play from Billy Gray to Jerry Lamb. Randall prevented a touchdown by diving and grabbing Lamb's heel for a split second. Lamb stumbled eight yards before falling on the 13, unable to regain his balance.

Griffing shot a 33-yard touchdown pass to Guy to round off a quick 67-yard expedition, all but one yard by air, less than two minutes later.

An early third-quarter fumble by Randall on the Ole Miss 18 was costly but only momentarily. Two plays afterward Arkansas got the tying touchdown on a five-yard pass from Moore to halfback Jesse Branch.

The game was six minutes older when the Rebs took the lead for keeps, just the time Griffing required to engineer an 80-yard charge. En route, he completed passes of 18 and 35 yards to Guy. He got the final yard himself.

Broyles did an unusual thing when the season ended. He turned down a raise in pay. He declined it and gave the money to his assistants. "I wanted them to have a nice raise," he said.

| Mississippi | 0 | 10 | 7 | 0 | 17 |
| Arkansas | 0 | 3 | 10 | 0 | 13 |

Mississippi—Touchdowns: Guy (33, pass from Griffing of 27, run of 6), Griffing (1, center sneak). Points after touchdown: Irwin 2. Field goal: Irwin (30, placekick).

Arkansas—Touchdown: Branch (5, pass from B. Moore). Point after touchdown: McNelly. Field goals: McNelly 2 (30, placekick; 22, placekick).

STATISTICS

Mississippi		Arkansas	Mississippi		Arkansas
Davis	LE	John	22	First downs	7
Hall	LT	Mazzanti	160	Net yards rushing	47
Robinson	LG	Howard	28	Passes attempted	18
Ross	C	Caveness	18	Passes completed	6
Dickson	RG	Trail	1	Passes had intercepted	2
Dunaway	RT	Adams	269	Net yards passing	123
Dabbs	RE	Lamb	429	Total net yards	170
Griffing	QB	B. Moore	2	Number of punts	4
Morris	LH	Branch	36	Punting average	38.2
Guy	RH	Worthington	1	Fumbles lost	0
Dunn	FB	Brabham	40	Yards penalized	13

Substitutions—Mississippi: Irwin (l), Champion (l), Wilkins (l). Lambert (l), Brown (r), Pettey (r), ends; J. Roberts (l), Ford (r), tackles; Kimbrell (l), Mattina (l), Lucas (r), guards; Dill, center; Weatherly, quarterback; Jennings (l), Crosby (l), Johnson (r), Smith (r), halfbacks; Randall, F. Roberts, fullbacks. Arkansas: Finch (l), Grizzle (l), Evans (r), Langston (r), ends; Tackett (l), Beutelschies (r), Bryant (r), tackles; Brasher (l), Jones (l), Hales (l), Johnson (r), guards; R. Hatfield, Polk, centers; Gray, quarterback; T. Moore (l), McKnelly (l), Sparks (r), Parker (r), halfbacks; Moody, K. Hatfield, fullbacks.

LIBERTY

Sportsman of the year he was in the valued opinion of *Sports Illustrated,* and if you read Alfred Wright's story in that weekly magazine about the Oregon State quarterback, you had to believe there were many cogent reasons for stating that Terry Baker did indeed emerge supreme.

He won the Heisman Trophy and the Maxwell Award. He was a unanimous All-America choice. He was Player of the Year and Back of the Year and he earned a $500 Earl Blaik Fellowship for postgraduate work from the National Football Foundation and Hall of Fame as one of the season's eight outstanding scholar-athletes.

Yet is even a man with these unheard-of decorations, and 4,980 career yards gained besides, expected to run 99 yards, two feet for a touchdown to bring his team a great victory in his final game?

Perhaps only Terry Baker.

The Liberty Bowl game between Oregon State and Villanova, before 17,048 shivering spectators in vast and frigid Philadelphia Stadium, was in the sixth minute. Bill Sherlock had punted from Villanova's 47 and Larry Glueck had grounded the ball barely 12 inches from Oregon State's goal line.

Here the official play-by-play report resumes tersely. It reads: "Baker around left end and down the sideline for 99 yards, a first down and a touchdown. Score: Oregon State 6, Villanova 0."

So it ended.

"I was afraid of a fumble unless I carried it myself," the left-handed, thin-haired mechanical engineering student told interviewers. "A couple of fellows blew in and hit me, but I got loose. Then another Villanova tackler bumped me on the sideline. But I was lucky. There was no pursuit to catch me after I turned the corner. A real break."

Quick downfield support formed as soon as Baker escaped from those who had a piece of him and couldn't hold on. Pursuit was hopeless.

Although Baker accounted for 260 yards of his team's total of 299, Villanova contained him well and emerged with unconsoling statistical superiority.

An apparent 12-yard touchdown run by fullback Billy Joe was erased because a backfield teammate was detected holding an Oregon State lineman. With time ebbing in the last quarter, Villanova's Wildcats swept the Beavers 61 yards before them, only to be halted by quarterback Ted Aceto's ball-losing fumble on the 9.

Both teams wore sneakers on the frozen turf.

"I hated those rubber soles," said Villanova captain Charlie Johnson. "We couldn't dig in. We had a 20-pound weight advantage per man and couldn't take advantage of it."

When Sandy Grady of the *Philadelphia Bulletin* went to the Oregon State dressing room, Coach Tommy Prothro told him, "This is the fourth bowl I've been in—three times a loser in the Rose Bowl— and I thought I was a goner again."

SATURDAY, DECEMBER 15, 1962

Oregon State	6	0	0	0	6
Villanova	0	0	0	0	0

Oregon State—Touchdown: Baker (99, left end).

STATISTICS

Oregon State		Villanova		Oregon State	Villanova
Burke	LE	McDonnell	11	First downs	20
J. Funston	LT	Johnson	176	Net yards rushing	246
Gnoss	LG	Calligaris	21	Passes attempted	10
Keeney	C	Moore	9	Passes completed	6
Cariaga	RG	Kowalski	0	Passes had intercepted	2
Neil	RT	Atkinson	123	Net yards passing	63
F. Jones	RE	Clifford	299	Total net yards	309
Baker	QB	Richman	5	Number of punts	3
Espalin	LH	Glueck	34.2	Punting average	41.3
D. Jones	RH	Merenda	1	Fumbles lost	4
Williams	FB	Rettino	80	Yards penalized	42

Substitutions—Oregon State: Seale (l), Miller (l), Frketich (r), McDougal (r), ends; Bonilla (l), Holley (r), Koeper (r), tackles; Nelson (l), Cole (l), Doman (r), A. Funston (r), guards; DeBisschop, Farrell, centers; Brooks, Clark, quarterbacks; Moreland (l), Sinyard (r), Sieg (r), halfbacks; Washington, Ruhl, Ankersen, fullbacks. Villanova: DeLone (l), Dinan (l), Barbaro (l), Michaels (r), O'Hara (r), Cutroneo (r), ends; Nask (l), Buben (l), Smith (r), Strofolino (r), tackles; McDonald (l), Armstrong (l), Bertozzi (r), guards; Ceppetelli, Reinoso, centers; Aceto, Sherlock, Dougherty, quarterbacks; Boyle (l), Thomas (r), halfbacks; Joe, fullback.

BLUEBONNET

Bobby Dodd was on record.

This was Georgia Tech's strongest starting line in his 18 years as head coach. Billy Lothridge, who scored 89 points, was the best quarterback the Yellow Jackets ever had.

This 1962 team was the finest bunch of two-way players to represent the school in his several decades at Tech. Further, he derived more pleasure coaching it than any other.

Nevertheless, when all was said and done at the Bluebonnet Bowl, Missouri had more points, 14 to 10. Various Tigers whisked through and around their adversary's enormous line for 258 yards.

Mr. Lothridge rarely was rushed so vigorously. He was able to complete only five of his 15 passes while sustaining four interceptions.

The scoring play that decided the game was an expertly executed reverse inside left end propelling Bill Tobin into the open for a 77-yard run. It came in the third period.

Victory was accomplished neither with mirrors nor passes.

"Missouri did to perfection the two things that win for you," Dodd said. "They tackled and blocked as the books say you should."

Missouri sent the ball aloft only seven times but had nary a completion . . . did it all on the ground.

The second time the Tigers got possession of the ball they scored. From Tech's 21 quarterback Jim Johnson faked a handoff to fullback Paul Underhill, rolled out to the right, cut in, and went over. That touchdown ended a 67-yard drive. Johnson was all but ignored in the flood of publicity for Lothridge before the game.

The Jackets got the equalizer in the second quarter. They moved 61 yards. Slippery Joe Auer turned the right corner for the last six.

After Tobin's run, Tech was far from finished, thanks in no small measure to Missouri's generosity. Fullback Andy Russell parted with the ball on the Tigers' 15, but Tech had to settle for a fourth down field goal of 26 yards by Lothridge.

Then, late in the conflict, Missouri rather recklessly tried to make a first down from Tech's 33 on a fourth-and-one situation. Failure to get it proved almost fatal.

Lothridge attempted to resurrect the Statue of Liberty play but couldn't bring it off because of another energetic charge. Instead, he tossed backwards to Auer and the left halfback, afforded fine protection, came within one man, tackle Dave Gill, of going all the way. Auer was nailed on Missouri's 32.

With two minutes to play, Tech stood at the 22. The Engineers' timeouts were exhausted now and Lothridge was passing stocking-footed after losing one shoe and tossing the other away. His second-down pass, aimed deep in the end zone to end Billy Martin, was underthrown. Russell grabbed it on the goal line.

It was Russell's eighth steal of the year, second of the game (both in the fourth period), and most important of his career. It was Russell's peel-back block, incidentally, which freed Tobin for his long gallop.

Missouri's All-America end, Conrad Hitchler, was a defensive pillar—voted outstanding lineman—in helping seal Tech's third straight bowl defeat after eight consecutive wins.

His nose was broken. When Hitchler heard he wouldn't play in the East-West game the following Saturday, he said, "I'll be in there. You can count on it. I feel like fighting wildcats."

SATURDAY, DECEMBER 22, 1962

Missouri	7	0	7	0	14
Georgia Tech	0	7	3	0	10

Missouri—Touchdowns: Johnson (21, right tackle), Tobin (77, left tackle). Points after touchdown: Leistritz 2.

Georgia Tech—Touchdown: Auer (6, right end). Point after touchdown: Lothridge. Field goal: Lothridge (26, placekick).

STATISTICS

Missouri		Georgia Tech	Missouri		Georgia Tech
John Sevcik	LE	Davis	10	First downs	13
Wallach	LT	Griffin	258	Net yards rushing	169
Phillips	LG	Guthrie	7	Passes attempted	15
Vermillion	C	Caldwell	0	Passes completed	5
Hertz	RG	Watson	2	Passes had intercepted	4
Gill	RT	Stallings	0	Net yards passing	68
Hitchler	RE	Martin	258	Total net yards	237
Johnson	QB	Lothridge	5	Number of punts	6
Roland	LH	Auer	35.6	Punting average	38.5
Tobin	RH	Jackson	2	Fumbles lost	0
Russell	FB	McNames	35	Yards penalized	5

Substitutions—Missouri: Oliver (l), Ritter (l), Palmer (r), James Sevcik (r), ends; Brown (l), Crumpler (l), Siekierski (r), Matthews (r), tackles; Lurie (l), Buerkle (l), Kubinski (r), Wyrostek (r), guards; Gilchrist, Jansen, centers; Krugman, Jones, quarterbacks; Turner (l), Leistritz (l), Crawford (r), Hinkley (r), halfbacks; Underhill, Otto, fullbacks. Georgia Tech: Sexton (l), Wright (r), ends; Ballard (l), Chapman (l), Farrington (r), tackles; Yates (l), Seward (r), guards; Matlock, center; Gann, quarterback; Bussell (l), Winingder (l), Gresham (r), Cooper (r), halfbacks; Toner, Mendheim, fullbacks.

Index